# THE KIBBUTZ MOVEMENT: A HISTORY

T0369752

# THE LITTMAN LIBRARY OF
# JEWISH CIVILIZATION

*Dedicated to the memory of*

LOUIS THOMAS SIDNEY LITTMAN

*who founded the Littman Library for the love of God
and as an act of charity in memory of his father*

JOSEPH AARON LITTMAN

*and to the memory of*

ROBERT JOSEPH LITTMAN

*who continued what his father Louis had begun*

יהא זכרם ברוך

'*Get wisdom, get understanding:
Forsake her not and she shall preserve thee*'

PROV. 4: 5

*The Littman Library of Jewish Civilization is a registered UK charity
Registered charity no. 1000784*

# The Kibbutz Movement
## A History

◆

VOLUME 1

ORIGINS AND GROWTH
1909–1939

◆

HENRY NEAR

The Littman Library of Jewish Civilization
in association with Liverpool University Press

*The Littman Library of Jewish Civilization*
*in association with Liverpool University Press*
*4 Cambridge Street, Liverpool* L69 7ZU, UK
*www.liverpooluniversitypress.co.uk/littman*

*Managing Editor: Connie Webber*

*Distributed in North America by*
*Oxford University Press Inc., 198 Madison Avenue,*
*New York,* NY 10016, USA

*First published in hardback 1992*
*by Oxford University Press on behalf of*
*The Littman Library of Jewish Civilization*
*First issued in paperback 2007*

*Catalogue records for this book are available from the*
*British Library and the Library of Congress*

*ISBN 978-1-874774-38-9*

*Publishing co-ordinator: Janet Moth*
*Design by Pete Russell, Faringdon, Oxon.*
*Typeset by Butler & Tanner, Frome and London*
*Printed and bound by CPI Group (UK) Ltd, Croydon, CR0 4YY*

*To my children and their contemporaries,*
*the younger generation of the kibbutz,*
*in the hope that study of the past*
*may provide inspiration for the future*

# *Preface*

THE kibbutz is a unique phenomenon, which has become the object of widespread interest, ranging from passing curiosity to detailed research. Many thousands of tourists, volunteer workers, visitors, and more serious students know the kibbutz as a multi-generational society with a variegated economic structure, struggling to adapt to the vicissitudes of the Israeli and world economy. They have seen its fields, orchards, and industrial enterprises, spoken to members of all ages, and taken note of the vitality of kibbutz children and the peculiarities of its educational system. All these observations have been and are being made at different levels of sophistication, from that of the tourists' hour to the detailed observations and analysis of the academic investigator. Kibbutz research is undoubtedly a growth industry, and the data bank of Haifa University's Institute for Kibbutz Research lists more than three thousand items, whose subjects range from childbirth to geriatrics, from interpersonal relationships to politics, and from detailed studies of individual kibbutzim to surveys of the kibbutz movement as a whole.

From this mass of impressions and investigations, a general picture emerges of the kibbutz as an established sector of Israeli society, with a way of life that is more or less standard as between different kibbutzim, and with institutionalized relationships between the kibbutz movement and the society of which it forms part. Today, as often in the past, the kibbutz is having to contend with serious social and economic difficulties. But as a social organism, and as a part of Israeli society, it seems to be here to stay.

Anything more than the most superficial of impressions will tell the outside observer that it was not always so. Tourists are still surprised, sometimes even shocked, by the prosperous appearance of the contemporary kibbutz. Some folk-memory tells them that it should be a semi-military outpost, defending the borders against hostile incursions, and inhabited by dedicated and ascetic pioneers. A short conversation with the veteran members of almost any kibbutz will indeed recall those early days, and may well open the floodgate to other memories—of social tensions within the kibbutz and hostility from outside it, of the transition from a closely knit group of young unmarried pioneers to an expanding child- and family-centred society, of economic and political changes. Many research works contain some reference to, occasionally even an analysis of, the historical aspects of their subject. There is a host of books, articles, and memorial pamphlets containing personal reminiscences of the kibbutz past. And in recent years a number of works have appeared, mainly in Hebrew, which use the methods of critical history to analyse particular aspects or sectors of the kibbutz movement or periods of its development.

This book is the first of two volumes which aim at a more general description and analysis than has so far been attempted. Its title—*The Kibbutz Movement: A History*—indicates its scope and its emphases. The expression 'the kibbutz movement' is used here, and throughout the book, to mean the totality of the communal societies which were created by Jewish pioneers in Israel and pre-State Jewish Palestine.[1] In this sense, nothing appertaining to the kibbutz is alien to my field of vision. On the other hand, the title speaks of 'the kibbutz movement' rather than 'the kibbutz'; and this implies that my emphasis is on the general rather than the particular—especially on such matters as the relationships between individual communities, and between the kibbutzim as a whole and the world around them. Therefore, much of the book is devoted to subjects such as the evolution of the various kibbutz movements, the pioneering youth movements, and the place of the kibbutzim in the politics of their time.

Such an account would be bloodless and perhaps even incomprehensible if I did not deal at all with the changing nature of the kibbutz communities themselves. Here, there is a methodological problem. Detailed historical research both of the Jewish community of Palestine and of the kibbutz movement is far from complete, and there are important gaps even within this relatively well covered period; but, although further research may require revision in detail, the general picture, particularly of the years covered in this volume, is clear, and rests firmly on published research. The social and economic history of the kibbutz, by contrast, is only now beginning to be the subject of critical research, as distinct from reminiscences and similar material. The investigations now in hand will enable

[1] A more exact definition of key words used to describe the kibbutz can be found in the Glossary, particularly under 'kibbutz' and *kvutza*.

others to complement and improve my work; but this book's emphases reflect the current state of the research.

My first aim has been to answer the classical question: 'What actually happened?'—to give a clear narrative account of the genesis of the kibbutz, and the way it grew from one tiny group in 1910 to reach a population of some 24,000 in 79 communities on the verge of the Second World War (and, in the second volume, to continue the story until the present day). But, particularly in the case of such an unusual phenomenon, narrative is not enough. I have attempted to analyse the historical forces which went into shaping these events, and to explain why the kibbutz came into being when and where it did, and how it changed and managed to survive. And, despite the limitations I have mentioned, I have added a further element: how did it look and feel? What was a kibbutz, and what did it mean to be a kibbutz member, in the circumstances whose description and analysis form the historical framework of this study? For the most part, I have tried to answer these questions by presenting descriptive material written at the time and reminiscences which I judge to be authentic; such recollections can sometimes give a more complete picture of the past than contemporary documents which take the surrounding circumstances for granted.

In general, I have adopted a chronological pattern. But certain themes transcend the limits of period which fit the general historical narrative, and I have not hesitated to follow particular developments or aspects of kibbutz life beyond the end of the period in which they mainly appear, or to trace their origins from an earlier point in time.

This book originated in a programme which I wrote for the Open University of Israel, whose directors kindly permitted me to use some of my material. I have made use of the work of many scholars, and often consulted them personally: I owe particular debts to Yossi Asaf, Eyal Kafkafi, Baruch Kanari, Elkana Margalit, and David Zayit. The final result is, of course, my own responsibility. Muki Tsur read much of the text at an early stage, and made several very valuable comments. Bridget Davies's reading of the first draft saved me from many solecisms, and Marion Lupu continued her work with skill and enthusiasm. The late Baruch Ben-Avram was unsparing in his encouragement and criticism. With his untimely death I lost a dear friend and colleague. Had he lived to see the whole of the manuscript, it would undoubtedly have been much better.

The staff of the archives at Ef'al, Hulda, Giv'at Haviva, Beit Berl

x    *Preface*

and the Lavon Institute provided essential services, and I found
peaceful sanctuary at the Oxford Centre for Postgraduate Hebrew
Studies.

The late L. T. S. Littman was most generous in his support, despite
his many reservations about my social philosophy and that of the
kibbutz. The late Dr Vivian Lipman, series editor of the Littman
Library until his death in March 1990, scrutinized the manuscript
with patience and sensitivity. I greatly regret that neither of them
lived to see the finished work. Connie Wilsack edited the manuscript
and saw the book through the press with great acumen and good
humour.

My greatest debt is to my wife, Alisa, and my children, for their
support and forbearance; and to the members of Kibbutz Beit
Ha'emek for my time and their tolerance.

H. N.

*Kibbutz Beit Ha'emek*
*September 1990*

# Contents

# Contents

# List of Tables

# Translation, Transliteration, Annotation, and References

ALL translations, except where otherwise stated, are by the author.

In transliterating Hebrew words, a modified version of the *Encyclopedia Judaica* system has been used, except in cases where an accepted English form exists (for example: Hechalutz rather than Heḥalutz). The divergencies from the *Encyclopedia Judaica* are that no diacritics are used: for example, *het* is transliterated as *h, tzadi* as *tz,* and no distinction is made between *aleph* and *ayin.* The definite article is transliterated as *ha* instead of *ha-.* The feminine singular form is indicated by *a,* not *ah* (*avoda,* not *avodah*).

Aids to the pronunciation of Hebrew words will be found in the Glossary, which explains Hebrew words and phrases not defined in the text, and provides background information on the various organizations which figure frequently in the narrative.

Books, articles, and other material cited in the footnotes are referred to by the author's name and a shortened form of the title. Full bibliographical details will be found in the References.

# Introduction

DEGANIA, the first kibbutz, was established in 1910 by a dozen men and women scarcely out of their teens. Its future was uncertain, its present dominated by the need to make a living from agriculture in the harsh climatic conditions of the Jordan Valley. Its members, as yet childless, created a closely knit egalitarian community where all, conferring together, decided the fate of each, and each bore the responsibility for all.

Like Degania in its early days, today's kibbutz is a voluntary society, administered by its members with no legal sanctions, by methods of direct democracy, in a spirit of close community and co-operation. The source of authority is the (usually weekly) general meeting of all the members. Goods and services are provided for the most part according to the principle 'to each according to his needs'. With insignificant exceptions all its members are Jews, but the great majority share no religious creed: their Judaism is a matter of culture or nationality rather than religious faith or practice. In all this the contemporary kibbutz is similar to Degania eighty years ago. But it is also very different.

Today's kibbutzim are complex and institutionalized communities. Economically, almost all of them are based on a combination of agriculture and industry. They are administered by a network of elected committees and officials, who hold their posts for a limited period of time, and whose policies are constantly subjected to public scrutiny. They have evolved a unique system of education, which has contributed much to their demographic growth, and the oldest kibbutzim have already reached their fourth generation. There are now some 250 kibbutzim scattered throughout Israel, from Kibbutz Dan close to the Lebanese border to Kibbutz Eilot at the southern tip of the country, with a total population of about 120,000. They are organized in three country-wide kibbutz movements, each of them with political affiliations.

This volume describes the first thirty years of the process which led from the pre-history and first hesitant steps of Degania to the kibbutz movement of today. I shall preface the detailed account of these complex developments with some remarks which may help to put it in a historical perspective.

By 1904, when our account opens, the Zionist movement was a recognized, though far from universally accepted, part of world Jewry, and its strength was growing steadily. For those who created the kibbutzim and reinforced them in later years, what was known as 'practical Zionism'—the belief that Jewish nationhood could be restored only by settling the Land of Israel—was a fundamental, almost unquestioned, assumption. It was a solution both to their personal problems as Jews—whether these consisted of physical danger, economic discrimination, or the cultural degeneration of Jewish life in the Diaspora—and to the same problems, writ large, in the life of the Jewish people as a whole. With the Balfour Declaration in 1917 and the growth of the Yishuv, and even more with the advent of Nazism and the closing of other borders to persecuted Jews, the Zionist solution seemed ever more persuasive. The whole of the development of the Yishuv, and of the kibbutz movement within it, can only be understood in this context.

Some of the implications of this fact form part of the history of the kibbutz throughout its existence. One is the interdependence of the kibbutz movement and the local agencies of practical Zionism (the Palestine Office of the Zionist movement and, later, the Settlement Department of the Jewish Agency). This symbiotic relationship was acceptable to both sides. Each of them contributed the appropriate means to their common end: the Zionist movement provided money and public and political backing; the kibbutz movement carried out the tasks of settlement, and educated a large reserve of devoted manpower.

Whatever their views as to the eventual political settlement in Palestine, all of the kibbutz movements—and, indeed, all the Zionist parties—were agreed on the central importance of Jewish immigration and self-defence. Since there was some violent opposition to Jewish settlement from a very early stage, self-defence was always part of the way of life of the kibbutzim. It came to special public prominence from 1936 onwards: the three functions which the kibbutzim had always taken on themselves—absorption, settlement, and defence—were now almost universally seen to be the priorities of the Yishuv and the Zionist movement. Supported by a politically sympathetic Zionist Executive, the kibbutz movement played a major role in fulfilling these tasks; and the results in public esteem, self-confidence, and demographic growth can be clearly seen. In the period with which this volume ends, the image of the kibbutz as a self-sacrificing élite dedicated to the service of the Yishuv and the Jewish people became part of the consciousness of every Zionist.

This image had long been accepted within the kibbutz movement itself, and was particularly important in a sector which, on the face of it, was not a part of that framework—the pioneering youth movements. In fact, it is quite clear that from the mid-1920s many of them were effectively under the control of the kibbutz movements, and formed an indispensable source of manpower for their growth and replenishment; and that, conversely, the kibbutzim provided senior educators, an educational ideal, and a practical solution to the problems of Jewish youth. It was this which gave the youth movements their inspiration and strength.

The implications of the kibbutzim's involvement in Zionism were not always entirely positive. One of them concerns their relationship with Jews of non-European origin. In the early years of Zionist immigration the old-established Sephardi community was an important element in the Yishuv. By the turn of the century, however, the Zionist 'New Yishuv' had attained dominance both numerically and in terms of social dynamism and political power. This group's intellectual and practical preoccupations reflected its European origins: increasingly so from the early 1930s onwards as the physical threat to the Jews of Europe became more evident.

It was within this social context that the kibbutz movement originated and grew. Accordingly, its main source of recruitment was in the European youth movements, and the pioneering movements which began to spread in the Yishuv during the 1930s were composed almost entirely of the children of European immigrants. It was only during the Second World War, when the Yishuv was cut off from Europe, that the kibbutz movements began to recruit young Jews in the Jewish communities of the Middle East. The European orientation of the Zionist immigrants also affected the situation of the one sizeable group of non-European Jews to be found in the rural sector—the Yemenites, throughout these years an underprivileged sector of the Yishuv. In the case of the kibbutz movement the position was complicated by the fact that, with their preference for the moshav, the Yemenites were competitors for land and other resources for settlement.

In quantitative terms, this question was not of great importance in these years: by 1939 almost 80 per cent of the Yishuv (and 86 per cent of its rural sector) were of European origin. It was only at a later period that it appeared in a new perspective.[1] But it coloured the ways of thought and action of the Yishuv and the Zionist movement, and the kibbutz movement within them, throughout the period covered in this volume.

This was not only the negative effect of the kibbutzim's involvement with Zionism. From the very first they were deeply affected by the political divisions in the Zionist movement, including the labour movement to which they were directly affiliated. When the three main kibbutz movements were formed at the end of the 1920s, they were divided not only by their concepts of what a kibbutz should be—its size, its economic functions, and the relationships between its members—but also of what it should do—its relationships with other parts of the Yishuv, and its political allegiance. From then on, although the structural differences between the kibbutzim gradually lessened, their political divergences became constantly wider and deeper.

In one sense, this is an expression of an element which will often be stressed in the following pages: the kibbutz movement was not only part of the Yishuv and the Jewish people, but also of a rapidly changing world, which particularly influenced the young people who founded the kibbutz movement and were at all stages its greatest potential for growth. Their reactions to these changes were in large part a function of the other universe of discourse of which they formed part—the international socialist movement. The principles of the kibbutz are clearly socialist, and despite some terminological disputes all kibbutz members perceived them as such. Thus, they added to their nationalism a universal dimension which helped to strengthen their convictions and facilitate the recruitment of young Jews who were sensitive to the social problems of the day. But this also had its negative aspect. In seeking allies in the socialist world for themselves and for the Zionist enterprise, the kibbutz movements were deeply affected by the growing split in the socialist movement which began with the establishment of the Third International in 1920. In an age in which contemporary events encouraged, even demanded, political commitment, it is not surprising that this split served to deepen the existing divisions between the movements.

[1] This question will be dealt with in more detail (including a closer examination of this period) in the second volume of this work.

Thus, their basic unity on the national and practical level was marred by political and ideological disagreements. To this should be added another factor, which will be discussed more than once in the course of this study: the influence of the different regions of Jewish life on the kibbutz movements, in terms of thought and action alike. Russian Zionism differed from that of Germany, and Galician Jewry from that of Greater Poland; and the source of these differences is to be found not only in the strength of the local leaders or in organizational factors, but in the varieties of culture, in the broadest sense of that term, in the different regions of the Jewish world. Such variations are reflected no less in the character and ideology of the different kibbutz movements and the youth movements allied to them.

I remarked in the Preface that the bulk of historical research about the kibbutz movements deals with its public and political aspects, rather than the development of the kibbutz community as such. This is, of course, not accidental: it reflects both the predilections of scholars and the nature of the material with which they dealt; for all of the kibbutz movements were informed by the belief that they were playing a vital part in changing the course of history, and devoted much thought and discussion to this aspect of their activities. I have none the less tried to give some idea of the development of the kibbutz community during this period. The picture which emerges is of a society inspired with ideals of equality, fraternity, and direct democracy, but often influenced by social trends not always foreseen or welcomed by its leaders. Some of these trends originated in worldwide developments such as technological change, others in cultural norms acquired in the Jewish communities of the Diaspora, while others again were a function of the spontaneous interaction of people living in a closely knit community. In looking at the social development of the kibbutz, one can see the mutual influence of such unplanned social trends and the overt ideologies of the kibbutz movements.

In more concrete terms, it may be said that the kibbutzim were not the embodiment of socialism and Zionism, but groups of individuals, subject to the stresses and afflicted by the weaknesses which affect any human being. If their leaders and propagandists sometimes spoke in superhuman terms, that is perhaps understandable; for many of the tasks which they undertook were supremely difficult, and demanded a high degree of self-sacrifice. In the pages of this volume, the words of the leaders appear more often than the thoughts and day-to-day actions of the ordinary men and women of the kibbutzim. But it was they who, by their faith and devotion, created and expanded the kibbutz movement, and made possible the achievements described here. It is they who are the real heroes of the story.

# I

# Background and Beginnings, 1904–1920

## ZIONIST SETTLEMENT AND THE SECOND ALIYA

THE first question must be: how did it all begin? It is not my purpose to try to locate the kibbutz in the long series of communal societies which have flourished and, for the most part, failed over the centuries. This book is limited in time and place to the specific historical circumstances of the development of the kibbutz itself. But, although that time begins in about 1904, and the place is in Palestine and Israel, the circumstances cannot be understood without a brief glance at the soil from which the kibbutz and its creators sprang: the Jewish people and the Zionist movement in the last two decades of the nineteenth century.[1]

The early 1880s witnessed the beginning of the mass migrations which changed the character and geographical location of the Jewish communities of the world. The Jews of Eastern Europe, fleeing from poverty and persecution, took advantage of the possibilities of modern transport and the help of their more fortunate brethren. They tripled and quadrupled the communities of Western Europe, and increased the number of American Jews from 280,000 in 1880 to a million in 1900. The vast majority of Jews went west. But a relatively small number, driven from the traditional areas of Jewish concentration by the same causes, took another direction. Of the Jews involved in emigration from Eastern European countries between 1880 and 1904, some 25,000 went to Palestine.[2] Their motives were varied. In many cases, they were continuing a long Jewish tradition of pilgrimage and settlement which can be traced almost throughout the Exile. Others saw themselves as the forerunners of a community which would

---

[1] For an account of the Yishuv and its development in this period, see Eliav and Rosenthal, *First Aliyah*; Laqueur, *A History of Zionism*, chs. 3, 4, and 6 gives a useful account of the development of the Zionist movement at this time.

[2] *Encyclopedia Judaica*, xv. 1608–11.

provide inspiration to Jews all over the world, and refuge in time of need. Many continued the tradition of settlement in the Holy Land which required them to live in the four holy cities (Tiberias, Safed, Hebron, and Jerusalem) and to hasten the coming of the Messiah by their piety. But this tradition itself had already been weakened by the economic and demographic pressures within those cities, and particularly in Jerusalem. In 1860, the first settlement outside the walls of Jerusalem was attempted. In 1878, the first attempts at agricultural settlement were made. During the following sixteen years, known in Zionist history as the First Aliya, the number of Jewish agricultural villages in Palestine grew to twenty-eight, ranging in population from the handful of settlers in newly founded Kfar Saba to more than 800 in Petah Tikva and Zichron Ya'akov: a total of almost 5,700, of a Jewish population of some 50,000.[3]

Conditions were far from easy for the new settlers. Politically, Palestine was part of the Ottoman Empire. The presence of foreign residents gave the Western powers an excuse to strengthen their foothold in the area, and the authorities at Constantinople were reluctant to permit any increase in their number. Thus, for long periods, permission to remain in the country could be obtained only by bribery, and there was constant danger of expulsion. In addition, land ownership and registration were subject to complex regulations, and there were high taxes on land and farm property. In 1891, alarmed by the influx of Jews and the growth of the new colonies, the Turkish government forbade Jews to purchase land; and, although such regulations could be circumvented by bribery and other ruses, they were a constant source of uncertainty. Nor did the existence of a central government necessarily mean security. Palestine was a peripheral area in the empire, and law and order were not stringently enforced. The farming community suffered particularly badly from the incursions of Bedouin tribes from across the Jordan.

On the other hand, the unsettled nature of the regime enabled the Jewish settlers to strike root in ways which would have been difficult perhaps even impossible, under a more efficient government. By the mid-nineteenth century, wide areas of cultivable land had been abandoned by farmers unwilling to grow crops for brigands to harvest. Their ownership passed to absentee landlords, who were prepared to sell at the rising prices engendered by the demand from the Jewish immigrants. Many farmers had retreated to hilly areas difficult of

[3] Eliav and Rosenthal, *First Aliyah*, i. 82.

access, where their land was close to their homes and more easily defensible. Thus, wide areas which were either unoccupied or cultivated by tenant farmers were made available for Jewish settlement. The geographic shape of the future Jewish state was already being determined.[4]

Even so, the Jewish settlers were unable to make their way unaided. Three separate agencies were involved in support for Jewish settlement at this stage: Hovevei Zion, a proto-Zionist organization of Russian Jews, which at a fairly early stage found itself unable to bear the expense involved in the upkeep of the settlements it had founded; the Baron Edmond de Rothschild, whose interest in Palestine settlement was partly philanthropic and partly religious; and the Jewish Colonization Association (JCA), founded by Baron Maurice de Hirsch, whose Palestinian operation was only part of a world-wide scheme to encourage Jews to engage in agriculture.[5] Rothschild's name was widely revered, and he became known as the 'father of the Yishuv'; but his methods of operation, which involved close supervision of the Jewish villages by a network of officials, tended to cramp the settlers' initiative. The JCA allowed the individual farmers much more initiative than the Rothschild regime, and promoted new methods of cultivation and settlement aimed at increasing productivity. By the turn of the century it had taken over the support of most of the colonies, and opened up a new area of settlement, in lower Galilee.[6]

During the First Aliya, Jewish agricultural settlement went through the difficult stages of foundation and initial economic development. As we shall see, the settlers of the Second Aliya were very critical of their predecessors. None the less, there were certain attitudes which were common to all of those who arrived in Palestine during these two periods.

All of them shared the political attitude encapsulated in the phrase 'practical Zionism'. Whereas 'political' Zionists, following Herzl, who had founded the Zionist Organization in 1897, believed that the key to the redemption of the Jewish people was in the political recognition of their right to Palestine (in the accepted phrase, the granting of a 'charter' by the Turkish authorities), practical Zionists, among whom were the philanthropic societies which had supported some of the

---

[4] Ben-Aryeh, 'Geographical Aspects', 86–96; Stein, *The Land Question*, ch. 1.
[5] Schama, *Two Rothschilds*, chs. 1–4; Eliav and Rosenthal, *First Aliyah*, i. 74–6.
[6] Aaronsohn, 'Stages in the Development of the Settlements'.

early Jewish colonies, believed that the major task of Zionism was the settlement of Jews on the land in Palestine. Some of them thought that political recognition was unimportant; others, that it would come as a result of the practical work of settlement.

The leaders and thinkers of the First and Second Aliya believed that their actions in settling in Palestine were the beginning of a new era in Jewish life. Culturally and morally, they intended to become the focus of a Jewish revival which was impossible in the conditions of poverty and dependence inherent in Diaspora life; and they saw Jewish Palestine as a potential refuge from persecution for the mass of Jewry. Moreover, both these groups shared a virtually unquestioned ideological assumption: the belief that the return to the Land of Israel implied a return to the land. This belief was couched in a variety of terms. Sometimes they stressed the need to change the character of the Jew, who for many hundreds of years had been forbidden to own land and had been cut off from productive occupations by legislative and other means. At other times they emphasized the state of the land itself; the demand to redeem it from the neglect into which it had fallen was presented as a moral issue. In these and other versions of Zionist ideology, the rural character of the Zionist utopia was taken for granted.[7]

The First Aliya showed that even in the unfavourable political, economic, and security conditions of the time, the creation of such a utopia was not an impossible dream. Furthermore, by the beginning of the century, some of the main lines of the development of the Yishuv were already established. Legally, the Jews took over the land by purchase. Economically, the purchase price and start-up capital were provided by agencies under the control of the Jews of the Diaspora. Geographically, the areas occupied were largely abandoned or neglected by their former owners. The first two of these three basic conditions of Jewish settlement (including that of the kibbutz movement) continued to apply until the establishment of the State of Israel, and the third until the late 1920s.[8]

Although the First Aliya laid the foundations of Jewish agriculture, not all of the settlers' ideals were realized in the way they originally envisaged. Many of them intended to live the life of noble peasants, all of whose wants would be supplied by their own labour on their family holdings. The realities of the Palestine agricultural economy

[7] Almog, 'Redemption in Zionist Rhetoric'; Near, 'Redemption of the Soil'.
[8] Stein, *The Land Question*, ch. 2.

forced them to abandon this ideal at an early stage. By the turn of the century almost all the *moshavot* were based on cash crops (mainly grapes and citrus fruit), and reliant to a high degree on hired Arab labour. Another widely held though far from universal ideal sprang from the belief that the new colonies should be an example of social justice and equality. Throughout the First Aliya there were various experiments in social organization, ranging from co-operatives of artisans to plans for communal settlement. In several *moshavot* the land was worked in common for the first period of settlement, though it was afterwards divided into individual holdings. And the Biluim, a small group of pioneers who in later years were thought to be the leading figures of the First Aliya, attempted to found a settlement based on co-operative principles.[9] Not one of these social experiments lasted for more than a few months, and by the time the pioneers of the Second Aliya began to arrive in the country they were scarcely even remembered. The social forms which evolved in the course of the Second Aliya were certainly not a direct continuation of anything in the preceding period: it was only much later that the co-operative ideas of some of the men of the First Aliya were used in order to add historical depth and continuity, *ex post facto*, to the kibbutz movement.[10]

## The Second Aliya

The men and women of the Second Aliya (1904–14) came, like their predecessors, mainly from Russia. But they were of a new generation, and had grown up in circumstances quite different from those of the First Aliya. They created the Labour Zionist movement and laid the ideological and structural foundations of the State of Israel. One of those foundations was the kibbutz.

Just as the First Aliya formed part of a wave of Jewish migration sparked off by a series of pogroms in Eastern Europe, so the Second Aliya was a proximate result of the persecution to which Russian Jews were subjected between 1903 and 1907. In this period, too, they formed a tiny minority of the Jews who left Russia. Jewish immigration to the United States between 1904 and 1914 numbered about 850,000. During the same period, the Jewish population of Palestine increased from 50,000 to some 80,000.[11]

[9] Braslavsky, *Workers and their Organizations*, 59–63, 66–70, 200–3.

[10] e.g. Luz, *Milestones*.

[11] *Encyclopedia Judaica*, xv. 1611.

It is hard to establish exactly how many of those who reached Palestine actually left it again during this decade. In the memoirs of the men and women of the Second Aliya, there is general agreement that only a minority of the immigrants stayed in the country. David Ben-Gurion claimed many years later that only 10 per cent remained; but the most reliable account of the statistics of the Yishuv estimates that 'a third or a quarter of the immigrants left the country in certain years'.[12] But, whatever the statistical truth, there is no doubt that disillusionment and despair led a high proportion to emigrate. The difficulties of adaptation to an unfamiliar climate and primitive living conditions also took their toll. The number who died from malaria and other diseases was far from negligible, as was the number of suicides. Thus, there was a process of selection and self-selection which weeded out all but the toughest, both mentally and physically. Those who remained were imbued with a degree of faith in the Zionist ideal, and determination to bring about its realization, which it is scarcely an exaggeration to describe as fanaticism.

Here, a word of caution is necessary. The phrase 'people of the Second Aliya' is frequently used in historical accounts of the period, and of the growth of the Yishuv. But this phrase does not usually refer to all the 30,000 people added to the population of the Yishuv during this enormously important decade. The accepted image of the 'people of the Second Aliya' is of the founders of the Labour Zionist movement, and, among them, the founders of the kibbutz who are the central figures in this chapter. But the whole of the labour movement probably numbered no more than 2,500 at the outbreak of the First World War.[13] We know of many who remained faithful to its principles in their early years in the country, but subsequently underwent a process of *embourgeoisement* (at least in the stringent terms used by their colleagues). Moreover, many of those who came to the country during this period were, in effect, the successors of the pioneers of the First Aliya; some settled in new or existing *moshavot*, many more swelled the numbers in the towns. In the course of the development of the Yishuv, the labour movement became a leading élite. By 1914 its members had already acquired many of the characteristics of such a group.

These people differed in several important respects from their

---

[12] Habass, *Second Aliya*, 17–18; Gurevich *et al.*, *Jewish Population of Palestine*, 21.
[13] Slutsky, *History of the Israeli Labour Movement*, 161–2. Even-Shoshan, *History of the Labour Movement*, i. 266–7, mentions an even smaller number: 1,500–1,600.

predecessors. Almost all of them were young: to take a typical instance, the founders of Degania, the first kibbutz, were on average 17 years and 6 months old when they arrived in Palestine, and Joseph Bussel, the acknowledged leader of the group, was only 16 years and 8 months.[14] They were mostly unmarried, and predominantly male. Here again, reliable statistics are hard to come by, but it is highly probable that no more than 20 per cent were women: at the peak of the Third Aliya, which certainly had a much higher proportion of women than the Second, more than 70 per cent of the workers were male.[15] Possibly most important is the fact that they came to maturity in Russia during the early years of the century: a time and place which were crucial in the history of the Jews, and, indeed, of mankind as a whole. As Jews, they were subject to the conflicting claims of almost every doctrine and dogma, from extreme orthodoxy in a variety of forms, through half a dozen variants of Zionism, to enlightenment and assimilation. As Russians, they were influenced by the revolutionary spirit of the period. Although at the time it seemed that hope for radical change had come to an abortive end with the revolution of 1905, in the years which preceded it virtually every variety of social doctrine had struggled for ascendancy among the Russian intelligentsia: populism and Tolstoyan thought, every type of anarchism from nihilism to the communalism of Kropotkin, social democracy of the Bolshevik and Menshevik varieties, liberalism, and more. Young Jews, seeking solutions to their own problems and to those of humanity as a whole, found themselves in an intellectual ambience in which the concept of revolution, or the building of a new society purged of the evils they saw around them, was a generally accepted ideal. Many of these young intellectuals found their way to Zionism and Palestine as a result of the failure of the 1905 revolution. In Palestine, they attempted to apply the social ideals acquired in their adolescence to the very different realities they now had to face. But even before the arrival of this significant reinforcement, the settlers of the Second Aliya had created the beginnings of a strong, politically conscious labour movement.[16]

From a very early stage, this movement was divided into two parties. The ideology of Poalei Zion ('Workers of Zion') was heavily influenced by the doctrines of Ber Borochov,[17] who interpreted the

---

[14] R. Frankel, 'Joseph Bussel', 83–103.
[15] *Pinkas Hahistadrut*, Feb. 1923, app. 8, table 1.
[16] J. Frankel, *Prophecy and Politics*.   [17] Ibid., ch. 7.

state of world Jewry in terms of a class analysis. The members of Hapoel Hatzair ('The Young Worker') maintained that this theory was not appropriate to the real situation of the Jews or the Yishuv: in their view, Zionism was first and foremost a moral and cultural movement. But, despite the ideological and personal rivalry between these parties, their approaches to the practical problems of the Yishuv were very similar. And one of the major areas of common ground between them was their criticism of the state of the Yishuv as they found it.

A major feature of the existing *moshavot*, which was criticized in circles far beyond those of the labour movement,[18] was their dependence on outside sources. Although many of them had been founded on the initiative of individuals or groups who aimed at economic self-sufficiency, virtually none had been able to attain this aim. Difficulties of acclimatization, lack of sufficient start-up capital, and the vagaries of the world agricultural market brought them to the point of failure: indeed, a number of villages were abandoned in the course of the First Aliya. Most of those that survived did so through the help first of Baron Rothschild and then of the JCA.

Although the policy of the JCA allowed more scope for the initiative of the individual, the farmer was still largely dependent on outside sources for economic development. Thus, instead of the Zionist enterprise being a new type of Jewish society which would provide leadership and inspiration to the Jews of the Diaspora, it turned out to be, in the eyes of its critics, a continuation of the 'Old Yishuv'— the pre-Zionist Jewish community of Palestine, which for centuries had been supported by the charity of pious Jews the world over. It looked now as if Zionism could prove to be equally subject to this dependence, albeit in a different form.[19]

Another matter on which the new immigrants criticized their predecessors was the question of Arab labour. The original concept of what the Jewish farmer should be had been based on the image of the Russian peasant: a smallholder whose crops would suffice to support himself and his family, with little reliance on cash crops. It soon became apparent, however, that this economic pattern was not suitable to the conditions of Palestine at the time. The *moshavot* came

[18] e.g. Ahad Ha'am (Asher Ginzberg), 'This is not the Way' (1869); 'Truth from the Land of Israel' (1891–3).

[19] On the differences in character between the Old and New Yishuv see Kaniel, *Continuity and Change*.

to rely on cash crops such as grapes and citrus fruit, which could not be cultivated by the farmer and his family alone. There was a need for seasonal labour; and, as seemed most natural to them, the farmers of the First Aliya employed the cheapest and most efficient workers—Arabs from the neighbourhood of their *moshava*. By 1900, this pattern of work and employment had become accepted, at any rate in the veteran *moshavot*. The Arab workers had become part of the local scene: so much so that many of them came to live in the *moshava*, the men working in the fields, the women as domestic servants.[20]

The men and women of the Second Aliya were surprised and shocked by this situation: surprised, because the image of the Land of Israel which they brought with them was of an entirely Jewish country; shocked, because they saw in the widespread employment of Arabs both a return to the very characteristics of the Diaspora Jew which, in their view, Zionism was to correct, and because the divorce of Jews from primary occupations would make their foothold in the country essentially precarious. But, for them, perhaps the most vicious aspect of the employment of Arabs was that it cut at the roots of one of their most cherished convictions—the belief in what came to be known as 'self-labour'.

One of the strands in Russian Populist thought inherited and developed by the pioneers of the Second Aliya was the personal application of general social and moral theories. For them, Zionism did not mean political activity or charitable work; it meant immigration to Palestine. Similarly, they believed that the moral, political, and cultural evils which resulted from the economic structure of the Jewish people could be cured only by creating a Jewish working class. This could not be done by legislation, or in any way other than that they themselves, the sons and daughters of Jews who had been divorced from productive work for many generations, should become workers; in this case, that they should become agricultural labourers.

Their criticism of the *moshavot* on this score was twofold. In the first place, the Jew suffered from a number of severe disadvantages compared with the Arab worker. He came from a different climate and culture, and had to become acclimatized while working to support himself. He lacked the infrastructure of housing, social framework, and care in times of distress which the Arab could take for granted. And, since he was used to a higher standard of living, his demands would always tend to be higher. Secondly, the fact that the employers

[20] Ro'i, 'Relations between Jews and Arabs'.

were Jews and the employees Arabs would increase the workers'
feelings of exploitation, direct them into nationalist channels, and
negate the moral claims of Zionism. In 1909, Aharon David Gordon,
the spiritual leader of the Hapoel Hatzair party, wrote: 'One thing
may be stated with certainty. The country will belong more to
whichever party [in the Jewish-Arab dispute] is able to suffer over it
more and to work on it more ... This is the conclusion of logic, of
justice, and the course of nature.' One of his political opponents,
Shlomo Kaplansky, leader of the Poalei Zion party, wrote in the
following year: 'The proper aim of national settlement—to populate
the country as densely as possible with Jews—has not even been
aspired to [by the settlers of the *moshavot*]. On the contrary, there
has been created an artificial conflict between Jewish property
and Arab labour: a class conflict which is deepened by national
differences.'[21]

These aims and ideological attitudes were common to the vast
majority of the Labour Zionist movement throughout the Second
Aliya and thereafter. The reality was very different.

There were two sorts of workers in the *moshava*: those experienced with the
hoe, who could make it 'sing' in their hands, whom the farmers knew and
were willing to employ; and the others, who were not known for their
expertise, who had to stand in the 'labour market' every morning, and were
unable to get any sort of work.

The 'labour market' was near the 'park' in the *moshava*. Every worker who
did not have a permanent job used to come early in the morning, with his
lunch (a bit of salt herring, half a dozen olives and a slice of bread) in a reed
basket on his arm, and stand by the fence. In this way, dozens of Jewish
workers would stand among the crowds of Arabs, and wait for their saviour.[22]

To the difficulties inherent in the situation was added the humili-
ation which many of the workers felt at the way in which the fortunate
ones were chosen: the farmer would feel their muscles, or give them
some demeaning task to try them out. But even those who were
disposed to employ Jews found it difficult to bear the losses which
this frequently entailed. Their main consideration was, and had to
be, economic. So the central preoccupation of the workers in the
Second Aliya was what came to be known as 'the conquest of labour'.

This phrase was calculated to apply the natural militancy of the

[21] Gordon, 'An Irrational Solution', 96; Kaplansky, 'Co-operative Settlement',
408-9.
[22] S. D. Yaffe in Habass, *Second Aliya*, 367-8.

idealistic young workers to the special circumstances of their situation, and was quickly adopted by the whole of the labour movement.[23] It contains an inherent ambiguity. On the one hand, it was a political and economic expression, encompassing the effort to compete with the Arab worker for the available jobs, to persuade the Jewish farmer that it was his duty to employ Jews and to encourage the Jewish worker to tackle as many different varieties of work as possible. But, equally, it became a moral term: it was the duty of the Jewish worker to 'conquer himself for labour', to persevere despite the objective difficulties, and by changing his nature to bring about 'salvation' for himself and for the Jewish people.[24]

The difference is exemplified in a well-known anecdote about Aharon David Gordon, the doyen and teacher of the workers of the Second Aliya. Gordon immigrated from Russia to Palestine in 1904, at the age of 48. Despite his age, he took his place with the workers, and rapidly became one of their spiritual leaders. He evolved a theory of nationalism and Zionism widely known as 'the religion of labour', which emphasized the moral aspects of the conquest of work, and laid stress on the regeneration of the Jew through physical labour and direct contact with nature. Although his philosophical writings were published throughout this period, his influence stemmed mainly from his personal example, and his quasi-paternal relationships with the young workers.[25]

It is said that Gordon was working with a group, digging holes in which to plant citrus saplings. Payment was by result, so most of the workers dug away furiously, in order to make as many holes as possible. Suddenly, they noticed that Gordon was far behind them. He was giving individual attention to every hole, for he believed that physical labour was a form of art, and ennobled the labourer only if he gave it his full attention. The payment for the work was only incidental to the moral elevation involved in the actual performance of physical labour.[26]

In order to 'conquer labour' in either of the senses of that phrase, the new immigrants had to overcome the objective difficulties described above. To this end, a number of stratagems were employed. One was

---

[23] Zemah, *In the Beginning*, 10, 16, 32.

[24] Kolatt, 'Ideology and Reality'.

[25] Schweid, *The World of A. D. Gordon*, 55–62.

[26] This is an apocryphal story, very well known in the labour movement now and in the past. Whether literally true or not, it is quoted here as typifying a difference in attitudes which was recognized and discussed throughout the period.

the establishment of training farms, where the workers could become acclimatized to their work and the conditions of the country before they had to compete in the labour market. Such was the farm at Sejera in Lower Galilee, established by the JCA in 1899. Similar farms were set up by the Zionist movement in the second half of the Second Aliya. One of them, Kinneret, on the shore of Lake Galilee, played a central part in the development of the kibbutz.

The workers themselves also played a major part in the invention of such stratagems. The political parties were not only ideological groupings; they also provided valuable social and psychological support to the otherwise isolated workers. Medical aid, help in finding employment and accommodation, Hebrew teaching, and other social functions were carried out (often only in the most rudimentary form) by the parties. From 1909 onwards, workers dissatisfied with party political divisions began to set up regional non-party organizations: Hahoresh ('The Ploughman') and, later, the Union of Agricultural Workers in Galilee, and similar associations in the coastal plain. These also promoted mutual aid and the spread of information, as well as aiming to raise professional standards and protect the workers' economic interests. Similar functions were also part of the work of organizations set up for more restricted purposes: for example, Hashomer, whose aim was to provide Jewish guards for the *moshavot* instead of the unreliable protection provided by the Arabs who had previously done this work. This organization, which demanded an exceedingly high degree of devotion, self-sacrifice, and discipline from its members and their wives, established funds for medical care, help in time of unemployment, aid to those imprisoned in the course of duty, and legal aid. Hashomer was also responsible for the widows and orphans of its members, many of whom were killed on guard duty or died as a result of the physical conditions in which they lived.[27]

## COMMUNES AND *KVUTZOT*

Another stratagem meant to alleviate the poverty, social isolation, and ill-health inherent in the process of the conquest of labour was the establishment of small groups known as 'communes'. A few such groups existed from the beginning of the Second Aliya. Here is a description of the group which came to be known as 'Haya-Sara [Hankin]'s commune', in Rehovot in 1904:

[27] *Hashomer Anthology*; Ben-Zvi et al., *Book of Hashomer*.

We hired an apartment—two rooms, kitchen and balcony. In the yard was an oven for baking bread. We fixed up beds made of planks and oil-cans. There was a rota for orderly duty; the orderly would get up early, prepare breakfast, and go out to work with the others. Someone else would bring water and wash the floor. We also took turns in kneading bread and keeping the stove alight. This was a job that everyone enjoyed, and nobody was willing to give up his turn. I cooked lunch and supper, and taught the boys to do the housework. Since I had time to spare, I also found work, as a seamstress. In the evenings we had a good time: every evening there were sing-songs, discussions, parties. We were invited to parties a lot. At first we accepted with pleasure, but soon stopped, since it was hard to get up early for work the following day. Our refusal upset the people in the *moshava*.

We didn't stay long in Rehovot. We lived well there, and used to go for long walks in the area on Saturdays. But we asked ourselves: 'Why did we come here, and what do we want? We were prepared for hardship, we were ready to go hungry—and now we have work, an apartment, good food, and money in our communal fund. Is that why we came? Surely each of us should do something for those who will come after us ...' So, one evening, after singing together for several hours, we examined our hearts and minds, and decided to split up. The following day we got our things ready, returned any remaining food to the shop, and went each his own way.[28]

Some elements in this account merit comment. Rehovot was a relatively prosperous *moshava* at this time, and there is no doubt that this prosperity was one of the reasons for the flourishing economic state of the commune. Culturally, however, there was a rift between the two societies: the younger generation in the *moshava* did not share the work ethic of the communards; indeed, although there are a few examples of farmers' children joining the pioneers of the Second Aliya, their values and aspirations were usually more in line with those of their parents. And, most important of all, the commune was not seen as an end in itself or a permanent association, but as a temporary means of easing the transfer to a life of work.

One more element should be noted before we leave the Rehovot commune. It broke up not because it was doing too badly, but because it was doing too well. Although the explicit ideology of the labour movement never advocated asceticism as an end in itself, it was impossible to achieve its aims without a high degree of devotion and self-sacrifice. From this account, and from other contemporary sources, it appears that such suffering was sometimes not only tolerated but welcomed.

[28] H.-S. Hankin in Habass, *Second Aliya*, 478.

In all these respects, the Rehovot commune was typical of the half-dozen such groups of which we know between 1904 and 1910.[29] In other respects it was less typical; for instance, in many of them there was one woman who served as 'house-mother' and did all the domestic chores. It is, however, something of an exaggeration to talk of a typical commune at this period. They varied in size, in the way their members were recruited, and in the extent and nature of their communal organization. In general, they were small; none that we know of had more than eight or ten members, and some as few as three. Members usually worked for different employers, but they lived together and shared their meagre earnings. And, as has been said, they were few in number, although it seems probable that there were others which left no mark on history.

In one sense, this also applies to those of which we know. Each of the labour parties produced a printed newspaper which contained detailed accounts of current events in the *moshavot* and other places of work. Neither of them mentions any of the communes, our knowledge of which is based entirely on later evidence. Thus, their influence on contemporary events was negligible, and they were ignored by the mainstream of the labour movement. It was only in later years that some of them were seen to have contained the seeds of important developments.

After the initial enthusiasm of the first few years of the Second Aliya, the ranks of the workers' movement were swelled by a new wave of immigrants fleeing Russia in the wake of the failed revolution of 1905. Soon, however, the tide of history seemed to turn. The annual rate of immigration decreased; and those who remained began to feel the effects of an extended period of hard work, illness, poverty, and lack of a permanent home. The workers' attempts to ease their lot proved to be no more than palliatives, and many left the working class or the country. The three years from 1908 to 1910 have entered Zionist historiography as 'the time of despair'.[30]

The belief that the Jewish worker was unable to achieve the exalted task of the conquest of labour spread both among the rank and file of the labour movement and in its leadership. In the autumn of 1910, each of the political parties held conferences. In both of them the

---

[29] For a detailed list of communal and co-operative groups from 1904 to 1914 see tables in H. Near, 'Towards Workers' Settlement' (summarized in Table 1 below).

[30] Even-Shoshan, *History of the Labour Movement*, i. 120–2; Katznelson, *Writings*, xi. 144–5.

atmosphere was pessimistic. In the conference of Poalei Zion, Ben-Gurion declared that he had reached the conclusion that the Ashkenazi worker could never become a farm labourer:

People who are not fit for work and have high cultural standards will never create a class of agricultural workers, despite all their ideals.... It is not because of adverse conditions in the *moshavot* that the workers are leaving, but because people of this type are incapable of becoming workers, and will never make a living as workers, either in the orchards or in field work.[31]

Ben-Gurion's conclusion was that the Jewish working class would be composed of immigrants from the Yemen and from Kurdistan, who could adapt themselves to the conditions of the country.

The same problem was discussed in the Hapoel Hatzair conference which took place at the same time. Here, a number of suggestions were made: to concentrate on the more remunerative agricultural work; to find ways of improving the workers' living conditions; or, again, to turn to the 'natural' workers from the Yemen and other Middle Eastern countries. The general feeling in both of these conferences was one of crisis. In the early days of the Second Aliya there had been plenty of young people eager to dedicate themselves to agricultural labour. Now there was, relatively, plenty of work, but the workers had succumbed to despair and disillusion.[32]

None the less, it was during the time of despair that a number of developments took place which led to the recovery of the Yishuv and, directly and indirectly, to the birth of the kibbutz. One of these was inherent in the process of despair. Several contemporary sources emphasize the fact that many of those who reached the Yishuv after 1905 were motivated more by a desire to escape from the tyranny of Tsarist Russia than by positive Zionist ideals.[33] Such people were the first to leave the country under adverse conditions. Others remained in Palestine but gave up the effort to become agricultural labourers. Thus, there took place a severe process of selection; those who remained true to their original ideals were the most convinced, the most persevering, and those most able to survive the gruelling physical conditions.

Among these was a handful of young men who later came to be known as the Romni group. It was created by four graduates of a

---

[31] *Ha'ahdut*, 2/1 (Oct. 1910), 6.
[32] All quotations from the Hapoel Hatzair conference, here and below (p. 29) are from *Hapoel Hatzair*, 4/2 (Oct. 1910), 21.
[33] Aharonovitz, 'To Clarify the Situation'.

Zionist movement called Hat'hia (Renaissance) in the Ukrainian town of Romni, who formed a commune the moment they boarded the ship on their way to Palestine towards the end of 1907. During the following year this group, now grown to five, worked as hired labourers in Petah Tikva, living communally: they shared wages and accommodation, but had no house mother and ate in the workers' restaurant.[34] They were known as particularly good workers, and managed to survive the period of decline thanks both to their success in adapting themselves to agricultural work and to their communal way of life. This group played a vital part in the establishment of the first kibbutz, Degania.

Another major link in this chain of events was the decision of the Zionist movement to take part in settlement activity in Palestine. This was a change of policy from that which dominated the movement in its earliest years: Herzl, the founder of Zionism, and his supporters had opposed any suggestion of supporting settlement in Palestine until the creation of a juridical framework which would ensure its future ('the Charter'). In the Zionist Congress of August 1907 this stance was modified, and the movement shifted in the direction of 'synthetic Zionism': a combination of political activity and colonization. As a result of this decision Dr Arthur Ruppin, a young sociologist active in the Zionist movement, was engaged to direct all the movement's activities in Palestine.

Ruppin was devoted to the Zionist cause, immensely active and inventive, and of a highly independent temperament; indeed, one of his conditions for accepting the post was that he be allowed *carte blanche* in applying the general policies laid down by the Zionist executive to the concrete conditions of Palestine.[35] Among his first actions on arriving in the country in April 1908 was the establishment of a training farm at Deleika (Kinneret) on the western bank of the Sea of Galilee, to be followed about a year later by two more: at Beit Arif (later Ben Shemen), not far from the Arab town of Lydda; and in the contiguous territory of Hulda.

In the language of the time, Kinneret was to be a 'preparatory farm' in two senses. Like the training farms of the JCA, it was to prepare unskilled workers to earn their living as farm labourers or proprietors. But there was a further intention: the land was to be improved, in preparation for sale or rental to Jewish farmers. (By

[34] Baratz, 'From Petah Tikva to Um Juni'.
[35] Bein, *Arthur Ruppin*, 88.

contrast, Sejera, the JCA training farm, was a permanent institution, whose most able graduates were offered holdings in new *moshavot*.) The process of settlement was to continue with the proceeds from these transactions, thus increasing the very small amount of capital available from Zionist funds.[36]

Conditions in Kinneret were primitive in the extreme. Israel Bloch, one of the group which started work in June 1908, described the first few months:

On the hill opposite the lake, we found a half-ruined *khan* which had been used by the sheikh [whose land had been purchased by the Zionist organization] to stable his horse, and had also served as a way-station for travellers. This ruin, which was full of dung, and in which scorpions and snakes went their way unhindered, served us as kitchen, dining-hall, and sick bay. We slept on the flat roof, in the gruelling heat, with no shade or cover. We brought water from the lake, and food from Tiberias or a nearby *moshava*. We took turns to cook. The food and sanitary conditions caused serious illnesses. We realized that we should not be able to continue this way, and although we had decided that we would not have women at the farm in its early stages, we invited Sarah Malkin to join us.... [On her arrival] our lives became more ordered, and we began to prepare the fields for cultivation.[37]

Sarah Malkin described her own experiences, a few weeks later:

The work in the fields and round the house progressed. In the farmyard they put up temporary buildings, and many of the workers slept on beds in the yard. The number of workers increased.... My work became harder and harder. I cooked in the open air, on a camp-fire between stones, with no shade or shelter—and it was a particularly hot summer. I cooked for thirty people, outside, even in the rain. The rain doused the fire, and got into the cooking pots.... Nobody talked about putting up a kitchen. It didn't even occur to me to raise the question, for I knew that we were still at the beginning, and all beginnings are difficult.[38]

The farm was managed by Moshe Berman, who had personally chosen the workers: the central group was the Romni commune from Petah Tikva. During the first few months his relationship with the workers was very good. In a letter to Ruppin dated 13 July 1908 he wrote: 'As for ... a workers' committee ... it is still too early to discuss it.... Perhaps we could create something like the Sejera collective, as they call it.... If you could work out an arrangement of

[36] Shilo, *Experiments in Settlement*, 125–9.
[37] Habass, *Second Aliya*, 404.
[38] Ibid. 497–8.

that sort, I would not disagree.'[39] In order to appreciate the significance of the reference to the Sejera collective, we must return about a year in time.

## Sejera

In September 1907, a small group (led, among others, by Yitzhak Ben-Zvi, who was to be the second president of Israel) founded a tiny secret organization known as Bar Giora whose aim was the protection of Jewish life and property by the Jews themselves. Shortly afterwards, most of its members found their way to the training farm at Sejera, where potential settlers had been trained under the auspices of the JCA for the past seven years. A leading member of this group was Manya Wilbushevitz (Shohat), one of the outstanding personalities among the many colourful characters who were to become leaders of the labour movement in the Second Aliya period.[40]

During her early twenties, Manya had been a member of the Social Revolutionary Party in Russia. One of the party's tenets was the practice of personal terror against the members of the oppressive Tsarist government and police. Manya became involved in an unsuccessful plot to kill the Russian minister of the interior. While raising money in Berlin to finance the operation, she was invited to Palestine by her brother. She went for an exhaustive tour of the country, and, in her words, was 'seized by an extraordinary love for the country—a love which filled all my soul, my mind and my heart'.[41] Because of her socialist principles she joined the Poalei Zion party, but was and remained a maverick in her political ideas. She came to the conclusion that the conquest of labour, as propounded by both the parties, was doomed to failure. The only way of settling the country was by the establishment of collective colonies. Twenty-five years later she wrote:

I had already had some experience with a collective, in Minsk. A group of us wanted to organize the workers without the help of the intelligentsia, and to that end we started a collective.... It was while living with this collective

[39] CZA, KKL A3/100.
[40] A concise account of Manya Shohat's early years (including the years of the Sejera collective) and a comprehensive bibliography is given in Shulamit Reinharz, 'Toward a Model of Female Political Action: The Case of Manya Shohat, Founder of the First Kibbutz'. Her title is misleading, however. As I maintain below, Sejera was not a kibbutz.
[41] Shohat, 'In the Beginning', 617.

that I learned that ... the collective provides the proletariat with its means for struggle.[42]

After returning to Russia for a short time to take part in the Jewish self-defence movement, Manya spent some time in France and America, studying methods of colonization and visiting a number of religious communes. Armed with this knowledge, she returned to Palestine, and, after an abortive attempt to establish a carpenters' co-operative in Jaffa, left for Sejera with the Bar Giora group, one of whose leaders was her future husband, Israel Shohat.

Eliahu Krause, the director of the Sejera farm, was an open-minded and tolerant man, and Manya persuaded him to try a social experiment. Instead of directing all the work under his own super-vision, as was the custom, he agreed to contract all the work on the field crops for a year to a group of workers; in fact, to the members of Bar Giora. They were to be given seed, tools, and working animals, and allowed to organize the work in their own way and on their own initiative—although Krause would continue to give them advice and lessons in agricultural science. At the end of the year, the equipment was to be returned to the farm, and any profit to be divided between the group of workers and management. This group came to be known as the Sejera collective.

The experiment was successful. A small profit was made, in contrast to previous years under more conventional methods of management. Manya had proved her point. But, in the short run, at least, her comrades in Bar Giora rejected the idea of workers' settlement as a central aim of the labour movement. The group left Sejera shortly after the end of the agricultural year and became the nucleus of Hashomer, a more widely based self-defence organization. But the experience of the collective had not been in vain. The same basic idea was used by Hashomer when it contracted to take on the responsibility for guard duty in the *moshavot*; the group of workers (in this case, guards) made an arrangement, as a collective entity, with the man-agement committee of the *moshava*, to do a defined job for a stated period of time—usually a year.[43]

---

[42] Ibid. Manya Shohat's reminiscences of the Sejera collective are confirmed by contemporary accounts. See e.g. 'Ben-Hava' (Moshe Smilansky), 'The Galilean Worker'.

[43] Gil'adi, 'History of the Movement', in *Hashomer Anthology*, 5–20. The text of several contracts between Hashomer and the *moshavot* is printed in Dinur, *History of the Hagana*, vol. i, pt. 2, pp. 815–35.

The story of the collective was known throughout the labour movement, and the idea of group contract work became an accepted pattern of social organization. Such a group was known as a *kvutza*. It is important to note just what the system was. The essential characteristic is communal production: the workers worked together and earned together as a group. Although in many cases they also lived together because of the nature of their work, this was by no means always so. Contract work of this sort was therefore different from the life of the commune, which was marked by communal consumption: its members frequently worked in different occupations, and even in different places. Throughout the Second Aliya, most contractual groups of both these types were temporary: they were formed for a particular purpose, at a particular time; usually 'from harvest to harvest'. When they had done their job, or the conditions changed, they would share out whatever money or property they held in common, and go their several ways.

The *kvutza* system began to spread in the agricultural year beginning in the autumn of 1909. There were in that year five working *kvutzot* and four defence groups, with a total membership of more than seventy—a significant development. Among them there were two of particular importance: those at Kinneret and Merhavia.

At Kinneret, the relationship between the workers and the farm manager, Moshe Berman, deteriorated when it became clear that his original optimistic estimates of the farm's profitability were exaggerated. Matters came to a head in October 1909 when he employed Arab workers to help bring in the harvest before the rains, and the Jewish workers went on strike: not in order to improve their wages or conditions, but as a protest against what they saw as a violation of the principles of Zionism.[44] Ruppin, who held overall responsibility for the farm, decided that the striking workers must leave Kinneret. As a concession to their demands, he suggested that they form a 'conquest group' ('conquest' here referring to the first cultivation, or conquest, of unworked or neglected land) on the pattern of the Sejera collective, and take over a relatively isolated part of the farm, that

---

[44] This was not the first clash between Berman and a group of workers on the issue of Jewish labour. In March 1908, he had employed Arab workers to plant the Herzl Forest at Beit Arif. A number of Jewish workers, including the Romni group, pressed him to employ only Jews; saplings planted by non-Jewish labour were uprooted in symbolic protest and immediately replanted. Contemporary accounts and later reminiscences are collated in R. Frankel, 'The Romni Group', 8–11.

surrounding the abandoned village of Um Juni. The strikers, among whom was the Romni group, refused the offer, as they felt they were not yet sufficiently experienced to accept the responsibility. But Hahoresh, the organization of farm workers in Galilee, chose a group which took on the work.

The Um Juni 'conquest group' attracted the attention of the whole of the labour movement. Its six members were specially picked to represent all the political and agricultural organizations with members in Galilee, and were the most experienced and responsible members of these groups.[45] Two women were attached to the group as cooks and 'house-mothers'; they too were specially chosen. Ruppin, writing to the committee of the Jewish National Fund (the owner of the property), requested that 'this modest experiment should be given no publicity', in case it be interpreted as heralding a new era; for, if it failed, the disappointment would be most harmful to the Zionist cause. Within the Yishuv, however, the very idea of publicly owned land being cultivated by a group of workers aroused great expectations, and great enthusiasm.[46] Berl Katznelson, who was to become one of the leaders of the labour movement, later described his reaction when he heard of Um Juni. He was working in Petah Tikvah when he heard a cynical observation to the effect that a 'workers' republic' had been established near Kinneret, and was doomed to be yet another failure. In his words, twenty-five years later:

One thing I knew: the revival of the Jewish worker would start from there. From then on I knew no rest, I went from one settlement to another, working on the way, until after several months of wandering I reached the place which had entranced me from afar. From a neighbouring hill, I looked down on this magical spot, within which lay the hovels of Um Juni. . . . Its magic has not grown less, nor have its people disillusioned me. To this very day I remember with gratitude how they allowed me, a young, inexperienced worker suffering from malaria, to join in their work—work than which I have never seen any more serious or more pure.[47]

The year ended, as had the year of the Sejera collective, with a small profit, and the dispersal of the conquest group. But the experience was not wasted. In view of its success, Ruppin sought out another group which would be prepared to take on the responsibility for Um Juni

[45] Katznelson, *Writings*, xi. 165.
[46] Shilo, *Experiments in Settlement*, 143–4.
[47] *Davar*, 25 Oct. 1935. Repr. in Katznelson, *Writings*, vii. 192–3.

under similar conditions. He turned to the group which had been expelled from the farm a year previously.

In the autumn of 1909, those involved in the strike left for the *moshava* of Hadera. From now on they were known, to their contemporaries and to history, as the Hadera commune. Each worked for a different farmer, and many had to sleep in their employer's barn in order to start work with the livestock before dawn. But they pooled their earnings and ate communally in a hired room. They were joined in the course of the year by a few new members. Here, under the leadership of Joseph Bussel, who had joined the commune in Kinneret, the group became consolidated and discussed plans for its own future and its place in the future of the Yishuv. Joseph Baratz, who joined them during this year, describes this period:

Thanks to our communal life, a feeling of intimacy between the members grew up. We talked a great deal about the 'commune'; for a certain time, this was the main idea [which was discussed]: communal life not just for a chosen few, but as a permanent social system, at any rate for the bulk of the pioneers who were immigrating to Palestine.

We did not arrive at this idea by a process of objective thought and consideration. It was more a matter of natural feeling: 'What is the difference between me and my comrade, and why should each of us have a separate account?'

Our chief aspiration was to be independent—to create for and by ourselves. We came to realize that it was a Sisyphean task to achieve this if we were working for somebody else, and we began to look back to Galilee.[48]

After some hesitation, the Hadera group accepted Ruppin's offer, and in the autumn of 1910 returned to Um Juni. On the way they took part in the conference of the party to which most of them belonged, Hapoel Hatzair. Their words on this occasion stood out in sharp contrast to the pessimism of virtually all the other participants. Tanhum Tanpilov, who had been one of the original four pioneers from Romni, said: 'I can say, on the basis of my own experience, that a Jewish worker can make a living in Palestine from the fruits of his own labour. Naturally, he must have strong muscles and be used to work.'[49]

Tanpilov's experience was, of course, not necessarily a basis for generalization to the whole of the labour movement. Tanpilov himself was not only an outstanding worker (as, indeed, were all the members

---

[48] Ehad Mihakommuna [Joseph Baratz], 'The First Two Years'.
[49] See n. 32, above.

of the Hadera commune, which was looked on as an élite group even at that time); he had also been a member of a commune ever since his arrival in Palestine in 1907. None the less, the contrast between the confidence that he and other members of this group exuded at the conference and the general air of despair of the other speakers is significant. The *kvutza* was pointing the way out of the trough of despair.

At the same conference Joseph Bussel, the acknowledged leader and ideologist of the Hadera commune, spoke of the basic dilemma of the workers of the Second Aliya, including those who had succeeded as agricultural workers.

Our ideal should be not to create an agricultural proletariat, but to develop an element of farm workers, whether they work for themselves or for others. . . . I mean a system which will truly give the worker individual freedom, without his having to exploit the work of others. Experiments of this sort are now being made in Galilee, and if we consider this question carefully we shall be able to discover the right method.

One of the major complaints of the workers, whether in the *moshavot* or the training farms, was that they were under the constant supervision of overseers or farm managers. This attitude had led to disputes, and even strikes. But they also rejected the only real alternative which the existing system could offer them: that they themselves should accept promotion within the system, and become supervisors or farmers in the *moshavot*. There were many who accepted these alternatives. Bussel and his friends saw such acceptance as a betrayal of the principle which informed all their ideas and actions: the belief in the moral superiority of a life of work, and in their own obligation (and desire) to continue in this way of life. Cautiously, but with the confidence born of his own experience, Bussel was suggesting a way out of this dilemma.

Other ways of solving this problem were widely mooted at the time. One of the strands in the profusion of social concepts which the settlers of the Second Aliya brought with them was the idea of cooperative or communal settlement. Two instances, each of which had important historical consequences, may be cited. The first is that of the Romni group, whose development after their arrival in Palestine has been traced in the preceding pages. One of the aims of the Hat'hia movement, from which this group originated, was 'to rebuild the Land of Israel on collective foundations'; and one of the central figures in the group said many years later that the original quartet's decision to establish a commune was no doubt influenced by this clause. Another instance is that of Joseph Trumpeldor, a soldier in the Tsarist army who was wounded in the Russo–Japanese war and taken prisoner in 1903. Having been much influenced by Tolstoyan ideas in his youth, he spurred his Jewish fellow prisoners into forming a movement for the creation of co-operative colonies in Palestine. In 1913 he and a group of his disciples reached Palestine, where they worked as a *kvutza* in the Galilean settlement of Migdal. Both these and other examples show that the idea of communal settlement was far from unknown to the people of the Second Aliya, even before the establishment of a single communal group.[50]

In the early days of this period, on the other hand, there was much opposition in both the workers' parties to the idea of workers becoming settlers. Many of their leaders maintained that once they left the ranks of the employed they would be on the slippery slope to becoming capitalists. By about 1906 the idea of workers' settlement had become generally accepted, though on certain clearly defined conditions. There were two ways in which a worker could legitimately become a farmer. One was the *moshav po'alim*, which was conceived of as a sort of satellite to one of the existing *moshavot*: the workers would continue to make their living as hired workers in the *moshava*, but they would live in their own village, each on a small family plot just big enough for a house and a vegetable garden. Thus, the problem of housing for the workers would be solved, and they would be able to supplement their income by growing their own food. Three such villages were founded during the Second Aliya, but two of them soon became small *moshavot*, and their inhabitants peasant proprietors like those of Petah Tikva or Rehovot. Only Ein Ganim, founded in 1908, retained the structure of a *moshav po'alim* for a number of years.[51]

The other way out of the dilemma of proprietorship was propounded by Franz Oppenheimer, a German sociologist with experience of settling farmers in East Prussia. He produced a plan for a co-operative village whose land would be owned by the Jewish National Fund and worked in common. The settlers would live in family units, each with a small plot for its own produce, and payment would be made according to the skills and productivity of each worker. The farm manager, who would train the workers and assess their capabilities

---

[50] *Israel Bloch*, 70; Laskov, *Yosef Trumpeldor*, chs. 3–6.
[51] Near, 'Towards Workers' Settlement'.

until they were ready for self-government, was an essential part of this scheme. It was approved by the Zionist Congress in 1909, and land acquired by the Zionist movement at Merhavia, in the centre of the Jezreel Valley, was allocated to it. In the autumn of 1909, at the same time as the 'conquest group' began work at Um Juni, a similar group of Hashomer arrived at Merhavia. Here the problems of self-defence were more serious than in the Jordan Valley at the time; the area had so far been free of Jewish settlement, and the local inhabitants, including the district governor, were anxious to keep it so. There were a number of armed incursions into Merhavia's fields, and the resulting fight led to some of the guards' imprisonment. The Hashomer group conquered the place in more than one sense: its members ploughed the fields in order to confirm their right to settle there; and they defended themselves and their property by force of arms. The following year, at the time when the Hadera commune was returning to Um Juni, the first permanent settlers arrived: a select group, chosen by the farm manager, who had helped train them at a JCA farm in Galicia, and who now accompanied them to their new home.[52]

In the year 1911/12 there were therefore three different types of contractual group (see Table 1): defence groups, of Hashomer; working groups such as that at Degania (as Um Juni was known from August 1911);[53] and settlement groups, of which the only example at this stage was Merhavia itself. From then until the establishment of the State of Israel, both of the latter types of communal framework— the settlement group (*kvutzat hityashvut*) and working group (*kvutzat avoda*)—continued to exist side by side, although both the relationship between them and the accepted terminology changed in the course of time (the defence groups ceased to exist with the disbanding of Hashomer in 1919). From now on, too, the term *kvutza* came to have the generic connotation of a communal group, whether permanently settled or organized for a specific purpose and limited in time, and it retained this meaning until the introduction of the word 'kibbutz' in the early 1920s. From this point, then, I shall use the word *kvutza* in this way.

[52] The best account of the settlement, development, and decline of the Merhavia co-operative is Rabinovitch, 'Social and Economic Life in the Merhavia Co-operative'; cf Shilo, *Experiments in Settlement*, 146–52.

[53] This Hebrew name, derived from a species of cornflower which grew profusely in the area, was chosen by the people of the *kvutza* themselves. Its adoption symbolized their attachment to the soil and emphasized that this locale was now a permanent Jewish settlement.

TABLE 1. Communal and Co-operative Groups during the Second Aliya

| Year | Type | Galilee | | Coastal plain | | Urban | | Total | |
|---|---|---|---|---|---|---|---|---|---|
| | | No. | Members | No. | Members | No. | Members | No. | Members |
| 1903/4 | Commune | – | – | 1[a] | 10 | – | – | 1 | 10 |
| 1904/5 | Commune | – | – | 1[b] | 18 | – | – | 1 | 18 |
| | Working group | – | – | – | – | 1[c] | 5 | 1 | 5 |
| | Total | | | | | | | 2 | 23 |
| 1905/6 | Commune | – | – | 1[b] | 12 | – | – | 1 | 12 |
| 1906/7 | Commune | – | – | – | – | 2 | 20 | 2 | 20 |
| | Moshav po'alim | – | – | 1 | 20 | – | – | 1 | 20 |
| | Total | | | | | | | 3 | 40 |
| 1907/8 | Commune | – | – | 1 | 4 | – | – | 1 | 4 |
| | Moshav po'alim | – | – | 1 | 22 | – | – | 1 | 22 |
| | Working group | 1[d] | 18 | – | – | 1 | 7 | 2 | 25 |
| | Total | | | | | | | 4 | 51 |

| | | | | | | | | | |
|---|---|---|---|---|---|---|---|---|---|
| 1908/9 | Commune | — | — | 1 | 3 | — | — | 1 | 3 |
| | *Moshav po'alim* | — | — | 1[c] | 20 | — | — | 1 | 20 |
| | Working group | 1[d] | 18 | — | — | — | — | 1 | 18 |
| | Defence group | 1 | 4 | — | — | — | — | 1 | 4 |
| | Total | | | | | | | 4 | 45 |
| 1909/10 | Commune | — | — | 2[f] | 18 | 1 | 5 | 3 | 23 |
| | *Moshav po'alim* | — | — | 1 | 20 | — | — | 1 | 20 |
| | Working group | 4[g] | 43 | — | — | 1 | 18 | 5 | 61 |
| | Defence group | 4[h] | 24 | — | — | — | — | 4 | 24 |
| | Total | | | | | | | 13 | 128 |
| 1910/11 | *Moshav po'alim* | — | — | 1 | 20 | — | — | 1 | 20 |
| | Working group | 3 | 44 | 3 | 46 | 2 | 26 | 8 | 116 |
| | Defence group | 3 | 30 | — | — | — | — | 3 | 30 |
| | Settlement group | 1[i] | 17 | — | — | — | — | 1 | 17 |
| | Total | | | | | | | 13 | 183 |
| 1911/12 | *Moshav po'alim* | — | — | 1 | 20 | — | — | 1 | 20 |
| | Working group | 2 | 15 | 3 | 50 | — | — | 5 | 65 |
| | Defence group | 3 | 22 | 1 | 25 | — | — | 4 | 47 |
| | Settlement group | 2[j] | 38 | — | — | — | — | 2 | 38 |
| | Total | | | | | | | 12 | 170 |

TABLE 1. *cont.*

| Year | Type | Galilee | | Coastal plain | | Urban | | Total | |
|---|---|---|---|---|---|---|---|---|---|
| | | No. | Members | No. | Members | No. | Members | No. | Members |
| 1912/13 | Moshav po'alim | — | — | 1 | 20 | — | — | 1 | 20 |
| | Working group | 3 | 47 | 5 | 74 | 5[k] | 60 | 13 | 171 |
| | Defence group | 3 | 24 | 3 | 30 | — | — | 6 | 54 |
| | Settlement group | 2[j] | 41 | — | — | — | — | 2 | 41 |
| | Total | — | — | — | — | — | — | 22 | 286 |
| 1913/14 | Moshav po'alim | — | — | 2 | 45 | — | — | 2 | 45 |
| | Working group | 9 | 89 | 9 | 109 | 3[k] | 32 | 21 | 230 |
| | Defence group | 2 | 54 | 1 | 6 | — | — | 3 | 60 |
| | Settlement group | 2[j] | 47 | — | — | — | — | 2 | 47 |
| | Total | — | — | — | — | — | — | 28 | 382 |

*Sources:* These figures are based on archival material, reminiscences, and press accounts from the period. Where there are no firm figures, I have made a minimum estimate. It is likely that there were similar groupings of which no firm evidence has survived. The table is thus a fairly accurate approximation, though the real number is probably greater. Further details and exact sources are to be found in the table in Near, 'Towards Workers' Settlement', and the list of sources attached thereto.

*Notes:* The Hebrew nomenclature for the terms used here is as follows: commune (of consumption): *kommuna*; defence group: *kvutzat sh'mira*; working group: *kvutzat avoda*, which also covered the 'conquest group' (*kvutzat kibbush*), a term indicating a group that had 'conquered' land not previously cultivated by Jews. Most of the groups contracted for a year's work 'from harvest to harvest', and then broke up, to disperse or re-form. The various specific groups mentioned in the text are indicated here by footnotes.

[a] The Rehovot commune (Haya-Sarah Hankin). [b] Petah Tikva. [c] Manya Shohat's *artel* (Jaffa). [d] The Sejera collective. [e] Ein Ganim. [f] Including the Hadera commune. [g] Including the 'conquest groups' at Um Juni and Merhavia. [h] All groups of Hashomer, including the defenders of Merhavia. [i] Merhavia and Degania. [j] Merhavia. [k] Mostly urban co-operatives organized by Poalei Zion.

The nomenclature of the early groups at Um Juni/Degania is of some importance. During 1909 it became clear to Ruppin that his plan for hiring out plots of the Kinneret farm was premature, to say the least, for there were no reliable hirers. He discussed a number of ways of involving the workers, who were the only element capable of carrying out the work while not demanding (or assuming) ownership of the land in the long run. Most of his ideas involved various methods of payment on behalf of the workers—long-term loans and the like; but all foundered on the rock of the workers' lack of capital. The solution was to contract the land, tools, and cattle to a group of workers who would continue to receive wages from the Zionist movement. Thus, the group was known as a *kvutzat po'alim* (workers' group; the word *po'el* specifically means a hired labourer).[54] This term still appears, anachronistically, to denote a kibbutz in many official documents.

From 1910 onwards there are no known examples of communes on the pattern of those described above. This does not mean that there was no communal consumption. In many of the Hashomer groups, there were married couples, and the wife would keep house for her husband; but the local conditions often dictated variations—in some places one woman cooked for a number of guards, in others the kitchen was completely communal. In Um Juni/Degania, there were both communal production and communal consumption from the first, and also in most of the other *kvutzot*. By the outbreak of the First World War, this was established as the standard model of a *kvutza*.

The Hadera group's contract at Um Juni/Degania for the year 1910/11 was renewed the following year. Meanwhile, the Zionist movement was building permanent housing in place of the dilapidated hovels which had been the original living quarters. When, in 1912, the new houses were ready, a fierce discussion arose: should the group stay to develop Degania, or should they move to new, more pioneering conquests? The day was won by Bussel, with the help of a highly respected veteran member of the commune, Tanhum Tanpilov, who is reported to have said:

Pioneering is not simply conquest, not just being first. We Jews have always been the first in every social movement, every revolution. What we lack is stability, the ability to preserve our conquests, to conquer ourselves and bind

[54] Shilo, 'Degania: First Model of Collective Settlement'.

ourselves to the soil and to the particular locality, to fight against the *wanderlust* which has afflicted us throughout the generations. We must remain here! It is our task to make the desert blossom, despite the malaria and the heat.[55]

From then on, the group's annual contract at Degania was renewed automatically. In practice, if not juridically, Degania had become a permanent settlement. At Merhavia, on the other hand, the situation deteriorated. There were constant clashes between the farm manager and the workers, who were of no less independent a turn of mind than those of Degania; and the situation could not be improved by removing the manager, who was an integral part of the system. Moreover, there was not sufficient land to provide the family plots which were to have produced a substantial part of the settlers' income in the first years, and the economic situation began to deteriorate alarmingly.

In December 1911, Ruppin, already concerned about the success of this supposed model for Zionist settlement, had suggested combining the Degania group with that of Merhavia. The workers of Degania replied:

The workers consider complete freedom in their work and in the development of their initiative to be essential for the existence of the *kvutza*. . . . In addition, they are opposed to two elements in Oppenheimer's theory: differential wages as between workers; and supervision by an official manager of a group of workers who have had several years' experience at their job.[56]

By 1914, most of the special characteristics of the Oppenheimer scheme had vanished from Merhavia, and it was occupied by a *kvutza* on the Degania model. In the labour movement this development was widely interpreted as the victory of a pragmatic approach over an abstract sociological theory.[57]

The last years of the Second Aliya, from 1911 to 1914, witnessed a sharp increase in the number of *kvutzot*. This was due in part to the success of Sejera, Degania, and the system of 'conquest groups'. There was now an organizational—and ideological—model for the conquest of work which largely eliminated or by-passed the difficulties

---

[55] *Tanhum*, 21. The use of the word 'pioneering' (*halutziut*) is anachronistic, since this term was not coined until the Third Aliya (Near, 'Redemption of the Soil and of Man'). But there seems no reason to doubt that this discussion took place, and that its general tenor was as described in the text.

[56] Quoted in Bein, *History of Zionist Settlement*, 67.

[57] e.g. Avner [Yitzhak Ben-Zvi], 'The Question of Collective Settlement'.

which had seemed insuperable in 1910. In addition, the growth of the *kvutzot* was helped by the steady increase in the number of *ahuzot*: associations of potential settlers in the Diaspora, who contracted the work on their land to groups of workers, hoping eventually to immigrate and settle on a developed farm. By 1914 there were twenty-eight *kvutzot*, whose members numbered some 380 (see Table 1). The great majority were 'conquest' or development groups. Only four were in sole charge of permanent settlements—Degania, Kinneret, Merhavia, and Gan Shmuel; and of these, only in Degania was there a group which had lived together in the same place for more than two years.

## Degania in 1914[58]

By 1914, Degania was no longer the tiny group which had originally taken on the responsibility for Um Juni. Around this group—still known as 'the commune'—the *kvutza* had grown both as a social organism and as an economic unit. Although people had left almost from the very beginning, the core of permanent residents gradually increased, and by 1913/14 it had reached twenty-eight. During that year there were forty-four names on the work roster[59]—some simply working visitors, others intending to stay permanently. Formally, they were all employees of the Zionist movement; for instance, apart from the members of the commune, each was accredited individually with his wages, less the cost of upkeep. In reality, however, this distinction made virtually no difference: all those living and working in Degania took part in all the activities.[60]

In the early years, the original members of the commune dominated both the rudimentary administration and the decision-making process. After a revolt by the younger members, they too were given a share in these matters; but tension between 'veterans' and 'youngsters' was a feature of life in Degania for many years to come.[61] The affairs of the *kvutza* were managed in an informal and, on the whole, egalitarian manner. Every evening, at a general discussion in

---

[58] Unless otherwise stated, the account of day-to-day life in Degania before the war is based on Dayan, *Twenty-Five Years of Degania*. Although his description is sentimentalized and contains a number of inaccuracies relating to himself, it is in the main factually accurate.

[59] Dayan, *Twenty-five Years of Degania*, 83; Katznelson, *The Kvutza*, 130.

[60] Dayan, *Twenty-five Years of Degania*, 86.

[61] Minutes of a general meeting on this subject in the archives of Degania Aleph, 23–6; cf. Katznelson, *The Kvutza*, 78–80.

which all could participate, the following day's work was allocated. These discussions often continued late into the night and were known to last even until the beginning of work the following morning. For work began early. The farm was based primarily on arable crops; and, with seasonal variations, the hours of work were 'from dawn to dusk', with a break of some two or three hours in the heat of the day. In order to prepare the draught-horses, several workers had to begin work two hours before dawn, and carry on for some time after dusk. Standards of work were high, self-criticism and mutual criticism frequent. One of the veterans tells of a young man who, after some experience in other *kvutzot*, was sent to plough in the biggest field— the 'long furrow'. At the end of each row, he would sit and smoke a cigarette. 'Nobody said a word to him. But in the evening, in the dining-hall, the atmosphere around him was such that the following morning he got up and left the *kvutza*.'[62]

Apart from the work roster every evening, there were general meetings of the *kvutza* at frequent intervals; the weekly roster, in which such work as guard duties, chores in the kitchen, and other non-specialist jobs were arranged in rotation; meetings on special problems, such as that mentioned above in which it was decided to stay in Degania; and, towards the New Year (September; also the end of the agricultural year) a series of meetings to discuss the state of the *kvutza*, and decide on general policy for the future. In a letter to a friend dating from 1916 Joseph Bussel speaks of a meeting which lasted, with short breaks, from Friday afternoon to Saturday evening. He adds: 'We decided, after a fine discussion, to continue our meetings every Saturday evening'; and thereby established a custom which is still practised in the great majority of kibbutzim.[63]

In contrast to the men of Hashomer, the members of Degania did not see the physical security of the Yishuv as their prime responsibility, but they felt themselves responsible for their own settlement. For several years, Lower Galilee had been subject to the incursions of tribes of Bedouin from across the Jordan, particularly at times of harvest. In November and December 1913, three Jewish settlers were killed, one in Degania, one in Kinneret, and one in Sejera, and guard duty became part of the regular life of the *kvutza*. This added much tension to the already strained work schedule; in a community where

---

[62] Zvi Rosenberg, in an interview with Muki Tsur; Tsur *et al.*, *The Beginning of the Kibbutz*, 34.
[63] Letter to Gershon, in the archives of Degania Aleph; ibid. 33.

malaria was virtually endemic, as much as half the work force could be idle because of illness on a given day.

Housing in Degania was no longer as primitive as it had been in Um Juni. Permanent housing was built within a walled yard, and contained the members' living quarters, as well as the dining-room, cowshed, barn, and so forth. The housing was well built (it is still in use today), but as the number of people grew, some of the men began to live in tents. Food was vegetarian (with the addition of fish when it could be obtained), its quality varying with the state of the economy and the competence of the cooks. In general, however, it was rather poor and badly cooked, and there were constant complaints of chronic indigestion and other food-related illnesses. Clothes were mainly functional, and taken according to need from the communal laundry. Until the mid-1920s the *kvutza* owned only a few 'good' dresses which were taken as needed 'for travelling'; and the wagon returning from Tiberias would stop when it met the one leaving Degania so that the good shoes suitable for town could be handed over to those who now needed them.

Cultural life was rudimentary. There was a certain anti-intellectual element, who believed that dedication to a life of work must be total; but there were also many devoted readers, and the general tone was cultured and tolerant. Sabbath evenings, festivals, and such special occasions as weddings were celebrated with folk-song and dance: some brought from the Diaspora, others newly composed and invented in order to fulfil the Zionist principle of creating a new Hebrew culture. In the first two years of Degania's existence, much Yiddish was spoken; but from 1913, with the arrival of a Hebrew teacher, Hebrew became the dominant language, in accordance with the accepted ideology.

Economically, the farm was still based on arable crops—half wheat, the rest divided between oats, sorghum, and various legumes. The practices and equipment used derived from European models adapted to local conditions. Mechanization was introduced in 1914 with the acquisition of a threshing machine. Experimental orchards—citrus fruit, olives, and almonds—had been planted, but they were still too young to yield fruit. Vegetables (cucumbers, carrots, and radishes) were grown for home consumption. At this time, the dairy herd and poultry were also considered part of the kitchen garden. In 1913 a number of cows had been brought from Beirut in order to begin the creation of a commercial herd; but an attack of cattle plague at the beginning of 1914 destroyed most of the stock, and it was many months until it was renewed. The combination of these developments with the uncertainties of the climate and other natural phenomena made economic progress unsteady. The farm had achieved comparative prosperity in the last pre-war year. But, as had become apparent during these years, this progress was precarious in the extreme.[64]

All these details are important, and serve to give some sort of picture of the *kvutza* at a vital stage in its development. It is much harder to describe what was, after all, the social cement of this very special society: what was known, and spoken of, as 'the spirit of Degania'. I shall close this description with two short pieces by people who were not at the time members of the *kvutza*. The first, dating from about 1913, is taken from the reminiscences of Aliza Shidlovsky, who came to Degania as an 18-year-old girl just before the war. She was not considered a good enough worker to be accepted for membership of Degania, but some years afterwards became one of the founding members of the first permanent group at the neighbouring *kvutza*, Kinneret.

If the members did not go out to the barn after supper, they would sit round the table, chatting a little, and singing a lot. Never since those days have I heard singing like that. It provided an outlet for the feelings of isolation and exile of this tiny group of people (we were 24 in all), and of each one of us individually. For there was no regular connection with any other settlement; the newspaper (the fortnightly *Hapoel Hatzair*) arrived very infrequently; the few books which people had brought with them were packed in their suitcases. The dominant feeling was that you were cut off from Europe, from the world, from your previous existence, and surrounded by a vacuum which you must fill yourself. The singing was shot through with all our doubts, all our suspicions that the passing day might bring no morrow. Often the singing would culminate in a *hora* no less strange—to the point of swooning. More than once I have seen Y.K. sinking onto a bench after the *hora*, all his strength used up. Bussel had to be taken out of the circle in a swoon. It was not just a dance, it was a wordless cry, a catharsis of all that had accumulated in the heart. And sometimes it also contained an element of reconciliation after

---

[64] The 'conquest group' made a modest profit in its year of operation (1909/10). In 1910/11 the farm made a profit of 566 Turkish francs, and in 1911/12 a loss of 805. The following two years saw profits of 841 and 9,212 francs, respectively. Dayan, *Twenty-Five Years of Degania*, 84; and cf. the work schedule of the *kvutza* in the archives of Degania Aleph.

harsh words between the members. To me, still a young girl, the *hora* was an open book in which I read all the difficulties of these people's lives.[65]

The second extract, by the Hebrew teacher, describes the Passover celebration in 1914, when he had been in Degania for about a year.

On the eve of Passover there was no special programme, but that evening revealed to me how deep were the spiritual ties between me and the people of the *kvutza*. I cannot remember if we read from the Haggada; but we sang a great deal—all of us. All were one great family, loving and beloved. We danced a lot, sometimes to the accompaniment of stirring songs, sometimes to the rhythmical tapping of many feet. Between the dancing, we played all sorts of party games . . . and all this—the singing, the games, the dance, and the excitement—together wove a web of fraternity and life partnership shot through with love, honesty, and joy.

On that night we drank a lot of wine and cognac. . . . We were all drunk. There is a saying 'in his cups shall you know him'. And in that evening I knew the quality of Degania. People became more elevated, and plumbed the depths of their noble souls. T. embraced a tree, and lectured on 'the new man in the *kvutza*'. Tanhum jumped onto a bench, and spoke in praise of the study groups and the high standard of culture in the previous year. In the course of his speech, he turned to me, suggested that I become a permanent member of the *kvutza*, and demanded that I say 'yes' immediately. The atmosphere was full of enthusiasm, faith, vision, and joy. I, too, was in an ecstasy of enthusiasm. It was the only time in my life that I have ever been drunk; but that fact has not dimmed the sense of that night's experience, which has influenced all my life ever since.[66]

## THE SPREAD OF THE *KVUTZOT*

It was noted above that from an early stage in its existence Degania became a model for other *kvutzot*. Even now, however, it was far from clear that it had become a model for settlement. The future of Merhavia was still uncertain. One other village—Gan Shmuel, near Hadera—was occupied by a communal group which intended to settle there permanently; but it had arrived at the spot only in the autumn of 1913, and was far from having proved itself.[67] Ruppin was still looking for new and more economical methods of colonization, and had discovered a group which had enough money to do what the *kvutzot* of Um Juni/Degania could not. In the agricultural year 1912/13, some twenty members of a movement called Ha'ikar Hatza'ir

---

[65] Habass, *Second Aliya*, 556–7.    [66] Ben-Yehuda, 'Life in Degania'.
[67] Habass, *Second Aliya*, 215; *Hapoel Hatzair*, 7/8–9 (11 Dec. 1913), 19.

(The Young Farmer) rented the Kinneret farm from the Zionist movement, with the intention of turning it into a moshav. Although these people were very efficient farmers, the group apparently lacked social cohesion and broke up before the end of the year. The farm was taken over by the group which eventually became the nucleus of a permanent *kvutza* on the model of Degania.[68]

Several of the communal groups of 1913 and 1914 were significantly different from Degania. The Poalei Zion party, disillusioned with the Merhavia experiment, promoted two new social forms: urban producers' co-operatives, modelled on the Russian *artel*; and an ambitious settlement scheme known as Ahva (Fraternity), which was to have comprised a network of enterprises ranging from an improved version of the Merhavia experiment to co-operative urban settlements and purchasing and marketing agencies. By 1914 it was already clear that the urban groups, most of them composed of new immigrants with little sympathy for the co-operative ideal, were on the decline. Ahva got no further than establishing a number of very successful *kvutzot*, more or less of the accepted type, when its development was halted by the war.[69]

Hapoel Hatzair, with the weight of opinion in the leadership of the Zionist movement and the labour parties behind it, continued to see the moshav as the form of settlement most likely to survive. By 1913 the principles of a new type of village—the *moshav ovdim*—had already been clearly defined. In contrast to the *moshav po'alim*, the workers' plots were to be big enough to support them without the help of outside work; the land was to belong to the Jewish National Fund; and the moshav as a whole was to be collectively responsible for its members' economic ties with the outside world.[70] At the outbreak of war, one such settlement, Nahalat Yehuda, already existed in embryonic form, and active preparations were being made for the foundation of another (Ein Hai).[71] It looked as if the Yishuv was moving in the direction of the doctrine which Yitzhak Wilkansky, the

[68] Shilo, *Experiments in Settlement*, 153–5.
[69] Near, 'Towards Workers' Settlement', secs. 2 and 3.
[70] Resolutions of the Judaean Agricultural Workers' Union, Dec. 1912, repr. in Katznelson, *At Work*, 119–20; cf. Katznelson's speech at this conference, *Writings*, i. 2–11. Although the phrase *moshav po'alim* was still used, the structure is unquestionably that of the *moshav ovdim*.
[71] Some of the settlers at Nahalat Yehuda were deliberately chosen to be the forerunners of this new type of community. They proved their dedication to the ideal of the *moshav ovdim* by transferring the ownership of their land to the Jewish National

manager of the Ben Shemen training farm, was actively promoting in his public activities: the *kvutza* for preparation of land and people for agricultural settlement; the moshav for permanent colonization.[72]

## *The War and the* Kvutzot

The proliferation of social forms towards the end of the Second Aliya was cut short by the advent of the First World War. This was a period of extreme hardship for the whole of the Yishuv. Its leaders were exiled, many Jews were imprisoned and tortured, men and animals were conscripted, crops were confiscated. Financial support from the Diaspora arrived most sporadically. By 1918, death and emigration had reduced the Jewish population to 56,000, little more than it had been at the beginning of the Second Aliya. Under these circumstances, most of the existing *kvutzot* broke up. On the other hand, a number of temporary communes were established in the *moshavot* in order to share whatever work and means of sustenance could be found; a few of the pre-war *kvutzot* managed to survive the war, and three of them eventually achieved permanent settlement;[73] and some half-dozen new *kvutzot* were formed during the war, but failed to outlast it.[74]

The *moshavot* of the coastal plain suffered particularly badly during this period, for their economies were based largely on grapes and citrus, which were unsaleable during the war. By contrast, despite the toll of suffering, of which they shared no small part, the established *kvutzot* survived the war reasonably well. The Jewish settlements of Galilee, where most of the *kvutzot* were located, grew mainly arable crops. Thus, they were able to supply the grain which was essential to the very existence of the Yishuv; and the price they could demand for their produce rose accordingly.

This situation created a number of dilemmas for the *kvutzot*. Concurrently with the rising demand for their produce, the people of Degania improved their methods of work and gradually expanded their economic capacity, and with it the need for working hands. Extra labour was available in plenty, for many of those thrown out of

---

Fund. Ein Hai was being worked by a 'conquest group' which intended to become a moshav, but the outbreak of war halted further development. On Nahalat Yehuda see Shefer, 'Nahalat Yehuda'. On Ein Hai (today Kfar Malal) see Tamir, *People of the Second Aliya*, ii. 219–20; Habass, *Second Aliya*, 469–70.

[72] Wilkansky, *On the Way*, chs. 1, 3–5, and 8.

[73] 'Ahva' in Yagur, 'Avoda' in Degania Beit, and the founding group of Geva.

[74] A. Friedman, 'From the Distant Past', in B. Katznelson (ed.), *At Work* (Heb.), (Jaffa, 1918), 22–32.

work by the depression in the veteran *moshavot* had come to Galilee. By 1917, Degania had some forty members, and at certain periods large numbers of seasonal workers were needed. This was one way of easing the plight of the unemployed and was accepted as a necessary evil. But the process of expansion led to a change in the structure of the *kvutza*, and wide dissatisfaction among its members. The general meeting was still the sovereign body, but day-to-day decisions about work and other matters were decided by a committee of four, instead of the spontaneous face to face discussions of the earlier days. There was tension between the veteran members and the more recent arrivals, and complaints that the ordinary member no longer felt full responsibility for the affairs of the *kvutza*. At a general meeting in February 1917, these questions were thoroughly aired. Bussel and others suggested returning to the earlier structure of the *kvutza*, forgoing some of its land, and restricting its number to ten families. This suggestion, which was partly put into practice in the autumn of 1919, expressed a basic attitude to the question of the relation between the *kvutza* and the outside world. In the words of one of the founders:

[I believe that we should] return to the past—not to the primitive way in which we used to live, but to the many positive aspects of our work then. We are not creators of ways of life for great multitudes; rather, we are an example for a small but idealistic group of people.[75]

None the less, it was patent that, while this was a possible long-term attitude, it ignored a number of very pressing current problems. One of these was the presence, literally at the entrance to the *kvutza*, of hundreds of starving and unemployed people. From the spring of 1917, Galilee was flooded with refugees, evacuated from Jaffa by the Turkish authorities in the face of the British invasion. Lacking any means of livelihood apart from occasional charitable donations, they lived in temporary shacks wherever they could find a resting-place—usually on Jewish-owned land, and often close to the few existing settlements.

Bussel was particularly sensitive to this problem; he spent much of his time during the last year of the war attempting to find work for these people in the neighbouring *moshavot*, and trying to set up an orphanage for some of the hundreds of children left homeless by the war. Indeed, his efforts in this work led directly to his death. In

[75] Tanhum Tanpilov, 15 Feb. 1917. Reported in minutes in the archives of Degania Aleph, 8.

August 1919, while he was hastening home after a meeting in Tiberias, the boat in which he was crossing the Sea of Galilee capsized in a sudden storm. Weakened by a recent bout of malaria and unable to swim to shore, he drowned at the age of 28.[76]

Degania's wartime experience exemplifies three different ways in which the *kvutza* could play its part in tackling the problems of the Yishuv: expansion; improvement of its own society and economy, in order to be a model to others; and work by its own members outside the *kvutza*—a concept known in later years as the 'mission' of the kibbutz. Degania tried, and later rejected, the first of these solutions, while adopting the other two.

During the same period the expansionist attitude became one of the hallmarks of Degania's neighbour, Kinneret. During the war it became a sanctuary of sorts for several dozen members of the labour movement, many of whom were already among its leading figures. Formally, it was run by the small *kvutza* which had taken over the farm in the autumn of 1913. But this group was constantly augmented by extra workers, some of whom worked with the *kvutza*, while others rented plots of land in the area. The atmosphere was different from that of Degania: rather than a small group bound together by a common past and ties of deep comradeship, these were people conscious of belonging to a common movement, in constant flux, ever seeking new ways of organization, and always conscious of their obligation to show the way to the rest of the workers of the Yishuv.

Not all their experiments succeeded. One such failure was the draining of a swampy area of Kinneret's land, carried out by unemployed workers during 1916 at the initiative of the Zionist movement. The contrast between the conditions of the swamp workers, whose living quarters and food were of a very low standard, and those in the farm—from among whose number the managers of the team were recruited—led to serious social friction, and the work was not completed. The veterans of the *kvutzot* and the organizers of the project were very severely criticized on the grounds that they were defending their interests against those of the refugees.

Another experiment, one which almost failed, took place in 1916. The scarcity of grain and the consequent rise in the price of the produce of Galilee's early harvest brought Degania the prospect of a profitable year, after a succession of poor yields and overall losses. The Galilean Workers' Union—one of several regional (non-political)

[76] Wurm, *Bussel Memorial Book*, 242–4, 299–300.

associations which had grown up from 1911 onwards in order to promote mutual aid and technical advancement among Jewish farm workers—demanded that all the *kvutzot* should participate in a scheme devised by a number of members of Kinneret for the collective purchase and equitable distribution of grain. At first Degania refused to take part in the scheme. One of its leading members is said to have remarked to Meir Rothberg, the organizer of the scheme, 'We view you as our enemy. At last we have the chance to pay off our debts, and you are preventing it.'[77] Only after the intervention of A. D. Gordon, and several days of reconsideration, did Degania join the scheme. This is generally considered to be the beginning of Hamashbir, the first of a wide range of co-operative purchasing and marketing agencies of the Histadrut.

Some of the leading members of Kinneret drew clear conclusions from the swamp incident. A few of them left the *kvutza*, membership of which—if it existed at all at this stage in any formal sense—was very fluid and noncommittal, as against the more clearly defined regime of Degania.[78] Others took some time to crystallize their ideas, which were expressed in 1919 with the establishment of the '*kvutza* of sixty'—a group composed of all the twenty members of the *kvutza*, together with forty new immigrants, who were to work together on equal terms both in agriculture and in other work (including the draining of the swamp). Kinneret had adopted the approach to the outside world which Degania had tried and rejected.[79]

It is at about this time that what may be called the 'myth of Kinneret' originated. In the historiography of the kibbutz movement, Kinneret is often given a special place as the originator of many ideas which later became incorporated into accepted doctrine.[80] As can be seen from the above account, there is some truth in this contention. But this fruitful period was a function of the people rather than the place; for it took place at a time when Kinneret was not, properly speaking, a settled community, but rather a place of refuge in which a number of original and talented people worked together, and began to work out a common ideology in reaction to the events of the time. In Degania, by contrast, the development of the community and its outlook was inextricably linked to the process of settlement.

[77] Oral testimony of Meir Rothberg, Aug. 1937, in the archives of Kibbutz Kinneret. Quoted by R. Frankel, 'The Kvutza and the Kibbutz', 83.
[78] Ibid. 61.    [79] On Kinneret during the war see ibid. 61–2, 81–7, 101–2.
[80] e.g. Rabinovitch, *Principles of the Kibbutz Me'uhad*, 56–7.

*Hashomer* [81]

The basic attitudes to the nature and function of the kibbutz which crystallized in Degania and Kinneret during the war foreshadowed events that were to be of major importance in later years. At the same time, also in Galilee but at some distance from the Jordan Valley, another section of the kibbutz movement was taking shape: the Hashomer movement began to establish settlements of its own, rather than simply guarding other people's property. This development had its origins a year or two before the war.

As we have seen, Hashomer adopted the system of *kvutzot* for guard duty, or for the initial cultivation of a newly acquired area. But this was not their only method of organization. Hashomer was a small and, necessarily, selective movement; in all, 105 people passed through its ranks in the thirteen years of its existence (1907 to 1920), and there were probably never more than 60 members at any given time. It demanded absolute discipline of its members; and, although it had a central committee and held frequent consultations, the word of the 'commander' was decisive in all military matters. At its annual meeting, the members would be given their tasks for the year; some of them would work in groups, others alone or in pairs in a particular area. [82]

The following extracts give some idea of the way of life of Hashomer, and the developments which led to its playing a further part in the history of the kibbutz.

The first is from the reminiscences of Keila Gil'adi, the widow of Israel Gil'adi, one of the commanders of the movement:

In Kinneret, Israel [my recently married husband] and I slept in an old, tumbledown, clay building, together with all the other guards. . . . Later, he fixed up a sort of mobile tent on a cart, and we would sleep in that. . . . When we actually got a room to sleep in, there were five of us in the one room— not to mention the frequent guests. I used to cook for us all, and we slept on the floor. . . .

We returned to guard duty in Sejera. One night, one of the guards woke us shouting 'Get up, Israel. Barel has been killed.' I was so upset that it made me ill, and this apparently had an effect on my baby, who fell sick. There were no medical facilities in the place, and after a few days he died. . . .

Again we were ordered to move, this time to Yavne'el. Here I lived in one room, together with five *shomrim*: they slept in the day, and I in the night.

---

[81] This section is partly based on Azati, 'Hashomer and its Attitude to Settlement'.
[82] *Book of Hashomer*, 474–5.

The room was stifling, with no floor, full of huge mice which were not afraid of us. This room, which was full of all sorts of bugs and insects, depressed me so much that on one occasion, unable to restrain myself, I told Israel that I was tired of this life. He was furious. 'How can you complain?' he said, 'when you assumed this responsibility knowing full well what it entails?' After this, he did not speak to me for several days, and I felt that he was right.[83]

The following extracts are from a letter from Mendel Portugali, one of the veterans of the movement, to his wife Tova, written in 1914 or 1915:

One hears of people who leave their former environment, and go to some distant place to live communal lives, pure, moral lives, lives without hatred and jealousy.... Not everyone is prepared to live such a life ... a life of fraternity. How I envy them! I would gladly live in a *kvutza* of this sort ...

We are now starting to implement the idea of the *shomrim's* village.... The basic idea is to have some land, to develop the market garden and other crops, and that a good proportion of the members will be able to be free from work for about six months in the year, for guard duty. But the most important thing is that the people living there should be close to each other ...

I like the idea of the village, for guard duty has ruined my health. The life of the guard has much that is poisonous in it, and there is much that we must change. There is, perhaps, some spiritual satisfaction in it at the beginning, when everything is new, but later one sees how empty the life is, and this emptiness leads to laziness and demoralization. Most of the veteran guards are broken, listless, and lacking in energy. There is nothing better than work, even if it is hard. He who works is always young in spirit.[84]

In these two extracts we see vividly the difficulties inherent in the life of the men, and even more of the women, of Hashomer. The idealism and devotion with which they had taken on themselves what they conceived to be the most pressing task of the Yishuv were eroded in the course of five or six years of military duty with its virtually unlimited demands. The problem of the wives and mothers was particularly pressing, and was compounded by the fact that Hashomer also took on itself responsibility for the orphans of its members: fifteen members were killed on duty and a dozen more died of illnesses or accidents. Thus the idea of a 'Hashomer village', modelled on the Cossack frontier settlements, began to take shape.

In 1916/17 land belonging to the JCA became available for Jewish

[83] *Hashomer Anthology*, 101–2.          [84] Ibid. 20–1.

settlement in Upper Galilee, close to the border between Palestine and Syria. Four sites were occupied by 'conquest groups'. One of them became the 'Hashomer settlement'. The social structure of this community (later Kfar Gil'adi) had not been finally decided, and most of its founders were in favour of parcellation into family plots after an initial period of communal living. During the Arab attacks on the Jewish villages of Upper Galilee in 1919 the site was evacuated, however, and when the members returned in 1920, they organized a communal dining-room, a communal clothing store, and everything necessary for communal care of the children. One of the members later recalled, 'I don't remember any discussion about these questions in the general meeting. It was obvious to all of us that this should be our way of life, for it was dictated by the realities of the situation.'[85]

This process, and the fact that Kfar Gil'adi continued to be a kibbutz after the initial period of settlement, reinforces the evidence of Mendel Portugali's letter, quoted above: communal life was adopted not only because it was an effective way of withstanding difficult conditions but because there was a model which could be imitated 'naturally', without the social and spiritual difficulties experienced by the members of Degania in evolving this social form. By the end of the war, Degania was both an established fact and a pattern for new settlement.

## *Women and Mothers*

As we have seen, women were generally taken on as 'house-mothers' in the earliest *kvutzot*: so much so that, in the first contracts between the *kvutzot* and the settlement authorities, the women were not mentioned: their expenses were borne by the *kvutza* as a whole, and they had no direct earnings. This was not acceptable to many of the women in the *kvutzot*, who demanded their right to take part in the conquest of labour and the other tasks of the Yishuv, no less than the men. The stories of Tehia Lieberman and Sarah Malkin, said to be the first women of the Second Aliya to work in agriculture, illustrate the process. On her arrival in Petah Tikva, one of the veteran *moshavot*, Tehia Lieberman was offered work as a seamstress, or in other 'women's' jobs. Scorning such work, she found employment with a sympathetic farmer, hoeing in the vineyard. Petah Tikva was largely under the influence of orthodox Jews, who looked askance at the idea

[85] Keila Gil'adi, in Poznansky and Shehori, *Women in the Kibbutz*, 32.

of women doing men's work—and, particularly, working together
with men. So she would hide her hoe in the field, and return by a
roundabout way after work. Her friend, Sarah Malkin, took on a
succession of agricultural tasks and 'women's jobs' in a number of
places before being asked to act as house-mother in the most difficult
and prestigious conditions of the conquest groups, at Kinneret in its
first year and at Um Juni. With the establishment of Degania she
became a member, but demanded to work in agriculture. When her
request was refused, she left the *kvutza*, to return only after many
years.[86]

The 'women's revolution' in Degania was effected by Miriam
Baratz, who had been house-mother of the commune in Hadera
together with Sara Malkin. When Degania's first cow was bought,
she demanded to be allowed to work with the dairy herd. The male
members refused to believe that a woman was capable of doing such
heavy work, and her request was also refused. Miriam took lessons in
secret from a woman in a neighbouring Arab village, rose early one
morning, and had finished the milking before the regular cowman
arrived.[87] Her right to work was established (and, it must be added,
acknowledged at once by the men of the *kvutza*); but it was only after
the birth of the first children that the *kvutza* completed its conception
of women's rights. In 1916 Joseph Bussel laid down the ideological
foundations of what became known as communal child care, and is
still the basis of education in the kibbutz.

Child care is not only the responsibility of the mother, but of all the women.
The essential thing is to preserve the principle of co-operation in everything;
there should be no personal possessions, for private property hinders co-
operative work. As for payment for child care, this must certainly be made
from the general fund, since in communal life all expenses should be paid
communally, and nobody can be exempted simply because he has no children.
In fact, all the expenses for child care should be paid for by the community.[88]

At the time, Degania was in the midst of a series of discussions
about the extent to which communal living was desirable, and the
technical details of its operation. This was, therefore, an extreme
point of view, which posited both completely communal forms of
consumption and the application of this principle to the exceedingly

[86] Lieberman, *Chapters in a Life*, 37–41; Malkin, *With the Second Aliya*, 20; Dayan,
*Twenty-Five Years of Degania*, 60.

[87] Baratz, 'Early Days in Degania'.

[88] In a general meeting in Degania, 1916. Repr. in Katznelson, *The Kvutza*, 3.

delicate question of education and child care. The actual process of putting this principle into practice was far from simple. In the early months, Miriam Baratz took the child with her to work; later, she cooked for her own family for a short time as a protest against the inadequacies of the food provided by the *kvutza*. Over the next few years, an organizational structure evolved in accordance with the dual principle of the mother's right to work and the *kvutza*'s duty to educate its children. In the earliest stages, one of the mothers would look after a group of children by mutual arrangement, enabling the others to work in the agricultural branches. Gradually the functions and position of the 'baby-sitter' were institutionalized, and child care became part of the regular work roster of the *kvutza*. The concepts of the *metapelet* (child-care worker) and the 'educational group' were born.

Until the invention of communal child care, it was generally supposed that the *kvutza* was a transitory phase which would yield to other forms of community, such as the moshav, as the number of families grew. But the emergence of a structure for child care—and, at a rather later stage, of communal education—put the seal on the *kvutza* as a permanent community.

## Degania in 1919

In the autumn of 1919, Degania carried out the reform which had been under discussion for more than two years and returned two-thirds of its land to the Zionist movement. At the same time another fundamental change took place. The contract with the Zionist movement was altered so that the members of the *kvutza* were no longer its direct employees but leased their land from the Jewish National Fund under a long-term contract. They had already bought much of the stock and farm equipment, and gradually purchased the rest. Although they still relied on the Zionist movement for development capital and expert advice in many fields they were now an independent body, exercising formal control over their own community and its economy.[89]

Despite its reduction in size, this was no longer the small, isolated, relatively homogeneous community of the early days described above. The process whereby those who left were replaced by new, younger members meant that there was now a wider spread of ages and places

[89] For the date see letter from Bussel dated June 1919, repr. in Wurm, *Bussel Memorial Book*, 241.

of origin. Moreover the feeling of isolation grew less once the land
they had relinquished was settled by a young and dynamic *kvutza*,
Degania Beit, and the neighbouring Kinneret developed as a permanent settlement. Gone, too, was the fear that 'the passing day
might bring no morrow'. Degania and the *kvutzot* established along
the same lines from 1917 onwards were now a recognized and
respected element in the labour movement and the Yishuv as a
whole.[90] In 1919, discussing whether the moshav was a better means
of absorbing new immigrants than the *kvutza*, Bussel expressed a
confidence to which the people of Degania had previously given voice
only in a minor key.

I perceive that, in the last resort, the *kvutza* is the only way which can enable
us to conquer agriculture. The young men who are about to arrive will also
have to adopt a communal way of life, which relieves the individual from
economic cares, and affords him the opportunity to live a productive life.
The same applies to the young women: they will not agree to the old ways
of work.[91]

Economically, there had been little development since 1914. It had
become clear that—partly because of the disruption caused by the
war—some of the experiments with fruit trees had failed. In the
balance sheet for 1919/20 neither citrus fruit nor any other orchard
crop appears, apart from olives and almonds. The dairy herd and the
poultry branch have grown, but they are still supplying the members'
needs and have not yet found an outside market. The main income
still comes from field crops, and it is sufficient to produce a reasonable
profit for the year.[92]

Degania's economic progress since 1914 can be summed up as solid
but not spectacular. Its social situation was more problematic. It had
avoided a potentially dangerous situation by rejecting the tendency
to uncontrolled growth which had typified the war years. But,
although the smaller Degania was more manageable and closer to the
original ideals of its founders, many problems remained. The death
of Joseph Bussel in his prime had left the *kvutza* without a leader of
vision who could suggest new and imaginative solutions to the

[90] These were Kfar Gil'adi and Mahanaim (1917), Tel Hai and Ayelet Hashahar
(1918), and Degania Beit and Kiriat Anavim (1920); Gurevich *et al.*, *Jewish Population
of Palestine*, 280.
[91] At the Agricultural Council of Hapoel Hatzair. Quoted in Wurm, *Bussel Memorial
Book*, 238.
[92] Balance sheet for 1919/20, in the archives of Degania Aleph.

problems posed by the post-war world. The approach proposed in the discussions of 1916—to concentrate on perfecting the *kvutza* itself, in the hope that others would use it as a model—could provide no immediate answer to the questions raised by the increase in immigration at the beginning of the Third Aliya in 1918. Public attention thus increasingly focused on other groups whose leaders believed that they did have such an answer. Moreover, some of the leaders of the *kvutza* believed that this form of social organization was suitable for an idealistic élite group, but that mass immigration would have to be absorbed through the family units of the moshav. A sizeable group, including two of the original Romni group, left Degania during this year to become part of the founding nucleus of Moshav Nahalal. In a general meeting of the members of Degania during this period, Degania was compared to an army which had lost its generals.[93]

For all these reasons, Degania itself lost much of its self-confidence and its public prominence during the coming years. But the idea of the *kvutza* as a means of settlement was born in Degania; and this was one of the major concepts which the men and women of the Third Aliya inherited from those of the Second.

## HISTORICAL ELEMENTS IN THE CREATION OF THE *KVUTZA*

From the foregoing account, a number of essential elements in the creation of the *kvutza* can be isolated. In describing them, I shall begin to give an answer to the question which arises from the historical account: why was it that the *kvutza* developed at this place and time, and in the way that it did?

I shall begin by mentioning some characteristics which are, in effect, part of the very definition of the kibbutz. We have seen the parallel growth of the communes and of the 'conquest groups', each based on an element of co-operation. Neither of these forms of social structure was a kibbutz. The first contribution of Degania to the emergence of the kibbutz was the combination of the community of consumption (the Hadera commune) with communal production (the first year's work at Um Juni). No less important is an element which characterized the founders of Degania from a very early stage: the factor of permanence. Unlike the members of Hashomer and the other

---

[93] Ben-Avram, 'The Formation of the Kvutza Ideology', pt. 1.

conquest groups, Degania had at its centre a set of people who since 1907 had been intending to live together as a close-knit community for the foreseeable future—perhaps, if a suitable organizational form could be found, even permanently. Indeed, some of the founders of Degania did live with their comrades of the Hadera commune until the end of their very long lives.

Degania was permanent in another sense. The decision to settle in a particular spot distinguishes it from all the communal bodies which preceded it. In one sense, this was a revolutionary departure within the labour movement, which had been firmly opposed to the 'peasantization' of the workers. But the fact that Degania's land was owned by the Jewish nation rather than by the settlers themselves enabled the *kvutza* to be perceived as a socialist unit. By 1914 the principle of 'workers' settlement' had become a major aim of the Labour Zionist movement.

To these elements—community in production and consumption, permanence in population and in location, and nationally owned land—should be added one characteristic which is certainly part of the existential definition of the kibbutz, although it is possible to imagine similar communities without it: the system of communal child care. This enabled the community to include parents, and to give at least a partial answer to the question of equality of the sexes. The two principles adopted by Degania—the mother's right and duty to work, and the community's responsibility for the care of its children—still obtain in the whole of the kibbutz movement.

Until 1918, the combination of all these elements existed only in Degania. Thus, although the Sejera collective and the other communal groups have an important place in the pre-history of the kibbutz, Degania has a right to the name which it traditionally bears: 'the mother of the *kvutzot*'.

None of this would have availed had the *kvutza* been an economic failure. Reminiscences of the first year at Sejera and at Um Juni both end with the phrase 'we ended the year with a small profit'. One of the aims of the labour movement in general was to free itself from the suspicion of living on the charity of the Jews of the Diaspora. This, in their view, was the characteristic blemish of the Old Yishuv,[94] and it had also crept into the Zionist settlements: crops were bought by the Rothschild organization at inflated prices; the settlers received

---

[94] The Jewish community of Palestine before the First Aliya, which continued to exist side by side with the Zionist settlements. See Kaniel, *Continuity and Change*.

cheap equipment and loans, though only under stringent conditions and constant supervision. Economic success was thus both a practical necessity and an ideological aim.

The economic success of the *kvutza* did not stem from its social structure alone. The Sejera collective, the conquest group at Um Juni, and the Hadera commune were all composed of some of the most experienced workers in the Yishuv. Other groups failed, despite their communal structure, because their members were unable to function as a social group or did not work well enough. The selection procedure at Degania was most stringent. Its members saw themselves as an élite; and, indeed, all the *kvutzot* which survived at this period formed self-selecting élite groups within the select group of which the workers' movement was composed.

A further essential element was the support of the Zionist movement for the *kvutzot*. This was both an ideological question and a practical necessity. All the workers of the Second Aliya believed themselves to be carrying out the aims of Zionism, and this perception was strengthened when the Zionist movement began to promote settlement in Palestine. In practical terms, the Sejera collective could never have been established without the active support of Eliyahu Krause, the representative of the JCA. And there is no doubt of the dominance and basic approval of the representative of the Zionist Organization, Arthur Ruppin, at virtually every stage of the evolution of Degania and the other kibbutzim which were founded in its image. Land for settlement, start-up capital, cattle and machinery, and legal support were all part of the infrastructure without which the settled *kvutza* would never have come into existence, and certainly would never have lasted.

None of these things was given simply out of sympathy with the *kvutza* and its objectives, but because it was seen as the best— frequently, indeed, the only available—instrument for carrying out the declared aims of the Zionist movement: settlement, absorption of new immigrants, and the establishment of Hebrew-speaking colonies which would promote the revival of Jewish culture. In all of these aims the founders of the *kvutzot* held views identical to those of the Zionist movement. From the point of view of that movement, and particularly of those in its leadership who had doubts about the desirability or efficiency of communal settlement, there seemed to be a mutual contract: the *kvutza* acted as the agent of Zionism, and in return was allowed to conduct its 'social experiments' without undue interference.

This interest in social experimentation was the result of the social and ideological background described above. To some degree, the whole of the labour movement was imbued with the socialist and revolutionary ideals which had surrounded its members during the formative period of their youth. But in the case of the founders of the *kvutza*, more specific influences can be detected. The ideological background and motives of Manya Shohat, the Romni group, and Joseph Trumpeldor have been described above. It was they who helped to focus these generalized ideas in a specific and practical direction.[95]

Thus, at the centre of many *kvutzot* were groups of men and women with clearly defined communal ideologies, even though not all defined themselves as socialists. On the other hand, many of these very people said in later years that the *kvutza* had been created not as a result of theories, but 'out of life', or because of 'the atmosphere of the Land of Israel'.[95] In part, these remarks can be dismissed as a sort of anti-ideological ideology; for these people were members of the Hapoel Hatzair party, which rejected Marxist and socialist terminology, and tended to extend this to a negation of any theoretical framework. But even a man such as Yitzhak Tabenkin, who emphasized the importance of ideology in his educational and political approach, said in later years:

The *kvutza* was the result of everything that the Jewish worker did in Palestine: in the conquest of work in town and country, in the conquest of the soil, the need for the *kvutza* always appeared; for we were alone and powerless, divorced from our parents and our environment, and face to face with the difficulties of life—the search for employment, illness, and so forth.... The conquest of work turned the individual to the *kvutza* from his very first day.[96]

Is it possible to reconcile these two versions of the place of ideology in the creation of the *kvutza*? One way of doing so is by considering the case of Trumpeldor and his disciples. Here was a charismatic leader, with an ideologically motivated group of followers, and a

---

[95] The degree to which the founders of the first *kvutzot* were motivated by ideology is discussed in Ben-Avram, 'The Formation of the Kvutza Ideology', and Frankel *et al.* 'Ideological Motives in the Formation of the Kvutza'. A different approach is adopted by Shafir, *Land, Labor, and the Origins of the Israeli–Palestine Conflict*. Unfortunately, this important work reached me too late to enable me to pay it the attention it deserves.

[96] *Kibbutz Me'uhad Anthology*, 27.

blueprint for the creation of communal societies. But on arrival in Palestine, he set up a commune on the same lines as the dozen or more conquest groups which came into existence at about the same time. This group broke up, not because it did not accord with his blueprint, but because its members were not able to stand the rigours of the life they had chosen.

Trumpeldor's group was an extreme example of ideology proving useless as a guide to the practical problems of creating a real community in the Palestine of the time. Groups whose plans for communal living were less clearly defined in advance could reconcile their practical actions with their principles more easily. What the founders of the successful *kvutzot* shared was not an ideology, in the sense of a detailed and rationally defended outlook on life, but a positive attitude to the idea of community. Within this framework of basic values, they could approach the actual details of community-building with a high degree of flexibility, and even of pragmatism.

These, then, were the factors which made the *kvutza* what it was: a settled place and a permanent core of people: co-operation in work and in consumption; communal child care; economic success, which stemmed partly from stringent selection of the members; the support of the settlement authorities; and a desire to live communally, combined with a flexible approach to the technical details of community-building. Together, these factors brought the *kvutza* into the world. What was needed for it to survive we shall consider in the next chapter.

# 2

# Expansion and Consolidation, 1918–1923

## THE THIRD ALIYA AND THE 'FELLOWSHIP OF THE ROADS'

THE First World War brought about far-reaching changes in the Yishuv, the Jewish people, and the Zionist movement. Its most immediate effect on the Yishuv was to weaken it, in numbers and in physical and moral strength. During the Second Aliya the Jewish population had grown from some 50,000 to just over 80,000. By 1918, after four years of economic stagnation, political persecution, and military dependence, a combination of emigration, exile, and starvation had reduced this number to 56,000. Thus, even in purely human terms, the conquest of Palestine by the British was an act of physical salvation. In political and spiritual terms, it was much more. Although the terms of the Balfour Declaration were deliberately vague, the Jews of Palestine and of Europe believed that the arrival of the British army would lead to the establishment of a Jewish commonwealth. There was an apocalyptic spirit abroad, and it was freely expressed in the discussions of the future which abounded in the labour movement during 1917 and 1918.[1] Phrases such as 'salvation', 'fulfilment of the words of the prophets', and other reminders of the biblical roots of Zionism were in frequent use. True, there were doubts and dissident voices, such as that of the member of Degania who killed himself in protest against the idea that a foreign army would offer the Jewish people its salvation.[2] But, in general, the hope offered by the British conquest and the undertaking given by the Allies was in such extreme contrast to the dark years of Turkish rule that the new regime was greeted with boundless enthusiasm.

European Jewry was in no less of a ferment. Many of its centres

[1] e.g. in Berl Katznelson's famous speech, 'Towards the Days to Come', in Feb. 1918; see Katznelson, *At Work*, 1–21; and cf. Shapira, *Berl*, ch. 4.
[2] Dayan, *Twenty-Five Years of Degania*, 157–8.

of population had been in the front line. Fighting, evacuation, poverty, and starvation had taken their toll. The factors which had led to the great migrations of 1880 to 1914 had not diminished; and in the countries formerly part of the Russian and Austro-Hungarian empires antisemitism was an endemic element in the nationalist traditions now triumphant. It is true that there were proposals to write the rights of minorities into the constitutions of the states created as a result of the break-up of the Austro-Hungarian Empire, but many Jews regarded such ideas with deep scepticism. In the event, these doubts proved fully justified.

By the end of 1917, news of the Balfour Declaration had reached the Jews of Eastern Europe. Like the Jews of Palestine, they did not know its exact terms, but it was widely believed that the British government had undertaken to establish a Jewish state. After two thousand years of exile, the Jews would be given the same rights as their neighbours (and persecutors) in Poland, Hungary, and the other new Eastern European states. To them no less than to the Jews of Palestine, it seemed that a new age was beginning. At the end of the war, the migrations which had marked Jewish life over the forty years before the war were resumed. As previously, a comparatively small number reached Palestine as against the general trend of migration westwards from the Eastern European countries. But even so, the number reaching Palestine was greater than in the Second Aliya: from 1918 to 1923 the population of the Yishuv increased by some 39,000—almost 8,000 per year, whereas the net annual increase in the Second Aliya had been about 3,000.[3]

In both historical and ideological writings, the people who came to Palestine in the Third Aliya are pictured predominantly, sometimes even exclusively, as young pioneers. It was, in a typical formulation, 'entirely a daring and independent operation of pioneers in their masses'.[4] These were young people who, inspired both by the Balfour Declaration and by the Russian Revolution to believe that the world was on the eve of a new era, formed small groups which began to make their way to Palestine—at first spontaneously, and later in the framework of a movement known as Hechalutz. Despite the hesitation, and even the active opposition, of the leaders of the Zionist movement, who were concerned that the economic infrastructure needed to

---

[3] Gurevich *et al.*, *Jewish Population of Palestine*, 21–4.

[4] Braslavsky, *The Labour Movement*, i. 163; and cf. Even-Shoshan, *History of the Labour Movement*, ch. 39.

absorb large numbers with no financial backing was still lacking in Palestine, Hechalutz became an irresistible force, which changed the nature of the Yishuv within a few years.

As in the case of the Second Aliya, this wave of pioneers was more limited than is generally believed, both in time and in numbers. Beginning with a trickle in the autumn of 1918, it increased in size and momentum until roughly the end of 1921. At the end of that period, of the 23,000 adults who had reached the country since the war, some 9,000 workers were registered in the Histadrut's census; and fewer than half of them were employed in the 'pioneering' occupations of agriculture, construction, and unskilled labour. It seems, therefore, that, even allowing for a considerable statistical error, the proportion of pioneers in the general population was no more than half. In the last two years of the Third Aliya, the number of immigrants who were of the pioneering type, or organizationally connected to the Hechalutz movement or the kibbutz, was even smaller.[5]

None the less, the changes which the pioneer immigrants brought about in thought and deed were so far-reaching that they left a lasting impression far beyond their numbers. Their impact on the kibbutz movement was even greater than that on the Yishuv as a whole. This chapter must open, therefore, with some account of their character and ways of thought and organization.

## Hechalutz[6]

The beginnings of the Hechalutz movement were in fact in accordance with the legend. The groups of young people who began making their way to Palestine immediately after the war—even though frontiers were closed and passports unobtainable, and civil war and violence still raged—can be seen as part of the trend to Jewish migration which was intensified by the sufferings of the war. Many of them, and particularly their leaders, had a background of pre-war Zionist activity, and their first formal organization had been in the framework

[5] The Histadrut census took place on 10 Sept. 1922 and was published in *Pinkas Hahistadrut* (Jan.–Feb. 1923), app. 8. The division of the Third Aliya into 'pioneering' and 'non-pioneering' periods was made by Eliahu Dobkin, general secretary of the world Hechalutz movement; see *Hechalutz Anthology*, 31–9. For a more detailed analysis, see Ben-Avram and Near, *The Third Aliya*, ch. 2.

[6] Descriptions and memoirs of the early years of Hechalutz are given in *Hechalutz Anthology*, sect. 2. On the antecedents and early history of Russian Hechalutz, see Margalit, *Commune, Society, and Politics*, pt. 1.

of one of the Zionist parties.[7] But they quickly attained a high degree
of independence, both ideological and practical. The name Hechalutz
('The Pioneer') was taken from the passage in the Book of Joshua
(vi:1–13) where the 'pioneer'—literally, the soldier—led the Israelites
as they marched round Jericho during the siege of the city; and its
symbolism was encapsulated in a phrase much quoted at the time,
'the pioneer goes before the host'. These young people saw themselves
as the vanguard of the Jewish masses.

A central figure in the organization and development of the Hechalutz movement was Joseph Trumpeldor, already mentioned in a
minor role in the previous chapter. Following the collapse of the
commune at Migdal in 1913, he spent some time working at Degania,
although he was never a member of the *kvutza*. With the outbreak of
the war, he did his duty as an officer of the Russian army, volunteered
for the Allied forces, and fought at Gallipoli as an officer of the Zion
Mule Corps. In 1917 he made his way to Russia, where he organized
groups for Jewish self-defence in the chaos of the revolution. After
the Bolsheviks seized power he began to work in Hechalutz, propounding a double message: the need for massive Jewish immigration
to Palestine; and the idea of the commune as the best way to facilitate
swift absorption of the newcomers and to build the country.[8]

During 1918 and 1919, small groups of Hechalutz members began
to make their way to Palestine. A number of training farms were
established, especially in the Crimea. There they began the process
of acclimatization to working life and communal society while waiting
for the opportunity to leave for Palestine. In August 1919 Trumpeldor
travelled to Palestine on what was to have been a pilot tour, to inspect
the conditions of absorption for the thousands of members of the
movement preparing themselves to immigrate. In the few months
that he was in the country, he accomplished two things which affected
the course of Zionist history. First, he was instrumental in achieving
unity in the labour movement. His first reaction to the labour movement was one of deep disillusionment because of the duplication,
mutual suspicion, and waste engendered by the existence of two
separate parties, Hapoel Hatzair and Ahdut Ha'avoda[9]. He wrote an

---

[7] Ze'irei Zion ('Young People of Zion'), which aimed at a cultural rejuvenation of
the Zionist movement and was later connected with the Hapoel Hatzair party.

[8] Laskov, *Yosef Trumpeldor*, chs. 11–15, gives a full account of Trumpeldor's
activities from 1917 until his death. On his activities before the war see ch. 1 above.

[9] A fuller account of the state of the labour movement at this time is given below.

open letter to the parties, suggesting a compromise between their declared standpoints on the question of workers' unity. Both Trumpeldor's personal reputation and the fact that he was known to represent thousands of young pioneers ensured that his suggestions were considered seriously. Indeed, not only did they get the negotiations under way again; they also formed the basis of the constitution which was actually adopted by the Histadrut, the comprehensive labour organization, in its founding conference at the end of 1920.

Trumpeldor's second accomplishment, the defence of Tel Hai in 1920 against marauding Arabs, cost him his life but made him a legend. Upper Galilee was thought by the Zionist movement to be an essential part of the territory of the Jewish national home, whose borders had not yet been clearly defined: its possession would give control of the sources of the Jordan, the use of whose water was of vital importance in the development of the country. For the labour movement, the fact that four settlements (three *kvutzot*, and one group which planned to establish a moshav) had been established in the area towards the end of the war was of almost equal importance. They were in a precarious state. The French, who claimed the area on the basis of wartime agreements, were unable to defend it, and the Jewish settlements were in danger of pillage and destruction by Arab irregular troops. The Yishuv was divided on the question of whether to reinforce the area or to abandon it as being indefensible. The labour movement was opposed to relinquishing it and sent whatever help it could muster. Trumpeldor, one of the few men in the Yishuv with significant military experience, was asked to investigate the situation and suggest what should be done. On arrival, he decided to take over the defence of the area, which was under constant attack by far superior forces. While participating in the defence of Tel Hai against an attack by a band apparently in search of plunder, he was mortally wounded. His reported last words, 'No matter; it is good to die for our country,' became a legend on which generations of pioneers have been, and still are, educated; for they embody the image of Jewish heroism which had been replaced during the long years of Diaspora life by unresisting martyrdom. Moreover, the success of the defence of Tel Hai, and the fact that the area was therefore subsequently included in British-controlled territory under the final terms of the Mandate, were held to prove the efficacy of two principles which also still inform the politics and defence policy of the Israeli labour movement: the moral imperative to defend any Jewish settlement, whatever its strategic or tactical importance; and the conviction that political borders are fixed by settlement.

All this was of vital importance to the later development of the kibbutz movement. Of more immediate influence, however, was another of Trumpeldor's ideas. When in Russia, he had discussed with his disciples the possibility of establishing 'Jewish legions'. In one version of this idea, these were to be military formations which would make their way through Southern Russia to the Middle East, help the British liberate Palestine from the Turks, and thenceforward constitute its defence force. In a later version, they were to be 'labour battalions', engaging in self-defence but with an emphasis on constructive work.[10] In both cases, these concepts combined three elements: firstly, communal organization, based on the principles which Trumpeldor had been advocating since 1905 ('the establishment of communist colonies in Palestine'); secondly, the aspiration to expand the movement as much as possible—a principle which Trumpeldor had espoused during his period at Degania, when he was already beginning to maintain that the small *kvutza* was not relevant to the real needs of Zionism, and which was confirmed by the circumstances of the post-war period; and, thirdly, the demand for self-sacrifice and devotion on the part of the pioneers who would make up the battalions.

## The 'Period of the Roads'

After Trumpeldor's death, the members of Hechalutz began to reach the country in increasing numbers. The reality they discovered there was hard in the extreme. The new immigrants carried with them their predecessors' vision of work and settlement on the land. But the Zionist movement did not have the means to settle such large numbers, or even to provide them with gainful employment. The situation was saved by the public works policy of the British government and the organizational ability of the leaders of the labour movement. Even before the confirmation of the British Mandate by the League of Nations in 1922, the military government began to develop the

[10] It is not clear whether the terminology of the Jewish Labour Battalion in Palestine (Gedud Avoda) was consciously modelled on that of the special labour units established by the Soviet authorities during the period of War Communism. Undoubtedly, however, many of the young pioneers, inspired by the example of the Soviet revolution, were conscious of the parallel. See B. Kanari, 'Planned Economy: Zionist and Socialist-Zionist', and Haim Golan, 'The First Year of Gedud Ha'avoda'.

country's infrastructure, in particular its road and railway system. In an extension of the social forms invented during the Second Aliya, the institutions of the labour movement contracted for the work involved—quarrying, stone-breaking, track-laying, masonry, and the like. This was then subcontracted to groups of workers, living and working communally wherever the possibilities of employment might take them. The new immigrants lived in tents supplied by the Zionist movement or the central institutions of the workers' movement, ate in communal kitchens, and pooled their meagre wages. This period (1919 to 1922) came to be known as 'the period of the roads'. It came to an end in 1923, when the British government applied a policy of retrenchment to all its colonial possessions, including Palestine. The state of virtually full employment was followed by an economic slump. Immigration was drastically reduced, and Jews began leaving the country. It was not until the spring of 1924, with the beginning of the Fourth Aliya, that some improvement in the economic situation was felt.

Politically, too, this was a period of stress within the labour movement. For many years, a group of the more recent immigrants had been emphasizing that the traditional parties, Hapoel Hatzair and Poalei Zion, had at least as much in common as divided them. This group, known as the 'non-party element', included men such as Berl Katznelson and Yitzhak Tabenkin, who were already prominent in the leadership of the movement. By 1917, they were propounding the view that the new situation called for new forms of organization, and in particular for unity between the two major parties. In 1919, under the leadership of the non-party group, a first attempt was made to attain such unity. The Ahdut Ha'avoda ('Labour Unity') movement was intended to be a comprehensive framework which would embrace all those who accepted the principles of Labour Zionism. As it turned out, however, the new organization attracted only the non-party group, the ex-members of Poalei Zion, and a very few members of Hapoel Hatzair. Most of the latter, fearful of being a minority in the new movement and hoping that the new immigrants about to arrive would turn their own party into the major political force in the Yishuv, remained aloof. So, at the beginning of the 'period of the roads', each of the major parties negotiated with the British authorities separately, subcontracted work to their own groups, and supplied and maintained their own basic equipment. Moreover, each maintained the administrative machinery required for absorbing and supporting the new immigrants: labour exchanges, sick funds, Hebrew classes, and printed material. Although many of the new immigrants quickly absorbed the local political culture and joined one of the existing parties, this duplication was clearly an administrative absurdity.

Pressure from the new immigrants combined with Trumpeldor's posthumous influence and the (theoretically) universally held belief in workers' unity to bring about a change. At the end of 1920, a comprehensive body was founded which embraced the whole of the labour movement. This was the Histadrut. The parties continued to exist, but the Histadrut took on administrative responsibility for many of the tasks which they had previously dealt with separately, and in competition. It was governed by a system of coalitions, but Ahdut Ha'avoda had a considerable majority within it from the first. This party, and its leader, David Ben-Gurion, who became secretary of the Histadrut in 1922, continued to dominate the labour movement until 1930, when the two major parties combined.[11]

The great majority of Hechalutz members joined what was later termed 'the fellowship of the roads'.[12] They lived in communal groups which would camp, move, break up, and be reconstituted according to the type and availability of work. In September 1920, six months after Trumpeldor's death at Tel Hai, a group of his followers met on the shores of the Sea of Galilee and, after a memorial ceremony, founded the Joseph Trumpeldor Labour and Defence Battalion, which came to be known simply as Gedud Ha'avoda ('The Labour Battalion'), or the 'Gedud'.

The ideology of communalism and pioneering fitted the historical development of the 'fellowship of the roads', a way of life that lasted for more than two years and was the seed-bed of many developments in the kibbutz movement which came to maturity at later stages. Some idea of the atmosphere that generated such developments can be gleaned from contemporary accounts.

I went by horse and cart to the 23rd kilometre on the Haifa–Jedda road, where I was to join a working party. On the way, I passed young men and women, sitting astride heaps of stones by the wayside, working with small hammers. By the side of every heap of stones [stood] reed baskets for the gravel. Many of [the young people] had bandaged hands, and their faces and

---

[11] See Tzahor, *On the Road to Yishuv Leadership*; Shapira, *Berl*, 49–53, 82–90; Shapiro, *The Formative Years of the Israeli Labour Party*, chs. 2 and 3.

[12] Margalit, *Commune, Society and Politics*, chs. 2, 3, and 4.

clothes were bathed in sweat, even though the sun was going down. Apart from them, the road was virtually deserted all the way. Not a Jewish village in sight—just the Arab villages in the distance, and ruins, concealing the secrets of the past.

I arrived at the camp: a big tent for the common meals, one or two huts, and a great many small tents scattered round the area. Small groups returned from work, bringing their tools with them. Some washed by the water-tub, for there were no taps or pipes. I found my friends, and watched supper being prepared—a fire, fuelled by dried thistles and cow-dung, surrounded by stones; and over it, an iron triangle supporting the pot. Thick smoke got into everybody's eyes. For supper—bread, soup, and tea. A poor meal, but I have never tasted better.

The following day, after tea, bread, and jam—to work! We had to make holes in the stones for dynamiting. I held the handspike, while my partner used the hammer. The sun shone relentlessly, the heat was stifling. My body ached, the skin on my hands was scratched and split. But I was happy to have reached my goal—a life of work. . . .

We joined up with another group, and for a time things were easier. But the rains came late, and all were approaching a state of exhaustion. The food was poor, and varied with the nationality of the cooks. . . .

'The porridge is burnt again,' someone would call out. 'What's happened to the cook? What's making her burn?' And in a few minutes, loud cries of 'Train!' The cry is echoed from all the tables: 'Train, train!' Everyone moves his plate to the middle of the table, and they are set together like a row of wagons, and pushed back to the kitchen. Everyone laughs and jeers. The noise booms, echoes, and resounds through the dining hall.

And the cook? A young girl, not long off the boat, who volunteered for kitchen duty . . . the 'train' cuts into her soul like an axe. She runs off to her quarters, and bursts into tears of frustration and depression. And at that moment she hears the first notes of a song . . . the burnt porridge has been forgotten, the pangs of hunger quelled with bread. It may be that the workers had no idea what injustice they had done to their comrade the cook. And, in truth, 'trains' did not occur very frequently; even if in most cases the porridge was badly cooked, and tasted of smoke, people were so hungry that they usually swallowed it unheedingly. . . .

We were overjoyed by the first rains, and burst into song—even when the storm blew our tents away. But illnesses began to spread. Sanitary conditions were primitive; the water was not boiled, although we did add chlorine. At work, we used to drink whatever water was available, even from open wells infested by frogs. All of us ran fevers, including me. I lay with a high fever and limbs like lead, in an open, wet tent. The girls looked after me . . . a cup of tea, a wet rag on my fevered brow, a blanket. . . .

The work comes to an end. It appears that we have a deficit. Stormy arguments: how can it be that with every extra metre of gravel, which we are working so hard to make, we lose money? We look around for a better place of work, and a different group to join up with.[13]

Although road-making was the central element, there were also other types of work—building, laying railway tracks, swamp-draining, and various sorts of agricultural work. Groups were made up on the basis of previous acquaintance, national origin, or party or youth movement allegiance; but there was a constant process of selection, and groups were re-formed and combined with others according to the type of work and relations between the workers. A new vocabulary also came into being. *Kvutza* now came to mean a settled co-operative community, on the pattern of Degania. The communal group with no fixed territory was called a *pluga* (plural: *plugot*). A group of *plugot* with a common administration, a number of which grew up in 1921 and 1922, was called a *havura* or *kibbutz*. Gedud Ha'avoda, according to this terminology, was the first country-wide *kibbutz*.[14] By the beginning of 1921 it was the biggest organization of *plugot* in the country, with some two hundred members. At the same time, the contracting agencies of the parties were absorbed by the Public Works Department of the newly established Histadrut, which was now the major contracting agency, dealing directly with the Mandatory authorities.

The list of the contract groups which obtained work through this office in August 1922 indicates their great number and variety. There were 77 in all, comprising 2,044 workers (among them 228 married couples, with 380 children). The biggest group was one belonging to Gedud Ha'avoda, with 186 members; but there were 3 others with more than 100. The smallest had only 5 members, and there were 17 groups with 10 members or fewer.

The names of these groups are themselves of interest. Thirteen seem to have had political connotations—for instance, Ahdut ('Unity'). Twenty-one names were symbolic ('Labour', 'Toil'), although some of these symbols were also connected with political groupings. Nineteen groups were named after people (usually the

---

[13] Eliahu Rappaport, in Erez, *Third Aliya*, 261–2. Although this account was apparently written some years later, it fits well with the same author's contemporary, but more literary, description in *Our Community*, 186–97. The section on the 'train' is taken from a description of the workers' restaurant in Hadera in a rather earlier period (Habass, *Second Aliya*, 272–3), but there is much evidence of the recurrence of such scenes throughout the Third Aliya. See e.g. Fishman-Maimon, *The Working Women's Movement in the Land of Israel*, 10–14.

[14] Near, 'The Languages of Community'.

leader or secretary of the group) or places of origin.[15] Ten bore the names of their current geographical location, and nine the trade of their members (builders, metal workers, carpenters), while four indicated a special social situation: families, women, homeless workers.[16]

One reason for the growth of such groups was the slow rate of agricultural settlement, which was limited by the straitened condition of the Zionist funds. None the less, the rate of expansion of agricultural *kvutzot*, permanent and temporary, was greater than in the Second Aliya. There were 42 such groups in 1921, and 48 in the summer of 1922. Of these, 24 were designated for permanent settlement as *kvutzot*; 7 of them had been founded during the Second Aliya, 4 during the war, and 13 during the Third Aliya.[17] The total membership of these *kvutzot* grew from about 600 in 1921 to 1,546 in 1923. Thus, despite the predominance of the road-laying and construction groups, this sector was also growing steadily, on the foundations laid by Degania before the war.

These figures show a steady growth not only in the number of *kvutzot*, but also in the numbers in each group. For instance, despite Degania's decision to remain small, the constant demands of increasingly intensive agriculture for more manpower led to an expansion from 31 members in 1921 to 43 in 1923. But the majority of *kvutzot* followed Degania's original policy and remained small: sixteen of them had an average of 30 members each.[18]

Even before the beginning of the Third Aliya, the effectiveness of this model at a time of mass immigration had been called into question. It was commonly accepted that the *kvutza* could be successful only if its members were a selected, experienced, and dedicated group: in

---

[15] It is often hard to distinguish between these cases. For instance, the Grodno group may have originated from that town, or have been led by a man of that name.

[16] *Pinkas Hahistadrut* (Jan.–Feb. 1923), app. 7, table 5. Although in some places the date is given as Aug. 1923, this is clearly a misprint, for the date of publication is certain.

[17] Ibid., table 6. These figures do not include all the *kvutzot* mentioned in the 1922 survey. Twelve of these were located in places destined for settlement as moshavim, although some of them later settled elsewhere as *kvutzot*. I have included only those *kvutzot* which were then working a defined area of publicly owned land which they had settled, or intended to settle, communally—although not all of them did in fact stay permanently on the site. The figures refer to the number of workers in agricultural settlements, which may exaggerate the number of members of *kvutzot*. But the overall numbers are reasonably accurate.

[18] Ibid.; and cf. Katznelson, *The Kvutza*, 15–34, 126–8, 131.

the words of its detractors and exponents alike, a handful of idealists. What, then of the masses?

## GEDUD HA'AVODA AND HASHOMER HATZAIR

### Gedud Ha'avoda

One widely accepted view was that the idea of the *kvutza* was not relevant to the new circumstances. Even some of the central figures in Degania reached this conclusion. In their view, the solution to the problem of mass immigration would be based on the family unit rather than on a type of society which was not viable without a long period of preparation. As we have seen, the idea of the *moshav ovdim* (in popular parlance, and in this book, the moshav) had evolved, and even been put into practice, by 1914;[19] but, for a variety of reasons, the first cautious experiments had not succeeded. In 1918, Eliezer Yaffe began to campaign for the establishment of the moshav, and the group which in 1921 founded Nahalal, the first moshav to become a permanent settlement, included some of the leading members of Degania.

Those who remained in Degania, and the handful of other groups which set up similar *kvutzot* at this time, began to see their aims in a much longer perspective. For them, the *kvutza* was still the solution to the problems of the Yishuv and the Jewish people. But it would take some time—and, no doubt, a change in historical circumstances—before a generation could arise which would fully accept its message. By 1923, this had become almost an article of faith in the veteran *kvutzot*. Here are the words of Joseph Baratz, who became the foremost spokesman of the *kvutza* after Bussel's death, in May of that year:

Those who criticize the *kvutza* always pose the question: 'What does the *kvutza* do to help mass settlement?' This is not a question which has ever occupied me very much. To me it has always been obvious that this way of life, of construction founded on community and moral values, is applicable to the masses, both of our own people and of humanity as a whole. But it is also clear to me that at the moment the masses, and even the so-called masses who are flocking to Palestine, are for the most part not yet capable of living the communal life. Our 'masses' are mainly interested in material progress and personal gain.[20]

---

[19] Above, ch. 1.     [20] Katznelson, *The Kvutza*, 19.

The breakthrough which heralded the link between the idea of the *kvutza* and the needs of a period of mass immigration found its expression in the writings and public activities of Shlomo Levkovich (Lavi), a veteran of the Second Aliya who had spent some years in various *kvutzot* and taken part in the experimental '*kvutza* of sixty' in 1919.[21] While accepting the principles of community and equality, his experience led him to far-reaching criticism of the *kvutzot*:

Perpetual poverty and cheese-paring, lack of development, arguments about trifles, continuous turnover of membership and unending problems—all this, and worse, is the lot of the *kvutzot*. They created a revolution, but their ideas have remained as poor as they were before. They have no notion of expansion, anything big frightens them, they reject anything new out of hand. To the concept: 'equal life for all' they never added 'full and rich life for all'. They made the step to communal life, to life without an unprivileged class, but failed to go on to create areas in which each individual can find himself or herself. Apart from the suffering within the *kvutza*, this leads to almost perpetual deficits: a profit is a miracle, scarcity is the rule, and they cannot obtain even the barest necessities. Family life is miserable. And, worst of all, there is no prospect of improvement. They have inherited from the past the desire ... for a quiet life—a warm, homely life—and with it fear of [new] people. And this fear makes them limit their numbers; this limits the amount of work done and the type of work available, and hence poverty is unavoidable.[22]

There was a considerable measure of truth in Lavi's contentions. The process of settlement brought with it a whole series of problems which had scarcely been foreseen in the pristine enthusiasm of the early days of the *kvutza*. It took several years to determine the quality of the land and the type of crops which could be grown. Many operations, such as clearing the land of stones, were long-term investments whose benefits were not immediately felt. Despite the devotion and experience of the settlers, they still had much to learn, and this fact expressed itself in their standards of productivity. Methods of irrigation, the key to intensive agriculture in the local climate, were primitive, and it was only in the late 1920s that large-scale projects were completed. For all these reasons, the Zionist movement had to continue to support the *kvutzot* financially to a degree and for a length of time that had not been foreseen either by the movement or by the workers themselves; and the suspicion that they had become subject

---

[21] Above, ch. 1.  [22] *Kuntres*, 57 (Oct. 1920), 9.

to a regime of 'patronage' no less demeaning than that of Baron Rothschild in the First Aliya was often voiced both within the *kvutzot* and outside them.[23] Part of Lavi's ideological stance was an explicit rejection of the ascetic attitudes of many of the people of the Second Aliya. Thus, his ideas formed a bridge to the new immigrants, many of whom (in Baratz's words) 'were mainly interested in material progress and personal gain' and considered neither morally reprehensible. There were also many Second Aliya veterans whose experience had led them to conclude, with Lavi, that 'poverty always corrupts'. So there was a wide audience for his suggestions. In practical terms, he advocated that the *kvutza* should aim at the maximum degree of social and economic autarky. In contrast to the veteran *kvutzot*, it should engage in industry and handicrafts, as well as in agriculture. In Lavi's words:

*a.* The *kvutza* organizes every aspect of its life independently, and, as far as possible, abstains from relationships with the exploitative market.
*b.* The *kvutza* does not renounce in the slightest degree any part of the essential culture or needs of its members.
*c.* The *kvutza* increases the number of its members to the maximum.

'All well and good,' I shall be told. 'But how can one organize such a big *kvutza* without jealousy, and without a management, which prevents the members from taking an active part in the affairs of the *kvutza*? How can you ensure that they will take each others' wishes into account?' In reply to this, and all other criticisms of my programme, I reply: expansion. What contraction failed to do will be achieved by expansion, by interest in every aspect of life, by the tremendous variety of types of people and types of work. There will be development, growth: the work will grow and the people will grow with it, there will be no need for one to give in to the other, for the will of one will not clash with that of his neighbour. Everything will make for the good, and the good is the same for all.[24]

Clearly, this programme—henceforth known as the 'big *kvutza*'— added conceptual and practical dimensions to the idea of the *kvutza*. At precisely the moment when Degania was deciding that it must limit its membership and give up some of its land, Lavi was advocating the establishment of *kvutzot* with three thousand members, based not only on agriculture but a wide variety of economic branches. It was, in effect, the model on which today's kibbutz is built.

Lavi's criticisms were not universally accepted. According to Lavi

---

[23] Bein, *History of Zionist Settlement*, 245–9, 259–60.
[24] *Kuntres*, 57 (Oct. 1920), 10–12.

the 'suffering within the *kvutza*' stemmed from the fact that the *kvutzot* were small, and their members lived in close proximity, with little or no privacy, and in a state of complete interdependence. But there were many who loved this way of life, and spoke of 'ideal relationships between the members'. Zvi Shatz, an author who lived in a succession of *kvutzot* and devoted much of his literary work to communal life, replied to Lavi's proposals:

The danger is not in 'perpetual deficits'; they will come to an end. On the contrary, the danger is in and because of satiety which can lead us to forget our community, and the achievements of the co-operative life. That is what we must beware of! [We should aim for] peace, not slumber or satiety, but spiritual peace, based on complete satisfaction in work, and on the constant creation of deep and wonderful bonds with mother earth and with one's spiritual brethren.[25]

In a meeting in 1923, Joseph Bussel's widow said: 'People talk about suffering in the *kvutza*. I would like to ask where on earth life is easier.' And Miriam Baratz added: 'In my view, the *kvutza* has already introduced a high degree of perfection into our lives.... I once heard it said that nobody can be bad in the *kvutza*. And, indeed, I have come to realize that in the *kvutza* one can educate oneself not to be bad.'[26] There was clearly a deep clash of values here. Nobody denied the facts which Lavi adduced. Life in the *kvutzot* was physically hard, living standards not much above the poverty line, and the members lived in cramped conditions with very little privacy. Yet Shatz, continuing the tradition of asceticism referred to in the previous chapter, welcomed the suffering and poverty which Lavi so firmly rejected; and the close relationships which Lavi believed to be restrictive were seen by others as pointing the way to social perfection. As long as this was so, the 'big *kvutza*' might become an important addition to the small one, but it was unlikely to replace it.

Lavi was deeply convinced of the need to establish a 'big *kvutza*', and to prove that his ideas were practicable. For this, he needed large numbers. Setting his sights on the young pioneers of the Third Aliya, in 1920 he joined Gedud Ha'avoda. He brought with him not only a set of well-defined social aims but also several years' experience in agriculture and public activity. Representing the Gedud at the Zionist Congress of 1921, he secured agreement to immediate settlement of

[25] Shatz, *On the Edge of Silence*, 98.     [26] Katznelson, *The Kvutza*, 27.

the Nuris area in the Jezreel Valley, which had only recently been acquired by the Jewish National Fund. In September 1921, 74 young men and women founded Kibbutz Ein Harod, and a few months later a similar number founded Kibbutz Tel Yosef, close by. The population of each of these kibbutzim soon increased to more than 150. This was the beginning of the realization of Lavi's concept of the 'big *kvutza*'.

Lavi was not the only member of the Second Aliya to join the Gedud. A number of veteran workers who had spent some time in the small *kvutzot* also joined him. The best known of these was Yitzhak Tabenkin, already prominent as a leader of the Ahdut Ha'avoda party, who was to play a central part in the development of the kibbutz movement. In addition, most of the members of Hashomer joined the Gedud, bringing with them Kibbutz Kfar Giladi and Kibbutz Tel Hai.[27]

Thus, the Gedud contained three separate and in many ways disparate elements: recent immigrants, mainly members of the Hechalutz movement; Second Aliya immigrants, such as Lavi and Tabenkin; and members of the defunct Hashomer. In its early stages, however, it seemed as if their common aims were sufficient to outweigh the differences of background, outlook, and temperament. The Gedud was seen both by its members and by the leaders of the labour movement as the spearhead of that movement. And so it was, in many respects. For the Gedud shared with the rest of the movement the central aims which had been elaborated by the Second Aliya and were still considered to be its most urgent tasks: the 'conquest of work', and agricultural settlement. The dimensions of the Third Aliya were far greater than those of the Second Aliya, the conditions under which it worked different, its terminology and organizational structure more complex. But its basic aims were still much the same.

The history of Gedud Ha'avoda was marked by a constant search for new ways of growth and sources of income, and by a readiness to take on the most adventurous and exacting tasks.[28] At different times its *plugot* engaged in road-making, quarrying, building, and laying railway tracks. One *pluga* built the first campus of the Hebrew

---

[27] With the establishment of Ahdut Ha'avoda, Hashomer was officially disbanded. The task of defending the Yishuv was assumed by the Hagana, under the control of Ahdut Ha'avoda and later of the Histadrut.

[28] There are several detailed accounts of the history of Gedud Ha'avoda, notably Margalit, *Commune, Society, and Politics*, and Shapira, 'The Dream and its Shattering'.

University, and many houses in Rehavia, the new Jewish quarter of Jerusalem. Others engaged in fishing in the Sea of Galilee, set up plant nurseries, tended sheep, picked grapes and oranges, planted tobacco, and prepared new areas for cultivation. At one stage there was a transport group, and a group for hauling water supplies. An unsuccessful application was even made for a civil aviation carrier's permit (at the initiative of a group from the former Hashomer, who saw the possibility of building the nucleus of the Jewish air force).

The very process of growth brought its own problems. There was always a degree of muddle, and even irresponsibility, in the Gedud's operations, particularly during its period of fastest growth (1921–3). The dynamism of its intake was matched by the large numbers who left. In fact, this was one of the inherent contradictions in the Gedud's function as the major absorption agency of the Histadrut: many of the new immigrants stayed in it long enough to become acclimatized to the country, learn the language, and get a basic training in a trade which they then practised elsewhere. The leaders of the Gedud complained that this was the reason so many of their operations ended in a loss. They demanded compensation from the Histadrut or the Zionist movement, or that the Histadrut should help in recovering the money which the Gedud had spent in training those who subsequently left. It is estimated that some 3,000 people passed through the Gedud during its first five years; but at no time did it have more than 700 members, and most of the time it numbered between 500 and 600. None the less, it succeeded in creating four kibbutzim, and a large *pluga* which eventually became a kibbutz; and, almost from the moment of its inception, it was a central element in the workers' movement, dynamic, challenging, and stimulating.

## *Hashomer Hatzair*[29]

The great majority of the pioneers who reached the country in the framework of Hechalutz were in their late teens or early twenties. In the language of the time, however, Hechalutz was not considered a youth movement. This name was reserved for a particular type of organization, represented in the Third Aliya primarily by the members of the Hashomer Hatzair ('Young Guard') movement. Members of this movement (which will be discussed in detail in a later chapter) began to arrive in the country at the beginning of the

---

[29] See Margalit, *Hashomer Hatzair*, chs. 1, 2.

Third Aliya. Within a year they numbered some four hundred. Many of them made or lost their own way in the chaotic conditions of the time. About half joined the working groups of movement veterans which became part of the 'fellowship of the roads'. Their education in the youth movement marked them off from the majority of the new immigrants. They shared a special, somewhat eccentric style of speech and thought, and a desire to evolve a way of life which would be a continuation of the youth movement experience. Their aspirations to a distinctive social and cultural life led them to keep aloof from the sectional organizations in the labour movement: they joined the Histadrut, but rejected overtures from Gedud Ha'avoda, and joined no political party. Throughout the Third Aliya, too, they were too preoccupied with the problems of acclimatization, and with defining their special identity, to maintain any strong links with their movement in the Diaspora. Their best-known group was a small *pluga* of twenty-seven young men and women who spent some nine months at Beitania Eilit, above Lake Kinneret, in 1920/1, doing a variety of agricultural jobs in the area. An edited and expanded version of their communal diary was published about a year later under the name *Our Community*. Its unusual style emphasized this group's special nature; but its content expressed aspirations common to many of the people of the Third Aliya—particularly the desire to settle as a permanent kibbutz.

The Beitania group combined with a number of others in the spring of 1921 to form a group called Shomria, which worked on the roads not far from Haifa until its settlement at Kibbutz Beit Alpha, in the Jezreel Valley, in 1923. Meanwhile, other groups were arriving, and in 1922 several of them combined to form what later became the founding nucleus of Kibbutz Mishmar Ha'emek. By the end of 1923 there were about 120 veterans of the movement in Beit Alpha, and a similar number in scattered *plugot*—altogether some 15 per cent of the kibbutz movement at the time.

## The Crisis and its Consequences

With the end of the government contracts in May 1923, the Yishuv entered a period of crisis. There was a high degree of unemployment. Immigration continued, though at a reduced rate, and accompanied by emigration in considerable numbers. The result was a net reduction in immigration of about 6 per cent in 1923 as compared with the previous year.[30] But the effect on the kibbutz movement was far greater than these figures would suggest. There is no exact account of the number of collective groups at the end of the Third Aliya, but a survey made by the Histadrut in August 1924 gives a very close approximation. At this date, the overall number of 'settled' *kvutzot* had grown from 24 to 32, and their membership from 1,150 to 1,409. On the other hand, the number without land of their own had decreased from 77 to 34, all but 7 in rural areas, and the great majority engaged in agriculture. Their membership had decreased from 2,044 to 1,340. No less significant is the fact that, in contrast to the fragmented character of the *kvutzot* in 1922, the time of their maximum growth, 10 of them, with a membership of 890, formed part of wider organizations functioning on a regional or country-wide level. All of them are described in the 1924 survey as '*kvutzot* preparing for agricultural settlement'. In short, the crisis had virtually eliminated the non-agricultural *kvutzot*, and strengthened the tendency among those that remained to enter a wider organizational framework, in order to ensure their survival and eventual settlement on the land.[31]

The effect of the crisis on Gedud Ha'avoda was rather different. From a very early stage, the Gedud was riven by internal disputes about its structure and function. The first clause in its constitution said: 'The aim: to build the country, by creating a general commune of the Jewish workers in the Land of Israel.' The notion was bold, to the point of arrogance: the Gedud would expand until it covered all of the Jewish working class and thus would eventually constitute the whole of the Yishuv. Organizationally, this idea was translated into the 'common treasury': each *pluga* or kibbutz would work in its own area of speciality but would contribute its produce or its earnings into the general pool. In this scheme, the big *kvutza* had its place, for the agricultural settlements would eventually become 'the granaries of the Gedud'. The urban *plugot*—most of them at this stage occupied in building or its ancillary trades—would eventually build houses for and/or earn money for the whole of the Gedud.

Shlomo Lavi opposed this idea almost from the first. For him, the vital aim was to prove that the big *kvutza* as he envisaged it was viable. For this, all possible resources—land, capital, manpower— had to be concentrated on the first such *kvutza*, Ein Harod. Although he believed that other such *kvutzot* would eventually be set up on

---

[30] Gurevich *et al.*, *Jewish Population of Palestine*, 13, 23.
[31] Katznelson, *The Kvutza*, 154–6.

this pattern, for the time being Ein Harod must have absolute priority. He could not deny the value of the other *plugot* in terms of economics and training for new immigrants; but he firmly rejected the idea that the country-wide structure of the Gedud should be perpetuated.

> The leaders of the Gedud see the centre of gravity in the common treasury ... in communal finances. This idea involves no real vision, no creative imagination. ... We have seen that some of our members who are engaged in one type of work display lack of interest in and consideration for the other branches; so we must confess that we did not properly appreciate the power of co-operative work, even though all our ideology is theoretically based on such power. ... The centre of gravity must be communal activity and communal production ... without this principle, the common treasury has no value whatsoever. The treasury becomes a substitute for the commune, and turns into an empty phrase, a phrase which has no real influence on our work or on our way of life.[32]

These two opposing views of the future of the Gedud could conceivably have co-existed had it not been for the slump of 1923, which hit the building trade very badly. The *plugot*—particularly the Jerusalem *pluga*—were in severe distress. The treasurer of the Gedud transferred funds which had been given by the Zionist movement as start-up capital for Kibbutz Ein Harod to Jerusalem. Lavi was incensed. In his view, the money had been given by the Jewish people, through the Zionist movement, for constructive purposes, and not to shore up the standard of living of a group whose very existence he thought unjustified. He wrote to the Zionist movement, accusing the treasurer of the Gedud of 'stealing public funds'.

The leaders of the Gedud, mainly of the Third Aliya, totally rejected this view and condemned Lavi's action as treachery. However, they hesitated to expel him from the Gedud. They valued his agricultural experience and his influence in the Zionist world very highly; and they feared that he would take with him the veterans of the Second Aliya, who played a significant part in the economic management of the Gedud's settlements. The dispute, which lasted for about eight months and involved all the members of the Gedud, was eventually brought to the Histadrut for decision.

The deliberations in the Histadrut were fraught with tension. The Histadrut itself was a new organization, still in the early stages of crystallizing its structure and procedures. It was controlled by Ahdut

[32] *Mihayeinu*, 34 (2 Sept. 1922), i. 446–7.

Ha'avoda, and Ben-Gurion was in the process of establishing himself
and his party in firm control over its machinery. Both the party and
Ben-Gurion himself had welcomed the idea of the Gedud as the
executive arm of the Histadrut in absorbing new immigrants, exploiting possibilities of employment for Jewish workers, and establishing
new settlements; but they strongly suspected that it aimed to compete
with them for the leadership of the Yishuv.

This suspicion was not ill founded. The very idea of creating a
'general commune' contained the seeds of a conflict with the Histadrut, which constituted an overall framework for those very workers
whom the Gedud hoped to recruit. More explicitly, the Gedud's
constitution declared that it would 'strengthen the Histadrut, and
influence it in the direction of the Gedud'. When this clause had been
adopted in 1921, one group had interpreted it as opening the way to
politicization and had left in protest. There was some ground for this
interpretation. From the time of the Histadrut's foundation, there
had been tensions between the Gedud and the Histadrut, stemming
from the natural frictions of day-to-day negotiations on terms of
contract, wages, and conditions as well as from conflicts of principle.
The leaders of the Histadrut tended to be pragmatic, interested in
efficiency more than in social equality. So they began to introduce
differential payment for specialized work, and demanded that professional managers be appointed for the less efficient *plugot*. The
leaders of the Gedud saw these tendencies as deviations from their
socialist principles. Apart from the veterans of the Second Aliya, the
majority of whom were members or supporters of Ahdut Ha'avoda,
most of them belonged to no party; it thus seemed a natural step
when, at the end of 1922, they put forward an independent electoral
list for the second conference of the Histadrut, with a platform
emphasizing the need for equality and democracy in the workers'
movement.

The veterans of the Second Aliya within the Gedud were divided
into two groups. Although most of the ex-members of Hashomer
had been members of the Poalei Zion party, they were by nature
oppositionist, sometimes to the point of eccentricity. Most of them
refused to join Ahdut Ha'avoda, and considered themselves to have
more in common with the young, adventurous, anti-establishment
majority in the Gedud than with their staider contemporaries. So
Lavi and his friends (mainly of the Second Aliya and Ahdut Ha'avoda
supporters) were in a minority, which quickly became known as 'the

opposition'. After a long series of internal squabbles, and attempts at conciliation by prominent figures from outside the Gedud, the Histadrut was asked to arbitrate between the two camps. Under the political circumstances, it is not surprising that the commission appointed by Ben-Gurion to deal with the matter showed little sympathy for the views of the majority. It decided that the differences between the two camps were irreconcilable, and that the only solution was to split up the Gedud and divide its property between the two factions. The 'opposition' concentrated in Ein Harod and in two *plugot* close by, and in June 1923 Gedud Ha'avoda split into two separate movements. The break-away group was called from now on Kibbutz Ein Harod ('kibbutz' here implying the federation of its three component parts), while the majority retained the prestigious name of Gedud Ha'avoda.

## THE KIBBUTZ MOVEMENT IN 1923

During the Third Aliya (1918–23), the Jewish population of Palestine had grown by about 66 per cent. The number of Jewish villages had grown by 77 per cent, but the percentage of the rural population in the Yishuv as a whole dropped from 21 per cent to 16 per cent. In the same period, the population of the kibbutz movement had grown by 312 per cent, and the number of permanent communal settlements by 120 per cent. Thus, the rate of growth of the kibbutz population was almost five times as great as that of the Jewish population at large, and the number of kibbutzim also increased far beyond the increase in the number of other villages (70 per cent).[33] The development of the kibbutz movement during this period is summarized in Table 2, which shows its population in the summer of 1923.

### Ways of Life, 1923

In describing the way of life in the kibbutz movement at the end of the Third Aliya, we cannot talk of a typical kibbutz, for there were considerable variations between different groups and settlements, both in their way of life and in their ideological outlook. Degania Beit, for instance, which took over the area given up by Degania Aleph, never accepted the view that the *kvutza* should limit its

[33] Gurevich *et al.*, *Jewish Population of Palestine*, 79; Ettinger, 'The Co-operative Groups'; Katznelson, *The Kvutza*, 154–6.

TABLE 2. Population of Kibbutzim and Moshavim, Summer 1923

| Movement | No. of settlements | Members of settlements | No. of *plugot* | Members of *plugot* | Total members |
|---|---|---|---|---|---|
| Ein Harod | 1 | 105 | 3 | 105 | 210 |
| Gedud Ha'avoda | 3 | 319 | 4 | 113 | 452 |
| Hashomer Hatzair[a] | 1 | 90 | 2 | 97 | 187 |
| Unaffiliated (rural)[b] | 22 | 555 | 4 | 132 | 687 |
| Unaffiliated (urban)[b] | – | – | 9 | 345 | 345 |
| Total kibbutzim | 24 | 1,056 | 22 | 792 | 1,891[c] |
| Moshavim | 9 | 534 | .. | .. | 534 |

*Sources:* Histadrut, *Report of the Agricultural Centre, 1923/4–1925/6*, (Heb.), (Jerusalem, 1925), mimeo, tables 4, 5, 6: *Pinkas Hahistadrut* (Feb. 1923), app. c, 25; *UAW Report, 1927*, ch. 14.

[a] These groups had as yet no formal affiliation.

[b] Including the *havurot* (groups of *plugot*) which were to disintegrate or merge with a country-wide movement during the next two years.

[c] There were also about 150 children of members at this time.

.. no data available.

numbers stringently; as a result, it continued to expand into the area originally allocated to a third Degania. However, it is possible to give some general account of social structure and customs in the three different types of kibbutz: the *kvutzot*, Gedud Ha'avoda, and the kibbutzim of Hashomer Hatzair.

In the *kvutzot*, there is clear evidence of a phenomenon which recurred throughout the history of the kibbutz movement: the tendency for each kibbutz to repeat within its own boundaries the stages of development which its predecessors had already gone through. Here, for example, is an account of the early period in the life of Kibbutz Ginegar, in 1922–3.

The only social institution which existed then, and for the first ten years of the *kvutza's* existence, was the general discussion; or, more exactly, 'the table'. It was 'the table' which discussed and decided; before it one could speak of personal or communal afflictions, from it the individual drew encouragement and consolation. Sitting round the table one could consider every aspect of our different economic problems, questions of work arrangements, housing, help for the members' parents, education, as well as problems of the labour movement, the kibbutz movement, and so forth.

The 'table' was all-powerful. The source of its power was in our conception of the *kvutza* as a family-type community. Between twelve and seventeen young men and women would sit together every evening after work, before or after supper, and exchange impressions and opinions. In the course of this discussion, in the most honest fashion, with the participation of all the members of the *kvutza*, all the questions of our life were decided. And, if you wanted, together with sixteen other pairs of arms you could embrace matters in the realm of eternity, of the salvation of the world and of the Jewish people. There was a kind of longing of each for his neighbour, a desire to sit together until late at night, and thus to penetrate the depths of the vision of communal life. Soul encountered soul. There was a yearning to become a sort of sea of souls, whose tributaries would flow together, and together create a fresh and mighty current of fraternity and comradeship.[34]

Ginegar was still at the stage which Degania Aleph had gone through some four or five years earlier. In Degania itself at this time, in contrast, one can see the beginnings of institutionalization. General meetings were still held at frequent intervals, but they were more formal, and tended to deal with matters which were considered more fundamental; the day-to-day running of the kibbutz (including the most difficult task, the allocation of work) was now the clear responsibility of individuals, although the network of committees and election to permanent posts which is the hallmark of the developed kibbutz had not yet fully evolved. Here is an account of this process as it took place in Kibbutz Geva in the mid-1920s.

We used to sit on benches in the dining-hall after supper. The work roster was arranged naturally; Haim would say 'You plough here, you go there,' and the others would divide the rest of the jobs among themselves. Usually Haim's opinion would be accepted, and confirmed round the table. Everyone used to come to the work roster. There, we discussed matters very thoroughly. Haim was work organizer for several years; he took the job over naturally— he used to get there first, and always had the last word. Some people worked in permanent jobs, but we never put up a notice to say who worked where [as happened in other kibbutzim]. We still don't. . . .

When I arrived at Geva in 1924, there was no secretary, no one wrote the minutes of the discussion. Yosske E. arrived in 1925, and later became full-time treasurer. He signed a promissory note for £20, and this became known only when it came due. K. made a great fuss about it: 'How could he sign without the permission of the general meeting?' The same problem arose about appointing a secretary. Ya'akov put forward the idea [which was,

[34] *The Book of Ginegar*, 136–7.

apparently, rejected]. He stopped coming to the general meetings, as was his practice when his suggestions were not accepted. At the annual general meeting (which lasted a whole day and the following evening on each Jewish New Year) someone suggested that Ya'akov should be called, and that if he refused to come he should leave the *kvutza*.[35]

One can already see a sort of morphology of the *kvutza* and the kibbutz. Starting as a close-knit, undifferentiated group controlled by a system of direct and universal democracy, it gradually became more formalized, although the basic pattern of frequent general meetings and the accountability of officials remained unchanged. In this area, too, there were parallel developments: for instance, there were many instances of long-term tenure of organizational posts, such as work organizer, treasurer, or farm manager; it was apparently only in the 1930s that the principle of rotation in such posts became firmly established.

Many of these developments occurred spontaneously in different *kvutzot*. Others were the result of exchanges of information in the meetings between representatives of the *kvutzot*, which took place almost annually until the establishment of the first overall kibbutz organization in 1925.[36]

The way of life in Gedud Ha'avoda was different in many ways. Here again, it is unwise to generalize: there were differences between the *plugot*, which varied in size, composition, and the political culture of their members; some of them were very similar to the *kvutzot* before they reached the stage of agricultural settlement. Generally, however, the centralistic tendency of the Gedud made itself felt. By 1922, each *pluga* was run by an elected committee. The central structure of the Gedud was pyramidal, with these committees electing the representatives of the *plugot* and kibbutzim to the central bodies of the movement. Thus, the spirit and practice of the Gedud were far from the extreme forms of participatory democracy favoured by the *kvutzot*.

The agricultural settlements of the Gedud were built on the model of Lavi's 'big *kvutza*'. With the large numbers which they had from the very beginning, they could not rely on the informal organization of the small *kvutza*. Although the general meeting was sovereign, the day-to-day running of the farm was from the first in charge of an elected committee, which appointed people to various posts—

---

[35] Shatner, *To Our Hill*, 19, 37, 53.          [36] Katznelson, *The Kvutza*, 15–49.

treasurer, work organizer, and those in charge of the productive branches. These latter were of great importance in kibbutz society, since (as in Lavi's concept) the work team played a vital role in the development of the farm and the community. As yet, none of the settlements in the Gedud had established an industrial enterprise, but sporadic attempts to do so were made throughout the 1920s in Ein Harod and Tel Yosef.[37]

Two more differences between the *kvutzot* and the Gedud should be emphasized. I have already spoken of the dynamic character of the Gedud, which expressed itself in the constant effort to expand. There was, therefore, no possibility—or desire—to try out candidates for membership over a long period, as was done in the *kvutzot*. The period of candidature in the Gedud was three months, and at its end the committee made its recommendation to the general meeting of the *pluga* or the kibbutz.

In some places the numbers and degree of instability were so great that the new candidates would have to stand on a bench during the meeting so that they could be identified.[38] Members were accepted by a simple majority, in contrast with many of the small *kvutzot* where a unanimous vote was required. Gradually, however, criteria for the acceptance of new members began to be accepted, though they were not always formulated—apart from the will and ability to work. Despite the protests of those who continued to believe in unlimited absorption as the way to build the 'general commune', such phrases as 'a real Gedudnik' or 'a Gedud type' became current. Some hint as to what such a type was is given by the story of Avraham Shlonsky, the poet, who was a member of Kibbutz Tel Yosef in the 1920s. He was socially accepted by the dominant clique in the kibbutz after he had successfully organized the local football team. When they discovered that he was a poet—one of his poems, to his dismay, had been published in his own name—he was ridiculed and ostracized as an 'intellectual' before being allowed back into their company. This was one expression of the Zionist determination to create a new, working-class culture in protest against the over-intellectualization of the Diaspora Jew.[39]

[37] On the democratic structure see Rokhel in Ex-Members ... *Gedud Ha'avoda*, 219–51; on industrial enterprises see Lavi, *My Story in Ein Harod*, chs. 43–4.

[38] Eliezer Cana'ani, in interview with Muki Tsur, Tsur *et al.*, *The Beginning of the Kibbutz*, 150; on unanimity in *kvutzot* see Shatner, *Sixty Years of Geva*, 46.

[39] On the '*Gedud* type' and opposition thereto see Lavi, 'Choosing Members', and A. Shlonsky in Erez, *Third Aliya*, 892–4.

The contrast between the Gedud and the kibbutzim of Hashomer Hatzair was marked. Here, as in the *kvutzot*, a standard morphology began to be apparent: Hashomer Hatzair's second kibbutz went through a period parallel to those of the first group in Beitania Eilit and the group from Ginegar, with their semi-mystical yearnings for social unity. Later, the group's preoccupations began to be more down to earth: places of work, possibilities of agricultural settlement, and housing (or, more correctly, 'tenting'). But these continued to be close-knit groups, deeply conscious of their common background in the youth movement, and they rarely accepted new members who lacked that background. Cultural activities played a vital role in their lives and they rejected the anti-intellectualist version of 'working-class culture' characteristic of many in the Gedud. Thus, several of these groups made a point of keeping communal diaries, which were meant to be the literary expression of their common social and cultural experience. An article in the Beitania group's *Our Community*, entitled 'The Feast', gives an elevated picture of the communal meal as an expression of social unity, with parallels from classical and biblical literature (including the Last Supper); but its practical import is the call for more cultured behaviour during meals, and the rejection of the rough-and-ready approach which characterized the Gedud in these matters.[40]

In the Second Aliya such differences in ways of life were little more than nuances which arose in the course of the evolution of a new and as yet untried form of society. By 1920, however, they had become central issues in the embryonic ideological stances of the future kibbutz movements. This is the way former members of Hashomer Hatzair expounded their concept of the kibbutz at a meeting of new immigrants in December 1920:

For us, our internal situation, the question of our social development, is the basis of everything, including all our thoughts about settlement. Our communal life is founded on no presuppositions; we are united on the basis not of a programme, but of our past before we reached Palestine, a past which brought us here, a growth through comradeship. What is our communal ideal? A living community can be created only if it is based on the relationship between man and man, and the questions which concern society at large also determine the development and work of the kibbutz: not problems of work or of economic structure, but of the relationships between man and man, and

[40] *Our Community*, 73.

between man and woman. They are the compass of every society, they determine which direction it will take and what its future will be. These are the questions which we put in the centre of our life.[41]

In contrast, here is Shlomo Lavi's contribution to the discussion:

The Gedud is the exact opposite of Hashomer Hatzair. The community does not concern itself with the individual's personal life. The basis is the upbuilding of the country, for which the commune is the best method—not the selection of members. That is the method we have decided on, for better or for worse. Is the commune a permanent way of life, or a transitional stage? That is a difficult question, and not everybody can face up to it. But it is certainly the right way just now. . . .

Economic affairs must be so organized that the individual can be liberated from financial worries in order to develop his personality. I interpret these differences of opinion as different approaches to the question of how each of us makes his obeisance to the laws of life.

These sentiments, with only minor variations, were common to all parts of Gedud Ha'avoda at the time. It is difficult to find a similar concise quotation expressing a consensus in the veteran *kvutzot*, the biggest section of the kibbutz movement at this period, for they were very varied in composition and outlook. Here are two sample statements, taken from a meeting of the *kvutzot* in May 1923.[42]

The fulfilment of this idea [of the *kvutza*] requires 'the whole man'; he must place all his will, his talents and his strength at the disposal of the *kvutza*. . . . Any kibbutz which does not recognize this moral element . . . which thinks that it can be built on the basis of economics, of technical superiority, efficient management, etc. . . . is not putting into practice the true idea of the *kvutza*. (Joseph Baratz, Degania Aleph)

In my view, we cannot say today whether the *kvutza* is *the* system or not. Moshavim are being established, and there are people who believe that they are also a possible system. As far as the *kvutza* is concerned, we must first of all find out whether it can live on its earnings. And it is precisely on this point that we are not sure that we have succeeded. Nothing else is needed than to establish a farm which is self-sufficient, and produces all it needs. At the moment we still don't have the strength to raise all the agricultural branches to a sufficient standard. (Levi Shkolnik (Eshkol), Degania Beit)

---

[41] Both this extract and the next are from notes taken at a meeting of new immigrants at Tira on the eve of the foundation conference of the Histadrut. Preserved in the personal archive of Ephraim Reisner, Ramat Yohanan, and reprinted Tsur *et al.*, *The Beginnings of the Kibbutz*, 150.

[42] Katznelson, *The Kvutza*, 16, 28.

To conclude this short description of kibbutz life in the early 1920s, something may be said about the relations between the sexes.

Towards the end of his life Joseph Bussel, summing up the achievements of Degania to date, said: 'The crowning achievement of the kvutza is ... equality, in the economic sense, and between men and women.'[43]

In this context, equality between the sexes has two aspects: political and occupational. From the first, women had unquestioned political rights within the *kvutza*. They took part in general meetings, and had the right to speak and vote exactly as did the men. This was in sharp contrast to the moshav, where the basic unit was the family rather than the individual, and it was virtually impossible for an unmarried woman to survive as a working member.[44] The occupational aspect was no less important in the eyes of the founders of Degania. The aim of the women who led the struggle for emancipation was to take a part in the struggle for the 'conquest of labour', alongside the men: to fulfil 'male' functions in the economic sphere. There were many barriers to this step, both on the part of their potential employers and in the attitudes of the male workers; indeed, in general, women's emancipation in this sense was a failure in the Palestinian Jewish community outside the kibbutz.[45] It was only by dint of conscious effort, in the first instance on the part of the women themselves, and in the course of time with the support of the kibbutz community as a whole, that a framework was created which enabled women to take part in agricultural work and at the same time to fulfil their functions as mothers.

This took place in several stages, some of which have been described above: Miriam Bussel's assumption of the position of milkmaid, and its immediate acceptance by the men of Degania; a retrograde step in 1913, with Degania's decision not to accept five graduates of the Kinneret agricultural school for women on economic grounds;[46] the changes in Degania's economic structure in 1919, whereby branches such as poultry, orchards, and market gardening were expanded or added to the previously dominant arable crops, largely in order to increase the number of agricultural jobs for women;[47] and the various steps which led to the institutionalization of communal child care. Parallel with these developments came the training of women for

[43] Wurm, *Bussel Memorial Book*, 237.            [44] Lieberson, *Life Chapters*, 117–38.
[45] Bernstein, *The Struggle for Equality*.        [46] Maimon-Fishman, *Fifty Years*, 20.
[47] Degania, general meeting, 1 Apr. 1919, 37.

agricultural work: at first in the Sejera training farm, later in the agricultural training school for women at Kinneret. By the end of the First World War, the right of women, including mothers, to work in agriculture, and the institutional arrangements which enabled them to do so, were an established feature of Degania.

In the perspective of the Second Aliya as a whole, these achievements were very limited. Indeed, Degania stood alone. The only other permanent communal settlement of the Second Aliya, Merhavia, was based on the family unit, in which the woman served as housewife. Other *kvutzot* were temporary, contained few couples, and had no permanent arrangements for child care. In Hashomer, a few of the veteran women were full members of the organization, but marriage to a member did not automatically admit women to membership, and most wives were not allowed to share their husbands' knowledge of the movement and its secrets. When the first settlement group formed a moshav at Tel Adashim, it was only after a revolt by the women that they were admitted to some degree of control over the community's affairs. And even in Degania, until 1921 the women were not officially employed by the Zionist movement. Most of them worked in what came to be called the service branches: cooking, child care, the clothing store. Women's work—including the 'feminine' agricultural branches, such as dairy farming and poultry—was recorded separately from that of the men, thus symbolizing a distinction between 'productive' and 'non-productive' branches which still exists throughout the kibbutz movement.[48]

This situation altered radically during the Third Aliya. Now, for the first time, there was a substantial number of women in the kibbutz movement, and there was no economic logic in confining them to 'women's work'. Moreover, they created communes and kibbutzim on the model not of Degania, but of the idea of Degania: a model in which men and women enjoyed equality in all respects, including their right to participate in the 'conquest of labour'. And, unlike their predecessors of the Second Aliya, many of them arrived in the country imbued with the ideals of the youth movement, including far-reaching concepts of sexual equality and the abolition of the bourgeois family. Several articles and discussions in *Our Community* spoke of the 'future family'; in effect, the substitution of the kibbutz for the nuclear family.

[48] Hashomer: Poznansky and Shehori, *Women in the Kibbutz*, 12–13; Dinur *et al.*, *History of the Hagana*, i, 897. Degania: The separate work rosters are to be found in the archives of Degania Aleph.

In short, the spirit of the youth movement was anti-familial. It was backed up by a radical approach to the question of employment. During the 'period of the roads', when the tone was set by veterans of Hechalutz, women worked by the side of men in stone-breaking and road-laying; and when they reached their places of settlement, many of them found a place in the agricultural branches. From photographs and verbal accounts of the period, a clear picture emerges: compared with the Second Aliya, women had achieved a considerable degree of emancipation in both occupational and political terms. It is from this period that the image of the Yishuv as a sexually egalitarian society, and the kibbutz as the supreme example of this egalitarianism, derives.

This image was not entirely accurate. There is very little reliable evidence about women's occupations at this time; but in 1926 the pattern set in the Second Aliya, whereby men worked in the 'productive branches' and women in the 'services', still applied in the veteran kibbutzim, though often not in the *plugot*, where there were few children.[49] It seems probable, therefore, that both the pressure for women's emancipation in this sense and its realization were centred in the groups of pioneers who arrived during the Third Aliya.

There is a good deal of anecdotal evidence about family life and personal relationships between the sexes during this period. Although the gender imbalance was less serious than in the Second Aliya there were still more men than women in the kibbutz movement. Even so, in particular groups, particularly among the selective *kvutzot* and the kibbutzim of Hashomer Hatzair, the problem could be extremely serious. For example, in Beitania Eilit there were only four women in a group of twenty-seven, and both the written sources and the members' reminiscences point to a high degree of erotic tension. Sometimes this tension was open, as in the account of competition for the love of a girl (followed by mutual renunciation) in *Our Community*; sometimes it was suppressed, or sublimated into work and interpersonal relationships in the communal framework. In Hashomer Hatzair, as in many of the European youth movements, there was a very strong strain of puritanism, which combined with the romantic ethos to reinforce this tendency: the woman was pure and untouchable, and could be approached only in the context of the group as a

---

[49] Rosen, 'Changes in the Status of Women', 77; and cf. Fogiel-Bijaoui, 'Motherhood and Revolution'.

whole. 'Soul encountered soul', but body kept aloof from body.[50]

Similar ambivalent feelings are to be found in almost all the kibbutzim of the Second and Third Aliya at an early stage of their development. Children were considered to be the joint responsibility of the group as a whole, and communal child care helped to knit the community closer together. On the other hand, although romantic love was not proscribed, it was felt to cut the lovers off from full participation in the lives of the community, and was often subjected to criticism. And this criticism was reinforced by the generally accepted condemnation of the 'bourgeois family'. Here are some examples:

We both believed, in our complete innocence, that ... true love must embrace the whole of mankind, and not be limited to a single couple. So we found an original solution: a boy did not love a girl; they loved The Young Man, and The Young Woman, united by a single social and national ideal which brought their hearts together. (Hayuta, widow of Joseph Bussel, on Degania Aleph, 1917–18)

We decided to 'share a room' (that was the phrase in those days). So, when the man who shared Yitzhak's tent was away, I moved my mattress in, and that was that.... No one talked of any sort of celebration. But Tanhum always said, 'When I get married, all the workers will come and dance.' Yitzhak said the opposite: marriage is a personal matter, and needs no ceremony. One Friday evening, there was a party to celebrate Tanhum's wedding—no ceremony, just a party, and lots of people invited.... Suddenly we saw the cakes: on one was written 'Haya and Tanhum', on the other 'Yona and Yitzhak' ... Yitzhak just got up and left. I didn't know what to do. In the end, I went after him. (Yona Ben Ya'akov, on Degania Aleph, 1920)

The practical joke which the guards played last night has infuriated some of our married couples. When they got up in the morning they found the children's hut, which has not yet been completed, arranged like the room of a petit-bourgeois family. Two beds made up tidily, slippers beneath them, next to the husband's bed a pipe, etc. Of course, what they meant was that our families withdraw and keep to themselves, and do not participate in the life of the big family—the kibbutz. Feelings ran high, and people said that it was a very tactless and objectionable thing to do. R. burst into tears as a result. (Second Kibbutz of Hashomer Hatzair, 1922)

In Beit Alpha there was an attempt to abolish rooms for couples. They took down the partitions in one of the huts, and couples and single people lived together. The reason was not shortage of housing, but ideology: the belief that we had to get rid of the barriers between us. The experiment lasted a

[50] *Our Community*, 21–3, 71; and cf. Ya'ari, 'Rootless Symbols', 64.

few months, and then the couples returned to their own rooms. (Beit Alpha, 1923/4)[51]

It may well be that the last of these passages reflects a much more extreme state of affairs than the writer is prepared to admit. Oral tradition has it that in many kibbutzim the far-going repressions of the early, puritanical period were often replaced by a flurry of sexual activity in the more relaxed and 'normal' atmosphere of the kibbutz after it had settled on its own land. Some even speak of 'a period of free love'. But in every case, with the appearance of the first children the nuclear family became an accepted—or at least tolerated—part of kibbutz life. It was still not socially acceptable to emphasize this fact too much. For instance, in most kibbutzim, husband and wife did not sit together at meals in the communal dining room or at kibbutz meetings, and this remained the norm until the 1940s. None the less, there was no serious attempt to carry to an extreme the opposition to the 'bourgeois family' expressed in the extracts above.

Clearly, the acceptance of the family unit was not the result of trial and error, but rather of social instinct, or ingrained cultural attitudes which dictated the limits of the social and personal revolution which these young people were prepared to carry out in their own lives. As one of them remarked in later years:

In relationships between the sexes there were very many inhibitions. In fact, the mentality of the *shtetl* remained unchanged. Below the surface, we all wanted to be like everyone else in the world, and every girl looked for a boy to marry, even though formally there were no marriages.[52]

In a deeper sense, however, it seems as if these limits were essential to the survival of the kibbutz. One can see how arrangements could have been made to care for the younger generation under a regime of multiple sexual partnerships, and it is impossible to say with certainty that such a regime could not have survived. But, given the sexual ethos of those who founded the kibbutz and of those who joined it later, it seems most likely that such a regime would have radically reduced the number of parents prepared to stay. In such a case, the rule would no doubt have become: married couples to the moshav.

---

[51] Tsur *et al.*, *The Beginnings of the Kibbutz*, 75, 181, 177; Erez, *Third Aliya*, 434. The latter is from a contemporary diary. All the others are later reminiscences which refer to the dates given in the text.

[52] Tsur *et al.*, *The Beginnings of the Kibbutz*, 177.

The outstanding example of faithfulness to the concept of the nuclear family is undoubtedly Yitzhak Tabenkin, who joined Kibbutz Ein Harod in 1921 and rapidly became one of the leaders of the kibbutz movement; as we shall see in later chapters, it is quite likely that had it not been for his personal role, the major kibbutz movement—the Kibbutz Me'uhad—would not have survived the crises of the 1920s and early 1930s. When Tabenkin arrived at Ein Harod he already had a wife and child, and it is certain that any attempt to abolish the nuclear family would have profoundly repelled both him and the other Second Aliya veterans who played a central role in developing this kibbutz. From his arrival in Ein Harod, Tabenkin maintained forcefully that the family was an essential component of kibbutz society. In historical perspective, therefore, it seems that, despite the tensions which it caused in certain periods, the acceptance of the nuclear family was a means of stabilizing and expanding the kibbutz.[53]

## The Kibbutz in the Yishuv

One should not rely too heavily on the accuracy of the statistical data quoted earlier, or on their significance. None the less, there can be no doubt that the growth and stabilization of the kibbutz movement were far greater than the corresponding processes in the Jewish population as a whole. By the end of the Third Aliya, kibbutz members had a firm factual basis for believing that the strength of the kibbutz movement was on the increase, and that it had already laid a firm social foundation for its own continued expansion. So it would not have been over-optimistic to forecast that the kibbutz would attain a majority in the rural Jewish population, or even in the Yishuv as a whole. On the other hand, statistics alone could not foretell the future. The factors which would determine whether the kibbutz would become stronger, disappear altogether, or remain a minority within a predominantly non-communal society cannot be expressed purely in numerical terms. I shall conclude this chapter by summing them up briefly.[54]

In 1920, the international Poalei Zion movement sent a delegation

[53] Fialkov and Rabinovitch, *Yitzhak Tabenkin*, 2–3; Katznelson, *The Kvutza*, 36–8.

[54] Detailed references to Hebrew sources for this summing-up of the situation of the kibbutz at the end of the Third Aliya can be found in Near, *Kibbutz and Society*, 44–9, on which it is largely based.

to Palestine to investigate the possibilities of development of the Yishuv. Its report listed the *kvutzot* and the size of their membership and gave detailed descriptions of their character and situation. It stated that 'in the course of its work, in the face of the contingencies of life, each *kvutza* has sought its own set of values, and built its internal life according to its own feelings, and the desires of its members'.[55] This description stands in marked contrast to the picture which emerges from the first book ever published about the kibbutz movement, Berl Katznelson's anthology *The Kvutza*. Published in November 1924, it deals mainly with the state of the kibbutzim at the end of the Third Aliya. One of the issues it deals with is a suggestion to adopt a standard constitution, to apply to every *kvutza* or kibbutz. Though this proposal was not accepted, the very fact that it was deemed possible shows that the structure of the communal groups had become crystallized, and to some extent standardized, during the previous three years. Similarly, while the statistical tables of the Poalei Zion report do not distinguish between 'conquest groups' and permanent communities, *The Kvutza* has separate lists of 'settled *kvutzot*' and 'groups preparing for communal settlement'. Again, while the Poalei Zion report does not refer to children in the *kvutzot*, by September 1924 there were already 190.

All this indicates that by the end of the Third Aliya the kibbutz was a more or less settled and permanent way of life. This does not mean that there were no differences between the different types of kibbutzim; but the word *kvutza* and the other terms signifying communal groups had acquired fixed meanings. All of them had in common such elements as common ownership and management of financial affairs, a general work roster, communal consumption (food, culture, and allocation of clothing), and communal child care and education. Moreover, the inter-kibbutz discussions of 1922 and 1923 show that in these matters there was a large degree of similarity between the various communal groups.

These developments stemmed largely from the fact that in most of the kibbutzim there was now a stable group of members who were prepared to bear the responsibility for the community. Even though there were many complaints about social instability in *The Kvutza*, the situation had changed since 1921 when A. D. Gordon had written: 'If, as I hear, the population of Degania Beit is completely changing this year, and Kinneret [and others] . . . can this be called human

[55] *Ha'adama*, 9 (June 1920), 241–55.

growth? And what about the human suffering these changes bring about?'[56] By 1924 virtually all the veteran *kvutzot* had a core of experienced members who formed the basis for the absorption of younger members, temporary workers, and the like.

A similar process of increasing permanence can be discerned in the relations between the kibbutzim and the Zionist movement. The future of the kibbutz no longer depended on one year's crop in Degania or Kinneret. There were fierce discussions in the Zionist executive about whether to increase kibbutz settlement or to freeze it at its current level. But nobody really doubted that it was the responsibility of the movement to support the settlements which had been founded under its auspices, insofar as it had the means to do so; and this was so despite financial losses, and bitter political and economic criticism. There was general, if not always explicit, agreement that Palestine would be settled by the members of the workers' movement, aided by capital nationally raised and nationally owned; and a central role in this process was allocated to the kibbutz. Both the kibbutzim and the Zionist movement found the financial losses which they continued to incur an oppressive burden, but the way in which each of them dealt with the problem was agreed and even institutionalized in periodic reports and meetings, committee-work and budgets.[57]

In brief, the kibbutz had passed the experimental stage and had become an integral and recognized part of the Yishuv. One indication of this is that phrases such as 'the kibbutz movement', which are not found at all in contemporary sources during the early years of the Third Aliya, were in regular use by the end of that period. This clearly reflected a change in the situation of the kibbutzim, rooted in their growth in membership, from 446 to 2,730. By 1924 the kibbutzim had become a movement.

No less important than the internal development of the kibbutzim was the change in their relationship with the outside world, and particularly with the Zionist movement and the Jewish people. This, the kibbutzim believed, was their greatest hope for the future. In 1923, at the depths of the economic slump, Hechalutz had 5,470 members in 224 local branches in the Jewish communities of Europe. In that year the conference of the biggest national section, in Poland, declared: 'This is the time for Polish Hechalutz to increase the number

---

[56] Gordon, *Letters and Notes*, 160.
[57] Bein, *History of Zionist Settlement*, 162–3, 212–14, 240–9.

of immigrants from its ranks,' and members of Hechalutz already in Palestine knew well that most would join the kibbutz movement. In the Russian section of the movement the majority faction had given this tendency clear ideological definition in its 'collectivist orientation'.

All of the facts so far described were a reasonable basis for a feeling of power and achievement in the present, and optimism with regard to the future. But in fact these feelings were mixed with a high degree of insecurity and apprehension. In Degania Aleph, for instance, although the social core was permanent and closely knit, the periphery was exceedingly volatile. In 1923 there were 43 members, 18 of whom had been members for no more than eighteen months, and 12 temporary workers, some of whom eventually became members: this was all that remained of the 356 people who had passed through the *kvutza* in the twelve years of its existence; and although 103 of them remained in the kibbutz movement, this was not of much comfort to the people of Degania in their struggle to build a stable and viable community.

The most serious blow to the kibbutz in this period was an event which was in itself a positive step for the workers' movement. The first two moshavim to achieve permanent settlement, Nahalal and Kfar Yehezke'el, were established in 1921, and six more had been founded by the end of 1923. From Degania Aleph alone, between 60 and 65 people left during this period to join a moshav. The existence of a new form of workers' settlement, legitimate in the eyes both of the labour movement and of the Zionist movement, created practical, ideological, and political problems for the kibbutzim.

One of the principal reasons for their social instability was without doubt their precarious economic situation. Even before the economic crisis of 1923 they had suffered from severe financial problems, and their standard of living was low. The reasons for this were partly objective—the difficulties inherent in the 'conquest of labour' and the 'conquest of the soil': climatic conditions, meagre accommodation, poor sanitary conditions, and so forth. But, equally, they sprang from the fact that, from the very earliest stages of settlement, they had to rely on allocations from the Zionist movement's Settlement Fund (Keren Hayesod), which was very often unable to provide the amounts required to carry out even its own relatively modest plans. Added to the cost of inexperience, all of these factors conspired together to produce a vicious circle of economic difficulties and attrition of membership which was broken only at a later stage.

These difficulties were compounded by the fact that the kibbutz was under attack from several quarters. The moshavim not only attracted kibbutz members who preferred a more individualistic and family-centred way of life; they also claimed that they were more efficient, and demanded to take the place hitherto occupied by the kibbutz as the chief means of Zionist settlement. Within the labour movement, this demand was given ideological backing by many in the Hapoel Hatzair party. No less important was the support given to the moshav by certain groups in the Zionist movement who used it as a stick to beat the kibbutz. In the Zionist Congress of 1920, and again in the 're-organization committee' which it established, the idea of settlement based on national capital was severely criticized, largely on the basis of the state of the *kvutzot* at the end of the First World War. This attitude was adopted by the Brandeis faction in the World Zionist Organization, and formed one of the main planks in its fight against the leadership of Chaim Weizmann.[58] With Weizmann's victory and the general enthusiasm aroused in the 1921 Congress by the beginning of the settlement of the Jezreel Valley the criticism died down, but it returned in the wake of the slump of 1923. As a result, the Zionist Executive appointed a commission to recommend future settlement policy. Although its recommendation to replace the kibbutz by the moshav as the major means of settlement was not fully implemented, this further intensified the kibbutz members' feeling that they were politically isolated. And so the moshav, whose establishment had been supported by many of the leaders of the kibbutz movement, and which was in many respects its ally, was used against the kibbutz by its enemies.

Finally, it was becoming clear that although in many ways the kibbutzim felt that they constituted a movement rather than isolated settlements or groups of communities, this feeling was far from untroubled. In the veteran *kvutzot* there was no general agreement about such questions as the desirable size of the community, its political connections, and its relationships with the rest of the kibbutz movement; and in some cases the relations between the *kvutzot* were strained as a result of boundary disputes and other local tensions. The Hashomer Hatzair groups had not established a country-wide movement, and had more or less abandoned their links with their mother movement in the Diaspora. The major kibbutz movement,

[58] On the Brandeis–Weizmann controversy see Laqueur, *A History of Zionism*, 458–62.

Gedud Ha'avoda, had suffered a major blow with the secession of Ein Harod; and, although it retained its organizational unity, in social and ideological terms it was increasingly a coalition of disparate forces. Party differences also added to the sense of disunity. Most of the members of the Gedud and the Hashomer Hatzair kibbutzim were not party members, and many were opposed in principle to party political activity, but in each of these movements there was a minority of Ahdut Ha'avoda supporters. There was also such a minority in some of the veteran *kvutzot*, most of whose members belonged to or supported Hapoel Hatzair. In short, there were already divisive tendencies which impaired the sense of underlying unity. Moreover, news of the economic crisis in Palestine led to a decline in the membership of Hechalutz in Europe at the beginning of 1924; and the disputes within the labour movement were echoed in the Diaspora to such an extent that the kibbutz/moshav controversy was central in the arguments which led to a split in the Russian Hechalutz movement in September 1923.[59]

Despite these problems, there can be no doubt that the Third Aliya saved the kibbutz from becoming merely an interesting but ephemeral episode in the history of the Yishuv. A number of factors stand out. From the first, the 'halo effect' gave the *kvutza* a high degree of prestige in the Yishuv and the Zionist movement and led the younger pioneers to see the process of agricultural settlement as 'natural'. Then there were the links between the various communities which were the beginnings of the kibbutz movement, and between that movement and the pioneer movements in the Diaspora. No less important was the new pioneers' deep conviction that they were building a new society based on the ideals of social justice, and their readiness to experiment, which together made possible the 'big *kvutza*' and the varied achievements of the Gedud. A final key factor, no less at this stage than at the beginning of the *kvutza*, was the fact that kibbutz society found it possible to accommodate the nuclear family, and was thus able to compete with the moshav not only in absorbing young pioneers but in retaining them in later life.

---

[59] For a detailed account of the development of Hechalutz and the youth movements, see ch. 3.

# 3

# The Pioneering Youth Movements: Origins and Growth, 1900–1935

THE development of the kibbutz from the end of the First World War is intertwined with the history of the pioneering youth movements in the Diaspora and, at a later stage, in the Yishuv. They supplied the reserves of manpower without which the kibbutzim would inevitably have entered a demographic decline. Their influence on the ideological development of the kibbutz movement was also great, and sometimes decisive. Conversely, they themselves were influenced, and eventually controlled, by the kibbutz movements, which supported them in myriad ways—as a social and educational model, as a source of senior educators, and as a link with the institutions of the Zionist movement and the Histadrut.

In this chapter I shall discuss the major youth movements which were connected with the kibbutz movement, from their beginnings until about 1930.

## HECHALUTZ

### Hechalutz in Russia[1]

At the beginning of the Third Aliya, the Russian Hechalutz movement was still in large measure an organization of 'pioneers on the way': groups of young Jews, ranging in age from 18 to 25, who united in order to prepare themselves for the journey to Palestine and make the journey together. Gradually, however, more permanent elements were added. Even in the chaos of civil war, rudimentary regional and even all-Russian organizations were set up. In the main Jewish centres branches appeared which engaged in propaganda for the pioneering ideal and helped the members on their way.

When it became apparent that the process of immigration, including the need for the permission of the Mandatory authorities, was longer

[1] This section is largely based on Pines, *Hechalutz*, and West, *Hechalutz in Russia*.

than had been expected, a number of training farms were set up, particularly in the Crimea. For this, the permission of the Soviet authorities was needed. At first it appeared that there was an identity of interest, for it was Communist policy to encourage 'product-ivization' of the Jews. But Hechalutz was under permanent suspicion of being Zionist, and therefore anti-Communist, and all its activities were in constant danger. By mid-1922 the movement was divided on the question of whether to attempt to function within the law or to go underground. The issue was partly a matter of expedience: legality would make the movement's work much easier, but it meant revealing the members' names and the movement's activities to the authorities, and being at their mercy if policy changed. But there were other issues which divided the factions. The 'legal' group advocated 'col-lectivism'—kibbutz rather than moshav—and made acceptance to their training farms conditional on acceptance of this principle; the 'illegals' were influenced by the Hapoel Hatzair ideology and rejected any such restriction.

By April 1923, controversy on these issues had become so bitter that the movement's two wings were unable to work together. The movement split into a 'legal' and an 'illegal' organization. This development was condemned by virtually all those in the labour movement who came into contact with Russian Hechalutz. Successive meetings of the world Hechalutz movement, which had been estab-lished in March 1922, called on the two movements to reunite. David Ben-Gurion represented the Histadrut at the Moscow Trade Fair in the summer of 1923 and used the occasion to make contact with the young Russian Jews.[2] He was quite appalled by the schism but failed to convince the protagonists. The two movements worked separately, with much rivalry and animosity, throughout the years of persecution and underground activity, until they were both liquidated by the Soviet authorities in the 1930s.

This quarrel was in part induced by the special conditions of Russia at the time: a tiny group of inexperienced activists attempted to guide the movement through constant danger and uncertainty. Partly, no doubt, it was an expression of the character of Jewish—particularly, perhaps, Russian Jewish—public activity; for instance, the Russian Hashomer Hatzair movement split on similar lines some months after Hechalutz.[3] But it also had an important ideological dimension. The

[2] Teveth, *Ben-Gurion*, ch. 16; Ben-Gurion, 'Hechalutz in Russia'.
[3] Raphaeli, *In the Struggle for Salvation*, 141.

left wing of the movement saw in the Communists' attempts to rebuild Russia on socialist foundations a parallel to the idea of constructive socialism in Zionist ideology,[4] and the language used by this group in the movement's deliberations can leave no doubt that they were deeply influenced by the Communist ambience.[5] This combination of constant pressure from their surroundings and isolation from the outside world (including Palestine) played a decisive part in determining their ways of thought.

After constant appeals to various Soviet authorities, the secretary of the 'legal' wing was granted an interview with Stalin, and as a result the movement's legality was confirmed.[6] But recognition was very precarious, did not apply to every region, and was in any case only temporary. In mid-1924 Soviet anti-Zionist policy became much more stringent and both wings were forced to lead an underground (though separate) existence. By the end of 1930 the movement had virtually ceased to exist. The proportion of immigrants of Russian origin dropped from 44.5 per cent during the Third Aliya to 18.7 per cent between 1924 and 1931, and no more than 1.5 per cent in the following decade.[7] This vital and dynamic community, from which had come the bulk of Hechalutz and the kibbutz movement during its first twenty years, was henceforth cut off from the outside world.

## *The Expansion of Hechalutz*[8]

Parallel with the decline of Russian Hechalutz came the growth of the other sections of the movement. In some places this was a spontaneous process, in that young Jews throughout Europe responded similarly to similar problems; in others it was the result of the migration of Russian Jews who had been in touch with the movement and now

[4] Pines, *Hechalutz*, 130–1.

[5] For example, in the 'April forum', which was the last meeting before the final split; ibid. 177–88.

[6] Apparently, the softening of the Communist attitude to Hechalutz stemmed from the fact that this was the period of the relatively liberal New Economic Policy (NEP), when the Soviet government was interested in winning the support of international Jewish organizations such as the Joint, the JCA, and ORT. Moreover, as remarked above, the aim of 'productivizing' the Jews was common to Hechalutz and the Communist party; ibid. 196–7.

[7] The number who arrived directly from Russia between 1924 and 1931 was much smaller than appears from these statistics, for many Jews of Russian origin had in fact settled temporarily in other countries on their way to Palestine; Gurevich *et al.*, *Jewish Population of Palestine*, 59.

[8] This section is based on Near, 'The Kibbutz and the Outside World', 88–96.

spread the pioneering idea in their new country or on their way to Palestine. The extent of this expansion is apparent from Table 3.

In 1921 the Mandatory government had introduced the 'certificate' system for regulating immigration.[9] Every six months, after negotiations with the Zionist movement, the British authorities would decide on the number of working-class immigrants to be admitted in the coming half-yearly 'schedule'. Immigration certificates were distributed up to this numerical limit according to lists prepared by the committees of the local Zionist organizations. They worked closely with Hechalutz, which would select its candidates according to its own criteria. Thus, Hechalutz acquired a semi-official status as the department of the Zionist movement responsible for the training and selection of working-class immigrants.

In certain regions this function was purely technical. For instance, in Galicia, Romania, and Germany, where the educational youth movements were the dominant force among the young pioneers, Hechalutz was, in effect, an administrative framework for arranging their training and emigration. Elsewhere, and primarily in Poland, the Jewish community was large and varied enough to permit the existence side by side of élitist movements such as Hashomer Hatzair and Gordonia and the mass-orientated Hechalutz. During the 1920s and 1930s, there were constant struggles in these regions for recruits, for the financing of training facilities, and—most of all—for immigration certificates.

The administrative machinery of the world Hechalutz movement had been established in 1922. Its secretary, Meir Bogdanovsky (Sheli), a teacher from Jerusalem and a member of Ahdut Ha'avoda, saw his task as primarily educational. In March 1923 the movement began to publish its journal, *Hechalutz*. From then on, differences in national movements' character and methods of work notwithstanding, it is possible to talk of a world movement with a common organizational structure and basic ideology.

Despite its connection with the Zionist movement, Hechalutz did not see itself simply as its junior section. In 1917, in an article which became one of the movement's basic ideological documents, Trumpeldor declared that Hechalutz should unite 'all the workers, whether they employ muscle or brain, provided that they derive their livelihood from their own labour, and not from the exploitation of

---

[9] Gurevich *et al.*, *Jewish Population of Palestine*, 23–4.

TABLE 3. Hechalutz Membership, 1923–1929

| Jewish community[a] | | 1923 | 1924 | 1925 | 1926 | 1927 | 1928–9 |
|---|---|---|---|---|---|---|---|
| Austria | Members | 120 | 202 | 700 | 400 | 350 | |
| (190,000) | Branches | 1 | 1 | – | 8 | – | |
| Bulgaria | Members | – | – | 20 | 21 | 20 | |
| (46,000) | Branches | – | – | – | 3 | – | |
| Czechoslovakia | Members | 100 | 190 | 420 | 440 | 405 | |
| (355,000) | Branches | 10 | 18 | – | 28 | – | |
| Galicia[b] | Members | 500 | 500 | 912 | 720 | 1,579 | |
| (800,000) | Branches | 25 | 65 | – | 124 | – | |
| Germany | Members | 420 | 604 | 1,050 | 1,040 | 510 | |
| (570,000) | Branches | 10 | 25 | – | 40 | – | |
| Greater Poland[b] | Members | 1,700 | 5,060 | 13,000 | 9,500 | 4,200 | |
| (2,500,000) | Branches | 71 | 280 | – | 392 | – | |
| Latvia | Members | – | 67 | 250 | 150 | 150 | |
| (95,000) | Branches | 3 | 6 | – | 12 | – | |
| Lithuania | Members | 450 | 1,000 | 3,000 | 2,400 | 560 | |
| (150,000) | Branches | 24 | 24 | 50 | – | – | |
| Romania | Members | 180 | 240 | 750 | 678 | 487 | |
| (800,000) | Branches | 10 | 13 | – | 21 | – | |
| Russia | Members | 2,000 | 7,000 | 13,000 | 14,000 | – | |
| (2,500,000) | Branches | – | – | – | – | – | |
| Total members (excluding Russia) | | 3,470 | 7,863 | 20,102 | 15,349 | 8,261 | 18,428 |

*1928–9 column:* There are no figures available for separate countries for these years, but the *Hechalutz Anthology* gives a total of 18,428 for 1929, of which 14,245 were in branches and 4,003 in training kibbutzim

*Notes:* These data are taken from contemporary publications and reports, as collated in *Hechalutz Anthology*, 185–209. As is often the case with statistics of youth movements, they may well be not entirely accurate; but they certainly reflect general proportions and trends. The figures for Russia are definitely exaggerated, and were not reflected in the immigration statistics; I have therefore not included them in the totals. A survey made in the autumn of 1926 gives a general idea of the national origins of the Hechalutz graduates then members of the Histadrut: Poland: 44.9%; USSR: 28.2%; Romania: 5.9%; Lithuania: 5.9%; Galicia: 5.4%; Germany: 3.2%; Austria: 2.4%; Latvia: 1.6%; Czechoslovakia: 0.9%; Bulgaria: 0.3%; various: 3.3% (*Hechalutz Anthology*, 218).

[a] The figures in parentheses show the approximate size of the Jewish communities in the 1920s, as shown in the *Encyclopedia Judaica*.

[b] Galicia is listed separately from the rest of Poland ('Greater' or 'Congress' Poland) here and in other sources because it was organized separately within the Zionist adult and youth movements. Cf. Mendelsohn, *Jews of East Central Europe*, 17–19.

others'.[10] This definition, which was adopted with minor variations by all the pioneering movements, effectively allied Hechalutz with the labour movement in the Yishuv. The recently arrived Hechalutz contingent that took part in the founding conference of the Histadrut at the end of 1920 saw themselves as a pressure group to ensure the establishment of an all-embracing labour movement. When they had achieved this object, they disbanded their separate organization. This act, and the ideology behind it, opened the way to the recognition of the special relationship between Hechalutz and the Histadrut. The resolution of the Polish movement at its 1923 conference, that 'all members of Hechalutz join the Histadrut when they reach the Land of Israel', became accepted doctrine in all parts of the movement. Hechalutz saw itself as the Diaspora branch of the Histadrut.

Despite this basis of common ideology, many of the developments which came about in the following years resulted from the particular social and economic conditions in specific countries. Poland, with the biggest Jewish community in Europe after Russia, led the way; what happened there requires more detailed analysis.

## Hechalutz in Poland[11]

With the cessation of immigration from Russia in the mid-1920s Poland became far and away the most important component of European Jewry. Up to the eve of the Holocaust it was the main source of manpower for the Yishuv.[12]

The Hechalutz movement in Poland began much as it had done in Russia, spontaneously, as a general movement of immigrants. Here, too, the realization that the process of immigration was lengthy and required psychological and technical preparation led to changes in the movement's character. The local branches in the areas of Jewish concentration became centres of propaganda and education for the ideas of Hechalutz, and various types of professional training were established for its members, usually with financial help from the local Zionist movement. From 1921 on the young pioneers set up dozens

[10] Trumpeldor, *Hechalutz*, 20–7.

[11] This section is largely based on Oppenheim, *The Hechalutz Movement in Poland*, and Sarid, *Hechalutz in Poland*.

[12] Polish Jews comprised 48.9% of all Jewish immigrants to Palestine between 1924 and 1931, and 40.5% between 1932 and 1942; in all, 41.5% of all immigrants from 1919 to 1942. The next largest groups were those of German origin, who reached 18.9%, and of Russian origin, 13.2%. See Gurevich *et al.*, *Jewish Population of Palestine*, 59.

of small farms: during the seasons of intensive agricultural activity they worked long hours, returning to their homes for the 'dead' seasons. This method was basically amateurish and led to heavy financial losses, and was more or less abandoned by 1923. Bigger training farms were also established, and a few of these lasted until the early 1930s. But the state of agriculture in Eastern Europe in general was such that these farms too became a heavy financial burden. Later, non-agricultural work was found in nearby towns. For a short period, during the 'period of the roads' in the Yishuv, agricultural training was almost abandoned in favour of more technical education, particularly in wood- and metal-work. But by the end of 1923 both agricultural and technical training were viewed as less important than the effort to educate a type of pioneer ready to fulfil any task. At the beginning of 1924, the movement was engaged in a wide-ranging debate on the aims and methods of its educational work which echoed a similar controversy in Russian Hechalutz some seven years earlier: was it to be a mass movement, or an élite group? In Trumpeldor's words, should it be 'a general professional organization, which aims to embrace, as far as possible, all the workers who have decided to migrate to Palestine ... or a sort of order of knights, bound by iron discipline?'[13]

## Hechalutz and the Kibbutz

These two views of the nature of Hechalutz in particular and the youth movement in general were widely debated in the early 1920s. The discussion was brought to an abrupt end at the beginning of the Fourth Aliya (Spring 1924) by the practical necessity of dealing with unprecedented numbers.[14] The realization that immigration was possible brought tens of thousands of young people to Hechalutz. World membership outside Russia rose from 3,500 in 1923 to 20,000 in 1925. The effect of this vast influx of new members can be judged from this description by one of the movement's leaders in Galicia.

We had no time to stand and consider, to investigate, think and decide whether to enlarge the movement or keep it small. While we were discussing the question, a great wave swept over us, and we were caught up and pulled along with its current willy-nilly.... We were in a very difficult situation. The theory of slow, step-by-step training was a good enough palliative for the time when there was no immigration; but we had to find a shorter way to train the pioneers who might be joining the builders and defenders of the

---

[13] Trumpeldor, *Hechalutz*, 23.      [14] See ch. 4.

homeland literally within a few days. . . . By some instinct, we grasped the beginning of a solution: *the kibbutz* [emphasis in original]. I do not know just what part the kibbutz in Palestine played in our decision. In point of fact, we had scarcely heard of it. We perceived its image as if through a screen, very nebulous, no more than the outlines of its different varieties. There was a longing to fashion a new type of life, to develop better relationships between man and man. Ideological foundations were very shallow, and we made no real intellectual effort to grasp its social significance. Our attitude was based more on longing than on logic and reflection. Most of our members were given only a short summer's training, they had not been prepared and educated for the kibbutz way of life over a number of years, as in the youth movement. We knew of the existence of collective bodies in Palestine: Gedud Ha'avoda, Ein Harod, the graduates of Hashomer Hatzair, and so on. But there was no consciousness of continuity, no obligation to draw personal conclusions or join any movement, and even the best of us did not find their way to the kibbutz movement.[15]

Although this very perceptive account refers specifically to Galicia, it describes events and reactions to them which were common to all the Hechalutz movements. A number of points may be emphasized. The 'great wave' of the Fourth Aliya caught the leadership of Hechalutz unaware, and brought to an abrupt end the controversy about expansion or limitation. Under the new circumstances of enforced expansion, the training kibbutz was a way both of preparing potential immigrants as quickly as possible, and of establishing a minimal criterion as to their suitability, in conditions which in some way approximated to those in Palestine. But they were still given only 'a short summer's training': at this stage, as we have seen, training was seasonal, in accordance with the agricultural calendar, and the trainee pioneers would return to their homes in the autumn. There was also as yet no institutionalized connection with the kibbutz movement, although certain local movements had established connections with particular groups of kibbutzim.[16]

Perhaps the most revealing remark in the above account is that about the motivation behind the adoption of the kibbutz idea: not rational, ideologically justified arguments, but 'a longing to fashion a new type of life'. Both this longing, and the 'nebulous' nature of the kibbutz image, 'perceived through a screen', continued to characterize the way in which young members of the pioneering youth movements

---

[15] Dov Stock (Sdan) in *Hechalutz Anthology*, 155–6.

[16] For example, Lithuania with Gedud Ha'avoda; ibid., 118; *Mihayeinu*, 30 (June 1922), i. 344–7.

saw the kibbutz for very many years after, even when their movements' ideologies were more clearly defined, and their knowledge much greater. The utopian longings of youth and the attraction of the idea of a new society such as a kibbutz are permanent ingredients in the relationship between the actuality of the kibbutz and those who identify it with their dream.[17]

Throughout the Hechalutz movement, then, the idea of 'training kibbutzim' was adopted as a reaction to the pressures of the Fourth Aliya. But the other element emphasized above was no less powerful, and the idea of the kibbutz as an educational ideal began to be part of the accepted doctrine of the movement. In this sense the Russian movement, which split on this issue, was only an extreme example of a general trend. One reason for the Russians' extremism was without doubt the fact that they were cut off from the Labour Zionist movement and the real kibbutz. In Poland and other countries, where there was much more knowledge of and contact with the Yishuv, it was accepted that Hechalutz was the equivalent in the Diaspora of the Histadrut and therefore educated towards membership of that organization. The leaders of the Histadrut itself went even further, and tended to demand complete Histadrut control of Hechalutz's policy. In spring 1924, when the Histadrut demanded the speedy immigration of all those preparing themselves to immigrate, the Romanian movement opposed it:

Hechalutz cannot direct its work in accordance with the temporary needs of the Yishuv, but only in the historical perspective of the construction of the workers' society in the Land of Israel.[18]

The Histadrut's response to this was delivered by David Ben-Gurion at the world conference of Hechalutz the same year.

The delegates from Romania think that our activities in Palestine at any given time should be guided not by the real requirements of our work, but by the 'historical perspective' of the lads in Czernovitz or some other *shtetl* in Romania. . . . Pioneers should be trained to be ready for work in Palestine *in all conditions* [emphasis in original]. I do not see Hechalutz as being separate from the Histadrut. Our movements in Palestine and outside it are one body, and Hechalutz is—at any rate, it should be—an organic part of the Histadrut. . . . The Histadrut's perspective is Hechalutz's perspective: we are

[17] Near, 'Utopian and Post-Utopian Thought'.
[18] *Hechalutz*, 1 (Aug. 1924), 28.

a single force, and its headquarters are in Palestine, for that is where the front is.[19]

Behind this exchange lies a fundamental question: should the youth movement in the Diaspora be independent, or is it simply the educational instrument of the adult movement which its members will eventually go on to join? This question will crop up again in other contexts. In the 1924 debate, Ben-Gurion's view was generally accepted. Not long afterwards a further development occurred which deterred adults and youths alike from bringing this controversy to a head.

Some of the national Hechalutz movements had received help from visiting kibbutz members or other representatives of the Labour Zionist movement. But this had almost always been for short periods, and usually as an adjunct to other activities. In the autumn of 1925 the first delegation of the Histadrut whose members were to spend a whole year in full-time educational work with Jewish youth arrived in Europe. Its most important component was a group consisting of half a dozen of the foremost members of Kibbutz Ein Harod, with Tabenkin at their head. Within a year this group had transformed Hechalutz, and particularly its Polish section, from a powerful but as yet amorphous organization, marked both by boundless enthusiasm and devotion and by severe internal differences and confusion, to a more or less unified, efficiently structured educational movement with a clear ideological commitment.

At roughly the same time as the arrival of the emissaries from Ein Harod, a group of young men and women managed to cross the border from Russia into Poland. These were the founders and leaders of a movement known as Dror (Freedom), who were close to the ideology of Ahdut Ha'avoda and wished to create 'an autonomous Zionist framework, based on activists who would devote their lives to Zionist work in the Diaspora and in the Land of Israel'.[20] Despairing of making any real progress in Soviet Russia, they transferred their activities to Poland, where they became involved in all aspects of the work of Hechalutz, from organizational work in the training farms and headquarters to propaganda and education in the movement's town branches. Thus, Tabenkin and his colleagues had ready to hand a cadre of professional leaders who lacked nothing but experience and

---

[19] *Kuntres*, 193 (Nov. 1924), 9.
[20] Maniv, *Dror Anthology*, 113; cf. Mintz, *The Lame and the Nimble*.

the knowledge which they had been unable to acquire in the Soviet Union. One of the new emissaries' first actions was to organize a series of special educational seminars. Here, the leaders of Dror, together with a number of outstanding members of the local movement, became full-time educators, propagandists, and organizers for the movement.

The message brought by Tabenkin and his colleagues fell on fertile ground. We have already seen how the idea of the kibbutz was adopted more or less spontaneously as a response to the stresses of the Fourth Aliya. This was also the organizational expression of the tendency of many young Jews to see the kibbutz as a social ideal, even if they themselves had very little knowledge of the realities of the kibbutz. The achievement of the educational emissaries of Ein Harod was to harness this idealism, and build round it an ideology and methods of organization attuned to their own outlook and leading to their own kibbutz. Together with the structural innovations of 1925–6—the dominance of an educational élite of young adults, supported by emissaries from the kibbutzim—the idea of the 'great and growing kibbutz' became an accepted part of the ideology of Hechalutz; and, concomitantly, it became regular practice for members to join Ein Harod (from 1927, the Kibbutz Me'uhad) on their arrival in Palestine.

*Immigration and Training*

A number of organizational changes served to underpin this development. In 1925, the first *kibbutz aliya* (immigrants' kibbutz) was formed in Poland. Until now members of Hechalutz had made their way to Palestine on receiving their immigration certificate individually or in very small groups with no commitment beyond the journey. They now began to travel as large, organized groups, with the intention of spending their first months together as a *pluga* to ease their absorption. In practice, the very first *kibbutz aliya* retained its separate identity even after the period of preliminary settlement, and became Kibbutz Ramat Hakovesh. This precedent was followed thereafter, and many similar groups of immigrants founded new kibbutzim or collectively joined already existing settlements.

Parallel to this development came changes in Hechalutz itself. As in the case of the *kibbutz aliya*, these were initiated by the Polish movement and adopted in other regions over the coming few years. The most important was the adoption of the principle of the permanent training farm. As we have seen, in the early 1920s the potential immigrants would spend one or more seasons on the Hechalutz training farms. Others would undergo what was known as 'professional' or 'individual' training, which might consist of an apprenticeship in some practical skill or a period of work as an agricultural labourer employed by a local farmer. In each case, the future pioneer spent long periods each year at home. He or she relied on family resources in time of sickness and while making final preparations for emigration, which often included earning part of the money for the journey if family assistance was not forthcoming. Indirectly, this meant that these young people's commitment to the idea of Palestine was liable to be undermined by the influence of their parents (many of them anti-Zionists) and the temptations of town life. These factors aggravated the decline in the strength of the movement during the crisis of the Fourth Aliya (1926–8). Furthermore, many of those who had withstood the general atmosphere of disillusionment with the Zionist idea and begun the process of preparation for a new life even in the uncertain conditions of that period succumbed to the very tangible attractions of family life and the prospects of a 'normal' career.

The response of the central group in Hechalutz, under the guidance of the emissaries of Ein Harod, was the establishment of permanent training farms. Here the trainees would remain from the moment they committed themselves to immigration in the Hechalutz framework until the time they left for Palestine with their *kibbutz aliya*. This innovation was quite revolutionary. From now on, the act of joining a training kibbutz involved a two-way commitment: the trainee pioneers cut themselves off from their former environment morally and financially; and the Hechalutz movement was committed to caring for them in times of sickness and unemployment, and equipping them for their future life materially as well as educationally. It was, in effect, the extension of the kibbutz movement to the Diaspora.

The idea of the permanent training farm was first put into practice in 1926 at Klosova, a small town close to the eastern border of Poland. Since 1924 it had been the site of a training establishment for members of Hechalutz from the district, but differed from most such centres in that the trainees were employed not in agriculture but in a stone quarry owned by a local Jew. In August 1926 its fortunes, like those of Hechalutz as a whole, were at a low ebb, for the crisis in Zionism and the Yishuv had greatly reduced the number of pioneers throughout Poland. The handful of people left at Klosova had finished the statutory six months' training, were considered fit to leave for

Palestine, and were entitled to home leave until immigrants' certificates became available.

At this point they were joined by one of the most forceful and colourful figures in Hechalutz. Benny Marshak, at this time about 17 years old, came straight to Klosova after participating in the first seminar of Hechalutz organized by Yitzhak Tabenkin and his colleagues of Ein Harod. With his unbounded energy and complete dedication to the cause of Zionism and the Hechalutz movement, he was able to persuade others and encourage them in time of trouble not only by the force of his unresting personality but by example, persisting in the hardest of physical tasks as well as playing a central role in the variegated social activities of the kibbutz. He persuaded the young men and women left in Klosova at the end of 1926 not to go back to their parents but to turn the kibbutz into their home until they were able to leave for Palestine. Round this core of dedicated idealists he recruited others until, with the renewed growth of the movement from 1929 onwards, its numbers reached two hundred and more, and it became the organizational centre of a number of 'satellite kibbutzim' in the vicinity.

The development of the permanent kibbutz was not merely a technical device. Klosova became a symbol and a model for the rest of Hechalutz, and was praised over the years in the most superlative terms. In Yitzhak Tabenkin's words:

The stone [of Klosova's quarry] was not only a way to earn money. It was first and foremost a method of changing the character of the Jew. They hewed out stone in order to hew out men, to make them pioneers, workers, communards, believers in the fraternity of man. . . .

What was the image of a human being in our movement? The unknown soldier, the Maccabi in us all . . . that was the image of the statue, embedded in the raw material, which you had to hew out for yourself, like a sculptor, by removing the superfluous parts of the rock. . . . It was an image of an ordinary man, simple in every way—in his actions, his way of life, his food, his clothing, in the way he rested, danced, hiked. And to achieve this simplicity one had to make a vast effort. . . .

In the training kibbutz people had an ideal, dearer and more beloved to them than their former way of life, more than their love for their home or their relatives. In this ideal they saw themselves not as they were, but as they ought to be. . . .

Klosova embodies the possibility hidden in every young man, in every ordinary Jew, to be a worker, to be other than what he is. There was a sort of legendary power in the rumour that ordinary people were quarrying stone, singing, dancing, living communally—and that they were not a chosen few: anyone could be like them. Not a legend based on a heroic figure or a leader commanding us to follow him, to accept his authority. No! The ideal said: 'You and I can become different: we can all reveal what is hidden within us!'[21]

In many respects, the legend of Klosova was not far from the truth. Here is a more prosaic description, written at the end of 1927. There were at the time some fifty trainees in the kibbutz, aged between 18 and 21.

Almost all of them are 'runaways', for anyone coming here has to run away from his family. This is the threshold of a new life, and they leave all their past behind them. Their families would even prefer them to join the 'Reds'. If they come to the kibbutz, they cut them off completely.

One of the main problems is that of sickness. At this tender age it is difficult to get used to hard physical work, and many fall ill. Today about 30 per cent of them are ill, and this is a real threat. Some of the young people, especially the girls, look on physical labour as a divinely appointed task, and work themselves to the point of collapse.... There is work to be done every day, and some of them work seven days a week. So it is not surprising that after a year or two a large proportion become weakened, especially since when several fall ill all the others try to do their work for them. This is undoubtedly a dangerous practice, but in the atmosphere of Klosova it's hard to raise the question. They simply won't understand you: work comes before everything else.

The hard winters are also a cause of much sickness. There is a severe shortage of clothes and footwear. I arrived here at the time of the first snow, and most of them were still going around barefoot in the kibbutz and going to work with their feet wrapped in rags, or in their cracked summer shoes. Many of them already had colds, rheumatism, and so forth. The 'runaways' usually come with one set of clothes and practically no underwear....

In the three rooms, one of which is the dining hall, they can just about fit 18 beds, very close together. So there's no place to sleep—they have to sleep two in a bed, and even use the benches, and take down the connecting doors at night to sleep on.

But all this suffering serves to draw these young people close together. You should see with what enthusiasm they dance the hora.... Even among the *hasidim* one doesn't see such ecstasy.[22]

In this letter, dating from an early period in Klosova's development,

[21] *Mibifnim* (Apr. 1934), 6–7, 12–13.
[22] Letter from Nahum Benari, 15 Nov. 1927, repr. in Dan, *The Book of Klosova*, 118–19.

several of its characteristic elements can already be seen: the stubborn independence of youths who refused to receive any support—even the most essential articles of clothing—from the families they had abandoned; the exaltation of physical work (not only in agriculture, or any specific skill, and for both sexes); the wretched physical conditions, which were considered not only unavoidable, but an intrinsic part of preparation for pioneering life; a high degree of mutual aid and an atmosphere of close community, bordering on ecstasy, which helped compensate for the hardships of life in the kibbutz. All this took place in an isolated spot which served to emphasize the independence and self-sufficiency of the community.

In all this, Klosova lived up to the slogan displayed prominently in its dining hall: 'The law of Hebrew pioneering is cruel in its practice, but wonderful in its essence.' And, although it was the most deliberately extreme of the training kibbutzim, the others were spurred by a similar combination of youthful enthusiasm and external circumstances to follow in its wake. By the end of 1927, the idea of the 'permanent kibbutz' had been adopted by the Hechalutz movement as a whole; and the other pioneering movements did the same, though more reluctantly, over the coming two years. Klosova itself, in conscious imitation of the ideology of the Kibbutz Me'uhad, declared itself to be a 'great and growing kibbutz', which would turn away nobody who was prepared to accept its way of life.[23]

Within a short time, this principle too was adopted by all the training farms under the influence of the Kibbutz Me'uhad. It was interpreted to mean that any young Jew or Jewess should be accepted for training; selection and education would take place in the course of communal life. Those who came straight to the kibbutz with no movement background were known as *stam halutzim* ('simple pioneers'). At the time of Hechalutz's greatest expansion, their proportion in its kibbutzim was as high as 30 per cent.[24] By contrast, the independent youth movements Hashomer Hatzair and Gordonia (of which more below) accepted for training only those who had been educated and selected in their town branches.

---

[23] On the Kibbutz Me'uhad see below, ch. 4.
[24] Otiker, *Hechalutz in Poland*, 179.

## THE 'CLASSIC' YOUTH MOVEMENTS

The great majority of the pioneers who reached the country in the framework of Hechalutz were in their late teens or early twenties. In the language of the time, however, Hechalutz was not considered a youth movement. This name was reserved for a particular type of organization, represented in the Third Aliya primarily by the members of Hashomer Hatzair, and later also by Gordonia and a wide variety of small movements. Before dealing with them in detail, something should be said in general about what came to be known as the classic youth movement.[25]

The youth movement is a product of a particular historical period, type of society, and social class. In the industrialized cities of Western Europe at the beginning of the twentieth century, groups of high-school students began to participate in spare-time activities which included hiking, folk song and dance, and wide-ranging discussions of the state of society and the place of young people in shaping its future. Sociologically, this age-group had only had the leisure and educational facilities to identify itself and formulate a special attitude to the world since the swift expansion of secondary education in the wake of the industrial revolution. Culturally, the youth movement was deeply influenced by European romanticism, and shared many of its characteristics: an accent on the self-expression of the individual; an emphasis on national characteristics, as opposed to the universal values of classical culture and education; and idealization of nature and the countryside. Psychologically, it eased the strains of adolescence by legitimizing the search for social intercourse between the sexes and providing peer-group support outside the framework of family and formal education. All of these movements were a small proportion of the age-group from which they derived, and most were very conscious of being self-selected élites. They quickly developed educational techniques and symbols based on games and scoutcraft. They met in small, exceedingly active groups, which they saw as an alternative to the official educational system.

Something of the spirit of the youth movement, with its claim to have created new and universally applicable values, can be seen from

---

[25] On the youth movement as a sociological and historical phenomenon see e.g. Manning, *Youth: Divergent Perspectives*; Paul, *Angry Young Man*; Laqueur, *Young Germany*. On the Zionist youth movements in Germany see Schatzker, 'The Jewish Youth Movement in Germany'.

the following extracts. Written in 1917, they became standard texts in the Hashomer Hatzair movement; but their approach and content were common to many of the wide range of movements which sprang up in the first two decades of the twentieth century.

In the youth movement there has been a flowering of the social form peculiar to this [historical] period: the youth group. In the movement, the youngster ceases to be an object of education and becomes simultaneously its subject and its object. Many youngsters emerge from their parents' home and their schools to develop into free, courageous persons struggling consciously for fulfilment as active individuals.

Thus, the youth movement liberates a complete period of life from the curse of achievement orientation, and gives the youngster the possibility of grasping the reins of his life, and directing it by himself. The youth movement puts before its members the ideal of activity and self-education throughout their lives....

We live in a community of youth, and life itself establishes its character. 'Pride, arrogance,' people will say. Well, we are not at all ashamed to confess: we exalt the spirit of youth above all else; for the values of youth are the very cream of culture....

We are young and strong. It is in the nature of youth to aspire continually to new forms of human thought. Endless longings for the highest and most exalted. What was achieved yesterday does not concern us today. Tomorrow is our future, the object of our desire.[26]

The first Jewish youth movement was the German Blau-Weiss, which grew almost contemporaneously with the first non-Jewish movement, the Wandervogel, both as a reaction of young Jews to the antisemitic tendencies of the Wandervogel and as an expression of their desire to find their cultural roots. By the time it reached its peak membership of some three thousand, in the early 1920s, it had evolved its own symbols and ideology, based on a variety of cultural Zionism. It influenced and was influenced by a number of young Jewish intellectuals, the most prominent of whom was Martin Buber.

## *Hashomer Hatzair*[27]

Hashomer Hatzair originated in Galicia in southern Poland shortly before the First World War. This area, then mostly part of the Austro-Hungarian Empire, had for many centuries been bedevilled by the

[26] Extracts from the journal of Hashomer Hatzair in Galicia and Vienna, 1917. Repr. in *Book of the Shomrim*, 43–4.

[27] This section is largely based on Margalit, *Hashomer Hatzair*, intro. and chs. 1 and 2.

conflict between its component ethnic groups (Jews, Ukrainians, and Poles), and its Jewish community had developed special characteristics which were seen as stereotypic throughout the Jewish world: a somewhat introverted intellectualism, a developed instinct for survival among conflicting ethnic and political groups, and a sardonic sense of humour. The hasidic movement and the local Zionist movement were both very strong in the province.

The founders of Hashomer Hatzair were drawn from the middle classes of Galician Jewry. The great majority attended Polish-language high schools, and many of them seem to have undergone similar experiences during their school days: a thorough grounding in European and Polish culture, attempts to be accepted as part of the Polish people, and rejection as a result of antisemitism. The result was an attempt to find their Jewish identity in the company of their peers, and the beginning of two independent organizations of young people: one, Ze'irei Zion ('Youngsters of Zion'), aimed at intensive Jewish and Zionist education; the other, Hashomer ('The Guard'), was modelled on the English scout movement but was Zionist in its ideology and took the members of Hashomer in the Yishuv as a role model.

These two movements united to form the new movement known as Hashomer Hatzair ('The Young Guard') in 1913, but much of its special character was crystallized in a few years' intensive activity in Vienna during the First World War. Galicia was in the front line of the fighting, and many Jews were evacuated to Vienna. Here, these young men and women, many of them separated from their families, sought a sense of identity and community: very frequently the movement came to replace the family. They began to create a social milieu and an ideology which sought to solve their problems as Jews and as human beings. In this search they were influenced by their contacts with the German youth movements, and particularly by the personality and teachings of Buber. The results can be seen in the following extract, which is the continuation of those quoted above.

In the bosom of the Diaspora we were educated; but our goal is to be the guardian of the Land of Israel. Our objective: to create a fearless Hebrew youth, aspiring to liberty and revival. In the bosom of nature, in the field and forest, we will awake to new life and liberate ourselves from the degradation of exile. We love labour, for in it, and only in it, is all our future ...[28]

[28] *Book of the Shomrim*, 44.

Taken together, these passages are typical of Hashomer Hatzair in its earliest period. It adopted the concept of 'youth culture' as developed in the German youth movement, and placed special emphasis on the educational group in which its members could find a new meaning and purpose in life. Many of its activities were modelled on those of the Scout movement—camping, rambling, folk songs. But their cultural content was Jewish and Zionist; the name of the movement combines the symbolism of the heroism of Hashomer with the concept of youth culture. And, under the influence of Buber and others, they translated these ideas into practical terms through the concept of 'self-realization': the view that general principles such as Zionism and socialism must be translated into terms of personal action—immigration to Palestine, and communal life.

The special historical circumstances—the end of the world war, and the beginning of the Mandate—gave them an opportunity to put this principle into practice. During the Third Aliya, some four hundred Hashomer Hatzair members reached Palestine, and about half of them joined working groups which formed part of the 'fellowship of the roads'.

It is not surprising that the first graduates of this very special educational system found it hard to assimilate to the dominant atmosphere in the labour movement. Their style of speech and thought, their desire to find their own direction, and their aspirations to a distinctive social and cultural life marked them off from the majority of the new immigrants. They were considered eccentric and 'bourgeois'—as, indeed, they were, compared with the graduates of Hechalutz, most of whom were of working-class origin. Something of their mode of expression can be seen in this extract from the Beitania group's collective diary, *Our Community*.

We are looking forward to our permanent settlement. And this hope, even though it is a little distant, stimulates my ability to concentrate, and my inner clarity. So far, I have kept silent. I could not speak to you, I did not yet know how to express the wild and savage thoughts which live and surge within me. I used to say to myself: 'Don't open your mouth! What will you say to others, when you don't yet know how to conquer the turmoil and chaos within you?' Now, when we are discussing settlement, I say to you: 'With you will I go, with you will I live, and succeed. I believe in our communal creation, in agriculture and through agriculture; and I believe that that alone will free me from the contradictions within me, and will guide me on the road to myself, to clarity and peace of mind.'

Devotion to one's friends ... I remember one moment. I was on guard duty. The night was pitch black. People were already sleeping in their tents. The lights began to dim. The tents were swallowed up in the darkness, one by one. Deep darkness came down and enveloped everything. A dreadful feeling took hold of me: darkness, darkness all around, and otherwise—nothing. I had the illusion that phantom spirits were wandering through the camp.... I turned my eyes to the hills. It was such a wonderful sight: the dawn was beginning. The sun began to rise, but not too brightly—the sky was slightly cloudy, and a pale, delicate red light rested on the hills. It was wonderful. Then I rang the bell, a pure clear sound, and woke up the camp.

A moment. One moment—and in it the essence of my relationship with human beings, with my comrades, with the kibbutz. I will say no more. I cannot.

I have told you of some things: tiny stations on my life's journey up to now. I shall not use exalted words to describe my unceasing struggle and the convolutions of my soul.

I want you to understand what I say to you in one word: liberation. Let us surmount the weaknesses that spoil our relationships with human beings.

Let us reveal together the holy mystery: the love of brothers and comrades.

Our aspiration is—wholeness. We shall come near each other not by lofty words, but only by spiritual communion. Let us try to love, and we shall succeed.[29]

This passage, which is characteristic of the book and of the way of life and thought of Hashomer Hatzair in this period, is couched in strange and grandiose terms. But its content is identical with the themes to be found in the much more down-to-earth literature of the rest of the kibbutz movement at this time, including that of Gedud Ha'avoda, which the members of Hashomer Hatzair refused to join for fear of losing their cultural identity. There is the aspiration to find a place of settlement, and begin a permanent life of common creation; the love of nature, with its mystical overtones; and the feeling of comradeship, both as a defence against isolation and danger and as a positive foundation for the co-operative community.

It was this combination of cultural singularity and pioneering devotion which persuaded the leaders of the labour movement and the Zionist authorities that these young people were entitled to create a kibbutz of their own. By 1923, when they founded Kibbutz Beit Alpha, they were acclimatized to work and were well able to overcome the difficulties of building a new kibbutz. They had come a long way from the introverted 17-year-olds of the youth movement in Vienna.

[29] *Our Community*, 54–5.

*Crisis and Ideology*

The Yishuv's gain was the movement's loss. Those who immigrated during the Third Aliya comprised virtually all the leaders and active members of its senior age-group. As a result, the movement in the Diaspora—both in Galicia and in the other areas of Poland—spent several years in search of a new identity. Three tendencies struggled for dominance: those who continued to see the movement as a general educational framework for Jewish youth, with no special aims other than character-building and the strengthening of Jewish consciousness; those who wished to turn it into a revolutionary political movement; and those who stressed the Zionist tradition, and believed that their future lay in Palestine. At first, the movement received little help from the members who had arrived in Palestine during the Third Aliya: they were too occupied with building their own communities to be able to expend thought or energy on external matters. Paradoxically, the links between the movement and its Zionist tradition were renewed with the help of a man whom the central group of movement graduates had rejected: Meir Ya'ari.

Ya'ari had been one of the movement's leaders from its earliest days. A few years older than most of the Galician evacuees, he had served in the Austrian army during the war. He had a dominating and complex personality. He could create a group and lead it to heights of common feeling, activity, and expression; but he also had a tendency to impose his own view on the group, and could be highly critical of those of whom he disapproved. He was the central figure in Beitania Eilit, and descriptions of life there show him initiating, judging, and manipulating the interactions within the group. He represented it in negotiations with the settlement authorities, and pressed strongly, both within the group and outside it, for it to settle as quickly as possible on its own land. But his authoritarian ways made him increasingly less popular. Shortly after the group left Beitania, a marathon discussion took place whose tone was so critical that at its conclusion he and his wife decided to leave.

Others less devoted or less gifted than he might have abandoned the movement whose members had treated him with such ingratitude. But Hashomer Hatzair was as much part of Ya'ari as he had been part of the movement. By 1924 he was again in Galicia, formally as an emissary of the Jewish National Fund but mainly in his old function of mentor to Hashomer Hatzair. During 1922 he had written an article entitled 'Rootless Symbols'[30] in which he rejected the romantic symbolism of Beitania and *Our Community* and demanded that it be replaced by the concrete demands symbolized by A. D. Gordon and his 'religion of work': physical labour and agricultural settlement. It was with this message that he returned to the movement and attempted to bring about an unequivocal decision in favour of pioneering Zionism in the ideological struggle then in progress.

But the pioneering message which had sufficed for a previous generation was not enough. Ya'ari soon became very conscious of the dangers inherent in the atmosphere of revolutionary fervour current among Jewish youth. His ideological defence against the threat of mass defections from the movement was his 'Theory of Stages': a combination of support for constructive Zionist activity in the present with a perspective of revolution in the future. According to this doctrine, the current situation of the Jewish people made it vital to build an alternative society in Palestine. This could not be done without collaboration with the bourgeoisie, in the framework of the Zionist movement, in order to raise funds for constructive work, represent the Yishuv before the Mandatory government, and so forth. This was the first, constructive stage. When the Jewish national home was firmly entrenched it would be time for the second stage: the kibbutz movement, and the youth movement with it, would then lead the revolutionary forces, overthrow the capitalist regime, and establish a true Socialist Zionist society throughout the Yishuv.

The place of the kibbutz in this new society was not very clearly defined; but it would certainly be of great importance. Its tasks in preparing the way were 'to be a prototype of the co-operative society ... to create economic positions in town and village; to enter as many productive branches as possible and to prepare the [working] class for self-management'.[31] On the other hand, it was quite clear to them that a socialist society would not come without a revolution; and when the time came, Hashomer Hatzair would take its place in the leadership of the revolutionary forces.

It was not only the ideology of the movement which ensured its survival and expansion over the next few years, however: its special educational methods were also a factor in this. The nature of the youth movement, of which Hashomer Hatzair was without doubt the

---

[30] *Hedim* (1923), 93–6; repr. in *Mekorot Hashomer Hatzair*, I (Mar. 1984), 60–9.
[31] Kibbutz Artzi, *Ideological Premisses*, 302.

outstanding example at this stage, can perhaps best be grasped by contrasting it with Hechalutz in rather more detail.

Except for a short period in 1922–3 when the controversy about expansionism or élitism was at its height, Hechalutz saw itself as a mass movement of young adults: a corresponding movement for younger age-groups (Hechalutz Hatzair) was founded in 1925; but Hechalutz itself worked among those aged roughly between 17 and 21, and urged them to begin their period of training for a pioneering life as soon as possible. Most of its members had only a primary school education, and some even less.

By contrast, the typical youth movement contained a much higher proportion of high-school students.[32] Its members were frequently recruited at the age of 11 or 12, and they continued to be members and leaders after reaching 18. It aimed to create close-knit groups whose members remained together, through an extended period of selection and education, throughout their movement life and frequently beyond. Many of its activities were based on scouting, which aimed to foster a love of nature, to strengthen the character of the individual, and to develop close relations within the educational group. These relations were often reminiscent of the happenings in Beitania Eilit and some of the smaller *kvutzot*.[33]

## Hechalutz as against the 'Classic' Movements

Most of this was rejected by Hechalutz. Even the terminology of the movements differed significantly. In the 'branch' of Hechalutz, the typical activity was a 'meeting', as contrasted with the 'educational

---

[32] Sources written at the time generally attest that Hashomer Hatzair's members were of 'bourgeois' origin, while Hechalutz and Hechalutz Hatzair were more proletarian; Gordonia, as we shall see later, occupied a middle position. The difficulties of classifying parents' status and the vagueness of the categories used in the movements' questionnaires make this virtually impossible to verify. The best indication of social status is, therefore, that used in the text: the standard of education. Even here, it appears that the situation was rather complex. Most of the leaders of Galician Hashomer Hatzair in its early stages were certainly high-school students, but the Warsaw branch always had a higher proportion of working-class youths. Among those on the training kibbutzim, the available figures for all movements show that the majority had worked before they reached the kibbutz, and that only a minority, increasingly small as the economic crisis deepened, had finished high school. Although the statistics are far from complete and show substantial regional variations, they would seem to substantiate the formulation used in the text. See Sarid, *Hechalutz in Poland*, pt. 2, ch. 2; Otiker, *Hechalutz in Poland*, 165–71, 196–200.

[33] Cf. e.g., the description of the *hora* in Degania, and the 'table' at Ginegar, in chs. 1 and 2.

activity' or 'discussion' in the 'nest' of Hashomer Hatzair. The number
of people in a Hechalutz 'branch' would be far greater, and there was
no attempt to preserve the identity of the educational group; indeed,
the leaders of Hechalutz condemned it as egocentric, and the use of
scouting methods as militaristic. From the first, Hechalutz was
opposed to any version of the idea of 'youth culture', or the autonomy
of the youth movement. It was dedicated to the cause of the welfare
of the Jewish people, and its members saw their own welfare only in
that context. The theory and practice of the other youth movements,
in contrast, began from a concern with the individual; and although
in practical terms the solutions which they advanced were very similar
to those of Hechalutz, their educational approach was therefore very
different.

Historical sources and reminiscences describe a wealth of activities
in the local branches of Hashomer Hatzair—as, indeed, in all the
classic youth movements.[34] Within the educational group there was a
varied programme, which depended on the age of the group but
would usually include games, singing and dancing, and some sort of
discussion or other intellectual activity. The members were required
to learn Hebrew, and something of the geography and history of the
Yishuv and of the history of the Jewish people. Current affairs, such
as politics, the state of the Zionist movement and the Jewish people,
were dealt with both in the educational group and the wider framework of the town branch in which several such groups would meet
together. The bigger branches had study groups, choirs, and orches-
tras. All the movements took part in fund-raising activities for the
Jewish National Fund, as well as for the support of their own meeting-
places. Rambles took place throughout the year, and the summer
camps—for the younger members close to their homes, for the older
groups in a national or even an international framework—were the
peak of the year's activity. In short, the movement required its
members to make it the centre of their lives, and it provided a range
and intensity of activities which made such devotion both possible
and exceedingly attractive.

It is significant that although descriptions of these sorts of activities
abound in the reminiscences and research works about the youth
movements that have appeared in recent years, it is difficult to find a

---

[34] See e.g. *My Notebook*, 1918 edn. and later editions throughout the 1920s; *Book
of the Shomrim*, 199–257; Zertal, *Spring of Youth*, 59–70, 185–276; Amit *et al.*, *From
Beginning to End*, 57–66, 193–232; Itai and Neistat, *Netzah in Latvia*, ch. 4.

parallel in material dealing with Hechalutz. There, the central experience was not in the local branch, but in the training farm; and that is what is remembered and described.

The best summary of the special character of the youth movement was written in 1927 by one of its opponents, Avraham Guberman, a former member of Dror who was at this time a central figure in Hechalutz. In a letter he wrote about conferences of the movement that he had attended he said that although the deliberations were of little moment, the time he spent there was most enjoyable.

I arrived late, and found accommodation with the youngsters from Hashomer Hatzair, in a big hall, sleeping on the floor.... I lay on the floor, and didn't sleep at nights. How could I? Among a hundred young men and women, in the ferment of youth, bearing dreams that encompassed the world? The spirit yearns, the body moves, one feels the will to come close, the need to unite, hand links with hand, feet tap and a song bursts forth—Youth!

There was beauty in the long intervals when the 'personages' and the 'all important' figures in the movement went off to ideological discussions, and the others stayed and waited ... then these lads and girls sat round in a circle, and a sad, yearning song came forth, expressing a longing for the remote, for the ultimate heights, for inexpressible things. The rhythm of the singing was superb, uplifting and alluring. More than once at these times I envied them mightily, and felt a deep regret. I saw before me the flower of our youth, souls moved by longing, I saw spiritual doubts and self-searchings in the very best sense—but on the other hand, I knew that they had locked away for themselves all this goodness and richness of spirit: no stranger may come near. At a time when the people is perishing for lack of an intelligentsia, when working-class youth is looking avidly for spiritual nourishment—at this very time they shut themselves up in their own circle, they refuse to go to the masses, and live their lives among their own sect. I remembered the Russian intelligentsia, who went to the people: their spiritual longings, their deepest yearnings led them to romanticize—but not to pure romance: to the romance of the people, of life with and among the people....

But even so, I loved them.... I said to my friends, 'I would gladly join their movement, if only for their songs.'[35]

By the beginning of the Fourth Aliya, Hashomer Hatzair had weathered the worst of the crisis. At the founding conference of the international Hashomer Hatzair movement in 1924, five national movements were represented—Poland and Galicia, Russia, Austria, and Czechoslovakia. There were also delegates from the movement's

[35] Letter from Avraham Guberman to Fania Bergstein, 28 Sept. 1927. In the personal archive of Fania Bergstein, Hechalutz archives, Lohamei Hageta'ot Museum.

kibbutzim; and although these kibbutzim, in their meeting at Beit Alpha before the conference, did not commit themselves to any binding framework, over the coming years there was a gradual increase in the number of educational emissaries to the Diaspora. The efforts expended in building up the movement began to pay off over the next few years. By the end of 1926 members of the movement had established two permanent kibbutzim (Beit Alpha and Mishmar Ha'emek) and nine working groups, and numbered close on 450. Meanwhile, the educational movement was growing apace: in 1924 it numbered 11,000 members in seven countries; in 1927, some 24,000 in fourteen countries; and in 1930, almost 35,000, in seventeen countries. True, this number is not strictly comparable with Hechalutz's 23,000 in 1930, for it included a high proportion of youngsters aged between 11 and 17. But it was a guarantee of increasing strength over the coming years.[36]

## Gordonia[37]

The third biggest of the youth movements, after Hashomer Hatzair and Hechalutz, was Gordonia. It was established in 1923–4 in Galicia, where Hashomer Hatzair had a virtual monopoly, by supporters of Hapoel Hatzair, with the objective of strengthening the Hit'ahdut— the Diaspora equivalent of Hapoel Hatzair. Named after the spiritual leader of that party, Aharon David Gordon, Gordonia emphasized the cultural values of Zionism and the essential unity of the Jewish people and rejected the Marxist social analysis and the politics of Ahdut Ha'avoda. But its leaders—or, more correctly, perhaps, its leader; for Gordonia was largely created and shaped by one man, Pinhas Lubianiker (Lavon), later to be secretary of the Histadrut and minister of defence in the State of Israel—also rejected the concept of 'youth culture' as propounded by Hashomer Hatzair and many of the smaller youth movements.

It is true that youth comprises a world of its own, distinct from the world of the older generation. There is no doubt that young people have a special psychological make-up ... their individuality has not yet been enslaved by the destructive and neutralizing influence of the social framework. But it is a mistake to assume that youth creates special ideals which distinguish it

---

[36] *Book of the Shomrim*, 215; Otiker, *Hechalutz in Poland*, app. c.
[37] This section is largely based on Margalit, *The Gordonia Youth Movement*; Ben-Avram, *Hever Hakvutzot*, 48–55. Statistics: *Encyclopedia Judaica*, vii. 806.

from the society in which it lives. The fact that the youth movement is divided as regards the very national, social, and religious ideals which divide the older generation proves that the concept [of youth culture] is an illusion. Youth is a psychological category, not an intellectual one. Its task is to create not new ideas, but rather a new relationship to ideals, a new approach to ideas which have already been expressed. The youth movement puts aspirations into practice; it does not create them. It derives its aims from the same sources as the society around it: the romance of the past, the inertia of the present, and belief in the future.

In other words: the spirit and faith which dominate this age are also the spirit and faith of the youth movement. Since the changing aspects of the spirit of the age are expressed and enacted in different ways, it is unavoidable that the youth movement, as an active social entity, will also bear the marks of this division.

Hashomer Hatzair believes that it is the task of the youth movement to formulate a political ideology and conduct independent political activity. Our movement ... confined itself from the very first to the political education of the individual, and left the task of political decision to the appropriate organizations.[38]

Despite this radically different ideological approach, Gordonia used many of the educational methods developed by Hashomer Hatzair. In particular, it placed a similar emphasis on nurturing close relationships between its members in the educational group. Between 1924 and 1929, it passed through the same stages of development which Hashomer Hatzair had undergone several years earlier, but in a much shorter period of time. First, it freed itself from the tutelage of the adult Hit'ahdut party and proclaimed itself an independent movement aiming at 'personal realization' of Zionism—that is, its members' immigration to Palestine. From 1927 onwards Gordonia's graduates were undergoing training on farms organized by the movement, and in 1929 it adopted the principle of the permanent training kibbutz. In 1927 Lubianiker was still expressing his opposition to 'kibbutzism' as a movement aim; but in 1929 he declared:

The *kvutza* in its pristine form is the only form of expression of the aspirations of the youth movement to an environment filled with cultural content—an environment which increases the creative powers of the individual and is free of the blemishes of centralized administration.[39]

[38] Lavon, 'The Principles of Gordonia as a Youth Movement' (Heb.), in *Hechalutz Anthology*, 325–32.
[39] Lubianiker (Lavon), 'Our Position in Hechalutz', *Gordonia* (June 1929).

Like Hashomer Hatzair, Gordonia saw the kibbutz as the realization of the social ideals of the youth movement. But Gordonia came into being at a different time and under different circumstances. The aim of its leaders was still 'to fashion a new type of life, to develop better relations between man and man'. But the kibbutz and its varieties were no longer 'perceived through a screen, very nebulous'. They knew of Degania, and that A. D. Gordon, their eponymous hero, had spent his last years there; and they knew, and rejected, the arguments of the proponents of the 'great and growing kibbutz'. In crystallizing their outlook, they were helped by a number of emissaries, themselves members of veteran *kvutzot*, including some of the outstanding intellectuals of Degania. Their allegiance to Hapoel Hatzair, which gave political backing to the *kvutza* and the moshav as against the big kibbutz, also buttressed their adoption of the *kvutza* as an educational ideal. The result was an extreme restatement of the concept of the small *kvutza*.

Why *kvutza* and not kibbutz? These are not two provisional terms with no defined content. Each of them has a special connotation, which has changed over time, but they are still fundamentally different.

Economically, the *kvutza* is more restricted than the kibbutz, more united and more stable. The kibbutz, on the other hand, is by its very nature volatile. Its membership is in a certain sense random.... But the most important difference is in the fundamental question: What is the objective of collective living? The *kvutza* says: 'We want to create new relationships between man and man, to create new cultural values, to build up the individual within society.' Thus the *kvutza* is an end in itself, not a means of achieving transient national or social objectives. Its end is a function of its immanent nature. The starting-point of the *kvutza* is cultural and humanistic. The kibbutz says: 'We are fighting for a socialist social order. Our aim is mass settlement. Therefore, the task of the kibbutz is to constitute a living example of the society of the future, and to ensure mass settlement.' The starting point of the kibbutz is ideological and political.

The *kvutza* is an organic creation, centred on the individual who creates a new reality based on free human social being. The kibbutz is a mechanical collocation, in whose centre is the 'management'. The individual executes 'tasks', just as the kibbutz as a whole executes 'tasks' for society.

The *kvutza* needs for its existence spiritual culture, psychological ties between its members, family-type feeling, a high degree of common emotion. The kibbutz requires no more than ideological partnership and doctrinal statements.[40]

[40] Lubianiker (Lavon), 'Our Position in Hechalutz', *Gordonia* (June 1929).

The first members of Gordonia arrived in Palestine in the summer of 1929. Within a year they numbered five *plugot*, with a total membership of about 150. Ideologically, they identified themselves with the 'small *kvutzot*'—those which had not joined either of the two major movements in 1927, and which included veteran settlements such as Degania, Kinneret, and Geva. Over the coming few years they developed close relationships with them, which resulted in the formation of Hever Hakvutzot, of which Gordonia was an integral part. This process, which was quite complex, will be dealt with in Chapter 4.

### THE SMALLER MOVEMENTS

#### Hechalutz Hatzair[41]

The patent envy of Hashomer Hatzair expressed in Guberman's letter, quoted above, was not only a matter of personal preference. He and his correspondent were leaders of the Hechalutz Hatzair (Young Pioneer) movement, which had arisen spontaneously in the early part of the Fourth Aliya, 1925–6, when young people below the age of 17 attempted to join Hechalutz, but were rejected because of their age. One of the members of the first group of emissaries from Ein Harod began to organize these groups, and by 1927 they had a membership of some three thousand, mainly in Poland. Not only was this a tiny movement compared with Hashomer Hatzair but it suffered throughout its existence from a chronic shortage of leaders, for its most active members left for the training farms at the first opportunity. Its leaders were opposed to the educational methods of the classic youth movements: scouting, and the fostering of intensive relationships within the group. None the less, its special relationship with the adult movement, and the belief that its members would receive priority in selection for the training farms, gave it an impetus which enabled it to survive. Its recruits were mainly working-class.

#### Hashomer Hatzair, USSR[42]

The founders of the Russian section of Hashomer Hatzair were among those derided by Trumpeldor in 1919 as 'young students [with] romantic revelations' who held that the youth movement should be

---

[41] This section is largely based on Bassok, *Hechalutz Hatzair*.
[42] This section is largely based on Itai, *Hashomer Hatzair in the USSR*.

selective, 'a sort of order of knights'. Very similar in social composition to the Galician Hashomer Hatzair, this movement, founded during the period of political freedom after the first Russian revolution in February 1917, was also a scouting movement with a socialist and Zionist ideology. Its historical background differed from that of the rest of Hashomer Hatzair. Its members grew up at the period of the civil war, and the beginning of the consolidation of Soviet power. In face of the day-by-day proof of the crucial importance of the power of the state and of political parties, they did not develop the anti-political attitudes of the majority of the movement in its formative period. They evolved an ideology of their own, based on the approach of Ahdut Ha'avoda and its corresponding party in Russia, and emphasized the importance of character-building education that would result in the personal participation of each of the movement's graduates in strengthening the Yishuv. Their youth movement experience brought them, like their sister movements, to believe in the creation of kibbutzim.

Not long after its formation the movement began to be subjected to the persecution which threatened all Zionists in Soviet Russia. By 1925, the fear of arrest had driven the leadership to give up work with the younger age-groups. Only the most dedicated remained in the movement; they had become a close-knit conspiratorial group.

Their first contact with the Yishuv was in 1923, when they met David Ben-Gurion during the Moscow Agricultural Fair. Ben-Gurion, who is said to have behaved bravely when faced with the possibility of being trapped by the Soviet secret police, advised them to get to Palestine with all speed. Thus began a tradition of personal loyalty to him on the part of this movement's leaders.[43] The first of them to reach Palestine arrived at the beginning of the Fourth Aliya. Deeply conscious of the need to provide support for their comrades in Russia, they maintained contact with them despite all the difficulties. Those who escaped or were expelled from Russia were absorbed unquestioningly into the movement's *plugot*. These groups jealously guarded their special identity, and their independence of the other *plugot* of Hashomer Hatzair. By 1926 there were half a dozen such groups which, in effect, formed a small independent kibbutz movement.[44]

[43] Ophir, *Afikim*, 33, 52–5.    [44] Ibid. 113–62.

*Germany*[45]

Like its non-Jewish counterpart the Wandervogel, the Blau-Weiss proved unable to withstand the social and partisan pressures to which it was subjected in the early post-war years. A few of its members found their way to Palestine: some founded Kibbutz Markenhof (later Beit Zera) in the Jordan Valley, and Kvutzat Zvi, at Yagur; others established workshops in Jerusalem and Haifa, which were unsuccessful, among other reasons because they refused to co-operate with the Histadrut on ideological grounds.[46] In Germany, the movement's leadership was split between those who emphasized its general educational character and those who aimed to give it a more defined ideological bent. During the early post-war years, the leadership took an authoritarian turn and attempted to build a new ideology modelled at least partly on Fascist ideas. The result was the decline and eventual dissolution (1926) of the Blau-Weiss, which left the field open to a number of smaller movements.

Two such movements had already been in existence since the early 1920s. The JJWB (Jung-jüdischer Wanderbund) and Brith Olim were pioneering movements similar in their aims and methods to Hashomer Hatzair but without its political ideology. The two movements differed mainly in their members' social background, and in 1925 they merged to become the biggest German Jewish youth movement committed to pioneering and the kibbutz. The united movement controlled German Hechalutz, which was essentially a technical framework with whose help its members prepared themselves for their future lives. In relation to the half-million strong German Jewish community, this was a tiny movement; in 1928 it had no more than thirteen hundred members. But its very selectivity produced a group of devoted pioneers with exceedingly high cultural and moral standards. From an early stage it came under the influence of the educational emissaries of Ein Harod and the Kibbutz Me'uhad, and when its first group of graduates left for Palestine in 1926 they joined Kibbutz Giv'at Brenner. This group, Kibbutz Herut, was deeply influenced by

---

[45] Sources for the German youth movements: Schatzker, 'The Jewish Youth Movement in Germany'; Reinharz, 'Hashomer Hatzair in Germany'; id., 'Hashomer Hatzair in Nazi Germany'.

[46] Weiner, 'The Co-operative Blau-Weiss Works'.

the writings of Martin Buber, and derived its name from an article by him.[47]

Not all the members of the JJWB accepted the union with Brith Olim. One group joined the remnants of the Blau-Weiss in 1926, and created a movement called Kadimah (Forward), which concentrated on non-political Jewish education while using the traditional youth movement tools of scouting and group activity. In its early stages it embraced both Zionists and non-Zionists, but by 1930 the pressure of world political events and the ideological evolution of its leaders combined to bring it to a Zionist stance. This, too, was a tiny movement, having at this stage no more than fourteen hundred members of all ages.

The creation of Kadimah in 1926 led to yet another split, this time of the more convinced Zionists, who formed a group known as the Zofim ('Scouts') based mainly in the Berlin area. Just as Kadimah changed its original stance in favour of a more extreme Zionist ideology, so this group gradually came to adopt the principles of pioneering and self-realization, and began to send its members to agricultural training for eventual immigration in the framework of Hechalutz. By 1930, some three hundred members of the German Hechalutz movement, almost all of them graduates of the youth movements mentioned here, were undergoing agricultural training.

Although still exceedingly small in comparison with the Eastern European pioneering movements, these organizations led a very active life and played a vital part in the spiritual and social development of their members. The problems which engaged them were different in many ways from those which troubled their East European counterparts. They still wrestled with the possibilities of assimilation, or, at a later stage, emigration to countries other than Palestine; many of them were attracted to Communism, particularly in the frenetic atmosphere of the end of the Weimar republic; and they tended to be particularly sensitive to the Arab problem. But, like the young Jews of Eastern Europe, they were affected by the changing situation in Palestine, and the figures mentioned above show that they shared in the revival of Zionist activity and immigration from 1929 onwards.

---

[47] The letters and other writings of some of its leaders are to be found in a most impressive collection edited and published by their comrades in Giv'at Brenner; *Herut: An Anthology of Letters.*

## THE YOUTH MOVEMENTS IN THE EARLY 1930S

By 1930 each of the kibbutz movements had created a permanent connection with one or more youth movements which ensured its survival and expansion. As these connections became permanent, the youth movements crystallized their ideological positions and defined and intensified the differences between them. Their arguments were made more acrimonious by their contrasting views of the function of Hechalutz itself.

Since 1921, Hechalutz had, in effect, been part of the administrative framework through which the Zionist organization channelled its support for the training of pioneers and distributed immigration certificates. But the leaders of Hechalutz and their mentors in the Kibbutz Me'uhad rejected the view that their movement should have a purely administrative function. They saw it as an educational framework destined to include the other movements and ultimately to supersede them. In their eyes these were bourgeois in origin and conception and as introducing unnecessary divisions into the kibbutz movement. In Tabenkin's words, 'anything which reminds [a kibbutz member] that he is of "bourgeois" or "working-class" origin, that his culture was once Hebrew or Yiddish, or Polish or Russian—reduces our stature and weakens us'.[48] The working class of the Yishuv, and within it the kibbutz, must be united, and abolish precisely those distinctions of origin and culture which the educational approaches of the other youth movements were designed to preserve; and the beginning of the abolition of such distinctions must be during the time of preparation for the pioneers' new life. In support of this strategy, despite the acknowledged fact of the connection between the Kibbutz Me'uhad and Hechalutz, its leaders called the bloc of training farms which their movement controlled 'the general bloc'. They spoke of the principle of 'comprehensiveness' (*klaliut*), whereby Hechalutz and the Kibbutz Me'uhad represented the general interests of the Histadrut and the working class as a whole, and should therefore be acknowledged as the overall framework for the preparation and absorption of pioneers. The smaller movements suspected, and with reason, that the Kibbutz Me'uhad meant to swallow them up, and resisted every attempt to infringe their autonomy.

By 1929, the relations between the movements had become more or less institutionalized. Hechalutz had become a federative body,

[48] Kibbutz Me'uhad Council, July 1929. See *Kibbutz Me'uhad Anthology*, 157.

providing services and immigration certificates to the different movements in accordance with their numerical strength.[49] Each movement
had its strongholds in particular social strata and geographical areas.
The autonomous movements had gone in the footsteps of Hechalutz
and adopted the principle of the permanent training kibbutz, although
they were rather less stringent in its implementation.[50] Under the
pressure of the expanded possibilities of recruitment, Hashomer
Hatzair even created a number of training and immigrant kibbutzim
for its 'simple pioneers' in 1927–8 and again in 1932–4. The Kibbutz
Me'uhad, in contrast, was as adamant as ever in its opposition to the
'closed' youth movements; but its own youth movement, Hechalutz
Hatzair, came rather closer to them in its educational practice, particularly in working with small educational groups.[51]

None the less, the distance between them was great, and was further
increased as they settled down to the role of providing reserves for
rival kibbutz movements. The next chapter will deal with the creation
and character of those movements.

[49] Oppenheim, *The Hechalutz Movement in Poland*, ch. 9.
[50] Sarid, *Hechalutz in Poland*, 382–9, 442–3.
[51] Bassok, *Hechalutz Hatzair*, 217–22.

# 4

# The Fourth Aliya and the Creation of the Kibbutz Movements, 1924–1930

## THE FOURTH ALIYA: PATTERNS OF SETTLEMENT[1]

THE Fourth Aliya, like other waves of immigration, was shaped by a combination of historical developments in Palestine and the Diaspora. It began in the spring of 1924, with the revival of economic activity in the Yishuv after a period of stagnation lasting nearly a year. Extensive planting of tobacco and the expansion of Jewish citrus groves brought the Yishuv to a state of full employment: the Histadrut issued a call to Hechalutz members still in their training camps in Europe to come immediately, in order to ensure the dominance of Jewish labour in these economic activities. But this spurt of pioneering immigration was soon swamped by the wave which gave the period its name in Zionist historiography: 'the bourgeois aliya'. This was the result of two events outside Palestine: the economic policies of the Polish government, which taxed Jews out of the small businesses that had been their traditional means of livelihood; and the new immigration laws of the United States, which put an end to the mass influx of European Jews to that country. As a result, in the years 1924 to 1926 more than sixty thousand Jews arrived in the country, most of them with what were known as 'capitalist certificates'; in contrast to the pioneers who were admitted in accordance with the possibilities of employment, they possessed at least £500 sterling[2] and were thought to be able to contribute to the development of the country.

And so, at first, they did. Businesses were started up, and plots of land were bought for agricultural development and building. Tel Aviv, which since its foundation in 1909 had been little more than a

---

[1] This section is based partly on Gil'adi, *The Yishuv in the Fourth Aliya.*
[2] This qualification was raised to £1,000 in 1928; see Gurevich *et al.*, *Jewish Population of Palestine*, 26.

Jewish suburb of Jaffa, underwent a construction boom. The economic and political complexion of the Yishuv began to change. During the Third Aliya, it had seemed that the course of history had justified the decision of the Zionist Congress of 1920: public funds, contributed by the Jews of the Diaspora and the Mandatory government, had provided capital; the new immigrants, organized in the Histadrut, had provided the manpower and enterprise for development and settlement. Now it began to look as if Brandeis had after all been right in his opposition to this policy, and private enterprise was the real key to development.[3] The settlement funds, which were one of the keystones of the Weizmann policy, succeeded in raising a mere fraction of the sums to which they had committed themselves. In 1924 and 1925 only two kibbutzim and three moshavim were founded. The change in the balance of economic activity in Palestine also had a political effect. In the Zionist Congress of 1925 the Labour bloc's representation went down from 21 per cent (in 1923) to 19 per cent, while the number of General Zionists, among whom were the economically conservative delegates, rose from 50 to 57 per cent.

The economic boom lasted only some eighteen months. In mid-August 1925, despite the rate and size of immigration, there was full employment in Tel Aviv. By October, there were a thousand unemployed, and their number continued to grow throughout 1926 and 1927; and a considerable proportion of them returned to the Diaspora. From the point of view of the Yishuv and the Zionist movement, the worst feature of the crisis was the fact that, for the first time since the beginning of Zionist immigration in 1880 (apart from the war years), more Jews were leaving the country than were arriving. It was only in 1928 that the two numbers reached a balance, and from 1929 onwards the number of immigrants exceeded that of emigrants: a feature of the life of the Yishuv which would remain constant until 1966, although the proportions were to vary tremendously. But the emigration from 1925 to 1928 created a vicious circle: development in Palestine was extremely restricted; and world Jewry became increasingly unwilling to finance further settlement activities or industrial development. The result was a crisis of confidence in the Yishuv and the Zionist movement alike.

To the labour movement, each of these phases was a severe blow. The short period of prosperity seemed to have destroyed one of its

[3] For details of the Brandeis–Weizmann controversy, see Laqueur, *A History of Zionism*, 458–62.

main ideological and practical mainstays: the belief that the Jewish worker organized in the Histadrut, and in particular the various forms of settlement on publicly owned land (which had now collectively begun to be called 'workers' settlement'), were the leading elements in building the Yishuv. And, although the slump showed that the simplistic views of the right wing were mistaken, the effect on the workers' movement was close to disastrous. In Berl Katznelson's words, 'There is a general sense of crisis, and it is transferred from Palestine to the Diaspora. The economic crisis in the Yishuv is becoming a crisis of Zionism.'[4] The Histadrut, backed by the Zionist movement, organized help for the unemployed and attempted to ensure a fair distribution of available work. But this was no more than a palliative. The dilemma of the workers' movement is well illustrated in an anecdote told by Rachel Yanait Ben-Zvi (the wife of Yitzhak Ben-Zvi, later to be president of the State of Israel, and a labour leader in her own right). At the depth of the depression, Ben-Gurion, then secretary of the Histadrut, was bitterly reproached by one of the unemployed. 'Why are you complaining?' he replied. 'Don't you feel good? How can you not feel good in our land?' All he had to offer at this time of crisis was the Zionist dream.[5]

In fact, however, there was more to offer. Even at the height of the crisis, it was widely realized that it affected mainly the towns and their inhabitants. Although the Polish immigrants had brought their capital with them, it was not sufficient to establish large-scale industry. Their money was invested in small workshops, in commerce, land, building, and their ancillary industries. The taunt of the labour movement during the time of prosperity that the number of lemonade kiosks and cafes in Tel Aviv exceeded the number of productive enterprises proved to have some substance: for, when it appeared that the productive investments were not paying off, the branches based on consumption, building, and land speculation collapsed. But there was a fair number of people who invested their money in a way which proved to have been far-sighted and productive. They bought land in and around the *moshavot* and began to develop Jewish agriculture— particularly citrus, a crop whose success and potential had already been proven. Between 1922 and 1925, 13 new *moshavot* were founded, eight of them in the Sharon district—the coastal strip north of Tel

[4] From Katznelson's speech at the Histadrut conference, July 1927. See Katznelson, *Writings*, iii. 118.
[5] Teveth, *Ben-Gurion*, 269, 894.

Aviv, whose soil and climate are extremely well suited to citrus-growing. Between 1924 and 1927, the area of citrus groves in Jewish hands grew from 1,100 hectares to 2,400 hectares. After four to five years, the new areas began to yield fruit which was eagerly taken up in the world market, thus providing both income for the farmers and a source of employment for the workers. Although the economic competition between Jewish and Arab workers was still fierce, the expansion of Jewish agriculture meant an increase in employment opportunities for those affected by the crisis in the towns. The transfer from town to country was one of the aims of the labour movement and of the Zionist movement as a whole. So there began to appear in the outskirts of the *moshavot* small groups of workers, 'refugees' from the towns or new immigrants, mainly from the pioneering youth movements, organized in ways very similar to the *kvutzot* of the Second Aliya or the working groups of the Third. If such groups had more than eight members, they qualified for help from the Zionist organization: tents, a small stretch of ground to pitch them, and a minuscule subsidy to help them exist; for even here there was not enough employment for all who sought it, and problems such as sickness, poor nourishment, and the difficulties of acclimatization to agricultural work continued to take their toll.[6]

Some of these groups had organizational affiliations of the type already seen in the Third Aliya: these were the *plugot* of Gedud Ha'avoda and Kibbutz Ein Harod, and the groups of the Hashomer Hatzair youth movement. Others, which until 1928 formed the majority, were formed spontaneously on the basis of previous acquaintance, or with the help of the employment exchanges and the Public Works Department of the Histadrut. Such loose federations of *plugot* were called *havurot* (singular: *havura*). Their members worked wherever work could be found, pooled their earnings, ate in a common dining-room (or -tent or -hut), and received monetary payment only if there was a surplus left when the *havura* broke up. This was a spontaneous movement, very similar to that of the 'period of the roads' five years earlier, though with different employers and types of work. Most of these people had not come to the *havurot* directly from the youth movement and did not link up to form country-wide movements. The number of members of such unattached groups grew from 375 in 1925 to 1,312 in 1926 and 1,226 in 1927. By 1928 the economic crisis had passed, the Zionist movement

[6] *UAW Report* (1927), 99–100; ibid. (1931), 17.

ceased its subsidies to the *havurot*, and their numbers dropped dramatically, to 100.[7]

During these years, the organized kibbutz movements also increased their strength, and continued to do so after the break-up of the *havurot*. In consequence, during the Fourth Aliya the kibbutz movement grew rather faster than the Histadrut as a whole. The presence of the *havurot* in the rural areas intensified the pressure on the Zionist movement to provide a permanent solution to their problems by increasing the area of settlement on nationally owned land. But the policy of the Zionist Executive, elected at the height of the capitalist boom and reflecting its ideological bias, was opposed to what it saw as speculative ventures as long as the veteran settlements had not yet become prosperous and independent. So during 1925 and 1926 the limited funds available were spent helping established settlements rather than establishing new ones. It was only in 1926 that a stretch of land in the western Jezreel Valley became available for settlement.

During the whole of 1927 all the communal groups working in the *moshavot* took part in the struggle for the employment of Jews, both as a means of survival and as an expression of the principle of the 'conquest of labour'. Their attempts to arouse public opinion by demonstrations and strikes achieved some success but were marred by clashes with the farmers and the police. The new Zionist Executive, which emphasized the need for economy, gave little help in what all kibbutz members believed to be the only long-term solution to their problems and those of the Yishuv—agricultural settlement. After the spurt of development in the western Jezreel Valley in 1926, settlement almost came to a stop until 1930, and for five years thereafter preference was clearly given to moshavim over kibbutzim.

The most discouraging fact was the decline in the population of the kibbutz movement. With the end of unemployment, the spontaneous growth of the kibbutzim and *havurot* ceased. From now on, the kibbutz movement consisted almost entirely of the agricultural *kvutzot* (which were not organized in a comprehensive movement until 1929) and the two country-wide kibbutz movements founded in 1927: the Kibbutz Me'uhad and the Kibbutz Artzi. All these communities felt that the Zionist establishment, on whom they relied heavily, was hostile to their views and interests. Arthur Ruppin, who had always supported workers' settlement, resigned from his post as director of

[7] See table 4 below.

the Zionist movement's Settlement Department in 1925, and returned to it only in 1929. In 1928 a report commissioned by the Zionist Executive recommended the cessation of support for the kibbutzim, and particularly for those modelled on the 'big *kvutza*'. And, worst of all, even after the economic recovery of 1928 the Zionist authorities refused for almost a year to recommend the resumption of immigration, with the result that only six hundred immigration certificates were granted for 1929. The effect of these historical and political processes on the pattern of Jewish settlement and the population of the kibbutzim is clearly reflected in Tables 4 and 5.

Table 4 shows how sensitive the kibbutz movement was to the changing historical circumstances. The swift growth during the period of the roads was followed during the recession of 1923 by a contraction. A year later, many of the pioneers who had arrived in considerable numbers at the beginning of the Fourth Aliya were still in the kibbutzim, but the crisis of faith of the 'bourgeois' period was reflected in the statistics. The losses of this time were more than compensated for during the crisis years 1926–7, but as soon as work became available again the *havurot* broke up and many people left the kibbutzim. This, too, is reflected in the statistics.

Table 5 shows that, despite the erosion in public support and the lack of means to translate whatever support there was into terms of agricultural settlement, the number of kibbutzim continued to grow steadily during this period. But the major competitor of the kibbutz, the moshav, was threatening to outstrip it, and both forms of workers' settlement were only just holding their own in comparison with those based on private ownership.

In all these events, one of the elements which has been emphasized in previous chapters—the symbiosis between the kibbutz movement and the Zionist movement, with its fund-raising and administrative machinery—stands out. Within the kibbutz movement, however, attention was focused on internal developments which stemmed largely from the events of the Fourth Aliya and reactions to them.

## GEDUD HA'AVODA AND EIN HAROD

The secession of Ein Harod and the events of the Fourth Aliya forced Gedud Ha'avoda to rethink the concept of the general commune. The Gedud was no longer the only (and soon, as we shall see, not the biggest) national kibbutz organization aiming at unlimited expansion.

TABLE 4. Kibbutz Population in Context, 1920–1928[a]

| | Adult population and no. kibbutzim | | | | | | | | | | Moshavim | | No. Histadrut members | Jewish population |
|---|---|---|---|---|---|---|---|---|---|---|---|---|---|---|
| | Gedud Ha'avoda | | Ein Harod/ Kibbutz Me'uhad | | Hashomer Hatzair | | Others | | Total | | | | | |
| | Popn. | No. | Popn. | No. | Popn. | No. | Popn. | No. | Popn. | No. | Popn. | No. | | |
| **1920** | | | | | | | | | | | | | | |
| Farms | — | — | — | — | — | — | 268 | 10 | 268 | 10 | — | — | — | — |
| Plugot | 88 | 3 | — | — | — | — | 203 | 26 | 291 | 29 | — | — | — | — |
| Total | 88 | — | — | — | — | — | 471 | — | 559 | — | — | — | — | 67,000 |
| **1921** | | | | | | | | | | | | | | |
| Farms | 402 | 4 | — | — | — | — | 247 | 8 | 649 | 12 | 80 | 1 | — | — |
| Plugot | 158 | 5 | — | — | 100 | 3 | 500 | 30 | 758 | 38 | — | — | — | — |
| Total | 560 | — | — | — | 100 | — | 747 | — | 1,407 | — | — | — | 4,433 | 72,000 |
| **1922** | | | | | | | | | | | | | | |
| Farms | 420 | 4 | — | — | 105 | 1 | 340 | 12 | 865 | 17 | 160 | 6 | — | — |
| Plugot | 172 | 5 | — | — | 206 | 2 | 1,500 | 72 | 1,878 | 79 | — | — | — | — |
| Total | 592 | — | — | — | 311 | — | 1,840 | — | 2,743 | — | — | — | 8,394 | 82,100 |
| **1923** | | | | | | | | | | | | | | |
| Farms | 319 | 3 | 110 | 1 | 90 | 1 | 495 | 16 | 1,014 | 21 | 534 | 9 | — | — |
| Plugot | 113 | 4 | — | — | 97 | 2 | 300 | 6 | 510 | 12 | — | — | — | — |
| Total | 432 | — | 110 | — | 187 | — | 795 | — | 1,594 | — | — | — | 9,000 | 89,700 |
| **1924** | | | | | | | | | | | | | | |
| Farms | 335 | 3 | 255 | 3 | 105 | 1 | 622 | 15 | 1,317 | 22 | — | — | — | — |
| Plugot | 331 | 5 | 180 | 3 | 127 | 4 | 657 | 23 | 1,295 | 35 | — | — | — | — |
| Total | 666 | — | 435 | — | 232 | — | 1,279 | — | 2,612[b] | — | — | — | 10,085 | 94,000 |

| | Adult population and no. kibbutzim | | | | | | | | | | | | Moshavim | | No. Histadrut members | Jewish population |
|---|---|---|---|---|---|---|---|---|---|---|---|---|---|---|---|---|
| | Gedud Ha'avoda | | Ein Harod/ Kibbutz Me'uhad | | Hashomer Hatzair | | Others | | Total | | | | | | | |
| | Popn. | No. | Popn. | No. | Popn. | No. | Popn. | No. | Popn. | No. | Popn. | No. | Popn. | No. | | |
| **1925** | | | | | | | | | | | | | | | | |
| Farms | 324 | 3 | 388 | 4 | 106 | 1 | 572 | 13 | 1,390 | 21 | | | 856 | 11 | – | – |
| Plugot | 285 | 4 | 127 | 3 | 152 | 5 | 375 | 12 | 939 | 24 | | | – | – | – | – |
| Total | 609 | – | 515 | – | 258 | – | 947 | – | 2,329 | – | | | – | – | 15,275 | 121,700 |
| **1926** | | | | | | | | | | | | | | | | |
| Farms | 369 | 3 | 467 | 4 | 195 | 2 | 657 | 13 | 1,688 | 22 | | | 911 | 13 | – | – |
| Plugot | 262 | 3 | 140 | 2 | 247 | 9 | 1,312 | 49 | 1,961 | 63 | | | – | – | – | – |
| Total | 631 | – | 607 | – | 442 | – | 1,969 | – | 3,649 | – | | | – | – | 19,588 | 149,500 |
| **1927** | | | | | | | | | | | | | | | | |
| Farms | 356 | 3 | 482 | 4 | 87 | 1 | 841 | 17 | 1,766 | 25 | | | 1,200 | 16 | – | – |
| Plugot | 90 | 2 | 497 | 11 | 320 | 5[d] | 1,226 | 48 | 2,133 | 65 | | | – | – | – | – |
| Total | 446 | – | 979 | – | 407 | – | 2,067 | – | 3,899[c] | – | | | – | – | 22,538 | 149,800 |
| **1928** | | | | | | | | | | | | | | | | |
| Farms | 260 | 3 | 590 | 6 | 139 | 2 | 793 | 16 | 1,782 | 27 | | | – | – | – | – |
| Plugot | – | – | 316 | 6 | 187 | 4 | 101 | 4 | 604 | 14 | | | – | – | – | – |
| Total | 260 | – | 906 | – | 326 | – | 894 | – | 2,386 | – | | | – | – | 24,000 | 151,700 |

*Sources:* This table is a corrected version of that given in Near, *Kibbutz and Society*, 418–19. For detailed references see Near, 'The Kibbutz and the Outside World', 506–23; also tables in *Pinkas Hahistadrut* (Jan.–Feb. 1923) and Gurevich et al., *Jewish Population of Palestine*, 268–80. The sources are kibbutz archives, Histadrut reports, and the like; but some estimates are included where no figures are available. It is of course impossible to give a completely accurate picture of a situation which was constantly fluctuating, even within a single year; but I believe there are no gross inaccuracies. The Jewish population figures are taken from Halevi, *Economic Development,* table 2.

<sup></sup>[a]As far as possible, the figures are for the autumn of each year.　　[b] And 150 children.　　[c] And 380 children.

[d] Not including the *plugot* of Hashomer Hatzair USSR, who joined the Kibbutz Me'uhad during the year.

TABLE 5. New Jewish Settlement, 1920–1928

| Period | Kibbutzim | | | | | Other | | | Total |
|---|---|---|---|---|---|---|---|---|---|
| | Gedud Ha'avoda | Ein Harod/ Kibbutz Me'uhad | Hashomer Hatzair | Other kibbutzim | Total | Moshavim | Moshavot | Urban settlements | |
| *Third Aliya* | | | | | | | | | |
| 1919/20 | | | | 1 | 1 | | | | — |
| 1920/1 | 1 | | | 1 | 2 | 1 | 2 | | 3 |
| 1921/2 | 1 | | | 2 | 3 | 5 | 2 | 1 | 8 |
| 1922/3 | | | 1 | 2 | 3 | 1 | 1 | 1 | 3 |
| 1923/4 | | | | 1 | 1 | 2 | 3 | 4 | 9 |
| Total | 2 | — | 1 | 7 | 10 | 9 | 8 | 6 | 23 |
| *Fourth Aliya* | | | | | | | | | |
| 1924/5 | | 1 | | | 1 | 2 | 3 | 4 | 9 |
| 1925/6 | 1 | | | 1 | 2 | | 2 | | 2 |
| 1926/7 | | | 1 | 5 | 6 | 3 | 2 | 1 | 6 |
| 1927/8 | | 1 | | | 1 | | | | |
| Total | 1 | 2 | 1 | 6 | 10 | 5 | 7 | 5 | 17 |

*Source:* This table is based mainly on Gurevich et al., *Jewish Population of Palestine*, 280–1, with minor corrections of detail.

But, even had its leaders been able to accommodate the idea of several general communes, the economic crisis made them doubt the plausibility of constructive socialism—the belief that it was possible to by-pass the capitalist stage of social development and build the Yishuv directly as a socialist society. They had seen the capitalist system buttressed by more than a year of prosperity and development; and, even though the crisis had to a great extent negated these achievements, it was clear by now that the 2,500 kibbutz members, only a quarter of them in the Gedud, who constituted less than 3 per cent of the Yishuv's population, were very far from expanding with the speed and inevitability envisaged in the original concept of the general commune. At the very least, the Gedud needed a new strategy for dealing with the Yishuv in the interim period; at the most, a new ideology to replace the idea of the general commune, which the course of events had shown to be impractical.

After a short period of undirected ideological ferment, two major groups emerged, both led by young men who had arrived in the country in the early days of the Third Aliya: the right wing by such men as Yehuda Kopilevich (Almog), Hanokh Rokhel, and Ze'ev Isserson (On), some of Trumpeldor's outstanding disciples; the left wing by Mendel Elkind, a brilliant organizer who had represented the Gedud in its relationships with the Histadrut, David Horowitz (an ex-member of the first Hashomer Hatzair group, who joined the Gedud in 1922), and Israel Shohat, one of the founders and leaders of Hashomer.[8] The rightist faction continued to believe in the Gedud's original aims, but now saw them in a much longer perspective. Their final aim was still a general commune *of* the Yishuv; but, meanwhile, they would continue to attempt to build their commune *within* the Yishuv. The prime aim was to build communal settlements, and to educate and absorb new immigrants, especially from Hechalutz.

The leftist faction drew much more radical conclusions from the events of the Fourth Aliya. Its leaders evolved a theory which applied a Marxist outlook to the realities of the Yishuv and of Zionism. They came to believe that the boom and slump were simply examples of

[8] The best known of these men in later years was Horowitz, who became the first governor of the Bank of Israel. Rokhel and Isserson were members of Kibbutz Tel Yosef all their adult lives; Isserson was active in the Histadrut and the Israeli Labour Party. Kopilevich was a member of Kibbutz Kfar Gil'adi, but spent much time and energy from the 1930s onwards in developing Jewish settlement in the Dead Sea area, where a young kibbutz now bears his adopted name (Almog).

the Marxist socio-economic prognosis, and that the future held a further series of such vicissitudes. The only way out was by revolution, and the only way to promote revolution was by political and educational means. They did not deny the value of constructive activities in themselves; but they tended to see them as secondary to the Gedud's political work, a means of providing logistic support for the standard-bearers of the revolution.

The contrast between the two groups is underlined in the following brief definitions of their aims. The right faction wanted to build

a kibbutz united in aim and method ... whose activities are centred on the type of construction which is a necessary consequence of its real nature and objectives: to build up the country and create a communist society by means of a social revolution.[9]

The leftist faction, of course, saw things differently:

Two paths lie open before us: to see the kibbutz economy as an end in itself ... or to put it at the disposal of a broader revolutionary concept.... We must always consider the achievements of the kibbutz movement from the point of view of the workers' movement in its broad historical perspective.... The kibbutz movement must be the avantgarde of the revolutionary labour movement ... not only a model social cell, but a fighting, conquering unit which bears within it the collective will of the workers' movement, and is at that movement's disposal in the war of [social] liberation.[10]

Each of these groups aimed at a social revolution. But, whereas the leftists wanted the Gedud to stand at the head of a workers' movement which would bring the revolution about by political means, for the rightist faction the revolution consisted in the expansion of the Gedud itself.

Several factors combined to strengthen the left, apart from the intellectual brilliance of its leaders. The younger members of the Gedud had been influenced at a formative time of their lives by the political and emotional impact of what they viewed as the beginnings of a double revolution: national liberation, symbolized in the case of the Jewish people by the Balfour Declaration, and social liberation, symbolized by the Bolshevik Revolution. Moreover, now that most Second Aliya people had left the Gedud, there was no group left in it which identified with any of the major Zionist parties. Those

[9] Isserson (On), *Mihayeinu*, 74 (Sept. 1926), iii. 409.
[10] Horowitz, ibid., 63 (Aug. 1925), iii. 207.

of the Second Aliya who remained were mainly the ex-members of Hashomer, who were anti-establishment in temperament and politics, and whose basic suspicion of the ruling Ahdut Ha'avoda was reinforced by the events of the Fourth Aliya. But these factors were probably no more than the background which ensured a sympathetic hearing to the members and sympathizers of two even more extreme anti-establishment parties: Left Poalei Zion which, while still maintaining its belief in Zionism, emphasized the importance of revolutionary and trade-union activity as against constructivism; and the 'Fraction'—the Jewish component of the semi-legal Palestine Communist Party. These were hard-line Communists, and therefore anti-Zionists. They saw the Arab workers as the local proletariat, and believed that it was the duty of the Jewish working class to co-operate with them against the imperialist British and their Zionist agents and helpers.

The atmosphere of despair then rife in the Zionist movement and the Yishuv eased the work of these parties. They were also helped by the attitude of the left faction, which refused to expel Fraction members from the Gedud even though their beliefs and propaganda were in clear conflict with its Zionist principles.[11] In two important respects, however, the left faction decided the fate of the Gedud at a relatively early stage. From mid-1923 several educational missionaries of the Gedud had been working in the European pioneering youth movements, and achieved a measure of success. In August 1924, when the two factions were beginning to crystallize, there was a decision to stop the Gedud's independent educational work and bring home most of its emissaries. The motives behind this decision are not clear, but it seems that it was an attempt to prevent the right faction increasing its strength by recruiting new members in the Diaspora. In this it succeeded, but at the cost of stifling the Gedud's possibilities of development; for without a constant flow of new members, a slow decline in numbers was inevitable. The other decision was a consequence of Marxist theory and the attempt to combine it with revolutionary practice. On the grounds that the future lay with the urban proletariat, it was decided to concentrate on the *plugot* in the towns—precisely at the time when there was economic and social stagnation in the towns and relative progress in the country. This

---

[11] Elkind led the opposition to the expulsion of Fraction members. It is not clear just when he actually became a Communist; so his insistence on the rights of the anti-Zionists within the Gedud may have been the result of naïvety or of cunning.

policy struck hard at the Gedud's economic situation. In the event, it meant that most of the left-wingers concentrated in the urban *plugot*, while the rightist faction continued to control most of the kibbutzim.[12]

I shall not pursue the controversy between the two factions in detail. It bred, among other things, a third faction, whose aim was unity of the Gedud at almost any price; a delegation of the Gedud to Soviet Russia, in the course of which its members suggested that the Gedud should advance Soviet military interests in Palestine, in return for Soviet support for Zionism; armed clashes between the ex-members of Hashomer and the Hagana in Upper Galilee, which stopped only when the Histadrut intervened; and the appearance of the two factions in separate electoral lists for the Histadrut conference of 1927. The cardinal fact is that the differences between the two factions proved irreconcilable. At the end of 1926 the Gedud split into two separate movements, each with its own *plugot* and kibbutzim: the right faction had 294 members, and the left 195.[13] The left faction, however, was already well on the way to abandoning Zionism altogether; within a year about eighty of its members had left Palestine for the Soviet Union. There they set up a commune called Vita Nova, which continued to exist despite great difficulties until its final liquidation in the purges of the 1930s. But the majority of the Gedud remained faithful to Zionism.

The defection of the left faction of the Gedud shocked the labour movement, whose leaders quoted it for many years as an example of the results of unthinking anti-establishment attitudes. The right faction, whose members continued to believe in constructive Zionism but were still highly suspicious of the Ahdut Ha'avoda leaders and their allies, maintained its separate existence until 1929, when it merged with the Kibbutz Me'uhad.

## Ein Harod, 1923–1927[14]

Immediately on its separation from Gedud Ha'avoda, Ein Harod found a new partner. It joined up with Havurat Ha'emek, one of the most energetic and efficient of the *havurot*, which was also orientated politically towards Ahdut Ha'avoda. Thus, from the first, Kibbutz Ein Harod comprised people from both the Second and the Third

---

[12] Near, *Kibbutz and Society*, 137, 165–7.
[13] *Mihayeinu*, 80 (Feb. 1927), iii. 493.
[14] This section is based on Near, *Kibbutz and Society*, ch. 4.

Aliyot. But they shared an overall philosophy, and were not rent by the temperamental and political differences which had afflicted Gedud Ha'avoda from an early stage.

Several of the leaders of the Gedud had stayed in Ein Harod. The two best known were Shlomo Lavi and Yitzhak Tabenkin. These men had many characteristics in common. Both were products of the Jewish Pale, largely self-educated in a wide range of subjects, and deeply influenced by the socialist and anarchist thinkers of their time. Lavi had been a member of Hapoel Hatzair, but his belief in the unity of labour had led him to join Ahdut Ha'avoda on its formation. Tabenkin had been a founder member of that party, having left Poalei Zion on his arrival in Palestine in 1911 to become a prominent member of the 'non-party element'. Each of them had acquired a personal and ideological following during their time in the Gedud. Yet, although they were allies, and had left the Gedud together, there were many differences between them. Some were exemplified in the course of the split in the Gedud. The act of agricultural settlement and the creation of a working community were central to the philosophies of both men. Lavi translated these concepts into practical terms in the creation and strengthening of one settlement, Ein Harod. This was to be the realization of his idea—one might almost say his blueprint—of the 'big *kvutza*'. Any deviation from or weakening of this plan was to be fought with all his tremendous single-mindedness and tenacity. This was at the root of his struggle inside the Gedud. Tabenkin, on the other hand, did not see the other parts of the Gedud as unnecessary or harmful. During the controversy he maintained, in contrast to Lavi, that inequality between the different *plugot* was intolerable. He therefore suggested a compromise whereby the money allocated to Ein Harod for its development should be sacrosanct, but the 'general treasury' should still be operated as in the original concept of the Gedud. It was mainly Lavi's obstinacy which prevented this or some other compromise from being adopted. By contrast, Tabenkin displayed both tactical flexibility and an understanding of the needs of the groups within the Gedud outside Ein Harod itself.

All these personal and ideological tensions recurred in the crisis which broke out in Ein Harod less than a year after it became independent of the Gedud. The new organization's political complexion was well known to the leaders of the Histadrut, and they were anxious that it should replace the Gedud as the prime instrument in absorbing and settling new immigrants and unemployed workers.

From the moment of its independence, there were a number of *plugot* affiliated to Ein Harod. Lavi believed that these should be abolished as soon as possible, and their members absorbed into Ein Harod itself. But there was constant pressure from the Histadrut to maintain, and even increase, the number of *plugot*. Lavi and his allies within the kibbutz disagreed violently: in their view, to maintain *plugot* outside the close vicinity of Ein Harod was tantamount to rebuilding the Gedud in another form. They were even more incensed when Ein Harod was asked to send groups to ailing *kvutzot* to save them from dissolution. To do this, they said, would be to turn Ein Harod into a 'country-wide kibbutz'—in today's parlance, a kibbutz movement; and it was precisely because they were against this idea that they had left the Gedud.

In the debate that followed, Lavi and his allies were in a minority at almost every stage. None the less, they attempted to gain the support of the Histadrut—on the whole unsuccessfully; on one occasion, however, with the help of Hapoel Hatzair, they persuaded the Histadrut Council to pass a resolution limiting the power of the kibbutz movement over its constituent members.[15] Only in 1926, with the collapse of his group of supporters, did Lavi give up the struggle. The discussion engendered by this episode is important because it prompted Tabenkin, who now emerged as the unchallenged leader of Ein Harod, to define his aims, and distinguish them from those of Lavi and the Gedud alike.

For Tabenkin, two issues were predominant: the centrality of settlement as an aim of every communal group; and the idea of 'conquest'—the belief that the kibbutz movement should strive to expand the places and types of work of the Jewish labourer, with limits fixed only by practical economic possibilities. In the Gedud, the idea of settlement was lacking, or at least not central to its aims; in Lavi's concept, although Ein Harod would expand indefinitely and would be an example to other similar communities, the idea of conquest—the direct responsibility of Ein Harod to strain every nerve in order to solve the problems of the Yishuv, as Tabenkin saw them— was missing.

By May 1925, the decision had been made: Ein Harod was to be a 'country-wide kibbutz', and in fact already comprised a combination of farms (Ein Harod, Ayelet Hashahar, Yagur, Gesher) scattered over

---

[15] At the Histadrut council in Gan Shmuel in 1926; ibid. 87. See also Hadari, *Kibbutz Ein Harod*, 106.

the north of the country, and of *plugot* in several locations between Jerusalem and Petah Tikva. By the end of that year, its 515 members were more than 22 per cent of the whole kibbutz movement; and the following year, at the height of the spontaneous influx to the kibbutz, its membership, at 607, had already passed that of the Gedud. When, in 1927, Ein Harod became the kernel of the new Kibbutz Me'uhad, it was the biggest kibbutz movement, with more than one thousand members.

This rapid, even spectacular, growth was due not only to the new movement's exceptional dynamism. An equally important factor was that which was symbolically represented in May 1924 when Ahdut Ha'avoda chose to hold its conference in Ein Harod. This decision made it clear that the party (and, therefore, the Histadrut) had chosen Ein Harod as its chief instrument in building the Yishuv, according to the theory of constructive socialism—the creation of a socialist society which would by-pass the capitalist economy, or eliminate it by competition. In practical terms, this meant that Ein Harod received priority in such matters as absorption of new immigrants and contract work supplied by the Histadrut's Public Works Office. The party's support of the 'great and growing kibbutz' was expressed in one of the main decisions of the conference, and Tabenkin and his friends spelt out the meaning of this concept in the discussions. In effect, it was a combination of the ideas of Shlomo Lavi and the Gedud. The kibbutz (in the sense of 'group of settlements') was to expand, with no limits except those dictated by the economic situation; and each individual component should, as far as possible, be built as a 'big *kvutza*', combining agriculture, handicrafts, and industry. True, at the present stage of development there would have to be *plugot* without land of their own. But every *pluga* should have as its aim to establish itself on the land, whether by joining an existing settlement or, when the economic situation allowed, by acquiring its own land.

The doctrine of the 'great and growing kibbutz' went further than this as it developed. At the 1924 conference, there was a discussion about a proposal to build workers' suburbs in and near the towns. Lavi suggested including land for agricultural development in each suburb. 'In that case,' he was asked, 'how will it be different from the kibbutz?' The reply, that it would in effect be a kibbutz, and that this would be the best way to build up the towns, is quite characteristic of the turn of thought of the men of Ein Harod then and subsequently. For they saw the kibbutz not as one possibility among others, but as the only certain way of building up the country. In their view, the *kvutzot* were inefficient, unattractive to the mass of new immigrants, and unable to expand quickly enough or to embrace all aspects of social, cultural, and economic life; the moshavim were essentially individualistic, and would tend to turn into *moshavot*; the *moshavot* had proved that they were unable to fulfil the basic Zionist commandment of employing only Jewish labour; and both they and the towns as at present constituted were capitalist societies, fundamentally inefficient and doomed to eventual extinction. This doctrine is a more sophisticated version of the idea of the 'general commune' advocated by Gedud Ha'avoda. Adapting a philosophical term used in other contexts, I shall call it 'kibbutz holism'.

In 1924, there was virtual agreement between the leaders of Ahdut Ha'avoda and those of the kibbutz on the central importance of the 'great and growing kibbutz'. But there was a catch in this agreement reminiscent of that in the agreement between Shlomo Lavi and the Gedud: whereas Tabenkin and his friends saw the kibbutz as the only method of absorption and construction, Ben-Gurion and others, who bore the main responsibility for the management of the party and the Histadrut, saw it as the main but not necessarily the only way. These differences began to be significant in the course of the coming years.

Tabenkin's prognosis, based on the experience of the Second Aliya as he read it, was simple. In the present conditions of the Yishuv, there was no place for immigration following the normal pattern. Jews who were not prepared for a high degree of self-sacrifice would not stay in the country. 'We need pioneers, not immigrants.'[16] Moreover, those who did stay would be able to survive only if they used the one tool which had proved itself able to support them in their struggle: the kibbutz. Thus, he argued, any attempt to develop an urban Jewish working class was doomed to failure.

Whatever the logic of these contentions, there was no clear evidence as to their truth or falsity in the realities of the Fourth Aliya. Certainly some of the processes foreseen by Tabenkin came to pass: three *kvutzot* were in such distress that they turned to Ein Harod, which rebuilt them in its own image; and there was more than one instance of a working group joining Ein Harod and developing from *pluga* to 'big *kvutza*'. But most of the veteran *kvutzot* remained faithful to their way of life, and several new ones based on the same model were founded at this time. Nor was there any real sign of moshavim

[16] Tabenkin, May 1925. See *Kibbutz Me'uhad Anthology*, 106.

changing to *moshavot*; indeed, there was one instance of the opposite process.[17] If we take as our criterion the overall structure of employment, it remained remarkably stable between 1924 and 1927; although the Histadrut grew from 10,085 members to 22,538, about two-thirds of its members lived and were employed in the towns at both these dates. It is true that Ein Harod grew at this time in terms of the overall statistics, but this was largely at the expense of the Gedud. The percentage of the kibbutz movement in the total population was also more or less stable.

None of this shook the faith of Tabenkin and his comrades in Ein Harod. They were convinced that the future of the Yishuv lay with them. And they began to spread this faith with missionary zeal from 1925 onwards, following the most important single act of Ein Harod's leadership during this period: the establishment of its connection with the Hechalutz movement in the Diaspora, and particularly in Poland. As we have seen, this movement had been cut off from the Gedud, and its attempts to renew the connection had been rebuffed. Ein Harod's delegation to the pioneering youth movements in 1925/6 was the beginning of a partnership which lasted until the Holocaust put an end to the Jewish youth movements; and this was undoubtedly the chief factor in the continued growth of Ein Harod and its successor, the Kibbutz Me'uhad.[18]

## THE FOUNDATION OF THE KIBBUTZ MOVEMENTS

### Kibbutz Artzi and Kibbutz Me'uhad

The first years of the Fourth Aliya created a state of alarm almost approaching panic in the kibbutzim. Their members saw the Zionist movement abandoning the basic approach to settlement and economic development without which their communities could never have come into being. They were apprehensive that they would now be unable to expand, even, perhaps, to survive.

One result of their fears was the attempt to defend their interests by creating an overall body which would be able to represent them *vis-à-vis* the Zionist movement and the Histadrut. Thus, in the spring

[17] Mahanaim, in Upper Galilee, founded as a *moshava* in 1899 and resettled by a 'settlement group' in 1917, became a moshav in 1923. It reached its final form, a kibbutz of the Kibbutz Me'uhad, only in 1939; Bein, *History of Zionist Settlement*, 375.

[18] Near, *Kibbutz and Society*, 169–71.

of 1925 there was established Hever Hakvutzot Vehakibbutzim (the Federation of Kvutzot and Kibbutzim), the first—and, even today, the only—kibbutz movement embracing all types of communal settlement and working groups. It included the existing movements, Gedud Ha'avoda and Ein Harod, as well as the small unaffiliated *kvutzot* and the kibbutzim of Hashomer Hatzair, as yet unaffiliated to any country-wide movement.[19]

This organization effectively ceased to exist within a year or so. Both of the existing movements were so strong, and so sure of their peculiar right to exist and lead the whole of the kibbutz movement—indeed, all of the labour movement—that they effectively denied its institutions any sovereignty over themselves or their constituent parts. But the basic problem it was intended to solve—how to ensure a higher degree of representation and support for individual communities and the existing inter-kibbutz groupings—still remained. During 1926 and the first months of 1927 there was a series of intensive discussions, which led to the establishment in 1927 of the two major kibbutz movements, the Kibbutz Artzi of Hashomer Hatzair and the Kibbutz Me'uhad.

By the summer of 1924, with the first international conference of Hashomer Hatzair, it had become clear that the movement had an organizational and ideological basis which linked it to Zionism and enabled the continuation of its educational traditions in that framework. The meeting of groups of movement graduates at Beit Alpha during that year served to renew their contact with the Diaspora, but they were not yet ready to create any formal framework in the Yishuv. In the course of the next two years the fruits of this recovery began to appear in Palestine, in the form of renewed immigration of groups from the movement. Despite the economic crisis, they established *plugot*[20] on the outskirts of Haifa and Afula where they worked as building labourers, and, when the crisis deepened, in the vicinity of the citrus-growing *moshavot*. By the beginning of 1926 there were some 550 members of Hashomer Hatzair in the country, nowhere except Beit Alpha in established settlements. (Mishmar Ha'emek, the second Hashomer Hatzair kibbutz, reached its place of permanent settlement in the autumn of 1926.) Unlike the immigrants of 1919,

---

[19] Id., 'Hever Hakvutzot Vehakibbutzim'; Ben-Avram, *Hever Hakvutzot*, 13–15, 26–7.
[20] In the idiosyncratic terminology of Hashomer Hatzair, the *plugot* (not yet permanently settled), settled kibbutzim, and the country-wide kibbutz movement were all denoted by the same term: kibbutz; Near, 'The Languages of Community'.

these new arrivals were well aware of the necessity to strengthen the mutual relationships between the groups and to maintain their links with the movement in the Diaspora. They therefore began a series of intensive discussions which resulted in the establishment of a 'country-wide kibbutz', the Kibbutz Artzi of Hashomer Hatzair, in April 1927.[21]

By mid-1926, Kibbutz Ein Harod had increased its membership more than six-fold since its secession from the Gedud, both by the addition of new *plugot* and kibbutzim and by absorbing individuals and groups into its existing communities. It was consciously fulfilling the role of a 'country-wide kibbutz': its leaders had clearly expressed their ambition to lead the whole kibbutz movement, and ultimately to unite all the communal groups in the country under its wing.[22] Their first aim was to unite with the right wing of Gedud Ha'avoda, which with the Gedud's final schism at the beginning of 1927 had become an independent movement. The negotiations failed as a result of nuances of expression in the proposed constitution, whose significance was quite clear: while the leaders of the Gedud were in almost complete agreement with those of Ein Harod on such questions as the primacy of agricultural settlement, they were still anxious to preserve their political autonomy. Since 1921 the Gedud had been struggling against the domination of Ahdut Ha'avoda in the Histadrut. Its leaders were not prepared to unite with a movement whose political sympathies (though not its formal allegiance) were so clearly with that party. It took two more years of independent but precarious existence to convince them that their place was in the Kibbutz Me'uhad.

The people who were anxious to unite with Ein Harod differed from those who had contributed to its growth over the previous three years. These had mainly been ailing *kvutzot*, and individuals or small groups fleeing from the economic crisis. The groups which took part in the negotiations of 1926–7 were strong in numbers and morale, mostly graduates of youth movements in the Diaspora, with a high degree of Zionist motivation and political awareness. In some cases they were already organized in 'country-wide kibbutzim' of their own.[23] All of them were close to the political outlook of Ahdut Ha'avoda.

[21] On the foundation of the Kibbutz Artzi see Margalit, *Hashomer Hatzair*, ch. 4.
[22] On the negotiations which led up to the foundation of the Kibbutz Me'uhad see Near, *Kibbutz and Society*, 106–15.
[23] e.g. the Pinsk group (later Kibbutz Gvat) which did not join the Kibbutz Me'uhad at this stage, and the graduates of Hashomer Hatzair in Russia, who did.

In order to unite groups of this sort, it was not enough simply to expand Ein Harod: a new beginning was required. The discussions which preceded the foundation of the Kibbutz Me'uhad in 1927 emphasized the desire to unite these half-dozen groups, based on common origin or chance association, into an all-embracing movement. On the day of its foundation in August 1927, the Kibbutz Me'uhad numbered 1,080 members, belonging to four kibbutzim and ten *plugot*. In it were united all of Kibbutz Ein Harod and three new groups of communal bodies.

Unlike Gedud Ha'avoda and the Kibbutz Me'uhad, the Kibbutz Artzi did not aspire to indefinite expansion. One of its prime objectives was to 'create an organic connection' with the youth movements in the Diaspora, and they were to be its only source of manpower. This was a principle accepted by all the groups which participated in the negotiations that preceded the movement's foundation. The most controversial issue in these negotiations was that of the new movement's political position. The graduates of the Russian section accepted the leadership of Ahdut Ha'avoda, and opposed any tendency to political independence on the part of the new movement. This view was rejected by the majority. Although they no longer believed in the extreme version of the 'youth culture' concept, they were still convinced that the youth movement, including the kibbutzim which it had created, should express its own world outlook on all aspects of society, including the political aspect. They rejected any connection with or control by a political party. But they were far from being a non-political movement. The following 'basic definition' was accepted at the founding conference:

The kibbutz is based on principles of political, social, and economic action. . . . [It is] not a political party . . . [but] an independent political grouping within the workers' movement in Palestine. . . . a prototype of the future co-operative society and an independent ideological and political collective.[24]

The development of Hashomer Hatzair from the romantic youth movement of the early 1920s to a point at which it could define its kibbutzim as 'independent political collectives' is at first sight paradoxical. True, the emphasis on 'the relationship between man and man had not been rejected.[25] In the words of the 'Ideological Premisses' of 1927:

---

[24] From the Ideological Premisses of the Kibbutz Artzi, 302.
[25] In the discussion at Tira, 1920. See above, ch. 2.

The essence of the kibbutz stems from its social life, in which it aims at complete integration of the individual and the community in a co-operative life-project covering all areas of life and the external relationships of the kibbutz. [The kibbutz] enables the individual to develop to the maximum, strives to solve the problem of the family ... and permits the development of deep personal and moral relationships.[26]

But politics was a major factor in this document, to a degree and in a form quite unthinkable only five years earlier.

The addition of the political element, which from now on would play an increasing part in the ideology and practice of this movement, was the result of a number of historical developments. The intellectual atmosphere of the Diaspora in the mid-1920s militated against the possibility of any mass youth movement's maintaining a non-political (or anti-political) stance: increasing economic deprivation and political persecution led to a vast growth of Communist influence, and the Zionist movements were compelled to present an alternative which viewed the problems of the individual in the context of society as a whole. On the other hand, the movement culture and ideology could not encompass the further step of identification with one of the establishment parties; its members were too conscious of their special character, too jealous of their organizational independence. Thus, having no external forum in which to crystallize their political views, they did so within their own movement. This tendency was strengthened by the fact that they saw Gedud Ha'avoda being torn apart and destroyed by internal political dissension. Their prime concern was to contain such dissensions within the framework of a united movement. They therefore adopted the principle of 'ideological collectivism', defined as 'a framework for continuous ideological action and discussion': a constant search for consensus, a reluctance to reach decisions opposed by a substantial minority, and a readiness to defer the resolution of conflicts or to reach compromises for the sake of movement unity—all this backed by unanimous support for the general movement line once a decision had been made. The movement was not a political party, in that it neither canvassed support nor recruited from outside its own ranks. But in all other respects— independent action within the Histadrut and the Zionist movement, alliances with other groups, adoption of an independent line on current issues—Hashomer Hatzair and the Kibbutz Artzi had all the characteristics of a party.

[26] Ideological Premisses, 302.

Two of the potential components of the Kibbutz Artzi were so opposed to these political formulations that they refused to join the new movement. Kibbutz Beit Alpha was almost equally divided between three political factions: those who accepted the Kibbutz Artzi outlook; supporters of Ahdut Ha'avoda; and the supporters of the left-wing Zionist party Left Poalei Zion. Its members concluded that if the kibbutz joined the new movement, it could not remain whole. The graduates of the Russian movement, on the other hand, supported Ahdut Ha'avoda and joined the Kibbutz Me'uhad at its inception. So the Kibbutz Artzi on the day of its foundation consisted of five groups, only one of them settled on its own land, comprising 286 members.

## Hever Hakvutzot[27]

All the kibbutz movements lost members in 1928 as possibilities of employment attracted those who had wanted to leave but had been unable to do so over the past two years. By the beginning of 1929, both the Kibbutz Me'uhad and the Kibbutz Artzi were receiving reinforcements from their youth movements in Europe. The situation of the unaffiliated *kvutzot* was much more critical.

The fact that people leave the kibbutz can almost be called a natural phenomenon. From the descriptions in the preceding chapters, it is easy to see that such factors as advancing age, ill health, or change in one's way of life (marriage, the birth of children, etc.) could alter an initial enthusiasm for communal life. In today's multi-generational kibbutz, this attrition can be balanced by the absorption of the younger generation, but in the early years of the kibbutz this was not yet possible. The Kibbutz Me'uhad and the Kibbutz Artzi found ways to strengthen their weak kibbutzim through their youth movements. In the veteran *kvutzot*, however, this solution was frowned upon. Their members believed that kibbutz life should be chosen freely by each new immigrant, after he or she had been in the country for some time and was able to weigh up the alternatives, and they consequently disapproved of the 'missionary' work of the youth movements. In reality, however, this work reached out to the vast majority of those who were prepared to join the kibbutz, and virtually all the new immigrants thus went to one of the two major movements.

At the same time, the established *kvutzot*, particularly in the Jordan

[27] This section is based largely on Ben-Avram, *Hever Hakvutzot*, 28–100.

Valley, underwent a steady process of development and agricultural intensification, and this led to a demand for increased manpower to cultivate the available area. The growth of the younger generation and the increased need of personnel for education and child care also strained the resources of the veteran *kvutzot* to an ever-increasing degree. From 1928 onwards, when economic circumstances were such that fewer individuals turned to the *kvutzot*, many of them began to employ hired labour in order to deal with their chronic shortage of manpower. Clearly, such a solution could be considered only as a temporary measure by people who claimed to be building a socialist society where there would be 'neither exploiters nor exploited'.

In the face of this dilemma, several of the small *kvutzot* adopted a solution for which there were a number of precedents in an earlier period: they turned to the Kibbutz Me'uhad or the Kibbutz Artzi for salvation. In exchange for the loss of their independence, they received reinforcements and an assurance of a wider collective responsibility for their future. However, most of the *kvutzot* attempted to solve their problems in concert with other communities similar in structure and outlook. In 1929, those of the former members of Hever Hakvutzot Vehakibbutzim who had not joined one of the major movements in 1927 met at Ginegar. Though not at the time proclaimed as such, this was the beginning of a third movement: Hever Hakvutzot. At this stage, however, it was not clear how they could overcome their crisis. Some speakers at the conference suggested joining the Kibbutz Me'uhad, as the first stage to the creation of a united kibbutz movement including the Kibbutz Artzi. Others expressed their apprehension that the Kibbutz Me'uhad, with its centralized structure and clearly defined ideal of the 'great and growing kibbutz', would destroy the special values of the small *kvutza*.

The struggle between these two groups in Hever Hakvutzot went on for several years. It was effectively resolved only in 1932, with the help of the Gordonia youth movement. When the first organized Gordonia groups began to arrive in Palestine in 1929 they were surprised to find the existing *kvutzot* far from the ideal picture outlined in their movement's ideology. Several of them employed hired labour, cultural life was not always intensive or elevating, and personal relationships within and between the *kvutzot* were often less than perfect. Many veterans had come to doubt whether there was any value in the small *kvutza* as such, and were prepared to attempt to unite with the Kibbutz Me'uhad. But, even in the face of these disillusionments and difficulties, the new immigrants did not abandon the two principles which informed their movement education: continued support for the ideals of Hapoel Hatzair as the inheritor of the mantle of A. D. Gordon; and belief in the *kvutza*, both as a way of life for themselves and as an important component of any future socialist society.

The first Gordonia group took over the site of Hulda, which had been abandoned during an Arab attack in 1929. Successive groups joined existing *kvutzot*, saving them from the choice between dwindling numbers and attachment to an uncongenial movement. This enabled Hever Hakvutzot, which was officially established as an independent movement in 1932, to survive and expand. In 1934, the movement adopted a constitution which defined Gordonia as an 'organic component' of Hever Hakvutzot.

## Ideological Emphases

With the establishment of the link between Hever Hakvutzot and Gordonia, the three kibbutz movements reached a form which remained largely intact until 1951. Many aspects of their outlooks and methods of operation have been described and analysed in the course of the historical exposition in this and previous chapters. I shall therefore add some notes on questions which have not been dealt with fully so far, and close this section of the chapter with a schematic summary of the varieties of kibbutz ideology and practice in the early 1930s.[28]

Every version of kibbutz ideology is utopian, in the sense that it incorporates a more or less clearly defined vision of the society it wishes to create and the place of the kibbutz within it. A comparative analysis of the varieties of kibbutz thought will start from these visions, and then consider the ways which were thought to lead to their realization.

The least clearly defined vision was that of the veteran *kvutzot*. Their aim was basically to increase the number of *kvutzot* and their influence on the world around them; in fact, a reasonable definition of their final aim is a phrase often found in their literature: 'a Land of Israel sown with *kvutzot*'.[29]

With the union between Gordonia and Hever Hakvutzot, this idea was defined rather more precisely. The leaders of Gordonia, who

[28] For the sake of comparison, the viewpoints of Gedud Ha'avoda and Shlomo Lavi are included, although by 1929 they no longer had any practical relevance.

[29] Z. Shatz, *On the Border of Silence*, 92, 98.

were influenced by the currents of socialist thought in the 1930s, spoke of a socialist society in which private ownership of the means of production would be replaced by a variety of social forms, of which the *kvutza* was the most important.

In the *kvutzot*, the words 'example' and 'exemplary' were in very frequent use. They encapsulated the accepted view of the relationship between the *kvutza* and the outside world. If the *kvutza* perfected itself, in terms of standards of work and efficiency and of relationships between its members, others would recognize perfection when they saw it and do likewise. This, in the view of the founders of the *kvutza*, was the only way that it could or should grow; and, as has been noted, until the early 1930s they even rejected as unethical any attempt to persuade others of the superiority of their way of life. The accession of Gordonia to Hever Hakvutzot put an end to the extreme version of this view, but the notion of the *kvutza* as an 'exemplary society' was also part of Gordonia's ideology: one of the functions of the youth movement was considered to be the selection and preparation of people whose standards of behaviour and interaction would be an example to the Yishuv, and even—in the context of the international socialist movement—to the world.

Such a process necessarily limited the number of people who could join the kibbutz. The Kibbutz Me'uhad totally rejected such limitation. Its view of the kibbutz utopia was like that of the Gedud in that it would consist entirely of kibbutzim; but whereas the Gedud aimed to create one big kibbutz covering the whole country, the Kibbutz Me'uhad foresaw a series of kibbutzim, each largely self-sufficient, though linked through the kibbutz movement and maintaining economic, organizational, and cultural ties on a national level. In order to reach this state of affairs, the kibbutz had to expand as quickly as it could, absorbing every person who was prepared to accept kibbutz life and could live up to its standards. In contrast to the Kibbutz Artzi and Gordonia, the Kibbutz Me'uhad rejected the idea of selection of members in the youth movement. Experience had shown, they maintained, that a wide variety of people joined the kibbutz; many of them changed in the process of absorption, and some contributed in unexpected ways to kibbutz life, and even altered it for the better. This 'constant process of becoming' was the true educational process, they claimed; and, although it engendered a high degree of social attrition, it should take place in the kibbutz rather than in the Diaspora.

The process of expansion would lead to social changes in the Yishuv which were very clearly forecast by the leaders of the Kibbutz Me'uhad. The terms in which this prophecy was couched are reminiscent of the Marxist 'law of polarization', with the kibbutz (called by its ideologists 'proletarian', 'working-class', even 'communist') in the place of the working class in the original Marxist schema. *Kvutzot* and moshavim would disappear, become *moshavot*, or join the 'big kibbutz'; and there would finally be a confrontation between the kibbutz and the capitalist sector, corresponding to (and, in fact, called by some kibbutz leaders) the revolution—whose outcome was, as in the Marxist original, in no doubt. All these forecasts were advanced in the framework of the doctrine of 'constructive socialism', whose aim was to build up the Yishuv as a socialist society; the class war was, therefore, not an attempt to destroy the existing system, but to improve on it. In Tabenkin's words, 'We are waging a class war, in terms both of struggle and of construction. Our way of struggle is competition with the other [type of] economy for success.'[30]

In contrast to both the Kibbutz Me'uhad and Hever Hakvutzot, whose approach was essentially incremental, the Kibbutz Artzi proclaimed a revolutionary doctrine, though it postponed its implementation until a later, as yet undefined, stage.[31]

There were further differences between the kibbutz movements on the questions of the nature and size of the kibbutz. The *kvutzot* rejected any tendency to unlimited growth, even though not all went to the extreme of those in Degania Aleph who in 1919 spoke of a limit of twenty families. But economic and social pressures led to a gradual increase in the number of members considered desirable; whereas in 1919 Bussel's aim had been a return to the undifferentiated self-management of the pristine *kvutza*, the emphasis was now on the possibility of deep mutual acquaintance and relationship, in the perspective of a long life together. At this point, the optimum was thought to be about sixty, although one or two *kvutzot* had already passed this number.[32]

Hashomer Hatzair believed in the 'organic' kibbutz. This concept had two elements: all kibbutz members must be prepared for communal life by a long period of education in the youth movement; and

---

[30] At the Third Council of Ein Harod, 1925. See *Kibbutz Me'uhad Anthology*, 106.
[31] See the account of the theory of stages in ch. 3.
[32] On the changes in the concept of the ideal *kvutza*, see Ben-Avram, 'The Formation of the Kvutza Ideology', 39–71.

the kibbutz was composed of groups of movement graduates, growing slowly and cautiously by the accretion of such groups. In the original, more extreme version of this view, the basis of the 'organic' structure of the kibbutz was education and selection in the local youth movement branch, so that any given kibbutz would be composed of groups who had a long history in common. In the course of time, however, groups for settlement came to be made up in the training farms, or even of people from the same area who happened to be immigrating at the same date. Nevertheless, there was always a strong local element in this selection which eased the process of absorption; and the requirement of previous movement education was still considered sacrosanct.

All of this was, of course, anathema to the Kibbutz Me'uhad. In principle, according to the doctrine accepted by the dominant group in this movement, new candidates for membership could be accepted from anywhere; their suitability for kibbutz life would be tested under the real conditions of kibbutz living rather than the artificial situation of the youth movement. Moreover, the new immigrant joined the kibbutz movement, and not one particular part of it: he could be sent to any settlement or *pluga* where he was needed, and even moved thereafter if the state of the kibbutz or the Yishuv required it. In practice, this extreme attitude was somewhat modified. During periods of restricted immigration (in fact, until 1948), preference was given to those who had undergone some training in the Hechalutz farms; and, from the time when the Kibbutz Me'uhad began to recruit new members from the youth movements, it was found more efficient in many cases to absorb and allocate them as groups.

The situation in the Kibbutz Me'uhad was complicated by the fact that among its founder members was the group from Hashomer Hatzair in Russia which had broken away from the Kibbutz Artzi because of their political differences. When the Kibbutz Me'uhad was founded they still believed in the concept of the 'organic kibbutz', and proclaimed their intention of converting the rest of the kibbutz to their viewpoint. Moreover, they felt a deep responsibility for the members of their movement who were still in Russia attempting to carry on their educational work under conditions of persecution and physical danger. When new immigrants from their movement arrived, the veteran members insisted that they join their groups, and not be subject to the overall direction of the Kibbutz Me'uhad.

As a result of their insistence, the definition of the 'open' kibbutz in the constitution of the Kibbutz Me'uhad was amended to read: 'The acceptance of members to a kibbutz is decided by the kibbutz, in accordance with its needs for labour, taking into account its economic *and social* possibilities [my emphasis; H.N.].'[33] This addition did not accord with the view of the majority, but was accepted as a compromise on the insistence of Berl Katznelson, who took an active part in the founding conference, in order to facilitate the foundation of the new kibbutz movement.[34] This meant that from the Kibbutz Me'uhad's first day, there were contradictions of theory and practice on these issues.

On questions of economics, one main issue divided the kibbutz movements. The founders of the *kvutzot*, and the young people of Gordonia at a later stage, believed that one of the major elements of their 'exemplary society' was direct contact with nature and the soil. They therefore refused to engage in industry. This principle was not accepted by either of the other movements. It must be added, however, that although experiments in non-agricultural branches were tried in various parts of the Kibbutz Me'uhad (a tannery at Ein Harod, quarries, transport contracting, carpentry shops), none really took off until the early 1940s, with the changes in the economy of the Yishuv which resulted from the Second World War.

The above comments do not cover two areas in which there were quite considerable differences between the movements: their relationships with the youth movements, and their political attitudes and connections. These subjects were so important at this and later stages that they will be dealt with in more detail in the following chapter, and appear only in summary form in Table 6.

UNITY AND VARIETY

During the decade following the First World War, seven separate varieties of kibbutz ideology developed and were embodied in organizational form. By 1930 three still survived, each buttressed by a nation-wide movement and supported by its own reserves in the youth movements of the Diaspora. Those who know the modern kibbutz may well feel that this very fact needs some historical explanation. The motivations of the three movements were similar, indeed in many respects identical. They derived from common ideological and

---

[33] Kibbutz Me'uhad constitution. See *Kibbutz Me'uhad Anthology*, 324.
[34] Minutes of the founding conference.

TABLE 6. The Kibbutz Movements in the 1920s and 1930s

| | Gedud Ha'Avoda | | Ein Harod/Kibbutz Me'uhad | | | Kibbutz Arzi of Hashomer Hatzair | Hever Hakvutzot |
|---|---|---|---|---|---|---|---|
| | Left | Right | Hashomer Hatzair USSR* | Majority | Lavi | | |
| Stated aims | General commune of all Jewish workers in Palestine | | Continuous expansion and absorption of immigrant workers ... economic and social union between workers in town and country in the independent farm, and in outside work | | | 1. 'To establish Jewish National Home in Palestine on a self-sufficient productive economic basis' | 1. 'The Land of Israel will be sown with *kvutzot*' |
| | Social revolution | Constructive socialism | | | | 2. 'To bring about the social revolution' | 2. 'The *kvutza* is essential for, and the full expression of, the realization of socialist Zionism' |
| Means | Combination of political, economic, and social activity | Agricultural settlement and hired labour** | Maximum absorption and expanding settlement | | Building Ein Harod as social and economic model | 1st stage: Educating youth to kibbutz 2nd stage: Social revolution | Building *kvutzot* as an ethical and social model |
| Type of social unit | According to circumstances – *plugot* and farms, exploiting all possibilities of employment | | 'Organic': youth movement groups form kibbutzim of their own; other units limited by social and economic considerations | 'Open': continuous growth limited only by economic possibilities | Continuous growth of the kibbutz unit limited only by economic possibilities | 'Organic': composed of groups created through education in the youth movement | 'Small' or 'intimate' |

| | | | | | | |
|---|---|---|---|---|---|---|
| members/unit, *c*.1930 | | | | | | |
| Economic structure | Conquest of every category of work | | Combination of agriculture, handicrafts, and industry. Combination of independent farm with outside work | | Not stringently defined; in practice, similar to the Kibbutz Me'uhad | Only agriculture |
| Movement structure | Centralized and pyramidal | | Youth movement retains separate framework in matters of education, immigration, and absorption | Centralized, but each unit has economic autonomy | No 'country-wide' kibbutz movement | Democratic centralism | Federative |
| Links with youth movements | Hechalutz, and 'Young Gedud' until 1924 | | Hashomer Hatzair USSR* | Hechalutz, Hechalutz Hatzair, Dror, Freiheit, Habonim, Noar Oved, Mahanot Olim | Hashomer Hatzair | Gordonia |
| Political connections | Independent lists to Histadrut elections | Opposed to Ahdut Ha'avoda | Ahdut Ha'avoda; after 1930, Mapai | | Independent. 'The kibbutz is an ideological and political collective with a crystallized political position' | Hapoel Hatzair; after 1930, Mapai |
| Terminology | *Plugot* and *meshakim* (farms) organized in the Gedud | | Kibbutzim or *plugot* organized in Kibbutz Me'uhad | *Plugot* and *meshakim* (farms) organized in Kibbutz Ein Harod/Me'uhad | Kibbutzim, organized in the Kibbutz Artzi | *Kvutzot*, organized in the *kvutza* movement = Hever Hakvutzot |

* Name later changed to Netzah.
** Hired labour: Kibbutz members' work outside the kibbutzim (in town, *moshavot*, etc.).

historical sources. Their basic values—Zionism, communitarianism, direct democracy, self-labour—were common to all. And, as subsequent developments have shown, they were at least potentially capable of development in directions which would emphasize their common characteristics rather than their differences. Why, then, did they choose to remain separate?

Generational differences played an important part in creating and perpetuating the differences between the movements. Both Gedud Ha'avoda and Hashomer Hatzair saw themselves as creations of the Third Aliya and consciously rejected the leadership of the Second Aliya. Although both generations were influenced by the revolutionary atmosphere of the countries of their birth, there were important differences between them. The first Russian revolution had failed; the creators of the *kvutza* were therefore deeply disillusioned with comprehensive solutions to mankind's problems, and their attitude tended to be cautious and pragmatic. By contrast, the leaders of Gedud Ha'avoda and Hashomer Hatzair saw themselves as part of a successful, world-wide revolutionary movement (in the broadest sense of that term), which was in the process of achieving both national and social liberation. It is no accident that the *kvutzot* found an ally in Gordonia, which came on the scene at a later date, when the revolution no longer seemed so invincible or untarnished, and evolved a world outlook deeply suspicious of revolutionary ideologies.

The men and women of the Second Aliya arrived in Palestine singly or in tiny groups. Their way and place of life, and often their organizational loyalties, were the result of a process of trial and error in Palestine itself. We find many of them moving from place to place, creating and leaving *kvutzot*, moving from the small to the large *kvutza* and from the *kvutza* to the moshav, as individuals or couples. Pioneers who arrived during the Third Aliya or later came in groups, and were already identified with a movement—usually one with a defined concept of kibbutz society. The movement, the group, and, finally, the kibbutz were their home, and it was of great importance to them to preserve it. If they changed their political views or their concept of the ideal kibbutz society, they rarely moved to another movement but preferred to change their own movement from within or, in the worst case, to leave with a group of like-minded comrades to form a new community based on existing social ties. Thus, the central model of political change in the kibbutz movement from the 1920s onwards is not individual secession, but group schism; and, for the same reason, dissident groups sometimes stayed in the same movement or kibbutz for many years, even though the kibbutz was ideologically split, and they were branded as 'oppositionists'.

Class origins were also of importance in crystallizing basic attitudes and methods of operation. The 'classic' youth movements were founded and led by high-school students, almost all of middle-class origin: only in this social stratum could there occur the confluence of cultural stimulation, leisure, and the *Sturm und Drang* of adolescence which produced the social, intellectual, and emotional ferment essential to the growth of such a movement. Working-class youths were more likely to be attracted to a mass movement such as Hechalutz, with its less demanding intellectual and social ambience. Although each of these types of movement made a deliberate attempt to break out of its own social grouping, these origins affected both their social make-up and the type of youth they recruited. And what was true of the youth movements became true of the kibbutz movements which their graduates created and joined.

These differences were further compounded by geographical divisions. The Russian members of Hashomer Hatzair shared many of the characteristics of their Polish and Galician comrades. But, since they grew up face to face with the realities of Soviet power, they never adopted the non-political or anti-political stance of the Galician section; such an attitude would simply have been a flight from reality. And, having seen for themselves the nature of the Soviet regime, they could not adopt the pro-Soviet ideology which was one of the hallmarks of the majority in Hashomer Hatzair from the late 1920s onwards. Their basic political attitudes were fixed from an early stage.

Geographical differences also accounted for differences in more intangible characteristics such as political culture and methods of social interaction. In this respect, each movement attuned its methods of recruitment, style of argument, and even its organizational framework to its own target population. Thus, from a very early stage, Hashomer Hatzair was dominant in Galicia, and Hechalutz in Greater Poland. Each worked in accordance with the special characteristics of the local Jewish community; and these characteristics were reproduced in the ways of life of their kibbutzim. To a very large extent, each area produced the type of kibbutz appropriate to its culture.

Despite these factors, the history of the kibbutz movements in their formative period provides little support for theories of anthropological or economic determinism. Sectoralism, whether regional, generational, or economic, was frowned on in the labour movement, and open identification of a kibbutz movement with a particular sector (such as that of Gedud Ha'avoda with the Third Aliya) was exceptional. Although influenced by the differing elements described above, the social make-up of most of the kibbutz movements cut across divisions of national origin, class, and generation. We have already seen that Gedud Ha'avoda was composed of three different social elements. By 1927, Hashomer Hatzair had branches in almost every European Jewish community, including Greater Poland, the stronghold of Hechalutz; and this fact was reflected in the composition of the Kibbutz Artzi. In 1923, the leaders of the Ein Harod faction in the Gedud were veterans of the Second Aliya, but many of their supporters were young men and women of the Third Aliya; and immediately after the secession they were joined by Havurat Ha'emek, a group composed entirely of Third Aliya pioneers. The distinctions between the left and right wings in the Gedud and the political divisions in Beit Alpha were not generational, economic, or cultural, but ideological.

Whatever the relative strength of the various sources of conviction—*Zeitgeist* or *Landgeist*, class origins or rational—they coalesced, in most cases, into a firm ideological mind-set. On a minimum of empirical evidence, a logical structure was built which became an article of faith: the superiority of the big kibbutz in absorbing immigrants, the greater social solidarity of the small *kvutza*, the indispensability of youth movement education for kibbutz life— each of these was held to be vital to the future of the kibbutz. A close examination of the arguments in favour of each of them will reveal a plethora of rhetoric and rational proof, and a minimum of empirical evidence: indeed, it may be argued that until the mid-1930s, when each of these alternatives had been tried for some years, the evidence was not yet available. But it was very rare indeed to find one of the ideologists of the kibbutz entering a plea of 'not yet proven', as Levi Shkolnik (Eshkol) did in 1923.[35]

This inner certainty is, in effect, only one aspect of a much greater inner certainty: the belief in the correctness of the kibbutz way of life and its ability to survive. We have seen that the kibbutz was under almost constant attack practically from its inception. The evidence from reality was at best ambiguous. Without a firmly rooted belief system couched in rational (or supposedly rational) terms, none of

---

[35] See above, ch. 2.

the kibbutz movements could have survived. And if this applied to the idea of the kibbutz as a whole, it applied *a fortiori* to the different varieties of that idea. The leaders and ideologists of the kibbutz believed that they held the key to the survival of the Yishuv and the Jewish people. They could not wait to see whether they or others were right; history would not wait for the completion of the experiment. Without a firmly entrenched ideology, the kibbutz could not have survived the crises of the 1920s. The struggle between the movements is the obverse side of their common faith.

Thus, history, geography, sociology, and ideology all contributed to the crystallization and differentiation of the kibbutz movements. One more factor must be noted: that of personality. Each movement produced, and was in large measure shaped by, its leaders. Without their devotion, faith, and ability, the movements would have lacked much of their strength and cohesion. But here again, there was an obverse side to these qualities. We have seen that the obstinacy of Shlomo Lavi was a prime factor in splitting Gedud Ha'avoda, and almost splitting Ein Harod. Yitzhak Tabenkin, while wiser and more flexible in tactical matters, was no less rigid in his basic ideological approach, and dominated his movement from the moment that it left Gedud Ha'avoda. As against Tabenkin and the Kibbutz Me'uhad, the leaders of Hever Hakvutzot were less self-confident and more self-effacing in relations with their comrades; while Meir Ya'ari led the Kibbutz Artzi in a more circumspect manner, as fitted a movement which still proclaimed its belief in the independence of the youth movement. As we shall see in future chapters, each of these men also contributed his share to the progress of the kibbutz movement, and to its continued division.

# 5

## After the Crisis: Recovery and Growth, 1927–1935

THIS chapter and the next cover the period of transition from the relatively stable world of the 1920s to a world already disfigured by many of the characteristic ills of modern times: economic crises, dictatorships, and the threat of war. For the Jewish people, these actual and potential catastrophes were compounded by the rise of Hitler, the growth of antisemitism throughout Europe, and the unwillingness of most of the world to grant refuge to Jews fleeing from persecution. Against this background, it seemed that the Zionist prognosis was being fulfilled, though in circumstances worse than any of the fathers of Zionism had foreseen; for in the spring of 1932 there began an unparalleled period of prosperity and development in the Yishuv, fed by and feeding immigration in numbers which were far beyond anything that had yet been known.[1]

The first signs of change in the Yishuv were far from encouraging. In August 1929 there was a series of Arab attacks on Jews in Palestine. They did much damage to a number of Jewish communities and villages, and no less to some of the assumptions on which Zionist policy had been based: the belief that Arab nationalism either did not exist or could be contained with ease by a firm hand on the part of the Mandatory government; and the confidence that support for the Jewish national home was an unalterable element of that government's policy. Although the actual destruction done by the riots was small compared with what was to come some seven years later, it proved to British and Jews alike that the third side of the Palestinian triangle was a force to be reckoned with. The British, whose policy was laid down in the Shaw, Hope-Simpson, and Passfield reports (1930–1),

---

[1] For a general account of the Zionist movement during this period, see Laqueur, *A History of Zionism*, chs. 7, 10, 11. The description of the progress of settlement is partly based on Bein, *History of Zionist Settlement*, ch. 7.

maintained that the cause of the riots was Jewish immigration and settlement, and the resulting Arab landlessness. Their conclusion was that Jewish land purchases should be restricted, and immigration stringently regulated in accordance with the absorptive capacity of the country. The Zionist movement accepted none of these conclusions or policies, and managed to have their immediate execution cancelled by the Macdonald letter of February 1931. From the Zionist point of view, the chief long-term effect of the 1929 riots was the new focus of British policy on problems of Arab landlessness, and the effects of Arab nationalism on the future of the Mandate. This trend came to fruition only at a much later date. But the potential threat to the future of the Yishuv was clear; and the reduction of the workers' immigration schedule from two thousand in previous years to nine hundred in 1931 showed how seriously political decisions could influence the development of the Yishuv and the labour movement.

The reaction of the Yishuv, the Zionist movement, and the Jewish people to the events of 1929 was vigorous, and, in the long run, positive. Despite the element of surprise, most of the Jewish settlements had managed to defend themselves; and those that were destroyed (with the exception of the Jewish community of Hebron, which was revived only in 1967) were rebuilt. The pioneering youth movements sent increased numbers of immigrants from the training farms. As a result, the adult population of the kibbutz movements rose from somewhat fewer than twenty-five hundred in 1929 to almost four thousand by the end of 1930—not far from the figures of the 'boom year' of 1927.

All of this, however, is dwarfed in the broad historical picture by other events which began in the autumn of 1929. The world economic crisis which began in the United States soon spread to Europe, and one of the results of the changes it brought was the rise and triumph of Nazism. Of more immediate interest to the Jews was the impoverishment of European Jewry, and particularly the Polish community, which came in its wake. In the long run, Hitler's accession to power was of more consequence to both Polish and German Jewry than the economic and social problems of either community. But between 1932 and 1935 Polish Jews fleeing from poverty and unemployment competed with German Jews threatened by physical persecution for the immigration certificates which would assure escape from their lands of birth and resettlement in Palestine.

From the beginning of the slump of 1929, an atmosphere of

approaching cataclysm was abroad in the world, particularly among
the Jewish people. Communists saw the predictions of Marx verified,
and prepared for the coming revolution. To them, and to many more
moderate democrats and socialists, it seemed that only the Soviet
Union could save Europe from conquest by the forces of violent
reaction. Antisemites blamed the world's ills on the Jews, and became
increasingly extreme and violent in their theory and practice. The
Jews of Eastern Europe, particularly of its largest concentration, in
Poland, had been suffering from a dual crisis, of poverty and endemic
antisemitism, ever since the granting of independence to the smaller
European states in the wake of the First World War. Now the sense
of crisis became even more acute; the looming threat of Hitler's
accession to power gave impetus to ever more extreme antisemitic
movements, while the economic depression made life increasingly
intolerable. It is not surprising that these events gave rise to forecasts
of a coming global war. In 1933, Yitzhak Tabenkin said: 'Our socialism
says: there is no peace, no middle way. There is a final battle. It may
last many years, but it will be final. All the economic and cultural
conditions are ripe.'[2] In the case of the Jewish people, this general
apocalyptic prognosis had special applications. Desperation bred
extremism. Many Jews were attracted to Communism. Within the
nationalist camp, extremist parties gained strength rapidly—particularly the Revisionist party, with its emphasis on military strength
and national unity.

Despite this generally gloomy picture, there was one bright area: a
number of factors combined to make Palestine one of the most
prosperous and attractive spots on the Jewish map, and certainly the
best hope of escape for European Jewry. These included the favoured
rate of exchange of sterling, the flourishing state of citrus fruit production, and, above all, the immigration of German Jews (much of
whose capital was transferred either individually or as part of an
agreement negotiated by the Jewish Agency with the German government) and the comparatively liberal immigration policy of the high
commissioner of Palestine, Sir Arthur Wauchope. In consequence, in
the spring of 1932 there began a new wave of Jewish immigration to
Palestine which doubled the population of the Yishuv in the years
from 1931 to 1935. As a result, the numbers in the Hechalutz movement and on the training farms also rose spectacularly. In 1933 Berl

---

[2] *Report of Kibbutz Me'uhad Council, Yagur, 1933* (mimeo), 76–7.

Katznelson spoke of the imminent 'conquest' of the vast majority of Jewish youth by the pioneering movements.[3]

The outcome of all these factors was that the Yishuv grew from 175,000 in 1931 to 350,000 in 1935.[4] The ever-growing wave of German immigrants and the associated influx of capital led to a cycle of development and modernization, full employment, and possibilities of further immigration which came to an end only with the economic crisis which followed the Italian invasion of Abyssinia in 1936.

For the labour movement this was a period of increasing power and confidence, together with a growing realization of the gravity of the problems for which the movement was assuming responsibility. The unification of the two major parties (Ahdut Ha'avoda and Hapoel Hatzair) in 1930 to form Mapai gave that party a majority of some 80 per cent in the Histadrut and enabled it to put into practice its intention of 'conquering the Zionist movement'.[5] Here, although the General Zionists were still the main power, there was a real possibility that they would be overtaken by the Revisionist Party—a radical nationalist group led by Vladimir Jabotinsky, who demanded the militarization of Jewish youth in order to realize what he believed to be the true aim of Zionism: a Jewish state on both sides of the Jordan River. Some groups in the Revisionist movement had been influenced by Fascist ideas, and they were widely viewed in the labour movement as Zionist fascists. Certainly, they were violently opposed to the strength and political influence of the Histadrut and the Labour Zionist parties.

By 1931, Revisionist representation at the Zionist Congress had reached 19 per cent, as against the Labour faction's 27 per cent. But this turned out to be the peak of the Revisionists' strength. In 1933 they had 17 per cent of the delegates and the Labour movement 41 per cent. Following the congress of 1935 Ben-Gurion, leader of the Labour faction, with 45 per cent of the delegates, was appointed chairman of the Executive of the Jewish Agency, thus confirming Labour's control over wide areas of Zionist policy. At about the same time, the Revisionists seceded from the Zionist movement. These events had a profound effect on many aspects of the development of

[3] In the discussion on Hechalutz in the Kibbutz Me'uhad Secretariat, Nov. 1933. Mimeoed version, entitled *On Questions of Our Movement in the Diaspora*, 12.

[4] Gurevich *et al.*, *Jewish Population of Palestine*, 30, 78.

[5] See Laqueur, *History of Zionism*, 314–20.

the kibbutz movement, ranging from the number of new settlements to its members' political attitudes.

## ECONOMICS AND SETTLEMENT

With the crystallization of the three major kibbutz movements and the break-up of Gedud Ha'avoda, there was no longer any dissent from the proposition that their main end was settlement—the establishment of new agricultural communities and the consolidation of those that already existed. This section will describe and evaluate their success in this enterprise, from the year of the foundation of the Kibbutz Me'uhad and the Kibbutz Artzi in 1927 until the end of 1935, when the Yishuv was on the brink of a new and decisive period in its history.

### Depression and Recovery

The year 1927 was the height of the economic depression which brought to an end so many of the hopes and plans of the Fourth Aliya. The labour movement, and especially the kibbutz movement, drew some comfort from the contradictory processes which took place during the crisis years: the fact that, during a major depression in the Yishuv, the agricultural sector continued to grow and even, relatively, to prosper; the spontaneous growth of the kibbutz movement as a reaction to the unemployment and despondency of the towns; and, perhaps most important of all from the point of view of the kibbutz, the continued immigration of groups of Hechalutz members at the very time when more Jews were leaving the country than were entering it. The result was a moderate growth in the kibbutz population: in absolute numbers, from 2,300 in 1925 to 4,097 in 1927; proportionately, from 2.3 per cent of the Yishuv to 2.7 per cent.[6]

None the less, the crisis caused grave damage to the kibbutz. Politically, it brought to power in the Zionist movement an executive unsympathetic to the ideals of the labour movement. This basic hostility was compounded by the drop in the income of the national funds, which virtually brought agricultural settlement to a halt for three years. In 1927, three kibbutzim and three moshavim were set up, on the basis of planning and funds dating from the period of prosperity. In 1928–9, only two kibbutzim and one moshav were established.

[6] Near, *Kibbutz and Society*, 418–19.

In 1930, the process of settlement seemed about to recommence—paradoxically, as the result of the Arab attacks on Jewish settlements in the autumn of the previous year: the pioneering youth movements responded by sending reinforcements in larger numbers than previously, and the Jewish communities of the world subscribed to an emergency fund, whose purpose was to restore the Jewish villages which had been destroyed in the riots and strengthen the defence capabilities of others. This aim was partly achieved: wooden huts were replaced by permanent buildings, and roads were built to isolated settlements. But apart from this, the kibbutz movement was helped relatively little by this moderate revival of Zionist finances: only one kibbutz was refounded in 1930, as against the creation of four new moshavim.

During the late 1920s, the leaders of the Zionist movement had seen the establishment of the expanded Jewish Agency as one way of relieving its economic distress and renewing the process of construction in the Yishuv. It was thought that by mobilizing support from wealthy and influential Jews who were not prepared to call themselves Zionists but were sympathetic to the Zionist idea, new sources of revenue would be opened up. The new body was inaugurated in September 1929. However, unfortunately for the grandiose plans of the Zionist leaders, this event was quickly followed by the great depression, which began in the United States just one month later, and spread to all the countries of Eastern Europe during the following year. Contributions to the Zionist funds declined immediately. This situation proved to be particularly unfortunate for the kibbutzim.

By now, the process of settlement had taken on regular administrative forms. The land was acquired by the Jewish National Fund (JNF) and allocated by its directorate to settlement groups (of kibbutzim or moshavim) according to priorities decided in consultation with the appropriate organ of the Histadrut, the Agricultural Centre (Mercaz Hakla'i). Start-up capital, livestock, and initial loans for equipment were provided by the Keren Hayesod ('Palestine Foundation Fund'). This body was responsible for the financial stability of the settlements until they were considered able to function independently. At that point, the amount they owed for financial support in their early years was calculated, and it was supplemented by a 'consolidating' loan designed to cover their basic needs in equipment and housing. From then onwards, they would pay rent to the JNF and begin to pay interest and return the money they had received from the Keren Hayesod.

This process of consolidation was first mooted in 1924, but the economic straits of the settlements and the national funds, and difficulties in negotiating the terms of the agreement, postponed its implementation until May 1935. This was not only a technical question. The ideology of 'workers' settlement' was deeply opposed to the notion that Jewish workers should be granted ownership of land or gifts of money by institutions financed by the Jewish people. Therefore, the repayment of loans and the payment of rent on nationally owned land became a matter of principle; and a settlement's ability to do so was interpreted as a sign of economic success:

During 1936, a major event in the affairs of the workers' settlements took place. The veteran kibbutzim and moshavim paid the first instalments of their debts to the JNF and Keren Hayesod.... It is not prosperity that enables the settlements to pay. Many of them are still struggling with difficult economic problems ... debts and high rates of interest ... lack of credit for development and working capital.... But they have decided that their debt to the national funds must be paid, together with their other essential expenditure.

These payments are a sign and symbol of the success of the workers' settlements, their economic progress and their healthy development. They prove that they can stand firm, and shoulder their responsibilities.[7]

This was the comment of the Agricultural Centre of the Histadrut when, in September 1936, the veteran kibbutzim and moshavim made the first repayments of their loans. The report of the Keren Hayesod itself said: 'Making this payment has become a ritual for the farmers, and each of them pays the money with all speed.'[8]

## Settlement

In 1930, the Keren Hayesod was still far from being able to consolidate its loans to the veteran settlers. Its income fell from a maximum of P£583,000 in 1926/7 to P£274,000 in 1930/1, and began to rise moderately only in 1933/4.[9] There were, however, many reasons for attempting to renew the momentum of settlement. Politically, the

---

[7] *UAW Report* (1939), 74.

[8] Ulitzur, *National Capital and Construction*, 64.

[9] Ibid. 37.

Zionist authorities were unwilling to create the impression that the Arab riots and British pressure were deterring them from extending the area of Jewish cultivation, particularly in view of the hostility expressed in the Hope-Simpson report. This factor was underscored by the fact that the JNF had purchased wide areas of land which could be occupied almost immediately. Further, there was a backlog of groups waiting for settlement—the surviving *havurot* of the slump period, and the pioneers who had arrived during the past three years, when settlement had virtually stopped. The Histadrut's Agricultural Centre had proposed a scheme known as the Thousand Families Plan, but the financial support to put it into operation was lacking.

This scheme was eventually carried out by a consortium of the Keren Hayesod with investors from England, Germany, and North America. It fulfilled only part of the hopes it raised: only 432 families were settled, instead of the thousand originally envisaged. The representatives of the company set up by the consortium proved to be rigid in their outlook, and suspicious of the intentions and ability of the settlers and of the Histadrut's negotiators. These suspicions were directed particularly at the kibbutz groups—so much so that, in the event, only two kibbutzim received support; and even this was scarcely more than nominal. This was a far cry from the trust and support which the Zionist movement had given so freely to workers' settlement, and first and foremost to the kibbutzim. In sum, though the Thousand Families Plan took some four years to come to fruition, it broke the impasse in settlement and helped to found ten new moshavim. But it left a residue of bitterness and suspicion in the kibbutz movement which was to have far-reaching effects.[10]

These feelings were strengthened by the next large-scale settlement scheme undertaken by the Zionist authorities, in the Hefer Valley (Wadi Hawarith). This valley lies between two major areas of Jewish settlement, on the coastal plain between Hadera and what has since become the township of Netanya. The land was purchased by the JNF in 1929, but settlement was delayed by the resistance of the Arabs who lived on, though they did not own, the land. The legal and political struggles over this area lasted almost four years; but the plan for Jewish settlement was ready by 1930, and the first group of settlers started working in the area at that time. This settlement

---

[10] Near, *Kibbutz and Society*, 275–7.

scheme differed from those that preceded it in that it was planned integratively, and emphasized the development of the area as a whole—including such matters as developing water resources and draining swamps. Land was allocated to settlers of different social origins. Of the twenty-four settlements eventually set up, eleven were devoted to what was defined as 'middle-class settlement', nine to moshavim, and only four to kibbutzim. Many of the middle-class settlements were up-dated versions of the pre-war *ahuzot*—citrus orchards whose owners took charge of them only when they began to give fruit, until which time they were tended by a contracting firm of the Histadrut (Yakhin).

The plan for middle-class settlement was partly designed to combat accusations of political bias on the part of the settlement authorities. It also came in response to the increased 'capitalist' immigration, particularly from Germany, which began in the spring of 1932. Palestine had become the most prosperous—and, with the increased immigration schedules from 1932 onwards, one of the most accessible—parts of the Jewish world; it was becoming clear that citrus was one of the country's most profitable products; and there was no doubt that the Hefer Valley was eminently suited to citrus growing. It was not surprising, therefore, that the Jewish Agency should encourage middle-class settlement, a much greater proportion of which would be financed by the settlers themselves than was the case in kibbutzim and moshavim.

The Hefer Valley plan was not the only framework for middle-class settlement. From 1933 onwards, groups of German Jews settled in villages which fitted none of the definitions accepted at the time. New immigrants, many of them with no agricultural background, developed a type of settlement based on intensive farming: mainly poultry and market gardening. The social structure of these communities was varied, but most of them adopted methods close to those of the moshav, based on family holdings, with a high degree of co-operation in marketing and other matters, though on privately owned land. The results of the events and tendencies described here can be seen in Table 7. This process drastically altered the numerical relationship between kibbutzim and other forms of rural settlement. In 1927, there were 24 kibbutzim, 10 moshavim, and 18 young *moshavot* (established after 1918); in 1935, there were 41 kibbutzim and 39 moshavim, in addition to the 22 *moshavot* and 8 middle-class settlements founded during this period.

TABLE 7. New Jewish Settlement, 1927–1935

| Year | Kibbutzim | | | | Moshavim | *Moshavot* | Middle-class settlements | Urban |
|---|---|---|---|---|---|---|---|---|
| | Kibbutz Me'uhad | Kibbutz Artzi | Hever Hakvutzot | Total | | | | |
| 1927 | 0 | 1 | 2 | 3 | 2 | 1 | 0 | 1 |
| 1928 | 1 | 0 | 0 | 1 | 0 | 1 | 0 | 0 |
| 1929 | 0 | 1 | 0 | 1 | 1 | 4 | 0 | 0 |
| 1930 | 1 | 0 | 1 | 2 | 4 | 0 | 0 | 0 |
| 1931 | 0 | 1 | 0 | 1 | 0 | 3 | 0 | 0 |
| 1932 | 3 | 0 | 1 | 4 | 6 | 6 | 0 | 0 |
| 1933 | 0 | 2 | 2 | 4 | 10 | 5 | 3 | 2 |
| 1934 | 0 | 0 | 0 | 0 | 4 | 0 | 4 | 2 |
| 1935 | 2 | 2 | 0 | 4 | 4 | 2 | 1 | 1 |
| Total | 7 | 7 | 6 | 20 | 31 | 22 | 8 | 6 |

*Source:* Based on Gurevich *et al.*, *Jewish Population of Palestine*, 280–1.

Not all of this was disadvantageous to the kibbutz. One of the innovations of the Thousand Families Scheme had been the introduction of a principle dictated by necessity: the demand that settlers themselves contribute financially to the settlement process. Although the leaders of the kibbutz movements feared that this would increase the inequality between settlers, particularly in moshavim, and reduce the number of new kibbutzim, it proved to be a positive method of surmounting the financial distress of the national funds. The *plugot* in the Hefer Valley and other places worked in the citrus groves, drained swamps, built houses in Hadera and Netanya, and saved enough capital to make the financial contribution to their eventual settlement demanded by the settlement authorities.

None the less, the rate of settlement achieved in this period was far from satisfying the demands of the kibbutz movements. The growing number of immigrants from Hechalutz and the youth movements increased the numbers in the *plugot*. In 1928, after the break-up of the *havurot*, there were 2.8 kibbutz members in established farms as against every 1 in a *pluga*. By 1935, the proportion had changed to almost exactly 2 to 1. The existence of a great and growing reserve army of pioneers who saw their future as members of settled kibbutzim was a powerful factor in the shaping of the policies of the kibbutz movements and the labour movement alike.[11]

[11] Ibid. 419.

*The Structure of Kibbutz Agriculture*

This period also witnessed important changes in the agricultural structure of the kibbutzim.[12] During virtually the whole period of Zionist settlement until the Second World War, the overall pattern of Jewish agriculture remained constant: roughly one-third of the land was devoted to fruit cultivation, while field crops were grown on the remaining two-thirds. Until the First World War, the fruit crops had been mainly grapes, but from the mid-1920s onwards this sector was dominated by citrus fruit: between 1927 and 1936, the area devoted to citrus increased nine-fold, and in 1936 reached 15,300 hectares—29 per cent of the area cultivated by Jews in that year.

The vast majority of the orchards, during every period, were in the *moshavot*, under private ownership. From the beginning the kibbutzim and moshavim, under the guidance of the Zionist movement, rejected this economic model. The monocultural economy of the *moshavot* of the First Aliya had made them dependent on the vagaries of the world market and, consequently, on philanthropic support. The farms which were set up in the Second Aliya—including the *moshavot* of Galilee, where the founders of the first kibbutzim learnt their farming skills—originally had as their model the self-sufficient family farms of Russia and Eastern Europe. This model soon proved to be impractical, and local conditions—the type of soil, and the lack of irrigation facilities—dictated the shape of the economy: extensive dry arable farming, based mainly on biennial rotation of wheat and barley with beans and sorghum. In this the pattern of Jewish agriculture at first differed little from that of the Arabs, apart from the gradual introduction of modern implements such as the European plough. The produce was sold on the local market. Degania and Kinneret adopted the same basic model: both the economic structure of the farm and the work methods of the kibbutz founders emphasized the primacy of arable crops. But from a very early stage additional branches were added, for social and economic reasons alike.

In 1925 Arthur Ruppin, the main policy-maker of Zionist agricultural settlement, wrote a short book describing the approach and achievements of the Zionist movement at that point.[13] After a brief historical introduction he devoted the first chapter to 'the principle

[12] The following outline of the development of Jewish agriculture is based partly on the historical survey in Gurevich and Gertz, *Jewish Agricultural Settlement*, 31–40, 57–69.

[13] Ruppin, *The Zionist Organization's Agricultural Settlement*.

of the mixed economy'. Ruppin gave three major reasons for the adoption of this principle: monocultural farms demand unequal numbers of working hands at different seasons, and therefore necessitate the employment of hired labour, usually Arab; the agricultural or commercial failure of a single crop threatens the very existence of the whole farm; and, considering the primitive state of transport and the marketing system, crops sold on the local market are more profitable. It is therefore wise, he counselled, to vary the crops grown and aim at the greatest possible degree of economic autarky. It was in view of these considerations, he added, that the Zionist movement's experimental farm at Ben Shemen copied and improved on the methods of the first mixed farms in Palestine, those of the German Templar sect, particularly in the production of milk and poultry.[14] He also listed other crops which had been tried in various places—notably vegetables, which were developed as a result of the conditions of semi-starvation during the war, and various types of fruit.

All this was relevant to the development of the kibbutz and the moshav. Even before the war, Degania had sent Miriam Baratz to Ben Shemen for several months to learn new methods of dairy farming, and made a number of attempts to plant fruit trees. There was, in fact, general agreement that it was necessary to increase the number of crops grown. But scrutiny of the minutes of the general meetings in which this question was discussed reveals a further dimension to Ruppin's purely economic reasoning.

Almost all of Ruppin's economic arguments were adduced, as well as some others. But the major reasons put forward for varying the kibbutz economy were ideological. There were no Arabs employed in Degania; but the pressure of seasonal work had led to the occasional employment of Jewish workers from Tiberias, and it was feared that, if the agricultural structure of the kibbutz were not changed, this might become a permanent arrangement. Some speakers emphasized the need for the kibbutz to exploit its members' initiative and ability to the maximum. The fact that at any given time 20 per cent of the labour force was ineffective because of illness was a further stimulus for providing alternative, less exhausting, sources of income. But the argument most frequently advanced was the need to promote social equality, both by creating new work branches alongside the

---

[14] Yitzhak Wilkansky, the manager of the Ben Shemen farm and an accepted authority on agricultural methods, argued the case for the mixed economy forcibly from 1912 onwards; Wilkansky, *On the Way*, chs. 2, 9.

prestigious, but physically very demanding, field crops, and by providing agricultural occupations suitable for women. In Degania's balance sheet for 1920/1, the following crops appear, in addition to the by now traditional field crops, milk, and poultry: vegetables, bees, citrus fruit, almonds, olives, and eucalyptus trees. Other *kvutzot*, both those established before the First World War and those set up in the first few years of the Third Aliya, adopted a similar pattern, with regional variations.[15]

The extension of the kibbutz movement with the settlement of the Jezreel Valley led to a further growth in arable crops, both because of the lack of irrigation and because it was necessary to cultivate extensive areas with comparatively little manpower. But a succession of natural disasters (droughts, mice, and diseases) confirmed the lessons of previous years: the kibbutz community could not afford to be dependent on a single type of crop. By the mid-1930s modern methods of cultivation had turned wheat and oats into profitable crops. The development of irrigation projects in almost every area of kibbutz settlement further encouraged the tendency to diversify the economy, in accordance with the demands of the market, the characteristics of soil and climate, and the initiative of the settlers. Thus, dairy herds and poultry were developed, and bananas and other fruit trees—including citrus, though in the context of a mixed economy— were planted. To complement this development, the Histadrut established a country-wide marketing co-operative, Tnuva, to channel the produce of kibbutzim and moshavim to the Jewish community. But Jewish agriculture was still very far from supplying all the needs of the Yishuv. Until the Arab revolt of 1936, the two economies were integrated to a great extent: some commodities (particularly vegetables) were largely produced in the Arab sector, while others (including various sorts of fruit) were imported from the neighbouring Arab countries.

## The Kibbutz Economy, 1929–1935

Table 8, which compares the kibbutz economy in 1929 with that of 1935, shows the practical implications of these trends. The total area

---

[15] Minutes of annual general meetings of Degania Aleph, Jan. 1917, pp. 5–7, 9, 15, 22; 31 Mar. and 1 Apr. 1919, *passim*; preserved in the archives of the kibbutz. The annual balance sheets of the kibbutz, also found there, reflect the gradual broadening of the economic structure of the community.

TABLE 8. Kibbutzim and Moshavim: Crops and Income, 1929–1935

| | 1929 | | | | 1934/5 | | | | 1935/6 | | | |
| | Area | | Income | | Area | | Income | | Area | | Income | |
| | ha | % | P£ | % | ha | % | P£ | % | ha | % | P£ | % |
|---|---|---|---|---|---|---|---|---|---|---|---|---|
| **Arable crops**[a] | | | | | | | | | | | | |
| Kibbutzim | 5,000 | 83.0 | 47,000 | 36.5 | 9,500 | 83.0 | 9,500 | 14.6 | 9,400 | 82.0 | 58,000 | 10.0 |
| Moshavim | 3,200 | 84.0 | .. | .. | .. | .. | .. | .. | 4,400 | 70.0 | .. | .. |
| **Fodder crops**[b] | | | | | | | | | | | | |
| Kibbutzim | .. | .. | .. | .. | 360 | 3.3 | 17,000 | 3.2 | 480 | 4.0 | 22,600 | 4.0 |
| Moshavim | .. | .. | .. | .. | .. | .. | .. | .. | 80 | 1.5 | .. | .. |
| **Vegetables** | | | | | | | | | | | | |
| Kibbutzim | 90 | 1.5 | 9,000 | 7.2 | 100 | 1.0 | 20,000 | 3.7 | 180 | 1.5 | 34,000 | 5.8 |
| Moshavim | 80 | .. | .. | .. | .. | .. | .. | .. | 200 | .. | .. | .. |
| **Fruit trees** | | | | | | | | | | | | |
| Kibbutzim | 340 | 3.5 | 12,000 | 9.4 | 740 | 7.4 | 48,000 | 9.0 | 860 | 7.6 | 59,000 | 10.2 |
| Moshavim | 180 | 4.8 | .. | .. | .. | .. | .. | .. | 900 | 14.0 | .. | .. |
| **Tree nurseries** | | | | | | | | | | | | |
| Kibbutzim | 7.5 | .. | .. | .. | 52.2 | .. | .. | .. | 54 | .. | .. | .. |
| Moshavim | 0.2 | .. | .. | .. | .. | .. | .. | .. | .. | .. | .. | .. |
| **Total field crops** | | | | | | | | | | | | |
| Kibbutzim | 5,600 | .. | .. | .. | 11,070 | .. | .. | .. | 11,350 | .. | .. | .. |
| Moshavim | 3,700 | .. | .. | .. | 7,800 | .. | .. | .. | 6,300 | .. | .. | .. |
| **Other branches**[c] | | | | | | | | | | | | |
| Milk | – | – | 33,000 | 25.7 | – | – | 120,000 | 22.5 | – | – | 128,000 | 22.1 |
| Poultry and eggs | – | – | 11,000 | 8.5 | – | – | 38,000 | 7.1 | – | – | 49,700 | 8.6 |
| Sheep and honey | – | – | 3,800 | 3.0 | – | – | 11,500 | 2.2 | – | – | 11,500 | 2.0 |
| **Total income**[c] | | | | | | | | | | | | |
| Agriculture | – | – | 116,078 | 90.3 | – | – | 332,372 | 62.3 | – | – | 363,412 | 62.7 |
| Industry | – | – | 860 | 0.7 | – | – | 79,000 | 14.8 | – | – | 90,000 | 15.5 |
| Outside work | – | – | 11,400 | 9.0 | – | – | 122,000 | 22.9 | – | – | 126,000 | 21.8 |
| Total[c] | – | – | 128,342 | – | – | – | 533,406 | – | – | – | 579,825 | – |

*Source:* Based on tables in *UAW Report* (1939), 202–21.
*Notes:* .. no data available; [a] Not irrigated; [b] Irrigated; [c] Kibbutzim only.

of agricultural land cultivated by the kibbutzim doubled, but non-irrigated arable crops still took up more than 80 per cent of the cultivated area in both years. In 1929, the majority of the remainder was devoted to cultivating a variety of fruits—in ascending order of area cultivated, bananas, citrus fruit, deciduous hard fruits, olives and nuts, and grapes. By 1935 the proportion of land under fruit crops

had risen to 7.6 per cent. This was mainly due to the addition of
nearly 300 hectares of citrus, which was now the most extensively
grown fruit; but almost all the varieties grown six years earlier still
remained part of the kibbutz economy. The general trend in the
country was quite different: the area of citrus fruit grew from 1,700
hectares in 1927 to 15,100 hectares in 1935, comprising 28 per cent
of the area under Jewish cultivation.

To an extent, the reason for the special nature of the kibbutz
economy was geographical: only about one-third of the kibbutzim
were situated in the coastal plain, which had proved to yield outstanding orange crops. But grapefruit had been grown in the Jezreel
Valley since the late 1920s, and the land and water available could
well have been used to increase this most profitable crop; and even
the kibbutzim of the coastal plain planted only very moderate areas
of citrus. The reluctance to adopt the farming pattern embraced
enthusiastically by the great majority of the Yishuv's farmers was the
result of a deliberate ordinance of self-denial. This policy, which
was in principle common to both kibbutzim and moshavim, was
expounded in an article by one of the officials of the Histadrut's
Agricultural Centre, discussing the planning of the moshav at the
height of the 'citrus rush':

We believe (as do all the settlement authorities to the best of my knowledge)
that the overall natural, historical, and technical conditions of the country
demand a variegated economy, and the greatest possible variety of branches
in each farm, even though not every branch is equally profitable.... This is
also important in order to spread out the risk over a number of branches....
The success of the citrus branch over the past few years is turning the settlers'
heads.... No explanation or demand for agricultural planning can hush the
clink of the shillings in the pocket of the orange-grower.... It is no small
achievement that in a new moshav in the 'classical' orange-growing area we
have persuaded the farmers not to plant citrus fruit, but to keep chickens and
cows, grow vegetables, etc.[16]

The point of view propounded here is in part prudential, deriving
from the need to insure against failure of a particular crop. But it also
contains an ideological element, based on the concept of the ideal
economic structure of the Yishuv espoused by the Zionist movement
from a very early stage. Both of these elements played their part in
determining the economic policy of the kibbutz movements during

[16] Halprin, 'On the Question of Planning'.

this period. The kibbutzim were even more faithful to this concept than were the moshavim. During the same period in which the kibbutzim increased their citrus groves by some 3 per cent, the corresponding figure for the moshav movement was 10 per cent. In the circumstances of economic distress and opportunity which accompanied the first years of prosperity, 'the shilling' spoke louder to the moshavnik than ideology and long-term interest.

Several elements other than field and orchard crops were to be found in the characteristic mix of the kibbutz economy. There were chickens and cows in Degania in its second year, and one of the founding groups of Gedud Ha'avoda was a shepherds' group which eventually settled at Kfar Gil'adi. In 1929, income from livestock (poultry, dairy herds, sheep, and bees) came to more than 40 per cent of the kibbutzim's income from agricultural produce. By 1935 this proportion had grown to some 52 per cent.

One other significant development should be noted. In 1929 the kibbutzim's agricultural production provided 90 per cent of their income. Six years later this proportion had declined to 62.3 per cent. Two branches played an increasing part in the kibbutz economy: 'outside work'—a continuation of the practice whereby the kibbutz members had worked for near-by farmers or in town when their community was still at the stage of the *pluga*; and light industry— woodwork, metalwork, industrial brick- and pottery-making, and the like. In 1935, outside work accounted for 22 per cent of kibbutz income, and industry for 15.5 per cent.

The question of outside work involved a number of dilemmas, both economic and ideological. In the mid-1920s, all the kibbutz movements saw it as a temporary method of absorption and settlement until the *plugot*, which could at that stage find no other employment, were allocated land of their own. Yitzhak Tabenkin expressed this point of view succinctly in 1927, when he spoke of a scale, with the *plugot* in the towns at the lowest point, *plugot* in the *moshavot*—where their task was to prepare their members for settlement—above them, while the establishment and strengthening of the big kibbutz should have first priority. From the early 1930s onwards, however, Tabenkin began to lay greater stress on work in the *moshavot* and towns as one of the kibbutz's contributions to the class struggle and to the Zionist cause in general. He contended that the kibbutz should not con- centrate on building its own economy, but should send its members to work outside its confines: this would be both a means of earning extra income and an expression of its involvement in the struggles of the labour movement. The other kibbutz movements approached the question with less ideological fervour, but by the early 1930s all of them were involved to some degree in hired labour in town and/or *moshava*, with a strong emphasis on the *moshava*.[17]

The prosperity of the 1930s changed the situation. Wages had always been higher in town than in agricultural work. As the possibilities of employment in town increased, workers left the *moshavot*, and in many cases their places were taken by Arabs; from 1933 onwards these were often migrant workers from outside Palestine, who depressed wages even further. The kibbutzim remained faithful, on the whole, to what they saw as a national interest—the 'conquest' of Jewish agriculture by Jewish labour. But there is no doubt that by preferring this to more profitable alternatives such as work in the building trade they were acting against their own immediate economic interests.

The changes in the kibbutz economy in the late 1920s and early 1930s were complex, and sometimes contradictory. But their end result was the economic consolidation and expansion of the settled kibbutzim. In 1929, the balance-sheets of 20 of the 23 veteran kibbutzim showed losses ranging from P£385 to P£15,788, and of the 3 which showed a surplus none made a profit greater than P£380. By 1936, 13 of these kibbutzim showed profits ranging from P£240 to P£2,609, and the greatest individual loss was P£3,014. This group as a whole showed a surplus of P£709. This can scarcely be called prosperity, but it certainly shows that the kibbutz movement was no longer in the situation of only three or four years earlier, when whole communities had been uncertain of their very survival.[18]

Many factors contributed to these developments. There can be no doubt that one of the most important was the devotion and self-sacrifice of the kibbutz members themselves. For instance, during the whole of the period, every *pluga* which was allocated land for settlement had to pay P£175 per family unit towards the initial equipment and capitalization, as against the P£340 loaned by Keren Hayesod; and this sum had to be saved by groups newly arrived from the training farms of Hechalutz in Europe with no resources of their own, often during a period of acclimatization, sickness, and lack of stable

---

[17] Tabenkin's 'scale': *Shorashim*, 2 (1980), 253; work in the *moshavot*: Near, *Kibbutz and Society*, 204–7.

[18] *UAW Report* (1939), 222.

employment. But the economic progress of the kibbutzim cannot be attributed solely to their members' own efforts, important as they were. External factors were important too. For the settled kibbutzim, the consolidation loans were a major step towards financial stability. These had been planned for several years, but the Keren Hayesod was able to grant them only as a direct result of the consolidation of its own finances, through a long-term loan of £500,000 from Lloyds Bank in 1934—undoubtedly in response to the general buoyancy of the Yishuv's economy.[19] Loans were also made to established kibbutzim which absorbed German immigrants, through a special fund financed through the Transfer Scheme, based on funds originating in Germany. But the increased availability of capital was only part of the story: the economic success of the kibbutzim was further aided by the growth of the non-agricultural sector of the Yishuv. Tel Aviv and Jewish Haifa each tripled their populations in the period under discussion, and many smaller towns and *moshavot* also grew, though to a lesser degree. This was the market for eggs, milk, grains, and fruit produced by the kibbutzim. Their progress was, at least in part, a function of the prosperity of the Yishuv as a whole.

Even in its improved state, the kibbutz movement faced severe economic problems, however. A third of its members were still living in *plugot*, under temporary conditions of housing and employment, and saving their earnings against the day when they would be allocated land for settlement. And even when the veteran kibbutzim received consolidation loans, the settlement authorities often underestimated the projected population on which the size of the loan was based, so the funds available were still less than what was needed. The constant pressure to absorb new members and expand the economy led the kibbutzim to strain their resources to the utmost, and the gap was only partly filled by credit facilities created by the Histadrut, the Jewish Agency, and the kibbutz movements themselves. In 1929, some 85 per cent of the capital invested in twenty-four settled kibbutzim came from institutional sources. By 1937, this proportion had dropped to 47 per cent. True, they were able to finance 13 per cent of their investment from their own savings; but this still left a gap of some 40 per cent (more than P£90,000), which had to be borrowed on short-term loans at high rates of interest.

The economic situation of the kibbutz movement in 1935 was

[19] Ulitzur, *National Capital and Construction*, 40–1, 57–9.

complex. In terms of productive capacity, manpower, skills, and managerial ability kibbutz society had progressed immensely over the past eight years. It was now firmly based, and undergoing a dynamic process of expansion, together with the economy of the Yishuv as a whole. It had developed a wide variety of products, mainly for the home market; and most kibbutzim were supplementing their incomes from this source by devoting a proportion of their manpower to outside work. There were also the beginnings of small industrial enterprises. Economically, therefore, it can be said that the kibbutz rested on firm foundations. But this state of affairs was not always reflected in its finances. The lack of cheap credit and the constant pressure to absorb new members combined to create new debts at high rates of interest, with the consequent danger of entering a vicious circle of financial commitments.

## Standards of Living

To what extent was this situation reflected in the standard of living of kibbutz members? Comparison of standards of living is notoriously difficult at the best of times, and in the case of the kibbutz simple statistical estimates are apt to mislead since they do not take into account the special features of the system: on the one hand, savings through bulk buying and cooking, communal clothing stores and laundries, and the like; on the other, a degree of waste which seems to be inherent in this way of life. None the less, some indications can be discerned.

Sir John Campbell, the League of Nations Commissioner for Refugees, visited a number of kibbutzim in 1927 as a member of the Zionist movement's committee of experts on agricultural settlement. He reported that the conditions prevailing in the great majority of kibbutzim precluded any possibility of luxury, or even of the most elementary comfort. Expenditure on food, clothing, and all other personal necessities was kept at an exceedingly low level. In many kibbutzim the prevailing standard was of flagrant discomfort, and even of poverty. Campbell's overwhelming impression was of an uncomplaining tolerance of almost unbearable living conditions.[20]

This was the nadir of kibbutz living standards, at the trough of the economic depression. At this time, the annual living expenses of an average kibbutz family were P£70–80. By 1936/7 the corresponding

[20] Quoted in Shatil, *Economy of the Communal Settlement*, 203–8.

figure was P£90–100; and this during a period when retail prices were on the whole very stable.[21]

This increase was not always reflected in the living standard of the individual, however. Some of the rise in expenditure can be attributed to the growing number of children, and considerable sums were spent on supporting the parents of kibbutz members. But it is clear from all accounts that by the mid-1930s Campbell's description did not apply to most of the kibbutzim. In 1936, the first year for which figures are available, the daily calorific consumption by adults in the developed kibbutzim had reached the quite satisfactory figure of 3,380. It seems, therefore, that the improvement in the economic situation of the kibbutz movement was reflected to a considerable extent in the members' nutritional standards.[22]

In so far as it is possible to compare this standard with that of workers outside the kibbutz, the picture is rather different. In 1934, the median daily wage in the building industry was 600 mils, and in agriculture 290.[23] Building workers' wages were roughly equivalent to those in Italy and the primarily agricultural countries of Eastern Europe, while the cost of most items of food was close to that in England.[24] So the standard of living of the agricultural worker (to which the standard of consumption of the kibbutz community was roughly attuned) was rather lower than that of Italy at this period of continued depression in the European countries.

In one respect—that of housing—we do have detailed accounts of the standard of life in the kibbutzim. Here is an extract from an article entitled 'The Third One', which appeared in the journal of the Kibbutz Me'uhad in 1934. The writer explains that she has been married for six years and has one child. For the past two years another woman has been living in her and her husband's room, separated from them only by a curtain.

I have not become used to it, and I never shall.... The sight of the curtain constantly reminds me that there is a witness to my spiritual life; for I still cannot distinguish between the life of the body and the spirit.... I live in

[21] Living expenses: ibid. 377. Stability of prices: Horowitz, *Development of the Palestinian Economy*, 132–8.
[22] *Yalkut Brit Pikuah*, 17 (Sept. 1941), 9; Shatil, *Economy of the Communal Settlement*, 206–9.
[23] 100 mils = P£1.
[24] Wages in the building industry: Horowitz, *Development of the Palestinian Economy*, 161; comparison with Europe: Preuss, 'Problems Related to Wages'.

perpetual anxiety, my heart shrinks within me. . . . Sometimes, when I come to his bed late at night, he embraces me, and I lay my head on his chest and relax. I am at peace. I lie still, frozen, unmoving; perhaps I need no more. I am full of dread that she may wake up. If she does, I have lost a whole world. I am afraid to move, scared to whisper into his ear the words which I have been saving up for so long. . . .

No doubt there are at this very moment many people in the world who conduct their intimate life in the presence of others. Perhaps they get used to it, treat it light-heartedly, ask 'What's all the fuss about? What's so tragic?' As for me, I shall never get used to it. I am myself, and this is my life, and at this moment I don't want to remember that there are many poor and oppressed and suffering people in the world. I shall fight desperately for my right to my own small happiness. . . .

My country, my kibbutz! I shall never betray you, my life and faith are bound up in you. But do you really demand this suffering of me? I shall live only once, I shall love only once. Will my love always be so intermittent, so blighted? . . .

My thoughts seethe within me: To cry out in protest? To accept the situation? The duty of absorbing immigrants, the holiest duty in the Land of Israel, involves the desecration—yes, the desecration!—of my love. Do I really have to make this huge sacrifice?[25]

This was far from being an exceptional instance. At the end of 1934, 80 of the 780 couples in the Kibbutz Me'uhad had a third person in their room. Of this movement's 3,600 members, 600 lived in tents; 400 lacked proper accommodation and lived in abandoned farm buildings. One of the leaders of the Kibbutz Me'uhad calculated that 60 per cent of that movement's members lived in 'perpetual hardship'. Although the Kibbutz Me'uhad suffered more than the other movements as a consequence of its policy of massive absorption, housing was scarce in all the movements. In 1936, when the situation had begun to improve slightly, 13 per cent of the members of the Kibbutz Me'uhad and the Kibbutz Artzi and 9 per cent of Hever Hakvutzot were still without permanent accommodation.[26]

The article quoted above created a considerable stir among the general public. An article by Moshe Beilinson, the editor of the Histadrut daily *Davar*, proclaimed that the kibbutz movement would pay dearly for the 'third'. Partly as a result of the public outcry, in 1935 a special fund was set up by the Jewish Agency and the Histadrut which built a number of special houses for new immigrants in the

[25] Rachel [Lilia Bassevitz], 'The Third One'.
[26] Zak, *Report to Bank Hapoalim.*

*moshavot*, including the *plugot* of the kibbutz movements. But tents, dilapidated huts, and other forms of temporary accommodation remained an accepted feature of the kibbutz scene for many years.

We may sum up this section by saying that the characteristics of the 'men of stone' that were the product of the education and self-selection processes in the training kibbutzim were translated into economic terms in the Yishuv. Faithful to their concept of a balanced economy, they resisted the temptation to make quick profits from the citrus boom. In contrast to the majority of Jewish workers, they took on the tasks which they and the Histadrut leaders considered most essential for the nation as a whole, without reckoning the financial cost. Conscious of the suffering and dangers of their friends and relatives in the stricken communities of Europe, they accepted the physical and emotional hardships involved in absorbing the greatest possible number of new immigrants. When the support of the Zionist authorities was insufficient, they invested their savings in the development of their farms at the expense of their own standards of living.

Moshe Beilinson was right, however: there was a price to pay. It was expressed most unambiguously in the figures of absorption into, and attrition of, the kibbutz movement. In each of the movements, the numbers of those who left the kibbutzim in the years 1932–5 amounted to some 40 per cent of those who arrived from the training farms.[27] The difficulties involved in maintaining 'pioneering tension', in the jargon of the time, frequently led to sharp differences of opinion within the kibbutz community, and between the individual kibbutzim and the leadership of the movement. This applied to all the movements, but was particularly marked in the Kibbutz Me'uhad, whose ideology and practice placed special emphasis on the duty of continuous expansion.

Similar tensions arose over the allocation of new immigrants. In view of the drastic reduction in the number of Jewish workers in the orange groves of the coastal plain in 1934–5, the Central Committee of the Histadrut demanded that all the new immigrants should be sent to work in this area. The kibbutz movements had interests of their own, among which was the strengthening of existing kibbutzim in other areas. The discussion was not only between the Histadrut and the kibbutz movements; they themselves were torn between their wish to build their communities according to a rational long-term

---

[27] Braslavsky, *The Labour Movement in the Land of Israel*, ii. 231–2.

plan and the principle of 'putting the kibbutz at the service of the Histadrut', which had been part of their ideology since the very beginning. In the end, the movements all compromised heavily in favour of the Histadrut's demands: they accepted a large measure of responsibility for the 'conquest' of work in the citrus groves, rather than seeking more profitable employment in other occupations.[28]

*Demographic and Geographic Developments*

Some further results of the historical developments at this time should be noted. The influx of German Jews changed not only the economic structure of the Yishuv, but also its social and cultural composition: by 1935, Jews of German origin, whose numbers had been negligible before 1933, numbered some 30,000 of the 350,000 in the Yishuv. The rapid growth of the pioneering youth movements—Habonim, Hechalutz, and the orthodox pioneering movement—and the less spectacular but steady progress of the German Hashomer Hatzair movement (founded in 1931) ensured that the kibbutz movement shared in this growth, though in very uneven proportions as between the movements. Between April 1933 and October 1936 the Kibbutz Me'uhad absorbed 1,555 members of German origin, Hever Hakvutzot 166, the Kibbutz Artzi 120, and the religious kibbutz movement 275 (see Table 9).

   Another aspect of the German immigration was that the advent of the Nazi regime had led to the creation of one of the most impressive educational institutions of the Yishuv: Youth Aliya. This was a scheme for saving the lives of German youngsters who were able to leave Germany, although their parents were unable to do so, and educating them. They were sent in groups to veteran kibbutzim, where educators who had gained their experience in the youth movement and the kibbutz cared for them under a special regime of half study, half work. The first group reached Kibbutz Ein Harod in February 1934. By the end of 1935 there were sixteen such groups, all except two in kibbutzim, comprising 564 youngsters. The period of training was for two years, and at its conclusion many of the groups proclaimed themselves *plugot* dedicated to settlement in the framework of the kibbutz movement which had cared for them since their arrival in the country. The first group to do so was among those which founded

---

[28] Shapira, *Futile Struggle*, 186–92; Lubianiker's speech, ibid. 186; minutes of Kibbutz Me'uhad central committee, 5 July 1934; *UAW Report* (1939), 240.

TABLE 9 . Population of Kibbutzim and Moshavim, 1927 and 1935

| | Kibbutzim | | | | | | | | | | Total | | Moshavim[a] | |
| | Hever Hakvutzot and independent | | Kibbutz Me'uhad | | Gedud Ha'avoda | | Kibbutz Artzi | | | | | | | |
| | Members | No. | Members | No. | Members | No. | Members | No. | | | Members | No. | Members | No. |
|---|---|---|---|---|---|---|---|---|---|---|---|---|---|---|
| Farms | | | | | | | | | | | | | | |
| 1927 | 841 | 17 | 482 | 4 | 356 | 3 | 87 | 1[b] | | | 1,766 | 25 | 1,200 | 16 |
| 1935 | 629 | 12 | 3,293 | 12 | — | — | 1,330 | 12 | | | 5,252 | 36 | 5,000 | 49 |
| Plugot | | | | | | | | | | | | | | |
| 1927 | 1,226 | 48 | 497 | 11 | 90 | 2 | 320 | 5 | | | 2,133 | 66 | n.f.a. | |
| 1935 | 702 | 16 | 1,329 | 10 | — | — | 1,391 | 17 | | | 3,422 | 43 | 400 | 7 |
| Total | | | | | | | | | | | | | | |
| 1927 | 2,067 | — | 1,979 | — | 446 | — | 407 | — | | | 3,899 | — | 1,200 | — |
| 1935 | 1,331 | — | 4,622 | — | — | — | 2,721 | — | | | 8,674 | — | 5,400 | — |

Source: Based on Near, Kibbutz and Society, 418–19 and tables in UAW Report (1927, 1931, 1939). Details of non-Histadrut settlements are taken from Gurevich et al., Jewish Population of Palestine, 268–82.

Note: Figures are for adult working members, men and women.

[a] Includes settlements not affiliated to the Histadrut (in 1935: 5 of Hapoel Hamizrahi and 8 'middle-class moshavim').

[b] Kibbutz Beit Alpha is included only in the 1927 figures of the Kibbutz Artzi; it did not join that movement until 1940.

Kibbutz Alonim in 1938, and many others followed suit in the years to come.[29]

The steady rise in the kibbutz population was not matched by a proportionate increase in settlement; while kibbutz membership doubled, the number of kibbutzim increased by less than 50 per cent. This stands in sharp contrast to the development of the moshavim: their adult population increased by 350 per cent, and the number of settlements by 230 per cent.

The changes were not only quantitative, however. One outstanding development was in the geographical distribution of the kibbutzim. Each period of settlement had added a particular region to the kibbutz map. The major areas of settlement for the Second Aliya had been the Jordan Valley and Upper Galilee, and for the Third Aliya the Jezreel Valley. At the beginning of the Fourth Aliya, a few kibbutzim had been established in the Western Jezreel Valley, but much of the kibbutz movement began to concentrate round the *moshavot* in the citrus-growing area in and close to the coastal plain. Between 1927 and 1935, with the settlement of the Hefer Valley and the establishment of permanent kibbutzim in the area, this region achieved an importance no less than that of those settled in earlier periods (see Table 10). These facts were to be of very great importance in the coming years.

TABLE 10. Regional Distribution of Kibbutzim, 1927 and 1935

| Region | 1927 | 1935 |
| --- | --- | --- |
| Upper Galilee | 2 | 2 |
| Jordan Valley | 5 | 6 |
| Jezreel Valley | 14 | 18 |
| Coastal plain | 1 | 14 |
| Jerusalem area | 2 | 2 |

*Source:* Gurevich *et al.*, *Jewish Population of Palestine*, 268–82.

[29] Absorption of German Jews: Kedar, 'The German Aliyah as an Apolitical Opposition'. Statistics: *Yediot Hamercaz Hahaklai*, 3 (Oct. 1936). Youth Aliya: *UAW Report*, 1939: 86–9

DEVELOPMENT OF THE KIBBUTZ MOVEMENTS

The kibbutz movements changed in many respects between 1927 and 1935.[30] The Kibbutz Me'uhad had always aimed to combine the central direction of manpower between settlements and of overall economic policy with a maximum of autonomy for its component communities, particularly in economic matters. In principle, however, the kibbutz member's first loyalty was to the Kibbutz Me'uhad as a whole, rather than to his own *pluga* or settlement. This principle was sometimes applied quite draconically. Some of the tensions which arose from the policy of maximum absorption have been discussed earlier. In these matters, the central organs of the kibbutz were the final arbiter, even though their decisions might be unwelcome, and even harmful, in the eyes of the members on the spot. Similarly, new immigrants were sent to *plugot* and established kibbutzim on the basis of need, without taking into account the immigrants' wishes or whether they shared a common movement or national background with the existing population. In the words of one of the leaders of the Kibbutz Me'uhad, those undergoing their training in the Diaspora were expected to create 'a living link with the Kibbutz as a whole', and not with particular groups of settlements. In the period of mass immigration, this policy was somewhat modified: reinforcements were sent to existing communities on the basis of common national or movement origin; the national grouping in a particular kibbutz was strengthened as a way of easing the difficulties of the adaptation period. Thus, concentrations of German Jews were created in Giv'at Brenner and Na'an, though care was taken not to build up a community with a homogeneous background. On the other hand, homogeneous communities were to be found in the *plugot* of the Russian sector of Hashomer Hatzair, which conducted its own absorption policy within the Kibbutz Me'uhad. In principle, the absorption policy of the Kibbutz Me'uhad contrasted sharply with those of the other two main movements, both of which believed in the 'organic kibbutz'—a fusion of groups with a common cultural and educational background. In practice, though, the movements were rather closer on this point than their ideological declarations lead one to believe.

Examination of the constitutions of the three kibbutz movements

---

[30] This section is based on Near, *Kibbutz and Society*, chs. 1, 8, and 9; Tsur, *The Kibbutz Me'uhad in the Settlement of Eretz-Israel*, vol. i, pt. 3; Ben-Avram, *Hever Hakvutzot*, 125–50; Margalit, *Hashomer Hatzair*, chs. 5 and 9.

reveals great similarity in their organizational structures. Each aimed at maximum autonomy for the individual kibbutz unit in its economic and social affairs, while exercising central control over such matters as the allocation of manpower, the mobilization of resources for work in the youth movement, and representation *vis à vis* outside institutions. Hever Hakvutzot's constitution, which was adopted in 1932, represented a compromise between the leaders of Gordonia, who wanted to tighten the movement's organizational structure, and the veterans of the first *kvutzot*, who believed in a far-reaching federalistic approach. In practice, however, the *kvutzot* of Hever Hakvutzot continued to enjoy a much greater degree of independence than the individual units in the other movements.

Other developments also reflect an increasing similarity between the movements. At the end of 1934, for example, the Kibbutz Me'uhad established the Kibbutz Me'uhad Fund as a way to channel monies levied from the more prosperous kibbutzim and *plugot* to the weaker and less established communities. The other two kibbutz movements followed suit during the following year. This step, while advantageous in itself, was clearly a severe limitation on the economic autonomy of the individual kibbutzim. Another step, originally taken by the centralistic Kibbutz Me'uhad in 1935 and soon followed by the other two movements, was the setting up of a series of central committees, in addition to the all-purpose General Secretariat. First and most powerful among these was the Economic Committee, which was empowered to examine the state of the individual communities, and also represented the movement on the financial bodies of the Histadrut and the Jewish Agency. This, again, was a significant strengthening of the movement centre as against its component parts.

Two other developments may be adduced as proof of the increasing similarity between the movements. Two of Hever Hakvutzot's most jealously defended principles were its opposition to the industrialization of the kibbutz and its defence of the concept of the 'small *kvutza*'. By 1935, each of these principles had been somewhat eroded. None of the *kvutzot* could be said as yet to have developed industry proper, but the item 'workshop' in the annual balance-sheet included such enterprises as carpentry or metal-work shops engaged in contract work, bakeries, small ceramic enterprises, and so forth. The accounts for 1935 are not available, but those drawn up in the autumn of 1936 show that 31 established kibbutzim of a total of 39 had some income from this source. True, 5 of the 12 kibbutzim of Hever Hakvutzot still retained their agricultural purity, but 7 had taken this first step on the road to industrialization.[31] On the question of size, the growth of the *kvutzot* had become so marked that in 1935 Hever Hakvutzot devoted a special conference to the issue.[32]

There is no doubt, therefore, that many of the differences between the movements which only five years earlier had seemed unbridgeable were now matters of emphasis rather than fundamental ideological divisions. On the other hand, it is important not to exaggerate the effect of these changes. There was, for instance, still a vital difference in the quality of kibbutz life between the communities of Hever Hakvutzot, whose adult population averaged 100, of the Kibbutz Artzi, with an average of 160, and of the Kibbutz Me'uhad, which had reached an average of 275 (including Giv'at Brenner, whose adult population of 565 seemed quite monstrous to the people of the *kvutzot*). On the level of movement organization, the differences of origin and ideology described in Chapter 4 were reflected in varieties of political culture rather than structure. Thus, the Kibbutz Me'uhad reacted to the world crisis by emphasizing the need to strengthen the kibbutz movement by disciplined action directed by a strong central authority; its leaders made much use of military metaphors in propounding this view. In the Kibbutz Artzi, by contrast, the dominant political culture stressed the need to strive for consensus, even at the cost of efficiency in the making and carrying out of decisions; this was a continuation of the traditions of the youth movement, in which the dialogue between the leaders and the rank and file played a central role. In Hever Hakvutzot, the key principle was decentralization: the centre of decision-making was in the *kvutzot* themselves, and the movement served as a federation of independent communities, making binding decisions only when unavoidable. The discussion of the size of the *kvutza*, which concluded with recommendations rather than decisions, is typical of this approach. Such an outcome would not have been possible in the Kibbutz Me'uhad, which would have reached a binding majority decision, or in the Kibbutz Artzi, which would have continued its deliberations, in the kibbutzim and in the movement's institutions, until general agreement was reached.[33]

[31] *UAW Report* (1939), table 22.
[32] Ben-Avram, *Hever Hakvutzot*, 129–35. No conclusive decisions were reached, except that recruitment must be cautious, and not indiscriminating as in the Kibbutz Me'uhad.
[33] Near, 'Authority and Democracy'.

Such differences served to reinforce several other elements which prevented the movements from emphasizing any tendencies to convergence, or from seriously considering unification. Among these were the well-known phenomenon of institutional persistence—the tendency for existing movements to ensure their survival by all possible means; the deeply felt differences of approach to the nature of the kibbutz community, which were still very evident; and, above all, the growing political differences between the movements. These were of such great importance both in themselves and in their historical consequences that they will be discussed in a separate chapter.

# 6

# Politics and Youth, 1927–1935

## THE POLITICIZATION OF THE KIBBUTZ MOVEMENTS[1]

If we ever create sectoral parties in Palestine, we shall destroy the basis of our constructive work in the Yishuv. The secret of our success . . . lies in our being able to establish a united front of labour, of the whole working class. Any attempt to replace this front, which includes all who live by their own labour, by a front composed of one type of settlement and opposed to other, competing types will undermine the moral and social basis of our existence.[2]

DAVID Ben-Gurion's words at the Hechalutz World Conference of 1924 encapsulate a point of view common to almost all the leaders of the labour movement and the kibbutz movements in the 1920s and early 1930s. Any attempt to form a party based on economic or generational groupings would reduce the Histadrut to a forum for resolving sectional interests and prevent it from acting in the general interest of the working class. The exception to this broad consensus was the left wing of Gedud Ha'avoda, whose failure was seen by the whole of the labour movement as a dire warning of the dangers of the politicization of the kibbutz. Thus, both fundamental ideological attitudes and the lessons of experience seemed to militate against the repetition of this process. None the less, by the mid-1930s each of the three kibbutz movements had developed its own political identity, which expressed itself in both ideological and organizational terms. This process of politicization, surprising at first glance, was of inestimable importance to the later development of the kibbutz movement.

Even the least ideological of kibbutz members believed that his or her actions were helping to shape the social structure of the Yishuv,

[1] This section is mainly based on: Ben-Avram, *Hever Hakvutzot*; Margalit, *Hashomer Hatzair*; Near, *Kibbutz and Society*; Zait, 'From Kibbutz Movement to Party Organization'; id., *Zionism and Peace*.

[2] *Kuntres*, 193 (Oct. 1924), 12.

and conversely, that the existence of his or her kibbutz depended on such bodies as the Zionist movement and the Histadrut, bodies which were controlled by political parties and motivated by political considerations. How, then, was the individual kibbutz to promote its ideals and protect its interests? Within the framework of the existing parties? By creating new political alliances and organizations? Or by alliance with the other kibbutz movements? For almost a decade, from 1927 to 1935, these fundamental questions were asked again and again, and received a variety of answers. They formed the background to the myriad discussions of particular issues which occupied the kibbutz movements during the same period—issues which sprang from their need to survive and expand, and from their sense of mission towards the Yishuv and the Jews of the Diaspora. Questions of means and ends, of organizational methods and political issues, were often interconnected in the historical process. Here, I shall analyze the way in which each movement's basic attitudes were formed—often before the period mainly dealt with in this chapter—and describe the process of politicization. I shall, however, describe not two movements, but five, each of which represented a different view of kibbutz politics: the Kibbutz Artzi and the Kibbutz Me'uhad; the veteran *kvutzot*, to be united in Hever Hakvutzot in 1929; Gordonia; and Netzah (the name adopted by the Russian Hashomer Hatzair movement after it broke away from Hashomer Hatzair in 1930).

## The Kvutzot *and Hapoel Hatzair*

On questions of political means, the veteran *kvutzot* stood at one extreme of a very wide spectrum. In their view, the *kvutza* as such had no political function, and its members could belong to any party they chose. In fact, most of them belonged to or supported Hapoel Hatzair, although there were a number of *kvutzot* that had a few members of Ahdut Ha'avoda, and even one (Kinneret) in which that party had a majority.

The leaders of the *kvutzot* believed that the building and improvement of their own communities was their principal contribution to the Zionist cause. But they were far from being indifferent to what went on in the wider community. From a very early stage they took part in public activities, party gatherings and the like: for instance, the conference of Hapoel Hatzair in 1913 took place in Degania, and expressed the fundamental solidarity between the party and the form of settlement to which it gave its support. Clearly, however, there was a conflict of interest involved. This is well illustrated in the annual general meeting of Degania in the autumn of 1924. Joseph Baratz, one of the founders and most respected members of the *kvutza*, said: 'I don't think [political] activity is a terrible thing [as do some of us]. I think it's very important—it's our connection with the broader community. If we were to stop it, Degania would lose much of its moral value and content'.[3]

Baratz himself was very involved in this question, and had been politically active, on and off, for many years.[4] A member of the Hapoel Hatzair party even before he joined the Hadera commune in 1910, he had been sent by the party on a number of educational and political missions within the Yishuv and abroad. At the time of the 1924 discussion he represented Hapoel Hatzair on the Agricultural Centre of the Histadrut (which dealt with such matters as the allocation of priorities for settlement and negotiations with the appropriate departments of the Zionist Organization), and was frequently away from Degania. So the discussion was of both public and personal importance to him. Ya'akov Berkovich, another veteran member, replied:

We've accepted new members and new responsibilities, and it's quite possible that some of the old-timers will leave. There simply aren't enough people to go out to work. . . . When things are in such a state, I look on public activities [such as political work] as a completely demoralizing factor. . . . I have no objection to them in a period of expansion. But at the moment, I have only one thought in mind: how to put the economy on a firm basis. I don't understand how anyone can think of anything else.

Other speakers repeated these arguments in various forms. So serious and outspoken was the opposition to political 'activism' that Baratz declared that he would give up his public duties and return to the *kvutza* at the end of the year, even though such a step was at variance with what he believed to be the correct policy for Degania.

I have quoted this discussion at length because of the light it throws on elements which appeared in kibbutz life again and again at different periods: the constant stress arising from shortage of manpower, especially of experienced workers; the tendency to give priority to the requirements of the kibbutz economy; and the tension between these essential components of kibbutz society and its desire to be of service to the Yishuv and the Zionist movement. To this should be added a further element, illustrated by the words of another veteran member in the same discussion: 'It's impossible to deny completely people's feelings and desires and aspirations—however much we may devote ourselves to our work.... In my view, we shouldn't aim to be like the Russian peasant, who knows nothing outside his work.' In the case of Joseph Baratz, his 'desires and aspirations' combined with constant pressure from the leadership of the labour movement to shape much of his future life, much of which was devoted to public activities of various sorts. In this respect he belonged to a small minority, both in Degania and in the kibbutz movement as a whole.

Throughout this discussion public activity was viewed not as a means of ensuring the interests of the *kvutza* (except in the general sense of strengthening its connection with the outside community), but as a duty, second only to the prime obligation of strengthening and perfecting the *kvutza*. Political activity, in fact, was seen as an act of service to the Yishuv—praiseworthy in itself, but liable to clash with the primary objectives of the *kvutza*.

This stance chimed well with the ideology of Hapoel Hatzair.[5] In the early post-war period, this party saw itself mainly as a cultural and educational movement whose aims remained, as they had been throughout the Second Aliya, the encouragement and organization of agricultural work and settlement.[6] But by the mid-1920s both of the parties seemed similar in their methods of organization, and the issues which concerned them; and when, in 1925 and again in 1927, Berl Katznelson raised the question of unifying the two parties, Hapoel Hatzair's leaders were hard put to find reasons for its continued separate existence. None the less, there were some matters of policy at issue between them. In matters of Zionist policy, Hapoel Hatzair was less 'activist' than Ahdut Ha'avoda. This expressed itself in a less critical attitude to the Mandatory power, particularly—in accordance with A. D. Gordon's virtually pacifist way of thought—in matters of defence; and in support for Chaim Weizmann and his policies in the Zionist movement. Moreover, in the belief that their party had a

[5] On Hapoel Hatzair and the *kvutzot* see Ben-Avram, *Hever Hakvutzot*, 22–3, 45–6, 92–3, 150–66.

[6] This reluctance to engage whole-heartedly in political activity in the accepted sense of the term had been one of the main factors which led A. D. Gordon and others to oppose uniting with Poalei Zion in 1919.

special responsibility for promoting agricultural settlement, their leaders took the settlement portfolio in the Zionist Executive from 1921 to 1925, a time when the leaders of Ahdut Ha'avoda refused to serve in a 'reactionary' executive.

Most important from our point of view was Hapoel Hatzair's opposition to 'mechanical' forms of social organization, and emphasis on 'organic' relationships. In practical terms, this approach led the party to oppose the large kibbutzim and the country-wide kibbutz movements and support the *kvutza* and the moshav. True, Hapoel Hatzair was in a perpetual minority within the labour movement. But the structure of the Histadrut, in whose executive bodies both major parties were represented, gave it disproportionate influence in certain departments—particularly in the key Agricultural Centre. Thus, Hapoel Hatzair's support ensured for the *kvutza* and the moshav a degree of political and practical backing greater than the number of their actual and potential members, and even greater than the real political strength of their patron party. The creation of Mapai in 1930 altered the formal configuration, but did little to change the power structure within the labour movement in this vital area. In the first few years of the new party's existence, executive responsibility within the Histadrut was changed very little: party patronage became personal patronage, and the patrons' predilections were not fundamentally altered by their broadened allegiance.

## Hashomer Hatzair

At the other end of the spectrum from the *kvutzot* stood the Kibbutz Artzi of Hashomer Hatzair. This movement's principle of ideological collectivism meant that decisions of the kibbutz movement taken after a 'long, and sometimes extremely exhausting, process of crystallization of ideas'[7] bound every member to at least passive support. The change which its adoption in 1927 brought about was well described by a not entirely unsympathetic political rival:

The Hashomer Hatzair conference has created something new—they have turned into a new political party, a political kibbutz movement: their members aren't allowed to belong to any party, they criticize all the parties violently. So what hope is there of uniting the youth movements?... Their new political system made our people furious. I don't accept it for a moment, either; but I understand their point of view. They want to see the fruit of their own

[7] Zait, *Zionism and Peace*, 48.

creation, the realization of their own ideas. Like all young people, who take the path they have blazed for themselves rather than being led and manipulated by others, they believe that their own way is the only right one.[8]

The members of Hashomer Hatzair indignantly denied that they had created a new party. In their view, the movement's prime task was educational, and the skills required for work with young people, and for building kibbutzim, were not consonant with the manipulation, propaganda, and compromise which were the hallmarks of a party. In practical terms, the movement's non-party character consisted in its refusal to set up independent political machinery, to canvass, propagandize, convert, and acquire new members. Its missionary work was done through the youth movement, and its political stance was the expression of the will of that movement and its graduates. But, despite all their denials, its leaders spoke in undeniably political terms, and the movement was an independent body in the Histadrut and the Zionist movement, pursuing its own policies and putting up its own lists for election.

In terms of political issues, the graduates of Hashomer Hatzair had already begun to define their own special stance even before the foundation of the Kibbutz Artzi. Their first attempt to create some sort of federative connection for their kibbutzim had been in the abortive negotiations with Gedud Ha'avoda, which took place in 1924. Although this attempt failed as a result of the Gedud's refusal to recognize the special social and cultural needs of the Hashomer Hatzair kibbutzim, the two movements revealed a number of affinities. Both treasured their independence of the Histadrut bureaucracy, with which they came into frequent and often frustrating contact. Both saw their vision of an egalitarian society being frustrated by that bureaucracy's compromises with the social realities of the time. And both were interested in applying their socialist principles beyond the bounds of kibbutz society to the Yishuv as a whole. As a result, the kibbutzim of Hashomer Hatzair supported Gedud Ha'avoda in its struggle against the Histadrut at the time of the 1923 schism; and on two occasions—in 1923 and 1927—the two movements put forward a joint list for the Histadrut elections.

---

[8] Avraham Guberman to Fania Bergstein, 1927. In file of Bergstein's correspondence, Hechalutz archive, Lohamei Hageta'ot Museum. This is the continuation of the letter quoted above, p. 123.

*The Arab Question*

The platform of the 'kibbutz list' to the third convention of the Histadrut in 1927[9] was supported by Hashomer Hatzair and the right-wing faction of the Gedud. One clause in the section on the trade unions (which were to be democratized and to include the kibbutzim) read: '*Contacts with the Arab worker*: In view of the common interests of Jewish and Arab workers in the class struggle, and of the future economic development of the Yishuv, the Histadrut should encourage the *joint organization* of Jewish and Arab workers.' This clause is the first formal sign of a tendency which was to become one of the hallmarks of Hashomer Hatzair and the Kibbutz Artzi: their special concern with the question of Jewish–Arab relationships. At this stage, however, it expressed an aspiration common to many on the left of the Labour Zionist movement, including some prominent figures in Ahdut Ha'avoda. In the spectrum of labour politics the extreme position was that of the Communists, who rejected Zionism altogether and viewed the Arab struggle against Jewish immigration and settlement as the expression of the interests of the Arab masses—so much so that they were prepared to ally themselves with Arab leaders whose social theory and practice were very far from theirs. Next came the Left Poalei Zion party, which, while accepting the principles of Zionism, rejected the emphasis of the mainstream parties on constructive work in the Yishuv and claimed that the struggle for the conquest of labour involved discrimination against the Arabs. One of their demands was that the Labour Zionist forces should ally themselves with the 'progressive elements' among the Arab workers. To this end, they advocated the establishment of joint Arab–Jewish trade unions, which would raise both the standard of living of the Arab workers and their political consciousness.

The attitudes of the major parties on this question had evolved during the Second and Third Aliya, when their main preoccupation was the construction of a Jewish agricultural economy based on Jewish labour. Under the circumstances, they gave scarcely more than cursory attention to the problems of Arab labour. By the mid-1920s, however, the situation had become more complex.[10] In certain sectors, and particularly the railways and telegraph services, where Jews and Arabs

[9] The text of the platform of the 'kibbutz list' appeared in *Davar*, 28 Nov. 1926. Reprinted in *Mekorot Hashomer Hatzair*, 5 (1987), 32–8.

[10] On the question of Arab–Jewish competition and co-operation in the economic sphere and its political implications, see Shapira, *Futile Struggle*.

employed by the Mandatory government worked side by side, they were organized in a joint union under Histadrut auspices. But in the *moshavot*, the struggle for Jewish labour continued unabated. It was not the classical struggle of an organized working class against the employers, however; the object of the leaders of the labour movement was to persuade the farmers that it was their Zionist duty to employ Jews rather than Arabs. The accepted methods of class struggle, such as strikes and picketing, were used here too; but to no small extent, their purpose was to influence public opinion, rather than to harm the employers' economic interests. Accordingly poets, artists, and other prominent figures were enlisted to support the picketers of the 1930s. But these tactics met with only limited success. Until the Arab revolt of 1936, Arab workers outnumbered Jews in most of the *moshavot*.

During this period, the question of the establishment of a joint trade union of Jewish and Arab agricultural workers in the *moshavot* was fiercely debated. On the face of it, it would seem that a joint effort to raise the standard of living of the Arab workers would reduce their effectiveness as competitors, and thus indirectly help the Jewish workers. Some leading figures in Ahdut Ha'avoda advocated the joint union for this reason. Hapoel Hatzair, on the other hand, was firmly opposed to the idea. Ideologically, its members saw in it a variation of the Marxist doctrine that class interests were of greater importance than national interests; and, indeed, this argument was one of the reasons why the joint union was a major plank in the platforms of the left-wing parties. In Ahdut Ha'avoda there was a struggle between the concept of the joint union and that of separate national unions in the framework of the Histadrut. The Histadrut conference of 1927 accepted the latter proposal; but its execution was slow and hesitant, and Arabs were admitted to full membership of the Histadrut only after the establishment of the State of Israel.

Hashomer Hatzair espoused the idea of the joint union in 1926, but during the late 1920s and early 1930s this policy was re-examined in a somewhat different context. From 1929 onwards, members of Hashomer Hatzair arrived in Palestine in ever-increasing numbers; membership of the Kibbutz Artzi leapt in one year from 362 to 800 and in 1934 it passed the 2,000 mark. But, in contrast with the earlier years, there was little agricultural settlement in this period: almost all these young pioneers spent their first years in the country in working groups in and near the *moshavot*, and took part in the daily struggle for employment to maintain a minimal standard of living. They quickly reached the conclusion that the demand of the majority in Ahdut Ha'avoda (including most of the leadership of the Kibbutz Me'uhad) for 'one hundred per cent Jewish labour' in the *moshavot* was unrealistic. On the other hand, they did not reject the concept of the conquest of labour, which they saw as an essential part of constructive Zionism. Their solution was to suggest that Arab membership of the joint trade union should be confined to those permanent Arab workers who, in their view, had become an established part of the *moshava* and could be effectively organized. Hashomer Hatzair was not alone in its advocacy of the joint union; but this particular combination of radicalism and realism marked it off from others—including some of the leaders of Mapai and the Kibbutz Me'uhad—who proposed similar policies.

The other plank in Hashomer Hatzair's Arab policy was the idea of binationalism. Again, this idea had been propounded within the movement even before the establishment of the Kibbutz Artzi; but it does not appear in the ideological platform adopted in 1927, since at this stage it did not command general approval. By 1933, the notion of a 'binational society . . . in Palestine and the surrounding area' had become part of the movement's official stance. It should be noted that at this stage this phrase was little more than a statement of final aspirations: the word 'state' was deliberately not used; for the 'binational society' was part of the concept of the post-revolutionary society which would be constructed after the 'second stage'. In this it was quite different from the superficially similar notion of 'parity' between Jews and Arabs which was the official policy of Ahdut Ha'avoda until 1929; 'parity' was not meant to be a permanent solution of the Jewish–Arab problem, but a means of coexistence until the Jewish community was sufficiently numerous and powerful to achieve the independence which was its ultimate aim.[11]

### 'Tightening the Line'

We have seen that one part of the basic ideology of Hashomer Hatzair—the 'theory of stages'—was determined in large measure by the radicalization of the young Jews who were its natural source of recruitment. This process continued throughout the 1920s. Between

[11] On the development of the binational idea in Hashomer Hatzair see Zait, *Zionism and Peace*, chs. 4 and 6; on parity, Teveth, *Ben-Gurion*, 563–7.

1928 and 1930, it led to a heated controversy on the subject known in the movement jargon as 'tightening the [movement] line'. This was a demand by the young leadership of Hashomer Hatzair in the Diaspora that the movement should take a more radical and independent line in political matters; in effect, that it should become a political party. This stand was firmly opposed by the veteran leadership, and rejected by the movement as a whole. But some of the tendencies already present in 1927—a Marxist world-view, support (albeit critical) for the Soviet Union, and opposition to any alliance between Labour Zionism and the social-democratic parties of the world—were reaffirmed and given a new emphasis.

Together, these four planks—the joint union, binationalism, opposition to the bureaucratization of the Histadrut, and radical Marxism—formed a platform which was to mark Hashomer Hatzair out increasingly from the other elements in the Labour Zionist movement over the coming years. None the less, its line on each of these issues had advocates, or close allies, within Ahdut Ha'avoda and Mapai; and, above all, its support for the principles of constructive Zionism kept it firmly within the ideological spectrum of the labour movement. Many of the leaders of the Kibbutz Artzi saw Mapai as the natural framework for their political activities; and the leaders of Mapai, who saw their party as an all-embracing framework in which a wide variety of ideological groups could find their place, were anxious to absorb the movement. Between 1930 and 1935 a series of discussions were held about the possibility of a merger between the two movements. They foundered on Hashomer Hatzair's insistence on the principle of ideological collectivism. They wanted to join Mapai as a movement, whereas Mapai's leaders were prepared to accept them as individuals, not *en bloc*; Mapai maintained that to accept the movement on its own terms could well turn the party into a federation of factions, rather than a united body determining its policies by majority decision.

## The Kibbutz Me'uhad

The Kibbutz Me'uhad followed a more hesitant and complex path to politicization than the Kibbutz Artzi, and this was reflected in the formula it eventually adopted. Although neither the Kibbutz Me'uhad nor its predecessor Kibbutz Ein Harod had any formal connection with the Ahdut Ha'avoda party, there were close personal and political ties between them. Thus, Tabenkin was one of the founding members of Ahdut Ha'avoda, and had been its first general secretary before he joined Ein Harod in 1921. Most of the Second Aliya veterans who left the Gedud together with him were also members or supporters of Ahdut Ha'avoda, as were most members of Havurat Ha'emek, which joined them after the split of 1923. Moreover, Ein Harod expected, and received, no less support from Ahdut Ha'avoda than the *kvutzot* and moshavim received from Hapoel Hatzair. The party's third conference, in 1922, had declared that there was 'a need for kibbutz settlements and labour battalions [*gedudei avoda*], directed by the Histadrut, and based on the aspiration to combine agricultural with other productive branches, collective and independent production and consumption.'[12] This was a declaration of support for the Gedud. The fourth conference, which took place in Ein Harod in May 1924, symbolized the transfer of the party's support from the Gedud to Ein Harod, but did not change the basic ideological stance expressed in this resolution.

As for Ein Harod, the unity between party and kibbutz seemed so fundamental that in the first two years of its independent existence (1923–5) virtually all the recorded discussions of the role of the kibbutz in the Yishuv took place in a party framework. Small wonder, then, that in the discussions which preceded the establishment of the Kibbutz Me'uhad in 1927 Tabenkin's view was: 'The party says: I think; the kibbutz says: I act.'[13] He believed in a threefold division of functions: the Histadrut was the organizational framework of the working class; the party gave it ideological direction; and the kibbutz executed the policies laid down in the political framework. Kibbutz members could and should be active in the party, but the kibbutz as such had no direct political function. All this, however, assumed a basic unity between the kibbutz and the party of the sort which had been proclaimed by both sides in 1924. Less than one year later, under the stress of the Fourth Aliya, this unity began to be disturbed. The leaders of Ein Harod continued to believe that only the kibbutz could solve the problems of the Yishuv; but the leaders of the party and the Histadrut had to deal with an influx of workers to the towns. Simple political realities forced them to face the fact that most of the Jewish working class in the Yishuv was outside the kibbutz. In January 1926 Berl Katznelson said:

[12] Decision of Ahdut Ha'avoda conference, Haifa, Dec. 1920, repr. in H. Hadari, *Kibbutz Ein Harod*, 122; decision of Ein Harod conference, ibid. 124.

[13] *Shorashim*, 2 (1980), 251.

It is [Tabenkin's] right to see the kibbutz as the seed from which the society of the future will grow. But can we, the whole community, forget our surroundings, ignore the new immigrants and the workers' lives, [and] exaggerate the ability of the kibbutz to absorb immigrants and the extent to which we have developed our settlements?... Is it possible for us today to put forward the notion that the kibbutz is a solution for every worker, an immediate answer to all our questions, a solution which can be achieved at once—and on these grounds to abandon all other activities?[14]

The ideologists of Ein Harod answered 'Yes' to all these questions. Thus began a process whereby the members of Ein Harod/the Kibbutz Me'uhad felt increasingly isolated in the labour movement and in their own political party. In 1929, when the creation of Mapai was being discussed, Tabenkin spoke of his feelings of alienation from the party, and his doubts about whether to support the merger with Hapoel Hatzair; for he feared that there would be a majority in the new party for those who opposed or mistrusted the kibbutz.

In the end, prompted by their belief in the concept of the 'mass party', Tabenkin and most of his comrades supported the creation of Mapai. But as Mapai moved ever further from the concept of kibbutz holism which underlay the thinking of Tabenkin and his followers, they began to be convinced of the need to take some sort of independent action within the party. In a sense, such action was forced on them by circumstances; for the interests of the kibbutz often clashed with those of other bodies or groups who held the same party allegiance. It is significant that the first serious suggestion that the Kibbutz Me'uhad should act independently in the Histadrut and the party was put forward in 1930, at a discussion of the decisions of the executive of the newly founded Jewish Agency. The representatives of the Histadrut were accused of having neglected the interests of the Kibbutz Me'uhad in the negotiations for allocating land for new settlement. The reaction of some kibbutz members was unprecedented in its extremity. There were demands that the movement should increase its activities in the Histadrut and the party, and that it should even send people to work as officials of these bodies and thereby acquire positions of influence.[15] This was a startlingly new departure. Until now, the leaders of the Kibbutz Me'uhad had viewed 'public activity' in much the same way as had the *kvutzot*, as a form

[14] At Ahdut Ha'avoda conference, Nahalat Yehuda, Jan. 1926. See Katznelson, *Writings*, ii. 132.

[15] Near, *Kibbutz and Society*, 276–81.

of service to the wider community. This had been one of the points of contention with Ben-Gurion in 1929. 'If you can't give more people to work in the party and the Histadrut,' he had declared, 'I'm afraid I shall begin to turn against the kibbutz.'[16] But, no less than the *kvutzot*, the Kibbutz Me'uhad had other priorities. Not only was there a chronic shortage of people with organizational ability in the kibbutzim themselves; it was also feared, with some justification, that the seductions of town life might prove too much for these emissaries from the kibbutz and tempt them to leave.

The first reaction to the suggestion that the Kibbutz Me'uhad should become an active force within the party was shocked opposition, from inside and outside the kibbutz. One of the veteran members of Ein Harod said:

We aren't a sect, not the cream of society. If ever we cease to see ourselves as the servants of society, part and parcel of our surroundings, we shall cease to exist. It is an illusion to think that we shall improve anything by sending people to work in public institutions. Our strength is not in the personal qualities of one or other of our members, but in the creative activities [of the kibbutz as a whole].[17]

At this stage, the idea that the kibbutz movement as such should play an active part in forming Histadrut policy was rejected by the leaders of movement and party alike. But this discussion was the beginning of a trend which was to become dominant over the next five years.

During this period, there was constant friction between the leaders of the Kibbutz Me'uhad and those of the Histadrut. The former accused the latter of not promoting their economic interests and of hostility or neutrality in the long-drawn-out struggle between Hechalutz and the independent youth movements. The Histadrut leaders countered these arguments with the accusation that the kibbutz was a 'sect', fighting for its own interests against those of the moshavim and other no less legitimate forms of settlement. These accusations were particularly resented by the members of the Kibbutz Me'uhad, who believed that they, and only they, represented the true interests of the Yishuv. None the less, they did their best to act as loyal party members. As far as possible, they abstained from joint consultation and action within the organs of the party and the

---

[16] In the central committee of the Kibbutz Me'uhad, 23 Jan. 1929.

[17] Aharon Tsizling at the Council of Kibbutz Me'uhad, Giv'at Hashlosha, 20 Nov. 1930; *Mibifnim*, 48 (Nov. 1930), 9.

Histadrut; and insofar as they were prepared to release members to work in the party apparatus, they did so in the spirit of service described above. But it gradually became apparent that this stance was in large measure fictitious. This was due in part to the cumulative effect of the constant clashes of interest built into the situation. But the trend was intensified and brought to a head by the dramatic changes in Europe and the Yishuv during these years.

## *Preparing for the 'Final Battle'*

Yitzhak Tabenkin believed that the apocalyptic vision of the world which he proclaimed from 1933 onwards had special relevance for the Jewish people. In his view, the coming war would be fought on many fronts. Internationally, the capitalist and Fascist countries would be arrayed against a bloc led by the Soviet Union. The Yishuv was under permanent threat of attack by the Arabs, and British support in this struggle was far from certain. And the Zionist movement—and particularly the labour movement within it—was endangered by the growth of Revisionism, which Tabenkin believed to be simply Zionist Fascism.

The leaders of the Kibbutz Me'uhad believed that their movement would continue to be the major source of pioneers for the Yishuv and play a major role in the coming struggle. How grave a problem this could be became clear when the first large wave of immigrants arrived in the spring of 1932. In October 1932, the Kibbutz Me'uhad's central committee was shocked by the news that 34 per cent of the new immigrants that year, all of whom had been trained and selected in the kibbutzim of Hechalutz, had not even bothered to see a kibbutz, but had gone straight to a town, moshav, or *moshava*. It soon became clear that these figures were not the result of some special circumstance, but a trend that threatened to become permanent. In the lengthy discussions which followed, the cause was attributed to the new immigrants' low cultural standards, which resulted from the general decline in education and culture among European Jewry. The cure was to be intensive 'cultural' education; and, indeed, plans were made for widespread education programmes, including seminars, lectures, and the dissemination of literature, both in the kibbutzim of the Kibbutz Me'uhad and in the Diaspora.

In the atmosphere of the time, it was more or less inevitable that the concept of 'culture' was interpreted largely in political terms. The members of the youth movements themselves demanded of the leadership a clear line on current political issues, as had long been the case in Hashomer Hatzair and Gordonia.

The demand for more effective education methods proved to be a further step in the politicization of the Kibbutz Me'uhad. An additional factor was that by 1934 the Kibbutz Me'uhad had acquired many of the characteristics of a mass movement. Its numbers had leapt from just over 1,000 in 1929 to 2,300 in 1932, and a year later it was approaching the 3,000 mark. Education could no longer be effected by individual persuasion, personal contact between the leadership and the rank and file membership, and a slow process of absorption: now, methods of mass persuasion and propaganda were required.[18] Preparations for the 'final battle' included ideological education, the heightening of movement solidarity, and a high degree of discipline. At the Kibbutz Me'uhad's conference in 1933, one of its leaders and ideologists spoke of the aspiration to maximum ideological unity.

If we add to our social solidarity by increasing our ideological partnership, this could enrich our life within the kibbutz, consolidate our community and educate our members, and be a fruitful influence on our activity in the Histadrut and the Party.... We need the courage to think independently, within the framework of overall responsibility to the working-class.[19]

Thus, parallel with the growing sense of disillusion with Mapai as protector and promoter of kibbutz settlement came a process of discussion and education which tended to stress the ideological solidarity of the Kibbutz Me'uhad. By 1933, the Kibbutz Me'uhad was well on the way to becoming an independent grouping within Mapai, its undoubted strength enabling it to defend its interests and present a united front to the leadership of the party. In that case, it was natural to ask whether it had not become a faction within the party, as its enemies charged. There seemed to be only one satisfactory reply: if it could find allies within the party who criticized the leadership on the same grounds, it would appear not as an interest group but as part of a movement for change within the party. In 1934-5 an issue arose which brought about just this constellation. It can best be viewed against the background of the issues with which the Kibbutz Me'uhad was concerned in the early 1930s.

In 1933, continuing the speech about the 'final battle' quoted

[18] Near, *Kibbutz and Society*, 269.
[19] Lev Leviteh, in Kibbutz Me'uhad, *Yagur Council, 1933*, 50.

above, Tabenkin said: '[The kibbutz] will play an important role in
guiding the movement in this war. We still have difficult days ahead
of us. They will try to close our schools, to kill our leaders, to destroy
the kibbutz and deny us land for settlement.'[20] Each of these issues
was a matter of current concern to the kibbutz. There was wide
support in Mapai for transferring the responsibility for the Histadrut's
educational system, which included the kibbutz schools, to the Jewish
Agency, and Tabenkin feared that this would destroy the independence of the kibbutz and the Histadrut in the educational sphere;
and, as we have seen, the Kibbutz Me'uhad often found itself isolated
in its struggle for land and capital for settlement. Each of these issues,
like the controversy about Hechalutz, bears a similar stamp: in each
case the direct interests of the Kibbutz Me'uhad were at stake; each
was seen by the leaders of that movement as a matter of national
rather than sectoral interest; and on each of them they were opposed
by the leadership of the Histadrut, or some part of it. The educational
work of the Kibbutz Me'uhad was based on the principle of 'comprehensiveness' (*klaliut*), according to which Hechalutz, guided by
the Kibbutz Me'uhad, represented the true interests of Zionism and
the Jewish people—in contrast to the 'sectional' youth movements
and the rest of the Zionist movement. Tabenkin was translating this
principle into terms of current politics.

The central issue for the members of the Kibbutz Me'uhad,
however, was, in Tabenkin's words: 'they will try ... to kill our
leaders.' This is a clear reference to the murder of Haim Arlosorov,
the head of the political department of the Jewish Agency, a few
months before the conference at which these words were spoken. At
the time, the labour leaders had no doubt at all that this was the act
of the Revisionists; probably of some member of Brit Habirionim, an
extremist group which had made Arlosorov a special target for its
invective. Although this event was exceptional both in its seriousness
and its results, it was not an isolated event. It came as the climax of
a number of clashes between the Revisionists and the Histadrut. Since
1930 the Revisionists had been active in attempting to organize their
own working groups in opposition to those of the Histadrut and in
demonstrating their strength at political meetings and parades. In both
types of activities there had been clashes, some violent, with Histadrut
*plugot* (mainly of the Kibbutz Me'uhad) or with Mapai members.

---

[20] Tabenkin, in Kibbutz Me'uhad, *Yagur Council, 1933*, 77.

In discussing some of these clashes in the central committee of Mapai, Berl Katznelson demanded that the Histadrut should in future eschew the use of violence. He was supported by a number of Mapai leaders, particularly those who had been members of Hapoel Hatzair. To Tabenkin and many others, this view was close to heresy. Revisionism was Fascism, and should be destroyed by any available means, including force if necessary. On this issue, which he saw as critical for the kibbutz and labour movements alike, the leadership of Mapai was a broken reed: Katznelson opposed taking action, and Ben-Gurion was not prepared to stand against him. (Although it appears that he was responsible for the organization of the Hapoel squads, which took part in a number of violent clashes with the Revisionists, in the face of Katznelson's threat of resignation from the central bodies of Mapai he did not force the issue to a decision.) In a discussion of the question in the central committee of Mapai (23 April 1933) Tabenkin accused *Davar*, the Histadrut newspaper, of 'stammering' on this matter, and protested against Ben-Gurion's absence from the country, which left the party leaderless. For him, this was a prime example of an issue on which the kibbutz should 'play an important role in guiding the movement'.[21]

## The Ben-Gurion–Jabotinsky Agreement

The opportunity to do so came in 1934. Ben-Gurion surprised all his colleagues by negotiating secretly with the Revisionist leader, Jabotinsky, and presenting them with a draft agreement between the Histadrut and the Revisionist movement for their ratification. This would have ended the constant struggles between the two organizations, but at the cost of recognizing the legitimacy of the Revisionist workers' movement, and setting up neutral (non-Histadrut) employment offices. Again, Katznelson and many of the ex-Hapoel Hatzair leaders supported the agreement. Tabenkin saw it as a betrayal of socialist principles: it recognized a Fascist movement as a legitimate sector of the Yishuv, and limited the right to organize freely and to strike. In the campaign which followed, the Kibbutz Me'uhad took the lead in the opposition to the agreement, and secured its rejection.

Here, for the first time, the Kibbutz Me'uhad had emerged from its isolation to political triumph, on an issue which was seen by the whole of the labour movement as of cardinal importance. In one

---

[21] Teveth, *Ben-Gurion*, 376–7, 413–14, 461–4; Shapira, 'The Debate in Mapai about the Use of Violence'.

sense, this issue was similar to those in which the Kibbutz Me'uhad had previously been engaged: the defeat of the Revisionists, whose workers were engaged in fierce competition with Histadrut workers for jobs and working conditions, was a vital interest of the Kibbutz Me'uhad. But in this case it was also widely agreed that the matter was of vital public importance, and that the stand taken by the Kibbutz Me'uhad sprang from its desire to protect the whole of the labour movement, and not itself alone. As Berl Katznelson remarked at the time, this incident marked a new stage in Labour Zionist politics.[22] The Kibbutz Me'uhad had come to the centre of the political stage, on a matter in which its own interests were widely identified (and not only by its own members) as being congruent with those of the Yishuv as a whole. In the course of the struggle, the Kibbutz Me'uhad's line was supported by the Kibbutz Artzi, Left Poalei Zion, and a wide range of active members and leaders within Mapai. The pattern for future developments had been set.

This applies in another sense too. Analysis of the vote on the agreement within the Kibbutz Me'uhad shows a relatively high number of abstentions. This is surely an indication of a feeling of distress at the struggle between the party and the Kibbutz Me'uhad. Here were the first indications of the strain which such ventures into national political leadership created within the movement, and which would eventually divide it completely.[23]

## Gordonia and Hever Hakvutzot[24]

It is paradoxical that Gordonia developed its ideology and declared itself the successor of Hapoel Hatzair just at the period when that party was losing much of its distinctive character; indeed, it was already well on the path which would eventually lead it to unity with Ahdut Ha'avoda in the creation of Mapai. Against this background, the demand of Gordonia to return to the pristine values of Hapoel Hatzair seemed vague and undefined. It was widely interpreted as a call to reject Ahdut Ha'avoda's overtures for unity; and, indeed, the leaders of Gordonia concurred in the creation of Mapai only with the greatest reluctance. In concrete terms, Gordonia had three major demands, one ideological and two practical. Ideologically, they were

[22] Katznelson, *Writings*, vii. 368–9.
[23] Rosolio, 'Controversy'.
[24] This section is partly based on Margalit, *The Gordonia Youth Movement*, chs. 6, 7, and 8, and on Ben-Avram, *Hever Hakvutzot*, 150–66.

faithful to the legacy of A. D. Gordon, who had firmly opposed the use of Marxist and class terminology with regard to the Jewish people and Zionism. (Gordon himself objected to the term 'socialism', although many of the party's leaders used it.) Gordonia's ideology was anti-Marxist, and its leaders interpreted the Gordonian tradition in terms of a non-Marxian socialism of the type advocated by many of the European social-democratic parties.

In practical terms, Gordon's opposition to 'mechanical' forms of social organization led Gordonia to reject the 'great and growing kibbutz' and propound a theory of 'organic' *kvutzot* very similar to that of Hashomer Hatzair. Its leaders also rejected the forms of mass education adopted by the Kibbutz Me'uhad in favour of the small 'intimate' group. Here again, they were very close to Hashomer Hatzair in their social and educational concepts, although they rejected the Marxist terminology which was common both to that movement and to the youth movements of the Kibbutz Me'uhad.

Thus, although members of Gordonia found themselves in the same party as those of Hechalutz and the other youth movements of the Kibbutz Me'uhad, there were fundamental differences of outlook between them, which were compounded by the struggle for the control of Hechalutz; for Gordonia constantly allied itself with Hashomer Hatzair in defending the autonomy of the smaller movements against the encroachments of the Kibbutz Me'uhad.

At the time of the establishment of Mapai, it looked as if these distinctive features of Gordonia's ideology and practice could make it a minority faction within Mapai: after all, class terminology was common among the leadership of Ahdut Ha'avoda, as was support for the idea of the 'big kibbutz', and specially for the Kibbutz Me'uhad. In fact, however, the issues which arose in the early 1930s were not nearly as unambiguous as might have been forecast. On the question of the use of violence in dealing with the Revisionists, both the leaders of Gordonia and the former leaders of Hapoel Hatzair remained true to two elements in Gordon's teaching—a tendency to pacifism, and an emphasis on the unity of the Jewish people as against class and political divisions—and supported Katznelson's position. While the Kibbutz Me'uhad adopted an increasingly pro-Soviet stance from 1933 onwards, Gordonia, together with Katznelson and Ben-Gurion, remained suspicious both of Russian intentions and of the effectiveness of a popular front led by Communists. Thus, on a number of concrete issues, the leaders of Gordonia came close to the leadership of Mapai and were firmly opposed to the policies of the other two kibbutz movements.

Although the establishment of Hever Hakvutzot in 1929 and its union with Gordonia in 1934 led to no formal affiliation with Mapai, and no change in the 'political neutrality' of the older members and *kvutzot*, this process was, in effect, the result of a clear understanding: in exchange for the accession of manpower which saved the *kvutzot* from the dangers of extinction, the members of Gordonia were allowed to put into practice their concept of 'ideological fraternity', which was very similar to the ideological collectivism of Hashomer Hatzair. Together with those veterans of the *kvutzot* who were active in the party at various levels, ex-members of Gordonia began to play a part in the deliberations of Mapai. Although Hever Hakvutzot had no formal connection with the party, there was no doubt of its place in the political system of the Yishuv.

## *Netzah*[25]

From the first, the leaders of Netzah (the Russian branch of Hashomer Hatzair) had rejected the non-political concept of the youth movement as propounded by the majority Hashomer Hatzair movement in its early stages. From 1927 to 1930 their position was anomalous. Politically, they supported Ahdut Ha'avoda, and saw their affiliation with the Kibbutz Me'uhad as a logical consequence of that support. In terms of youth movement values and their belief in the 'organic' kibbutz, however, they were still very close to their mother movement, and remained affiliated to the world federation of Hashomer Hatzair movements. The leaders of Hashomer Hatzair invested a great deal of effort in attempting to persuade them to remain in the movement, but to no avail: they rejected both the notion of ideological collectivism and the concrete policies of the majority in their movement. In 1930 they left it, and became an independent movement affiliated to the Kibbutz Me'uhad. Shortly afterwards they adopted the name Netzah (an acronym of *Noar Tzofi Halutzi*—Pioneering Scouting Youth).

Their enthusiasm for Ahdut Ha'avoda, and afterwards for Mapai, was far greater than that of the veteran leaders of the Kibbutz Me'uhad. They were among the first to demand that the movement should define its position on the unity of the labour parties, and they declared openly that their youth movement educated not only to

[25] This section is based on Near, *Kibbutz and Society*, 388–54 and ch. 13.

socialism and the kibbutz but also to Mapai. Within the party, most of them continued to express admiration for Ben-Gurion, although there is no evidence that they supported him on the issue of the projected agreement with the Revisionists. They supported the moves towards increased participation by the kibbutz in the general political system, but with one important reservation. In the words of one of their leaders: 'In my view, the kibbutz should make collective decisions on political questions. Of course, this is a two-edged weapon: there is a danger of our cutting ourselves off from the rest of the [working] class, and that would be alien to the spirit and essence of the movement. Even so, we should not abstain from political discussion within the kibbutz.'[26]

'To cut oneself off from the working-class' meant, in this context, to become an independent political force within the Histadrut— precisely the direction towards which the leadership of the Kibbutz Me'uhad was beginning to lean at this time. Thus, at the same period in which the leadership of the Kibbutz Me'uhad was feeling its way towards becoming an alternative to the leadership of the labour movement, there was within the same movement a small but well-defined group whose instincts were to rely on that leadership. This group was not only at odds with Tabenkin and his allies on many issues of internal kibbutz policy; it was able to command its own reserves of manpower, and controlled an independent youth movement. In terms of the declared pluralism of the Kibbutz Me'uhad, this was certainly no ideological deviation. But there can be no doubt that it conflicted with the course on which that movement's leaders were embarked in 1933.

## Movement Politics: A Comparative Analysis

To conclude this section, we can now sum up the parallel processes of politicization in the three major kibbutz movements. Each of them began as a non-political movement whose primary concern was agricultural settlement and the education of young Jews in the Diaspora to that end. None of them altered these basic aims, but each evolved its own answer to the question posed at the beginning of this chapter: what is the most appropriate framework for the kibbutz to influence the wider political system? The simplest case was that of the Kibbutz Artzi. Despite its rather

[26] Elik Shomroni in Kibbutz Me'uhad, *Yagur Council, 1933*, 65.

obfuscating terminology, this movement was fundamentally a party from the day of its establishment, though of a type which must be very rare, if not unique, in the history of democratic politics: it was a non-recruiting party. Its other characteristic principle, ideological collectivism, is far from unknown in the history of politics: it is the Communist theory of democratic centralism under a different name. It should, however, be added that in its actual workings it functioned very differently from the Communist parties. The definition in the founding document of the Kibbutz Artzi—'a framework for the continuous crystallization of the movement's ideology'—was perfectly accurate.

In this respect, the Kibbutz Artzi provides a very clear contrast to the other non-recruiting party, Gedud Ha'avoda. In the absence of a self-denying ordinance such as that of Hashomer Hatzair, the Gedud broke up as a result of a long series of fierce controversies followed by decisions which it was not in the power of a voluntary body such as a kibbutz movement to enforce. There seems no doubt that the Kibbutz Artzi learnt the lesson of the Gedud well.

Hever Hakvutzot offers two models of political activity in the kibbutz: neutrality and service. In the first, neither the kibbutz nor the kibbutz movement as such has any political function: political activity is the right of the individual, not of the collective. In the second version, which we have seen at a very early stage, political activity is not a right, but a duty: it is one of the many ways in which the kibbutz puts itself at the service of the broader community. This was the view of an influential minority within the veteran *kvutzot* and it was also the practice (if not necessarily the theory) of Gordonia, from the time that that movement adopted an attitude of support for the leadership of the labour movement in the early 1930s.

The Kibbutz Me'uhad underwent a process of change from a politics of service, essentially similar to that of the veteran *kvutzot*, to one of leadership. At this stage, however, its opposition to the notion of a kibbutz party was more than verbal, and there was no group within the Kibbutz Me'uhad which questioned the commitment to the mass party, Mapai. In view of the widespread reluctance to see the kibbutz as a faction within the party, the aspiration to leadership was expressed in two ways: participation in policy-forming bodies of the party, and a constant search for political partners. At this stage, this search was connected with particular issues; it was only later that it expressed itself in a permanent alliance.

What were the reasons for this process of politicization? Despite the differences between the movements, some underlying causes may be perceived. In one sense, the Kibbutz Me'uhad serves as a paradigm for all the movements. In analysing the issues which it saw as vital, I emphasized their connection with the existence and progress of the Kibbutz Me'uhad as a movement for settlement, education, and absorption of immigrants. When it appeared that these interests could not be promoted without political support, there was a gradual progression from the politics of self-defence to the politics of leadership; the interest of the kibbutz was increasingly seen as a function of the public interest. Likewise, the Kibbutz Artzi, having evolved its 'theory of stages', went on to heighten its left-wing orientation in response to the demands of its constituency, the young people who were recruited to its ranks. Failure to do so would have meant that neither the educational movement nor its kibbutzim could have survived. The same applies to the veteran *kvutzot*. For the leaders of Gordonia, politicization was a matter of ideological choice; for the veteran *kvutzot*, the link with Gordonia, and the tacit acceptance of its political activities, was a matter of survival. In each case, therefore, there was a clear link between the process of politicization and the basic needs of the kibbutz movement.

One more factor should be noted. In the cases of Hashomer Hatzair and Gordonia, it is clear that the decisive element was the youth movement itself: more exactly, that generation of young people within the youth movement whose political perceptions led to the change of line. A closer examination of the process in the Kibbutz Me'uhad shows a marked similarity to the other two movements. In the discussions which preceded the establishment of Mapai—in the 1930 discussion at Giv'at Hashlosha, and in the Yagur conference of 1933— recent arrivals from Hechalutz and the youth movements (and recently returned emissaries) demanded a clear and radical political line. The reason is clear: the environment in which these young people lived and worked made them constantly aware of the overwhelming influence of world political factors on the Jewish people and the Yishuv. They had no patience for the long view espoused by many veteran kibbutz members who believed with perfect faith in the eventual triumph of constructive socialism, much as their religious forebears had believed in the eventual coming of the Messiah. If the young people could not be convinced that the kibbutz and the kibbutz movement could affect the course of current events, they might well defect to a movement

that did claim to do so, such as the Communist party. The proximate
cause in the process of politicization was, in every case, the youth
movement. But it could well be said that the ultimate cause was the
*Zeitgeist*, speaking through the mouths of the younger generation.

It remains only to sum up the issues which the movements considered to be of importance. Here, we must ask to what extent any or
all of them mapped out a distinctive policy, in contrast to the other
movements and their closest allies, the leaders of the labour movement.
Table 11 compares these policies with those of the three leading
non-kibbutz figures in Mapai: Ben-Gurion and Katznelson, undoubtedly the two most authoritative men in the party (and both formerly
leaders of Ahdut Ha'avoda); and Joseph Sprinzak, formerly the central political leader of Hapoel Hatzair. It shows how varied their views
were, and how far they were from being in any way united politically.

TABLE 11. Political Attitudes in 1935: Kibbutz Movements and
Labour Leaders

|  | Kibbutz movements | | | | Labour leaders | | |
|---|---|---|---|---|---|---|---|
|  | Kibbutz Me'uhad | Netzah | Gordonia | Kibbutz Artzi | Ben-Gurion | Katz-nelson | Sprinzak |
| 'Comprehensiveness' in Hechalutz | + | − | − | − | + | − | − |
| Support for Weizmann | ± | ± | + | ± | ± | ± | + |
| Binationalism | − | − | − | + | − | − | − |
| Joint (Arab–Jewish) trade union | − | − | − | + | − | − | − |
| Use of force against Revisionists | + | + | − | + | ± | − | − |
| Support for Ben-Gurion–Jabotinsky agreement | − | − | + | − | + | + | + |

*Note:* +: supported; −: opposed; ±: neutral, wavered, or changed policy.

### THE EXPANSION OF THE YOUTH MOVEMENTS

The steady growth of the Yishuv in the late 1920s and in the period
of prosperity from 1932 to 1935 was paralleled by similar developments in the youth movements abroad: as in 1924–5, the possibility of
immigration stimulated Zionist aspirations. Numbers in the training

kibbutzim grew steadily to a peak of 21,000 pioneers in more than a thousand kibbutzim, and a total of 89,500 movement members in twenty-five countries in 1935.[27] Thereafter, with the economic recession, the Arab revolt, and the restrictions on immigration, the whole of the Zionist movement, including its youth movements, entered a period of crisis. This chapter will conclude, therefore, with a sketch of how the youth movements described earlier developed over this later period. It should be noted, however, that a number of new youth movements were established at this time, both in the Diaspora and the Yishuv. They are not considered at this juncture because in general they became a significant factor in the development of the kibbutz movement only at a later stage. A detailed description is therefore postponed till Chapter 8, even though some of their history coincides with the events described in this section.

## Hechalutz in Poland

It was not only the ideology of the 'great and growing kibbutz' which led to the constant expansion of the training kibbutzim in the early 1930s. From the resumption of immigration in 1929, and even more from 1932 onwards, the steady increase in the membership of Hechalutz—and indeed of all the Zionist youth movements—led to constant pressure to accept more members. In 1931–2, when growing unemployment and the antisemitic policies of government agencies in Poland made it impossible to maintain the kibbutzim in their original form, their members embarked on what they called, no doubt in deliberate imitation of the Yishuv during the Third Aliya, 'the period of the roads'.[28] Carrying their tools and a minimum of domestic equipment, the young people walked from town to town in search of work. By doing so they not only ensured their physical survival but also increased the public impact of the movement; for their first contacts, and in many cases their places of work, were with the local Jewish community. By broadening their web of contacts in this way, they became a recognized and influential factor within Polish Jewry. At this stage, history was on their side. The contrast between the growing poverty and dangers of the Diaspora, the impenetrability of the rest of the world, and the prosperity and relative accessibility of the Yishuv was obvious to all. Palestine was widely viewed as a

[27] Memorandum submitted to the Zionist Congress of 1935 by the World Hechalutz Organization. Repr. in Otiker, *Hechalutz in Poland*, app. c.
[28] Braslavsky, 'On the Roads'.

promising place of refuge, and Hechalutz as the best way to obtain
the treasured immigration certificate. As one of the emissaries of the
Kibbutz Me'uhad reported in 1932: 'People are hungry for emigration
to Palestine, hysterical to go.... The *shtetl* is in decline, there is no
work, no chance of studying, no help from [relatives in] America or
the Argentine.... Fathers encourage their sons to join the training
farms. They are looking for any way of getting to Palestine—even by
bicycle or on foot.'[29]

Even in the context of the demand for unlimited devotion and self-
sacrifice which were built into the ideology of Hechalutz, the training
kibbutzim did not always achieve unequivocally positive results. One
of the emissaries of the Kibbutz Me'uhad wrote in 1930:

[In the training kibbutzim] pioneering means suffering, even if it is unnecessary.... It is no wonder that so many are sick. People are being prepared not
for work, but for illness. It is very hard to explain these problems to
the people in charge here—they can't and won't understand (especially in
Klosova).... Much the same applies to their understanding of the principles
of kibbutz life. They have little desire to learn about the problems of collective
living. There is a sort of 'kibbutz dogma'. They tend to demand absolute
conformism, and are in danger of emphasizing the trivial at the expense of
the essential. They aren't concerned about the constructive side of life in the
real kibbutz—economic progress, child-rearing, the practice of communal
life. They know little of all this, and perhaps it doesn't interest them ... but
when they heard that one of the girls in the *pluga* in Petah Tikva dared to go
to the cinema with someone who isn't a kibbutz member and the kibbutz
didn't react, there were stormy discussions about it. It proved that the kibbutz
was deteriorating, they said, and that those who are to join it next year must
bring it back to the principles of pure communism.[30]

Such phenomena were apparently built into the isolated and introverted life of the training kibbutz; and although the emissaries from
the kibbutz movement were able to put matters in a more balanced
perspective, there were never enough of them to withstand the many
harmful influences to which the kibbutzim were subject. Moreover,
the fact that the length of the period of training was undefined, and
depended on decisions quite beyond the control of the local Hechalutz
authorities, created perpetual tensions within the system. In general,
the trainees spent between one and two years on the farm; but at

[29] Aharon Berdichevsky in the Kibbutz Me'uhad central committee, 29 July 1932.
[30] Letter from Hershl Pinski, 6 Feb. 1930. Repr. in Dan, *The Book of Klosova*,
225–6.

times of reduced immigration, as from 1936 to 1939, this could be lengthened to as much as four years. In this context, the training period turned into a semi-permanent way of life. Relations between the sexes, usually no less puritanical than those in the early kibbutzim, caused serious problems in many cases. So, too, did the relationships with the local Jewish communities, whose religious leaders found much to disapprove of in the life-style of the free-thinking pioneers. Many of these problems were compounded, particularly in the kibbutzim connected with the Kibbutz Me'uhad, by the presence of a number of 'simple pioneers' with no previous education in the youth movement.

Some of the problems involved in this situation are hinted at in the following extract from a report of an emissary of the Kibbutz Me'uhad. It describes the process of selection of candidates for emigration at Klosova in 1930:

There were very many people at the general meeting, expectant and tense. I opened the discussion. I explained the situation in Palestine and in the movement, and the reason why this compelled us to choose the immigrants. The central committee had allocated 70 certificates to this kibbutz, out of 260 possible candidates.... The general meeting had to choose a special committee, with broad prerogatives, which would have the confidence of all the members. The committee sat for three whole days and nights.... The criteria it applied were: length of time in training, attitude to work and society, knowledge of Hebrew, ability to withstand the hardships of life in the training kibbutz, suitability to be a member of the Histadrut, the working class, and the kibbutz. All these factors were summed up, and the deciding question was the degree to which he or she was able to fulfil the current demands of the Yishuv and the kibbutz. So some who had been in training for some time had to stay, while a few, who had been there for only seven months, were granted their certificate on the grounds that they would be of exceptional value to the kibbutz [in Palestine]. In fact, a considerable proportion of those who stayed had been on the farm between a year and eighteen months.[31]

The criteria for selecting the new immigrants were largely applied by those who had lived with them over the previous months. Whereas this undoubtedly made it possible to exercise more specific judgements than mechanical criteria such as time spent in training, it had some very definite disadvantages. Many, particularly among the 'simple

[31] Lev Leviteh, report to Hechalutz seminar, Dec. 1930. Dan, *Book of Klosova*, 206–8.

pioneers', were motivated less by ideals of equality, community, and socialism than by the desire to escape to Palestine from a life that was becoming increasingly intolerable. These people would attune their behaviour to what was expected of them. But very often their training experience made them disillusioned with the kibbutzim, and they revealed this only after arriving in Palestine.

One of the results was a great and unexpected increase in the number of graduates of the training kibbutzim who left the kibbutz after their arrival in Palestine. In the years between 1932 and 1939, all the youth movements attempted to combat this phenomenon by increasing the number of emissaries and the intensity of educational work in the training kibbutzim. But none of them was able to send anything like an adequate number.

Throughout this period, the struggle between Hechalutz and the independent youth movements continued unabated. The leaders of Hechalutz continued to develop Hechalutz Hatzair as a younger section of their movement that would share its ideology and educational approach, and demanded that its graduates should have priority in admission to the training farms. The independent movements fought this move, and managed to defeat it in the world Hechalutz movement. It became clear that although the Kibbutz Me'uhad had a clear majority in Polish Hechalutz, the other movements outnumbered it in the world movement. From the mid-1930s the Kibbutz Me'uhad attempted to increase its influence by a new tactic. In certain countries, notably Lithuania, local conditions had led to the establishment of joint training farms in which graduates of different movements received their training together. The Kibbutz Me'uhad tried to force the adoption of this system in the whole of Hechalutz, particularly in Poland. The other movements resisted strongly, on the ground that such establishments would be dominated by the Kibbutz Me'uhad. This and similar issues were to have been discussed at the conference of Polish Hechalutz in 1932; but, alarmed by the prospect of being steamrollered by the Kibbutz Me'uhad's automatic majority, the other movements boycotted the conference. The questions at issue were subsequently brought for decision to the central bodies of Mapai and the Histadrut—a move which emphasized the degree to which the centre of power in all the movements had shifted from the Diaspora to the Yishuv. Here too, however, no clear decision could be reached; for, while the Kibbutz Me'uhad remained the strongest single pioneering movement, it was never able to defeat an alliance of all the other movements, each jealous of its own autonomy. So the institutional *status quo* remained in being until 1939.[32]

The controversies about the nature of Hechalutz and its policies were not only a function of power struggles between the movements. Criticism was also voiced from within the labour movement by people whose general approach was favourable to the Kibbutz Me'uhad. One incident, whose later consequences were of very great importance in the further development of the kibbutz movement, was sparked off by Berl Katznelson's incognito visit to a number of training kibbutzim in the summer of 1933.[33] In his report to the Central Committee of the Kibbutz Me'uhad, he spoke of the low cultural standards on the training kibbutzim; of the belief that 'the more cruelty, the more pioneering'; of the resultant inefficiency, disorder, and illness; and of the 'regime of fear' resulting in submissiveness and hypocrisy on the part of many of the trainees, who would pretend to a fervent belief in the kibbutz simply in order to obtain the coveted immigration certificate. The result, he claimed, was that no more than 30 per cent of the trainees actually settled in the kibbutz, and that as many as 65 per cent knew no Hebrew when they arrived.

These criticisms were indignantly rejected by Benny Marshak, the leader of Klosova, now settled at Kibbutz Giv'at Hashlosha, Tabenkin, and others. Certainly it was true, said Marshak, that the more one was prepared for cruelty, the higher the degree of pioneering which one could achieve. The training kibbutzim and the emissaries did indeed select people for immigration according to their suitability for the kibbutz—and quite rightly so; for the kibbutz was the only sector of the workers' movement which remained faithful to the pristine aims of the Histadrut. Tabenkin added that the 'power of the certificate' was apparently necessary in order to influence young people in the right direction: 'Education involves the suppression of certain human characteristics, and that arouses resistance.'

This discussion reveals a deep conflict of values. For Tabenkin and Marshak did not deny the facts which Katznelson had discovered in

---

[32] Sarid, *Hechalutz in Poland*, pt. 6, ch. 5.

[33] Shapira, *Berl*, ch. 12. Katznelson's report and the ensuing discussion were printed in the minutes of the enlarged central committee of the Kibbutz Me'uhad at Ramat Hakovesh, 23–6 Nov. 1933: Kibbutz Me'uhad archives sect. 5, box 1, file 6, 26. They were repr. as 'On Questions of our Movements in the Diaspora' (mimeo), (Ein Harod, 1933). The quotations in this section are taken from this report, unless otherwise attributed.

the training kibbutzim. On the contrary, they defended both the draconian means which were used, and the end: the creation of the Klosovan 'man of stone', as against Katznelson's idealized Second Aliya pioneer, whom he described as 'the opposite of a philistine, the opposite of slovenliness, cowardice, submissiveness'. In this context, it is no wonder that he defended the rights of the autonomous youth movements, which prided themselves on putting the individual at the centre of their concerns. And it is equally no wonder that his defence of a pluralistic approach incensed Tabenkin, whose educational approach had always been, in his own words, monistic.

One question remains, however. Just five weeks earlier, Tabenkin had addressed the same forum on the same subject, and had condemned what was going on in the training kibbutzim in almost the same words as Katznelson's: the trainees were 'living a lie', standards of cleanliness and behaviour were low, and cultural activity less than minimal.[34] What incensed Tabenkin was not what was said, but who said it; and, particularly, the conclusion that the Kibbutz Me'uhad's educational monism, and its claim to a monopoly in Hechalutz, were not justified. This was not simply a discussion of educational and moral issues. It involved a conflict of vital interests.

Although Katznelson had argued all these issues at length with the leaders of Hechalutz in Warsaw, the most important discussion took place in the central bodies of the Kibbutz Me'uhad in Palestine. This is only one example of a distinct shift in the locus of power in all the movements. It was most perceptible in Hashomer Hatzair. Although this movement's leaders continued to speak of the autonomy of the youth movement, this had gradually become a fiction. The age gap between the ordinary movement member or leader and the leaders of the Kibbutz Artzi was becoming wider, and the latter's influence proportionately stronger. The need for emissaries from Palestine was more acutely felt as the movement's numbers grew, and their influence became accordingly greater. The changes in Polish and Galician Jewry, where educational standards were rapidly falling, made the contrast between the members and the leaders even more marked. The youth movement became the 'reserve force' of the kibbutz movement.[35] And if this was so in Hashomer Hatzair, it was so *a fortiori* in the other movements, virtually all of which had at various

---

[34] Minutes of Kibbutz Me'uhad council, 19 Oct. 1933, p. 243. In Kibbutz Me'uhad archives.

[35] Margalit, *Hashomer Hatzair*, ch. 9.

stages rejected the concept of the independence of the youth movement.

## *Netzah*[36]

The Russian section of Hashomer Hatzair, now known as Netzah, was an apparent exception to the subordination of the youth movements to the kibbutz movements. In 1927 almost all its leaders were living in a number of *plugot* scattered over the Yishuv. Their membership of Ahdut Ha'avoda effectively shut them out of the Kibbutz Artzi, whose members were forbidden to join the existing political parties. But, in all respects except their political allegiance, they were an aberrant element in the Kibbutz Me'uhad. Not only did they believe in the 'organic kibbutz' and the educational methods of the youth movement, but they proclaimed their intention to convert the whole of the newly established movement to their point of view—an attitude which the veterans of Ein Harod and their disciples considered to be immature impertinence.[37] As we have seen, their presence had some effect on the wording of the new movement's constitution; and they continued to support their comrades in the Diaspora with advice and even with educational emissaries, and to control the process of their absorption within the Kibbutz Me'uhad. If this had applied only to the Russian movement, it would perhaps have been of little moment; for, having lost its natural source of growth in the younger age-groups, this movement was doomed to extinction. No more than a few hundred of its members reached the kibbutz, and most of them eventually settled at Kibbutz Afikim in the Jordan Valley. But from a very early stage members of the Russian movement had helped to create local movements in Latvia and Lithuania, both of them at this point democracies where Zionist activity was permitted. In 1930, when they left Hashomer Hatzair to create their new movement, they were joined by the national Hashomer Hatzair movements in Latvia, Lithuania, and Austria: all of them countries whose political culture favoured social democracy as against the leftward trend which was already becoming marked within the majority of the world movement.

[36] On Netzah's struggle within the Kibbutz Me'uhad, see Near, *Kibbutz and Society*, 341–54.

[37] In the event, they themselves adopted the ideology and practice of the 'great and growing kibbutz', and their central settlement, Afikim, became one of the biggest and most dynamic in the movement. But they never abandoned their educational concepts or their organizational independence.

Thus, by 1930, Netzah was an independent youth movement with several national affiliates; and, although an integral part of the Kibbutz Me'uhad, it preserved its own power base within that movement. Its graduates were concentrated in a number of *plugot* which were formally at the disposal of the central committee of the Kibbutz Me'uhad, but their plans for settlement or for amalgamation with other groups were in fact determined by (or with the advice of) the central bodies of Netzah. This was an extreme deviation from the theory and practice of the ruling group in the Kibbutz Me'uhad. In their view, each member or potential member of the movement must be prepared to go wherever the need was greatest, at the decision of the central committee, even if this meant detaching the individual from his or her former friends, or even from a *pluga* which he or she had considered a permanent home. There were many precedents for such actions; for instance, the central committee refused to permit the concentration of Klosova graduates in a single kibbutz—despite the contention of Benny Marshak, the leading figure of Klosova, that such a concentration would promote the interests of Klosova and Hechalutz. But all the central committee's attempts to apply this principle to Netzah were resisted firmly.

The controversy about educational methods between the autonomous youth movements and Hechalutz now took place within the Kibbutz Me'uhad itself. The leaders of Netzah rejected the concept of an educational mass movement. They attempted to convince the leaders of the Kibbutz Me'uhad to adopt Netzah and its structure as a model for all the educational activities of the Kibbutz Me'uhad. The central bloc stood firmly behind Hechalutz and its younger movement, Hechalutz Hatzair, even to the point of creating a branch of Hechalutz Hatzair in Lithuania in competition with the well established branch of Netzah.[38]

These questions were discussed with varying degrees of heatedness in the central bodies of the Kibbutz Me'uhad for some five years, until in 1932, at a meeting of leaders and educational advisers of all the European movements connected with the Kibbutz Me'uhad at Danzig, it looked as though agreement had been reached: Netzah would give up its autonomy in matters of absorption and settlement, and in return would be allowed to expand and, in effect, to become the youth movement of the Kibbutz Me'uhad. This agreement was never carried out, however. The extreme devotees of Netzah in the

[38] Near, *Kibbutz and Society*, 303–4.

Diaspora, and the leading ideologists and educators of Hechalutz Hatzair, now in Palestine, demanded 'interpretations' which effectively cancelled the original bargain. Although the conferences of the Kibbutz Me'uhad in 1933 and 1936 decided to cancel Netzah's autonomous status, the decisions were never put into effect; and, equally, Hechalutz and its satellite movements remained the chief educational body of the Kibbutz Me'uhad except in the few countries where Netzah was firmly established.

From one point of view, this incident underlines the vitality and power of the youth movements. But it was their final achievement of this sort. For from now on Netzah was, in effect, a kibbutz movement within a kibbutz movement, governed by its 'contact office' in Kibbutz Afikim no less than the Kibbutz Me'uhad was governed by its executive committee in Ein Harod, and relying on its reserves in the Diaspora for its continued existence. This offshoot of Hashomer Hatzair, which had first brought the concept of the autonomy of youth to Eastern European Jewry, was the last to put it into practice within the kibbutz movement.

## *The German Youth Movements in the 1930s*[39]

During the late 1920s, a new factor began to be important on the German scene. Since its establishment in 1927, the international Hashomer Hatzair movement had been interested in expanding its activities to new countries, and Germany was an obvious candidate for these plans. From early 1928, graduates of the movement visiting Germany from the Yishuv—mainly people in Germany on other business rather than emissaries sent for the purpose—had been creating and developing contacts with existing groups and movements, particularly the Zofim (the Jewish Scouts). By 1930, Hashomer Hatzair virtually dominated the Zofim, and had contacts in other movements such as Kadimah, which was now quickly moving towards a Zionist position, and even in Brith Olim, still dominated by the Kibbutz Me'uhad. It had also created a group of sympathizers and supporters in the adult Zionist organization. But its very success engendered a reaction. Brith Olim and the emissaries from the Kibbutz Me'uhad were anxious to preserve their virtual monopoly on pioneering youth in Germany, and to extend their activities to such unattached movements as Kadimah. The official Zionist organization

---

[39] This section is based on J. Reinharz, 'Hashomer Hatzair in Germany', and id., 'Hashomer Hatzair in Nazi Germany'.

feared the extremism of Hashomer Hatzair, with its uncompromising demands for 'self-realization' in the kibbutz and its Marxist sympathies. The relations between the two movements reached a state of open warfare at the end of 1930, when Hechalutz, under the control of Brith Olim, dismissed the Hashomer Hatzair emissary.

One reason for the ferocity of the struggle between the movements was the special nature and situation of the German youth movements at this period. Neither the Zionist prognosis of the German Jews' plight nor the pioneering solution commanded general agreement. The youth movement ethos commended itself only to a tiny minority: most young German Jews still saw their future in the country of their birth, and sought to solve their problems by such approaches as those of traditional (cultural) Zionism, or occupied themselves with the political problems of the German people. The youth movements themselves were in a constant state of ideological tension, and open to influences of all sorts. In Poland even the minority who could be attracted to Zionist youth activities formed a considerable mass in absolute numbers. In Germany, by contrast, the number of young Jews who were potential recruits for the youth movements was relatively limited. The result was a struggle not for unattached youth, but for influence over and control of existing groups.

Between 1928 and 1931, the emissaries of Hashomer Hatzair used their special talents and experience to create deep and lasting ties with small groups in the existing movements and mould a cadre of local leaders able to play a vital part in the work of the movement. In August 1931, breakaway groups from the Kadimah and Zofim movements formally established a German branch of Hashomer Hatzair numbering some 250 members, as against the 1,800 in Brith Olim. The struggle between these movements, each with its own educational methods and its special ties with one of the kibbutz movements, continued unabated until the establishment of the Nazi regime in 1933. By this time, despite the hostility of the major forces in official Zionism, Hashomer Hatzair had managed to increase its numbers to about 460.

One of the focal points of this struggle was the attempt by both sides to gain the support of the Werkleute, a movement based on a small, select group (Der Kreis) within yet another successor movement of the Blau-Weiss. Deeply influenced by Martin Buber, these young people created an ideology which combined religious and socialist elements with the idea of the *Gemeinschaft*. In many senses this was the intellectual élite of the German youth movements, and their decision to set up their own kibbutz (Hazorea) within the framework of the Kibbutz Artzi was definitely a moral and educational victory for Hashomer Hatzair, as well as a welcome addition to its kibbutz movement.[40] It is noteworthy that as this group grew closer to the Kibbutz Artzi, it gradually adopted the ideological and political attitudes of that movement; its own special emphases, such as religious socialism and the philosophy of Buber, were played down and eventually abandoned in favour of the political Marxism prevalent in the Kibbutz Artzi.

Meanwhile, events in Germany and elsewhere were moving at a speed which made these struggles seem parochial. In March 1933, Brith Olim combined with the majority faction of Kadimah to form a new movement, Habonim, whose graduates joined the Kibbutz Me'uhad. In the following month, two outstanding members of the Kibbutz Me'uhad, Enzo Sereni and Eliezer Livneh, arrived as emissaries to Habonim and Hechalutz, and these movements became focal points for young people seeking an escape from Nazi Germany.

Paradoxically, the German Zionist youth movements flourished between 1933 and 1938. In line with the Nazi policy of encouraging Jewish emigration they were allowed to continue their work, though under strict supervision. With the help and inspiration of the representatives of the Kibbutz Me'uhad, the local leadership of Habonim and Hechalutz, recruited and crystallized before 1933, took on the organization and education of thousands of young Jews who saw Palestine as their only hope, and the pioneering movements as the best way of getting there. The network of training farms within Germany was vastly expanded, and extended to several neighbouring countries. The religious movement, Bachad, adopted a similar attitude, and succeeded in arranging for the emigration of many hundreds of religious pioneers.

Hashomer Hatzair fared less well. This was partly because it came on the scene relatively late and existed as an independent movement for less than eighteen months before Hitler's advent to power. Its local cadre, while talented and devoted, was therefore much smaller than that of Habonim, and less able to cope with the challenges of the time. Moreover, the leaders of Habonim, afraid that Hashomer Hatzair would poach their members as it had done in the past, kept

[40] Although Hazorea formally joined the Kibbutz Artzi only in 1938, its general direction was clear by 1934, when it set up an independent *pluga* near Hadera.

them out of positions of influence in Hechalutz. But, most of all, the leadership of the world movement, with its centre in Palestine, failed to recognize the urgency of the situation. They therefore did not send the extra educational and organizational forces which their German comrades were constantly demanding; and indeed, in 1933/4, at a time when the potential for expansion was greater than ever before, the movement had to make do with its local leadership for almost a year. It remained a small and 'intimate' movement, with all the advantages in educational depth and social consolidation which this implied—but also with the tragic consequence that it failed to reach many young people who could have been saved from the Holocaust.[41]

Hechalutz continued to function even after the Kristallnacht of November 1938, though under increasingly irksome surveillance by the Gestapo. With the deportations of Jews to the East in 1941, the youth movements ceased to exist, except for sporadic meetings and a certain amount of underground activity. For almost eight years they had carried on their activities under conditions of increasing tension and danger, and had succeeded in saving tens of thousands of Jews from the Holocaust. By the beginning of 1938 more than twenty-three thousand young people had undergone training in the Hechalutz farms and eventually reached Palestine, and by 1944 more than eleven thousand had been brought to the country in the framework of Youth Aliya. A considerable proportion of the German immigrants went to the kibbutzim, the majority to the Kibbutz Me'uhad and the Kibbutz Dati, the religious kibbutz movement.[42]

The influx of German immigrants changed the different kibbutz movements to varying degrees. For the Kibbutz Me'uhad, the change was fundamental: thanks to the arrival of the German Jews it achieved by 1936 a population of some 5,000, making it at last a mass movement in reality as well as in intention. Moreover, this new element had a cultural background quite different from that of the Polish and Russian Jews who had dominated the movement up to now. The religious kibbutz movement, in contrast, was dominated by immigrants from Germany from its very beginnings. Although the changes in the other movements were less emphatic, the addition of considerable numbers of German Jews added an important new element to their demographic composition.

[41] Carmel, 'Hashomer Hatzair in Germany'.
[42] Braslavsky, *The Labour Movement of the Land of Israel*, ii. 25.

HISTORICAL INFLUENCES ON THE DEVELOPMENT OF
THE YOUTH MOVEMENTS

'Every social movement [in Zionism] over the past fifty years ... has
been a youth movement,' said Berl Katznelson in 1934.[43] That most
of the groups within the labour movement were originally composed
mainly of young people is no doubt true. But both the ideological
underpinnings of the youth movements described in this chapter and
their connection with the kibbutz movement added dimensions which
call for closer examination.

Some elements of the ways of thought and action common to many
of the youth movements of the twentieth century are particularly
close to the kibbutz ideal: the return to nature as a reaction against
industrialization; the vision of a new society, unmarred by the injust-
ices and contradictions of the old; the creation of very close social
ties, from which arose the notion of a *Gemeinschaft* which could be
continued in adult life; and all this against the background of a search
for cultural roots which stimulated a host of variants of nationalism,
ranging from the patriotism of the Boy Scouts to the fanaticism of
the Nazis. To all of this, which applied in varying degrees to all the
youth movements of Europe, Jewish and non-Jewish alike, must be
added two elements which are specific to pioneering Zionism: the
opportunity to create a new society by direct action, without the
struggles and compromises of political activity; and the challenge
implicit in the demand of the pioneering movement for 'self-realization', or personal enactment of its principles.

From the point of view of the kibbutz, the appeal to youth was
unavoidable. From the moment that Degania decided to become a
permanent settlement, the cycle of attrition and the need for reinforcements was inherent in its situation; and this applied with even more
force to the larger kibbutz movements, for which expansion was an
ideological tenet. Such reinforcements could come only from a
segment of society which was prepared to adopt the kibbutz way of
life; and, in view of the occupational distribution of the Jews, for
most adults this would mean a change of profession as well as of
country. It could scarcely be expected that many adults would vol-
untarily undertake to change their way of life in such a drastic, painful,
and dangerous manner. Thus, when Tabenkin spoke not of the
working class but of 'the Jew who becomes a worker' as the chief

---

[43] Katznelson, *Writings*, vi. 290.

component of the workers' movement and the kibbutz, his forecast was well rooted in the social and economic situation of the Jews. Young people might not come to the kibbutz; older people certainly would not.[44]

All these elements were part of the theory and practice both of Hechalutz and of the youth movements. But each movement emphasized and gave priority to different aspects of what may be seen as one complex. In part, these variations stemmed from the differences in social and cultural background which have been mentioned above. For the Jews of Western Europe and the Eastern European intelligentsia who were attracted to the youth movements, assimilation was a possibility, and the cultural aspects of Zionism were of first importance; to the mass of Polish Jewry it was no more than a peripheral phenomenon, of far less importance than the struggle for a livelihood and for elementary human rights in the face of a violently antisemitic environment.

In part, however, the differences stemmed from moral attitudes which ran deeper than cultural or social conditioning. These were given their classic formulation in the controversy between Berl Katznelson and Tabenkin: did the social and political end justify the educational means? What were the rights of the minority in a democracy? Could indoctrination be justified—or successful? In that discussion, the two systems were presented almost as ideal types. In fact, however, the dichotomy between them was far from complete. For instance, not all the training kibbutzim of Hechalutz were equally extreme.[45] And among the autonomous youth movements both the objective conditions and the psychology of youth dictated a high degree of 'cruelty' in all the training institutions. Between 1927 and 1932, all of the youth movements had adopted a number of principles once thought to be typical of the extreme Hechalutz, such as the permanent training kibbutz, and the 'obligation of realization' (the demand that every movement graduate should join a kibbutz). In 1933, Benny Marshak said: 'We must live today with the feeling that the individual has no value, especially if he is a worker.'[46] Such a

---

[44] *Kibbutz Me'uhad Anthology*, 156–7; and cf. Near, *Kibbutz and Society*, 241–3.

[45] For instance, Grochov, near Warsaw, prided itself on its cleanliness and its consideration for the individual, despite its poverty and the rigours of training; its trainees contrasted its atmosphere with the 'grimness' of Klosova. See letter from Zeltka Gitlis, Grochov, 13 July 1932, repr. in Segal and Fialkov, *The Fields of Grochov*, 162–3; and cf. Sarid, *Hechalutz in Poland*, 453, 457–61, 489–503.

[46] *Mibifnim* (June 1933), 75.

saying would have been anathema to youth movements of all types only two or three years earlier. In the face of the threat of Nazism, and the gravity of the international situation, there were now many who were prepared to try 'to find a synthesis between two apparently contradictory positions: the task and the man, economic and social considerations, quantity and quality, the *halutz* and the youth movement member'.[47] None the less, Hechalutz and the youth movements continued to emphasize the differences between them and waged a continuous struggle for resources which they could have used better in concert. The reason was clear: each of them had its own interest in strengthening the kibbutz movement to which it was attached. Unity, or even a high measure of concord, between those movements could have led to further rapprochements between the youth movements. The reasons why this did not happen are to be found not in the Diaspora but in the Yishuv.

There can be no doubt that the pioneer movements made a vital contribution to the Yishuv and the kibbutz. In March 1937, almost 43 per cent of the members of the Histadrut, 46 per cent of the members of the moshavim, and 78.5 per cent of the adult kibbutz population were graduates of youth movements, including Hechalutz.[48] Their educational influence on tens of thousands of young people who never reached the kibbutz, or even Palestine, was considerable. But it pales into insignificance beside the stark fact that every Jew who left Europe between the wars was saved from the Holocaust. In this perspective, the expansionist aims of the Kibbutz Me'uhad certainly seem to have been most suited to the exigencies of the time. The coming catastrophe makes such questions as the cultural standards of the training farms or the degree of democracy in the movement look irrelevant as against the need for survival. To have saved more than fifty thousand souls is a very considerable achievement.

There was, however, a marked contrast between the rhetoric of Hechalutz and its effectiveness. Even at the time of its greatest expansion, in 1935, its membership never reached more than some 8 per cent of Jewish youth of the appropriate age.[49] It was therefore, in

[47] Elik Shomroni, cited in Ophir, *Elik: Streams of Life*, 215. The phrase quoted was written in 1939 but refers to the early 1930s.

[48] Statistics from *Pinkas Hahistadrut* (1938), in Bassok, *Book of Hechalutz*, 506.

[49] The Jewish population of Eastern Europe in 1935 was about 4 million (not including the relatively 'Westernized' communities of Czechoslovakia and Hungary).

fact if not in intention, an élite group. Nor is this very surprising. The 'severity' of the training camps was, as Tabenkin himself remarked, a means of selection no less than of preparation.[50] Hechalutz wanted to encompass the masses, but they were not prepared to compromise in order to accommodate its unspoken demands.

As for the ideological struggles between the movements, from the vantage point of the present they seem of less importance than they did to the protagonists. Both types of movement claimed to have the more effective educational system, and each believed that the differences between them were crucial. But their fortunes waxed and waned not with the perfection or failure of their educational methods, but with the fortunes of Zionism and the chances of immigration; and the differences between the movements in percentage of absorption in the kibbutzim were negligible.[51] The expansionism of the Kibbutz Me'uhad certainly attracted greater numbers. But the very fact that the various types of educational approach and organization were effective with particular constituencies shows that the *de facto* pluralism of the pioneering movement was attuned to the pluralist reality of the Jewish communities. Hechalutz's demand to impose its own approach on all of the movements created tensions and controversy which were without doubt harmful to the general cause. However important ideological conviction was as a spur to action, the energy which it generated was not necessarily put to the most efficient use.

It appears, then, that the strength of each of these educational systems led to an inherent weakness: the dynamism of Hechalutz to arrogance, and the intensive education of the autonomous movements to limited numbers. Each hoped to encompass all, or most, of Jewish youth in the Diaspora. Tabenkin fully concurred with Berl Katznelson when he said in 1933: 'The conquest of the people for Zionism is near. The training facilities of Hechalutz can encompass the whole

---

Assuming that the demographic composition of Poland was roughly correct for all these countries, about 30% of these were aged between 14 and 27 in 1935, and 20% of this number between 18 and 21: 240,000 in all. Yet the number of this age-group on the training farms was 21,400, or only 8.3% of the potential. Population statistics: Mendelsohn, *Jews of Eastern Central Europe*, 23 (Poland), 178 (Romania), 244 (Latvia), 255 (Lithuania). Hechalutz membership: Otiker, *Hechalutz in Poland*, app. c. Demographic analysis of Polish Jewry: *Encyclopedia Judaica*, v. 1515–17.

[50] Kibbutz Me'uhad Council, Ramat Hakovesh, 23 Nov. 1933, 26.

[51] Statistics compiled by the Histadrut show that for the kibbutz movements as a whole, the number who left the kibbutzim in the years 1933–5 was 42%–44% of the number who joined; Braslavsky, *Labour Movement of the Land of Israel*, ii. 231–2.

younger generation of the Jewish people.'[52] And Meir Ya'ari of Hashomer Hatzair claimed: 'The kibbutz movement, in so far as it is orientated towards the whole of the Jewish people, must embrace all Jewish children in its educational activities, even though it can encompass only part of the Jewish working-class in Palestine before the social revolution.'[53]

That they failed in this ambition was due in large measure to circumstances quite beyond their control. None the less, the growth of the kibbutz movements testifies to a substantial degree of success. True to the nature of youth, their reach exceeded their grasp. But, considering all the difficulties under which they worked, they grasped a great deal.

[52] Kibbutz Me'uhad Council, 23 Nov. 1933, 12.
[53] *Book of the Shomrim*, 113.

# 7

## Glimpses of Social History: The Kibbutz Community, 1920–1935

PREVIOUS chapters have dealt mainly with ideological and economic aspects of the development of the kibbutz movement in its formative period. Documentary sources and the reminiscences of kibbutz members alike emphasize the centrality of these issues in the life and thought of the kibbutz at this time: these were people who had adopted their way of life after much reflection, discussion, and self-examination; and they were most conscious of the need to prove that it was economically viable. But many other factors also affected the quality of day-to-day life in the kibbutz: methods of organization and social interaction, varieties of cultural expression and educational approach. The purpose of this chapter is to illuminate some aspects of kibbutz society in the fifteen years from the start of the movement's expansion in 1919/20 until 1935, at the height of the economic boom. The first section is an account of the development and crystallization of kibbutz education. The second consists of a number of concrete examples of the kibbutz way of life—or, more accurately, ways of life—at this period; while the third gives a detailed description of three kibbutzim in 1935. This is far from being a systematic account of kibbutz society at this time, but it does afford some valuable and interesting glimpses of social history.

### PATTERNS OF EDUCATION: THE 1920S AND 1930S[1]

It was not only in matters related to the youth movements that the kibbutzim had to concern themselves with education. By 1927, when the two major kibbutz movements were established, there were 472 children in the kibbutzim. By 1931 this number had increased to 624,

[1] Much of the material in this section, including the translations of all but the last extract quoted, is based on R. Porat, *History*, and id., *Together but on our Own*.

by 1935 to 1,057, and by the beginning of 1936 to 1,666.[2] If in the early days of Degania the problem of the younger generation could be defined as simply one of child care, as the children grew up their educational needs, and consequently the organization required to supply these needs, became very much more complex.

For the pre-school ages, all the kibbutz movements adopted the system of child care which had evolved in Degania in its early years. In their very early days the children were cared for in a 'babies' house'. Within their first year they usually became part of a *pe'uton* (toddlers' group) which varied in size but usually numbered no more than eight, in charge of a *metapelet* (nursemaid).

## Sleeping Arrangements

Although Degania took the lead in the invention of child-care arrangements, its child population was cut drastically with the departure of the group which founded the first moshav, shortly after the first World War. Both in numbers and in social inventiveness, the kibbutzim of Gedud Ha'avoda took the lead in matters of education and child care as in other fields of kibbutz life. The first addition to the standard arrangements for pre-school child care was the invention of what came to be known throughout the kibbutz movement as 'communal sleeping'. This was first practised by the members of Kibbutz Kfar Gil'adi, who had had to leave their recently established home in 1919 during the fighting which included the Tel Hai incident. On the way back to Kfar Gil'adi they had to stay for some time at Rosh Pina; accommodation available there did not permit the children to sleep near their parents, so the children all slept in one room. Tova Portugali, their *metapelet*, later wrote:

When we finally got to Kfar Gil'adi, we decided to continue such arrangements as part of our educational system. In addition, this decision also helped solve many of our housing problems. Until the first buildings were ready, the children lived in an attic above the cowshed. Finally two rooms with a large opening between them were allocated to them. The children all took their showers in one of the rooms. It was in these rooms that they met their parents, since the latter had no private corner of their own. The children ate separately, but their parents frequently visited them at mealtimes and at bedtime.[3]

[2] *UAW Report* (1927), 180; ibid. (1931), 197; *Hovrot Statistiot*, 2 (Feb. 1935), 4 (Feb. 1936).

[3] Ben-Zvi *et al.*, *Book of Hashomer*, 354.

The change in the system was at first an improvisation, designed to overcome the physical difficulties of life in temporary conditions. In the coming years, however, 'communal sleeping' became part of the ideology of most of the kibbutz movements. At Kfar Gil'adi itself the arrangement was made permanent at the insistence of the young, ideologically extreme members who saw in it the logical expression of the principle that the children belonged to the whole community, and not to the parents alone. Others like them helped to confirm the principle as part of the educational system of Gedud Ha'avoda. Eventually it was adopted by all the kibbutzim except Degania and a few other veteran *kvutzot*; and it remained the rule in virtually the whole of the kibbutz movement until the early 1960s.

## *Schools: Kfar Gil'adi and the Kibbutz Me'uhad*

Hashomer also pioneered the kibbutz kindergarten, at first in the 'conquest' group at Tel Adashim, later at Kfar Gil'adi. This also was created in temporary conditions, but rapidly became part of the accepted educational set-up. Indeed, the kindergarten was seen to be a natural extension of the *pe'uton*, to be formed by combining a number of smaller groups when the children reached an appropriate age—usually 3 or 4.

The kindergarten stage marked the introduction of a phenomenon which remained part of the kibbutz educational scene for many years. While the *metapelet* who worked with the youngest children was looked on as a sort of surrogate mother, kindergarten and school teaching were thought to be more professional tasks. Accordingly, although the children's physical needs were still supplied by members of the kibbutz, the teachers from kindergarten upwards frequently came from outside the kibbutz, and were employed by the Histadrut rather than the kibbutz itself. Thus, there could be—and in many kibbutzim there was—a long succession of teachers, not all suited to the difficult task of teaching a group of children in an isolated settlement who had inherited no educational tradition, and sometimes under the most difficult conditions.

The teachers sent by the Cultural Committee of the Histadrut to Kfar Gil'adi were highly devoted men and women, most of them believers in various forms of progressive education. These they attempted to apply, each in his own way, to the special conditions of the place: a remote community, in wild and untamed countryside, influenced strongly by the romantic and demanding tradition of

Hashomer; a small number of children, of many ages and at different stages of development; few school-books or other learning aids; and an adult community struggling hard to build a viable farm and a socialist way of life. The result was a mixture of formal and informal education, emphasizing the values of community, mutual aid, labour, and self-defence; a curriculum centred largely on local studies, the kibbutz and its natural surroundings; and an integration of children's activities at school, at work, and at leisure into the cultural and economic activities of the kibbutz. Here is a description of the situation in 1930:

We have twenty children. Eleven are of kindergarten age, eight of school age, and one is a girl of 14, who works mornings on the farm and comes to school in the afternoon. The children are responsible for the maintenance of the building and for the orderliness of their quarters. They perform all the required chores in the classroom, but in their bedrooms they are expected only to make their beds, do the dusting, and so on. When it comes to preparing the food, the children do only whatever can be done outdoors such as peeling potatoes, sorting out peas and beans, and the like. Almost a third of the day is taken up by manual labour. The kindergarten children participate in the housework the same as the school children. There isn't much that one can learn from jobs like these, but there is no better method for the socialization of children than working together. In addition, we run the vegetable garden. We had to overcome several difficulties before we set it up, but we have succeeded. Thus, we have assured ourselves of a place where the work is steady and can be done systematically.

Participation in work on the general farm, especially in seasonal jobs, is also extremely important. It is in this milieu that the process of socialization takes place, and, to a certain extent, the learning gained from working on a real farm. This also gives the child the opportunity of being with his or her parents, a rare treat. Moreover, it is only on jobs like these that the child gets to feel like a real worker, conscious of the worth of his or her effort and of the contribution it makes. There are many side benefits in this type of work, which give the child great joy and are not easily forgotten: the long walk to the fields, the meal out there, the singing at work, and various other events.[4]

These practices were institutionalized and given a theoretical basis by Mordechai Segal, who was the principal of the school from 1933 until 1939, when he founded the first kibbutz teachers' training facility, the Teachers' Seminar of the Kibbutz Me'uhad. The experience

[4] From a report on Kfar Gil'adi in 1921 by the teacher, Baruch Bernstein. Repr. in R. Porat, *History*, 65–6.

that he acquired in Kfar Gil'adi and the ideas he developed from it became the basis of the educational theory of the whole of this movement.[5] Education was to be integrated into the life of the kibbutz. Both primary and secondary schooling were to take place in the children's home kibbutz: the curriculum was to be built in widening circles around local studies, and the children were to be integrated gradually into the cultural and economic life of kibbutz society as a whole. Thus, for instance, from an early stage the children took part in the celebration of the festivals with the whole kibbutz. There was a small children's farm, to familiarize the children with agricultural work; but as soon as the children could be integrated into the day-to-day work of the agricultural branches, they worked together with the kibbutz members.

As has been said, the model evolved in Kfar Gil'adi became the pattern for the whole of the Kibbutz Me'uhad. Tabenkin was also a strong advocate of locating education entirely within the kibbutz community. In 1926/7, when the Cultural Committee of the Histadrut attempted to establish a joint school for all the children of the Jezreel Valley from kibbutzim, moshavim, and towns, he decried the plan:

We must not turn all the workers' children into artificial orphans. A kibbutz has to maintain communal education, and that is the *raison d'être* for the children's house, but not for a central orphanage.

From a purely technical point of view it is easier to concentrate children in one spot than to teach little groups of children separately. But no settlement that has the potential of a kibbutz will agree to remove its children beyond its boundaries. The Cultural Committee would like to deal with each child as a separate unit, but the kibbutz exists, and desires to continue to exist. A settlement is made up of its families and its children. . . . A kibbutz has much more to offer to education than the finest school. The idea of a central school, unaffiliated with any settlement, is inspired by teachers. They regard society and parents as harmful superfluities that must be extirpated. We are accused of conducting experiments in settlement, in social relations, and in education, but these experiments constitute our very lives, and are not the result of abstract logic. On the contrary, the separation of the child from society is opposed to any substantive need.[6]

[5] Although Segal's educational theory was to a great extent evolved in the course of his educational work in Kfar Gil'adi, he was also influenced by the theories of John Dewey during his studies in 1931/2. Apparently he was also taught by teachers of the Deweyan school before his arrival in Palestine. See R. Porat, *History*, 132-3, and verbal communication from Prof. Moshe Kerem.

[6] At an inter-kibbutz discussion in 1923; see Katznelson, *The Kvutza*, 36; R. Porat, *History*, 72-3.

Practical considerations caused this extreme stand to be somewhat modified. Because of its size, Ein Harod was able to man its school, first established in 1924, with members of the kibbutz. They had little formal training as teachers, and lacked the enthusiasm for progressive education which many of the Histadrut teachers brought with them. In terms of curriculum and the number of hours of instruction, therefore, they tended to model their work more on their memories of their own schools (or *hadarim*) in the Diaspora. Even so, the informal atmosphere of the school, the individual attention given to each pupil, and the breadth of interests of the teachers gave it a special character of its own. Since it was less integrated into the life and work of Ein Harod, it could more easily absorb pupils from the neighbouring Tel Yosef after that kibbutz joined the Kibbutz Me'uhad in 1929. Eventually, this developed into a joint day-school for the children of both these kibbutzim. Thus, within the Kibbutz Me'uhad two separate models existed side by side: the integrated school, in which the children studied and worked in their own kibbutz for all their school lives; and the regional school, where classes were conducted jointly but the children worked and spent their leisure hours in their home kibbutzim.

## Schools: The Kibbutz Artzi

In Beit Alpha, the first kibbutz of Hashomer Hatzair, both the local situation and the theoretical background of educators and kibbutz members were different from those of Kfar Gil'adi and Ein Harod. By 1926 Beit Alpha had ten children of school age. Their numbers were complemented by the absorption of the siblings of kibbutz members, orphans from outside the kibbutz, and a handful of children from neighbouring kibbutzim. Together they formed the 'children's community at the foot of Mount Gilboa'.[7] This institution was run mainly by members of Kibbutz Beit Alpha and Tel Yosef, some of them graduates of Hashomer Hatzair and all firm believers in progressive education. Their aim was to apply the theories of Siegfried Barnfeld, John Dewey, and others to the creation of a new type of educational system whose essence was guided self-instruction and an emphasis in both social and intellectual education on physical work and agriculture: children aged from 10 to 13 worked three hours a day, those from 13 to 16 worked five hours. Methods of instruction

[7] Ron-Polani, *Until Now*, ch. 2; R. Porat, *History*, 101–5.

were varied, but centred largely round study projects conducted separately in each age-group.

Despite the tremendous difficulties which stemmed from the children's disparate backgrounds and lack of a common educational tradition among the teachers, the 'children's community' lasted from 1926 to 1929, breaking up only in the atmosphere of suspicion and mistrust engendered by the split in Gedud Ha'avoda and the conversion of its left wing to Communism. (One of the immediate causes of its dissolution was the discovery of a secret Communist cell among the children.) Its main permanent contribution to kibbutz education was the invention of the very concept of the 'children's community' (*hevrat yeladim*), which is still a central motif in the educational theory and practice of all the kibbutz movements.

The outstanding innovation of the Kibbutz Artzi, which is still the basis of its education at high-school level, was the 'educational institute' (*mosad hinukhi*), today a boarding school for children aged 12 and over from a group of neighbouring kibbutzim. The first of these was founded in 1931 (with the financial help of some of the movement's sympathizers in the Diaspora) in Mishmar Ha'emek, following a wide-ranging discussion of theoretical and practical issues connected with education in the kibbutz. Until 1939, all the children of high-school age in the Kibbutz Artzi lived, worked, and studied in the Mishmar Ha'emek institute, visiting their home kibbutzim and their parents for one day each week.[8]

Instruction in the institute was based mainly on 'projects', each of which was explored for varying periods of time—several weeks or months, as the case warranted. They dealt with the sciences and humanities as fields that are both linked and complementary. The various academic subjects, such as arithmetic, chemistry, physics, history, and geography were studied systematically on a level suitable to the various age-groups. Younger children devoted their studies to matters relevant to their life experience: the house, the farm, nature, and climate. As the children grew up, the subjects expanded to the region, the country, and the world, viewed in their geographical, historical, social, economic, and political aspects. Thus, the scope of the students was continuously being widened and they were simultaneously becoming more involved in the adult world. They were being educated to become partners in the ideological and social norms of their community.

[8] R. Porat, *Together but on Our Own*, 35–62.

These instructional activities were integrated into a highly intensive programme of work on the children's farm, academic and artistic learning, and social activities. The aim was to reproduce the 'youth society', which was the central concept of the Hashomer Hatzair youth movement. It was, however, firmly under the aegis of the kibbutz movement and the parent kibbutzim, so as to prevent such deviations from the accepted norms as occurred in the first 'children's community'. Its educational theory was derived from the two major intellectual influences on Hashomer Hatzair—Karl Marx and Sigmund Freud—reinforced by eclectic theoretical support from Dewey, and, in later years, Jean Piaget and others. In short, the educational institute was an attempt to reproduce, in a controlled and sophisticated fashion, the youth movement experience which the founding members of the kibbutzim of Hashomer Hatzair had undergone in their own adolescence. Indeed, the original plan was to establish a single institution for the whole of the Kibbutz Artzi, thus eliminating the supposedly harmful influence of the older generation,[9] and creating the 'children's republic' advocated by Gustav Wyneken and other theorists of the youth movement. From 1939, however, institutes began to develop on a regional basis, thus preserving the connection with the parent kibbutzim and with the pupils' parents.

*Education in the* Kvutzot[10]

In the *kvutzot*, although the problems were similar in essence, the different theoretical approach of educators and kibbutz members led to different practical solutions. The small number of children of school age led to the establishment in 1927 of the 'House of Communal Education' in Degania. This was a school initially for children from the two Deganiot and Kvutzat Kinneret, although children from *kvutzot* established in the area during the 1930s also studied there. In its curriculum and methods of teaching, this was a more conventional establishment than those so far described. Although the project method was used in the younger classes, there was throughout an emphasis on nature study, and the children worked at their home kibbutzim. Here as in other kibbutz schools, there was a 'children's community', modelled on the kibbutz, in which the children enjoyed a wide measure of autonomy. But, like the Ein Harod–Tel Yosef joint

---

[9] These theories, which were not confined to Hashomer Hatzair, roused the wrath of Tabenkin, as expressed in his remarks quoted above, 244–5.

[10] See R. Porat, *History*, 135–9.

institution, it never became a boarding school, and the children returned to their home kibbutzim each day. As the size of the *kvutzot* increased, extra-curricular activities began to take place more frequently in the individual settlements, each of which created a 'children's' and 'youths' community' of its own.

## Similarities and Differences

Education has been one of the central concerns of the kibbutz since its earliest days. It is not hard to see why. Unless the character, the will, and the social values of its members were particularly strong, a voluntary community would have difficulty in maintaining an identity distinct from the society around it. And, as the founding generation very soon realized, this applied no less to the second generation than to the first:

When we saw our first children in the babies' playpen hitting one another, and even grabbing toys for themselves—we were seized by fear. 'In that case,' we said, 'being educated in a communal society is not enough to uproot all traces of egoism.' So, little by little, our original utopian social concepts were destroyed.[11]

The educational systems of the different youth movements and the kibbutz movements alike were adapted to the different concepts of what the kibbutz should be and do. The Kibbutz Me'uhad, like Hechalutz, imitated the structure and methods of recruitment of the 'open' kibbutz: education to kibbutz life took place in the constant process of growth and social change within the kibbutz itself. In the course of this process, the kibbutz community was improved by the addition of new blood, new ideas, and new ways of action. Similarly, the children of the kibbutz took part in as many of its activities as was practical, contributed to its economic and cultural progress, and became part of a multigenerational community. The leaders of Hashomer Hatzair, on the other hand, attempted to separate the 'children's community' from the adult world, just as they themselves had built their movement in rebellion against the world of their parents, and used many of the methods of intensive social education which had been developed in the youth movement in the Diaspora in order to do so—though of course they could not practise the same process of self-selection among their children. The educational system of Hever Hakvutzot began pragmatically, in tune with the

11 Smetterling, 'Conclusions'.

temperament of the veterans of the *kvutzot*. With the union with Gordonia, many of the elements of youth movement education were added.

Thus, each of the three main systems was adapted to ensuring the survival and strengthening of a particular type of kibbutz. In this way, the differences between the movements were perpetuated and given ideological depth. But it should be stressed that, with all the differences between them, each of these types of kibbutz was a species of the same genus. Each educational system stressed the love of nature, adaptation to physical work, and desire and ability to live in a close-knit egalitarian and democratic community, the love of Hebrew, and Jewish cultural values. In youth movement and kibbutz alike, there was a common infrastructure of values and educational methods. I shall conclude this section with a quotation from the reminiscences of one of the first children of the kibbutz. The incident took place in Kibbutz Ein Harod, but it could easily have happened in any kibbutz at any time during the 1920s or 1930s.

From the very earliest days the way of life of the children's community began to take shape: everything was organized by the children, together with the teachers. They worked together with us in everything, cleaning the house and in seasonal work in the fields.

Apart from the two cooks, all the work in the house was done together by the teachers and the children. Shoshana the teacher taught the little ones the three R's, natural history, and so forth. She also bathed them, and sometimes even soaped our backs for us on Sabbath evenings.... We had a work roster, a committee for controlling the general meeting, a social committee, a cultural committee, and a studies committee. From time to time there was a general meeting of all the children, to discuss matters that affected all the children's community. Its decisions were binding on all, children and adults alike. Once Moshe the teacher got furious with one of the lads, and said he was 'no better than a carter'. The boy replied: 'Perhaps I did something wrong, but it's no disgrace to be a carter.' He brought Moshe before a 'jury-trial'. The trial went on for weeks.... The 'prosecutor' and the 'defendant' spoke exhaustively on the question of 'carters' and physical work. We brought Shimonovitz's poem 'The Carter's Jubilee' as evidence. Moshe explained why the word was an insult in Petah Tikva, where he grew up, and spoke of his fear that in the course of time Ein Harod could become a sort of Petah Tikva, where people lived on the work of others. Finally, the 'defendant' apologized for his inaccurate use of the word, and the incident was closed.[12]

[12] Reminiscences of Zerubavel Gil'ad, in the archives of Kibbutz Ein Harod. Repr. in Tsur, *The Beginning of the Kibbutz*, 194.

COMMUNITY AND CULTURE

## The Bell

The kibbutz bell was not usually bell-shaped. More often it was a piece of metal piping, or an outworn ploughshare, rung by the night watchman at the end of his duty. This was not its only function; and even this, its most commonplace use, could be the subject of controversy.

The bell was first used by the Hashomer Hatzair groups in the big camp at Shomria (it seems that there was no bell in Beitania Eilit), and by the movement's second kibbutz before it settled at Mishmar Ha'emek.

I am still exhausted after last night's discussion. At midnight, when I was fast asleep, I was suddenly woken up by the loud peals of the bell. I was sure that a fire had broken out. I rushed outside, half naked, but everything was quiet.... I asked what was going on.

'Shh ... don't make a noise,' they whispered. The bell is calling us to a discussion.' I was amazed. A discussion at midnight? I went back to my tent and dressed. The dining-room was in semi-darkness; somewhere, in a corner, a little oil-lamp blinked. People sat huddled together on the floor. From one of the corners, somewhere in the depths, arose Y.'s voice, as if from the nether world, shrouded in the mysteries of past generations. A tremor passed over me. Head bowed, in the tone of the high priest worshipping in the Holy of Holies, the speaker cast some disjointed phrases into the darkness.

'I called the meeting ... (long silence) ... because I ... that is to say—we, every one of us ... (long silence) ... the community—one family (long silence).'

Everybody's head is bowed. Only heads can be seen, bowed down to the ground. I put my head between my knees and listen.

I shall never know what was said afterwards, since I fell asleep, and woke up only when the guard came in to light the stove. What a shame! Everyone says that it was a most profound and beautiful discussion.[13]

This is, of course, the first stage of kibbutz life, similar to (indeed, according to some, in imitation of) Beitania Eilit. Two years later the same man wrote: 'Our discussions have slowly been losing their special flavour.... The dining hall is fully lit ... we talk more loudly, sit up during the discussion and speak to the point. Something has changed in us—some say that something has been spoilt.'[14]

[13] 27 Feb. 1922. From the diary of a member of the founding group of Mishmar Ha'emek, repr. in Gadon, *Paths*, i. 344–5.
[14] 20 July 1922; ibid. 349.

Other kibbutzim did not go through this stage. For them, the bell had a different use. One of the leaders of Gedud Ha'avoda wrote:

The big kibbutz cannot exist without strong internal discipline. This was proved at an early stage in the Gedud's existence. The first element in this discipline is every member's duty to work six days (apart from illness or a journey, or periods of unemployment). A man who works by himself, who is not a kibbutz member, can afford to work less. It is not so in the commune. All the members, whether they are working or not, have their needs supplied by the commune equally. Any deviation from or infringement of this principle is liable to create a class of slackers, who live at the expense of others. No 'depression' can justify anyone evading work. Of course, we must rely on the members' own sense of responsibility, but one should not put temptation in people's way. If we hadn't kept this rule religiously, we should have caused ourselves grave problems. It would have been enough to let one person off work because of 'depression', or any other subjective reason, and an epidemic of idleness would have spread through the camp, and made the whole work schedule more difficult.[15]

We established discipline according to 'the call of the bell'. The members had to get up when it rang, and work a certain number of hours per day. Even though in many places the Gedud worked under its own management, at piece-work rates, we had to establish 'the discipline of the bell' in order to prevent chaos in the work schedule, and to enable us to check the work. The bell provoked a great deal of criticism at first. 'It's like a barracks', people said. But anyone who has a close acquaintance with these things knows that in order to organize work and prevent waste everyone must go out to work at the same time, and finish at about the same time. Permanence leads to punctuality.[16]

By contrast, here is an extract from a description of life in Kvutzat Hasharon, a group whose first members reached the country in the mid-1920s and which eventually became part of Hever Hakvutzot.

At first we didn't ring the bell. It was thought to be wrong: the bell was appropriate to a factory, not to the *kvutza*. The night watchman used to go into the hut or the room and call out in a loud voice, 'Wake up, wake up.' He didn't knock on the door, just went straight in. There was no room for

[15] This refers to the practice in some of the smaller *kvutzot*, and many of the kibbutzim of Hashomer Hatzair, of allowing members to take days off when they felt too depressed to work, without requiring any further justification. For instance, the diary quoted above carries the following entry: 'A. is in a deep depression, no-one knows why. He has not gone to work or come to the dining-room for several days. Sometimes he can be seen wandering about the farmyard at night. Who knows what he is suffering?' (20 Feb. 1923; ibid. i. 347).

[16] Hanokh Rokhel, in *Gedud Ha'avoda*, 225–6.

privacy—he shook each person until he or she got up and dressed. At mealtimes, one of the cooks would go out to the huts and call everybody to eat. She would call 'Come and eat' until her voice gave out.

When the bell was installed, there was a crisis. The women wept. When people said that it wasn't so terrible, that it was impossible to run from place to place and call everyone, they didn't agree. 'A bell is impersonal,' they said. 'When the cooks or the night watchman call you, that's an expression of a personal relationship.'[17]

## Mutual Relationships

Attitudes to the bell are, of course, only one expression of different types of mutual relationship within the kibbutz community. Here is an extract from the house journal of Ein Harod, in the early 1920s:

In the last two general meetings of Ein Harod, a miracle occurred. Two or three members took heart, and tried to raise the painful question of the inner state of the *pluga*, and all the things which have been seething in the minds of many members recently. These were 'activists', and what they wanted was that for once the question should be posed as it really is, without embroidery, looking directly at the truth without fear, without any desire to obscure anything, to cover anything up, or to deceive ourselves with soothing words.

But these people felt that they had a hard task, and did not have the strength to carry it through. They stood in the meeting, and, so to speak, asked for help: 'Let the others come and carry on what we've started.' But nobody carried on. The others kept silent. Their voices remained isolated, and their strength failed them.

Why? Why did everybody remain silent? Why did everybody not say what pains him, what disturbs him? Why did we let the anger and dissatisfaction within us bubble and seethe like poison, polluting our lives, and creating the dangers of evil judgment and distorted thought? Why?[18]

In contrast to this description of a big kibbutz, where open and intimate expression in the general meeting was the exception, in the smaller *kvutzot* it was the norm. Here is an extract from the house journal of the second kibbutz of Hashomer Hatzair (later: Mishmar Ha'emek) from about the same date:

I think that the reason [for our social problems] is lack of truth in our mutual relationships. If a person conceals his real opinion of his neighbour but tells it to someone else, then it is dishonest, and causes a decline in our social

[17] Avraham Cohen, in interview with Muki Tsur; Tsur *et al.*, *The Beginning of the Kibbutz*, 148.
[18] *Mihayeinu*, 33 (Aug. 1922), 430.

standards. Obviously, one can keep one's opinion hidden for a short time; but only in relation to people with whom we are not living permanently in a community. In a kibbutz, where our lives are communal in every sense, such a relationship cannot last. . . .

If this is so, we cannot act as if people's negative characteristics will simply pass away! If we do not point out each other's mistakes and shortcomings— we shall not be able to achieve anything, and the common values which we have acquired so far will be lost. . . .

So I say: among the factors which can improve the internal state of the kibbutz we must give priority to improving the individual. And among the ways to do this, one of the most important is to reveal the facts, and show up the mistakes and negative aspects of each individual. It must be done 'with wisdom'. . . . But it must be done![19]

One of the ways in which the small *kvutzot* tried to improve themselves was by sessions of open mutual criticism. These were not always universally approved of.

I cannot shake off the terrible feeling of oppression which I've had ever since the first evening of our discussion. For a long time now my faith in the complete ability of our general discussions to illuminate and improve our mutual relationships and resolve personal differences has been shaken. But this time, it was too much for me.

The way in which people spoke about L. was intolerably cruel. I don't belong to any 'clique', so I'm free from all subjective judgement on the matter. So I can say that, to the best of my knowledge and feeling, things were said out of complete lack of sympathy to L.—and perhaps even worse. Which of us could hear such harsh criticism and react calmly, and not reach the conclusion which L. did? [Apparently to leave the *kvutza*].[20]

## Cultural Life

The above extract is from the 'Book of the *kvutza*' of Kvutzat Hasharon, a collective diary similar to *Our Community*, though less formal; the members wrote spontaneously in a book kept specially for this purpose, and their words were neither edited nor published. The purpose was to create 'a sort of "book of life" of our own, in which everyone will write whatever is in his heart'. Such diaries were kept in several kibbutzim, though the practice was far from universal:

[19] From the journal of Kibbutz Mishmar Ha'emek, 1928. Repr. in Tsur *et al.*, *The Beginning of the Kibbutz*, 139.
[20] From the *Book of the Kvutza* of Kvutzat Hasharon, in the archives of Kibbutz Yif'at.

in Degania, for example, one such was begun but very quickly discontinued.[21] But as the kibbutz community grew, the need to provide information and spread ideas became increasingly important. Some of the biggest kibbutzim had local news-sheets from a very early stage, in addition to the informative and ideological movement journals; but they did not become widespread in the kibbutz movement until the late 1930s. More usual in the 1920s and early 1930s were wall newspapers and oral newspapers.

In Tel Yosef the written news-sheet and the oral newspaper were both in use: *Mihayeinu*, ('From our life') the journal of Gedud Ha'avoda, became the local news-sheet of the kibbutz after the breakup of the Gedud; and between 1931 and 1935 there were some forty editions of the oral newspaper. Here are some extracts from the latter which shed light on one aspect of cultural and social life in an established kibbutz at this time.

There is no need to waste words on explaining the necessity of [the reading-room]. It is sufficient to adduce the masses of people who are constantly there in these short evenings; there isn't even room to turn around. That is enough to prove that it is a real necessity.

The reading room should be a place in which the members can sit in comfort after an exhausting day's work, in a quiet corner, next to a table full of varied reading matter, representing all the printed material produced in the Yishuv and outside it....

'Comfort' does not mean silk-covered armchairs. Heaven forfend! But it does mean a roomy hall, with plenty of light, tastefully arranged, with suitable pictures etc., so that people should not have to stand up while reading, as they do now, or not come at all because there is not enough light.... Members can help by contributing all sorts of newspapers [which the kibbutz cannot afford to buy]—from relatives and friends, from the parties, and so forth ...

In our reading-room there should be room for reading-matter of all sorts, representing all shades of thought: pro- and anti-Zionist, nationalist and assimilationist, working-class and bourgeois, serious and humorous, so that we may practise the injunction: 'Know what to reply to the non-believer.' The general rule must be: put in everything, take out nothing.[22]

The author warned his hearers that the reading room might be closed if material were removed, or if there were not enough volunteers to carry out, in their spare time, duties such as arranging the papers and

[21] Dayan, *Twenty-Five Years of Degania*, 99.
[22] Shimon Ben-Shalom in the oral newspaper of Tel Yosef, 103 (7 May 1931), 109 (7 June 1931), 125 (18 July 1932). My thanks to his daughter, Galila Mor, for drawing my attention to this material and allowing me to quote it.

cleaning the room. Two months later, he appealed to the public through the oral newspaper to avert the danger that two extra rooms, originally promised as an extension of the reading-room, might be allocated to the infirmary (in a process which he claimed to be undemocratic). His appeal was apparently successful. But within a year papers were disappearing, and not enough volunteers could be found to keep the place tidy.

These extracts show something of the difficulty of organizing any sort of cultural activity, even in a relatively large and well-established kibbutz such as Tel Yosef. But they also show that, by dint of devotion and tenacity, such activities could be successful, and that institutions such as the oral newspaper had a vitality and perseverance of their own, provided that a handful of enthusiasts were prepared to bear the quite considerable burden of promoting them. Failing that, life could be humdrum and frustrating.

Our life continues as usual ... every day has its own work, every evening its general meeting, discussion, committee-session. And so pass weeks and months.[23]

Once again, nothing of interest. The evening begins, and people start to play cards, since there's nothing to read, not even a newspaper. Some play chess, others write or draw. Yehudit, the only woman who doesn't take part in these games, gets bored, and goes to bed early. Very bad. I hope something changes soon, that new members will come, or that we'll get some books. At least, something must change, for evenings like this are liable to do harm to the group.[24]

Such institutions as libraries and reading rooms, established at a fairly early stage in the bigger kibbutzim, were of very great importance. In the first years of Degania Beit many spent Saturdays (their only free day) reading. 'The greatest pleasure in reading was exchanging views with the other members. A book which gave pleasure would sometimes be read aloud. There were many discussions on general literary topics. Often they would touch on more abstract questions, and go on far into the night.'[25] A report from Ein Harod in 1926 says that 'of the 200 members living in the kibbutz, 172 use the library, and 50% are regular borrowers'.[26]

[23] Letter from Abba Zalman Lifschitz, 1922. In the archives of Ein Harod.
[24] From the collective diary of Kvutzat Hacarmel. In the archives of Kibbutz Ramat Yohanan. Repr. in Tsur *et al.*, *The Beginning of the Kibbutz*, 216.
[25] Recollections of Daniel, founding member of Degania Beit; *Degania Beit*, 35–6.
[26] Edelstein, *Mibifnim*, 7 (May 1924), 122.

Much of the cultural activity of the kibbutz, then as now, centred on Sabbath and the festivals. At this stage, there was no religiously orthodox kibbutz. But it was common ground to all kibbutzim that one of their most important functions was the continuation of Jewish culture, and its revival in a new, secular form. The first step in this direction was the universal adoption of the Hebrew language. Although in some places much Yiddish or Russian was heard in informal conversation, from a very early stage all the official business of the kibbutz—general and committee meetings, correspondence, work allocation, and all cultural activities—was conducted in Hebrew. When Hebrew was well established as a lingua franca, it was possible to develop communal forms of culture. Here, for instance, is Friday evening in Geva, a *kvutza* established in 1921, as recalled by one of the first children born there:

On the Sabbath eve there were always white cloths on the table, and some cultural activity.... Most frequently, people would just sit around and sing. They would wash up, put the small children to bed, and come back to the dining-hall. Haim Rosen sat with all the members round him. He could sing Yiddish, Russian, and Hasidic songs....

On Sabbath eve he always wore a white shirt. Somehow, Sabbath was important to him, though he worked every Saturday morning; he would apply fresh tar to the wheels and woodwork of the carts, so as to avoid [wasting time by] doing it on a working day....

There was something festive about Haim Rosen on Sabbath eve: clean-shaven, sunburnt, with a deep-furrowed face. The people would gather round him like butterflies and begin to sing, sometimes in unison, sometimes in harmony. They were all fanatically anti-orthodox, they worked on the Sabbath, but they sang Hasidic songs: 'Purify our hearts,' and 'Thou art one and Thy name one', and so on.[27]

One can already see the beginnings of a cultural tradition, even though the Friday evening ceremony of *kabbalat Shabbat* had not yet taken on the more or less permanent form including such elements as Bible and poetry readings which was adopted by Geva and many other kibbutzim from the mid-1930s onwards.

There was a wide variety of experimentation with the traditional Jewish festivals, often in an attempt to revive their agricultural associations. Here is an extreme statement of this point of view, contrasted with that which stressed the continuity of Jewish social and cultural

[27] Nahman Raz, quoted in Shua and Ben-Gurion, *Sabbath Anthology*, 242.

forms. It is taken from the diary of a young member of Degania Gimel, a group later to settle in the Jezreel Valley at Kibbutz Ginegar:

The festival of spring, the festival of birth—mother earth, the life-giver. The wheat-fields are shining, soon they will turn yellow, and the anemones are laughing their last red laugh. The harvested sheaves are arranged neatly, like the tents of a military camp. Everything is waiting for the harvester, so that we can begin 'to reap in joy'. Yesterday I harvested beans, and tomorrow is the holiday. I have been looking forward to it; it's a long time since I was in festive mood.

I wanted for once to celebrate my own festival, ours, and not our fathers' who went forth from Egypt. In Degania Gimel the field lies beyond the railway tracks, next to the fields of Hauran. There one can taste the taste of the festival, without any connection with dead historical memories ... but in the farmyard of Degania Gimel this year they celebrated the Passover just like our ancestors in Berdichev or Tarnow. What noise, what a commotion! The yard was full of pillows, blankets, beds, boxes, boots, and all sorts of rags. The rooms are gloomy—for two days we've been sleeping without sheets, and the dirt is frightful. All in honour of Passover—not my festival. If only you knew how much it infuriates me—but I didn't get cross, only a little upset because they desecrated my festival.... On Passover eve everything was just as in my mother's house. I tried to work alone in the fields and think about *my* festival. There were *matzot* and, of course, jollity: plenty of wine. I drank a lot on Passover eve, but I had no festival.... We sat by the tables a short while, and then the dancing began. We couldn't celebrate the festival of Berdichev—we're complete apostates—so we danced.... But I got fed up with that soon enough.

The next day I had to work in the kitchen. I was occupied all day, and that saved me from being sad. But it will come soon enough. People will gradually come to realize that our forefathers' festivals are empty for us. We must create our own festivals, not specially on the day we came forth from Egypt.[28]

This approach was not generally adopted. Until the early 1930s, when more formalized modes of celebration were devised, the more or less improvised Haggada was the general rule. 'We read a humorous Haggada, laughing at everybody in the kibbutz, eating, drinking, and dancing.'[29]

Purim, too, was treated as a 'local celebration', combining traditional elements with references to the kibbutz. The group later to settle at Mishmar Ha'emek celebrated the festival in this way in 1925:

[28] Diary preserved in the archives of Kibbutz Ginegar.
[29] El'azar Halivni. See Tsur, *The Beginning of the Kibbutz*, 224.

*Purim is nisht kein yomtov, un kedachass is nisht kein krank.* [Yiddish: Purim is no festival, and malaria is no disease.] So they say, but we've disproved it. Malaria is certainly a disease—and what a disease! As for Purim, this year we surpassed ourselves, and showed what talents are hidden within us. We produced an opera, a real opera entitled 'King Ahasuerus and Queen Esther'. Half the kibbutz took part, those who can sing and those who can't. It was made up of forty different operas, from *Aida* to *The Barber of Seville*, fitted together to our own text. Apart from the usual orchestra the music was accompanied by pots and pans and the wash-kettle from the laundry. The sounds of our revelry could be heard from Hodu to Cush [From India to Ethiopia: the limits of Ahasuerus' realm, in the Book of Esther] and made a deep impression on all of us—and even more on our neighbours, some of whom said that the performance was unforgettable.[30]

In Ein Harod, an impressive ceremony was devised for the Feast of Tabernacles, with a torchlight procession, a water-dance by the well, bonfires, and singing and dancing, with the participation of children and adults. Attempts were made to revive Shavuot, the Feast of Weeks (traditionally the time of the Giving of the Torah, but also the Festival of the First Fruits) as an agricultural festival. This brought protests by the rabbinate and pressure by the Zionist movement to abandon the ceremony because it involved riding on a Holy Day and infringing orthodox custom.[31] Together with the search for new ideas to symbolize the special nature of communal society while preserving a measure of cultural continuity, there was continuous self-criticism.

Is [our Passover] really our own way of expressing the Feast of Freedom and of Spring? As for the other festivals, we have still found no proper way of dealing with them. We celebrate them formally, with no real spiritual connection with their symbolic content.

There is a powerful desire to express our life in cultural terms. So, on the recent Harvest Festival [Sukkot], we stood in the dark before the gate to the cave, which was decorated with foliage. And the cave was lit with row upon row of candles—and one stood unawares on the tips of one's toes, listening intently to the sound of the water as the children drew it from the well in their pitchers.[32] It was like the moment when the worshippers of the planets and the astral signs[33] achieve unity with their gods ... but only for a

---

[30] 20 Mar. 1925; Gadon, *Paths*, i. 349–50.

[31] Liebenstein, 'Labour Festivals and Religious Tradition'; N.Y., 'With the Festival'.

[32] This part of the ceremony echoed the water-drawing ceremony during the Feast of Tabernacles (Sukkot) in biblical times.

[33] A stock phrase for 'idolator'.

moment, of course—the sound of the crunching of sunflower seeds among the crowd round the well awoke one from one's reverie ... for above our heads there are no planets or astral signs, and we have no god with whom we can unite.[34]

The writer does not condemn such ceremonies; he merely points out that they could not celebrate what he termed 'primitive nature festivals'. 'We are not simple enough, we lack the direct link with nature. We are cursed by consciousness, the consciousness of the "second I", the I who observes, criticizes, and strives to "create" nature festivals, who writes articles about nature festivals.' He does not suggest that such ceremonies should be abolished. But he maintains that there should be a greater emphasis on cultural activities through which the kibbutz community can achieve a more direct spiritual experience, such as literature and music:

Look around you in the dining-hall when those strange notes are heard, the sound of the violin, which always turns one's mind immediately to the 'other side' of life, to the source of all life. Look at them all, how changed they are, eyes downcast, concentrated within themselves, and what silence, holy silence there is in our dining-hall.

This is perhaps the only time when there is something of the house of prayer in our dining-hall. And this should also be the character of the dramatic art, when we develop it in our community.

From this mosaic of cultural activities, no one general theme emerges other than a profound desire to build a new society, with a cultural life satisfying to the community and appropriate to its values. In this framework, there was room for many different approaches, and a very wide variety of cultural forms.

### WAYS OF LIFE: THREE KIBBUTZIM, 1935

By the end of the period of prosperity in the Yishuv, the kibbutz had evolved a settled and, in the main, standardized way of life. 'All beginnings are hard', as the popular saying of that time has it, and the members of a young kibbutz could indeed expect to go through many years of deprivation and hard work. But a visit to a veteran kibbutz, or even a young one which had developed quickly during the economic boom, might afford them a vision of a future which,

[34] This and following extracts are by David Maletz, 'On the Way to a Cultural Ambience'.

while far from luxurious, could offer satisfaction in many fields—
economic, cultural, and social.

This vision, and some of the obstacles in the way of its attainment,
will be illustrated here by a broadly painted description of the ways
of life of three kibbutzim, one from each of the kibbutz movements,
in 1935. They were chosen not because they were necessarily typical—
indeed, it is hard to say exactly what a typical kibbutz was—but
because there is sufficient documentary and oral evidence available
for a reasonably detailed account. None the less, other sources confirm
that the following, admittedly impressionistic, descriptions of Giv'at
Brenner, Mishmar Ha'emek, and Hulda are on the whole characteristic of many communities at similar stages of development during
this period.

## Giv'at Brenner

Of the three kibbutzim to be described, Giv'at Brenner, situated close
to Rehovot, is in many ways the least typical. Its name ('Brenner's
Hill') commemorates the Hebrew author Joseph Haim Brenner, one
of the leading figures of the Second Aliya, who was murdered in 1921
during the Jaffa riots. Founded in 1928 by the conjunction of three
*plugot* of the Kibbutz Me'uhad, it suffered severely in its early years
from lack of water and because its members had difficulty in finding
employment in the nearby citrus groves. None the less, it grew
quickly, and from 1932 onwards became one of the main absorption
centres for the German Jews who joined the kibbutz in increasing
numbers. It was one of the outstanding examples of the 'great and
growing kibbutz', always eager to absorb new members, to expand
its economy, and to diversify its social and cultural life. While it had
not yet reached the status of 'the biggest kibbutz in the world' on
which its members pride themselves today (when its population is
close on two thousand), by October 1935 it was already the second
biggest in terms of its members (382), and the third in terms of overall
population including children (545). Its very size and dynamism
enabled it to produce a unique record of life in the community. Every
day its members would receive a duplicated sheet from which they
could learn 'what's on in Giv'at Brenner'. An analysis of its contents
during 1935 gives a fascinating insight into kibbutz life at the time.
It forms the basis of much of the following description.[35]

[35] Copies of the news-sheet are preserved in the archives of Giv'at Brenner and of
the Kibbutz Me'uhad at Ef'al. I owe special thanks to Moshe Tzemah, one of the

With its growth in size, the *pluga* (as its members still called it) had developed a sophisticated organizational structure. As in every kibbutz, the general meeting met almost every Saturday evening to decide on issues of moment. Current issues were decided—and, if necessary, brought to the general meeting for confirmation or resolution—by an elected general committee, known as the *mazkirut* (secretariat). In Giv'at Brenner this was mainly an administrative body, comprising the general secretary and three other office holders. In addition, there was a *mo'etza* (council) consisting of twenty-seven members who met weekly and discussed questions which could be dealt with without recourse to the general meeting.

The daily news-sheet reported the discussions and decisions of the council and the secretariat, gave information about developments in the community, including notices of future events, and served as a sounding-board for the expression of opinion. An analysis of the subjects which appeared in the course of 1935 gives a detailed indication of the issues with which the members of Giv'at Brenner were concerned in their day to day life. Culture and economics far outstrip the other subjects. Economic matters predominate mainly by virtue of the information provided in the news-sheet: the end of the harvest of a particular crop, completion of a building or other form of investment, details of crop yields, and so forth. In the cultural sphere, there are notices of coming events, such as Hebrew lessons, literary circles, choir rehearsals, or visits of theatrical performers. Virtually no day passed without some sort of cultural event, from elementary Hebrew lessons to discussions of political and philosophical issues.

The contrast between the ways in which these two types of subject were dealt with is also instructive: economic issues were more controversial, requiring more decisions in the council and secretariat, while cultural events were an accepted part of kibbutz life, requiring few administrative decisions, though they fairly often formed the subject of an article. Relations with the kibbutz movement, problems connected with the absorption of new immigrants, and educational questions often appeared in the reports of council and secretariat, in notices of coming activities, and as the subject of articles. Each of these was the subject of constant concern and action, and required

---

founders of Giv'at Brenner and now a member of the staff of the Kibbutz Me'uhad archives, for explaining obscure points and for adding a great many valuable details of Giv'at Brenner's social history.

much administrative attention. The contrast between the number of articles on interpersonal relationships (which included such problems as the acceptance of gifts from outside the kibbutz, and other forms of inequality between the members), and their virtual non-appearance in the reports of the administrative bodies points to the existence of a series of problems which were widely discussed, but with which the official machinery of the kibbutz was unable or unwilling to deal.

Towards the end of the year elections were held. Twenty committees were appointed. These ranged from the smokers' committee, whose three members estimated the needs of each smoker and distributed cigarettes accordingly, to the eight members of the educational council. In all, about a hundred people—almost a quarter of the total membership—sat on these committees. Clearly, Giv'at Brenner was attempting to spread the obligations of democracy as widely as possible.

One item which does not appear in the daily news-sheet should be mentioned in this context. In sharp contrast to any similar kibbutz house-journal today, there are neither announcements of coming general meetings nor accounts of the meetings and their decisions. Such accounts were, in fact, kept in the minute book of the general meeting. But it was assumed that all the members would participate in every meeting, and that an announcement of the time and agenda on the notice board would ensure maximum attendance. There was therefore no need to tell the members what had happened at the weekly meeting. It was assumed (on the whole, correctly) that they had all been there.

Two other important characteristics of this kibbutz emerge from the contemporary documents. The commitment to form a centre for the absorption of German Jewry was one of the main factors in Giv'at Brenner's rapid growth. But it also led to great social strain and involved considerable investment in manpower and money: extra demands for accommodation, for teachers and leaders for the Youth Aliya group, for Hebrew classes, and the constant need to train the new arrivals for their work.

In the economic sphere, there was a constant effort to enlarge and vary the kibbutz's sources of income. The agricultural crops produced included cereals, vegetables, a tree nursery, citrus fruit, a dairy herd, poultry, and bees. In August 1935, 14 per cent of the members' work was devoted to these branches. In addition, a wide variety of non-agricultural branches had already been developed: a metalwork shop, involvement in a co-operative bakery, a jam factory, a workshop for producing building blocks, contract work for the carpentry shop, a guest house, and even a cafeteria in Rehovot. But all these enterprises together employed only 13 per cent of the kibbutz's total work force: the greatest single category of productive employment was outside work, mainly in the orchard groves and building sites of Rehovot, which accounted for 33 per cent of kibbutz employment. As against some 60 per cent of work that was income-producing, 17 per cent was devoted to the social services (for example, in the kitchen and clothing store or the organization of cultural activities), and 7 per cent to child care. Some 10 per cent of the members did not work during this month because of illness or convalescence. Economically, there-fore, Giv'at Brenner was an example of the kibbutz model which figures prominently in the ideology of the Kibbutz Me'uhad: a combination of agriculture, industry, and outside work, a mixed economy constantly expanding both in numbers and in variety of occupation.

It should not be thought, however, that Giv'at Brenner's success was simply the result of the application of a standard model. Much of it was due to the driving force of a small group of founder members, among them the outstanding figure of Enzo Sereni. Having gained a doctorate in philosophy at the University of Rome, he came to Palestine as the result of his analysis of the situation of the Jewish people, and joined Giv'at Brenner at a very early stage in its develop-ment. Not only was he a constant stimulus within the kibbutz itself, urging the members to ever greater effort, expansion, and economic development; he also used his connections with Italian Jewry to obtain loans and help to buy land for the kibbutz. He was concerned not only for the material development of the kibbutz but also with the quality of life, from the standard of food to cultural activities; and there is no doubt that it was at least in part his influence which helped to create the wide range of cultural creativity noted above. At the same time, he was active in the politics of the kibbutz movement and the labour movement, and for several years after Hitler's rise to power worked with the Zionist youth movement in Germany. He was killed in 1945, after parachuting into Italy to try to make contact with the remnants of the Jewish community there. Without Sereni, Giv'at Brenner would have been a poorer place in all senses of the word. Both in this case and in every other kibbutz, social developments were determined not by adherence to abstract principles but by the devotion and human qualities of the people who constituted kibbutz society.[36]

Dan Vittorio Segre, who came to Giv'at Brenner a few years later as a young refugee from Italy, sheds some interesting sidelights on life in the kibbutz. His comments on his relationship with Sereni bear witness to the way in which devotion to the cause of Zionism and the kibbutz could be interpreted by an outside observer as fanaticism and rigidity. He also mentions an aspect of kibbutz life at this time not usually mentioned: the contrast between the public showers, which emphasized the overriding character of the communitarian ethos, and the lavatories—the only place where a young man, living in a room with four others, could be alone behind a locked door for a short while.[37]

This necessarily impressionistic account of Giv'at Brenner in 1935 will conclude with a selection of items from the daily news-sheet, which may be of some help in sensing the ambience of the kibbutz, and the day-to-day concerns of its members, at this time:

— Giv'at Brenner was frequently criticized by economic experts and authorities from outside the kibbutz, including those of the kibbutz movement, for its high rate of investment despite the uncertainty of its economic future.[38] After a visit by a member of the economic committee of the Kibbutz Me'uhad, who criticized the high expenditure of the kibbutz, one of the members asked: 'How can it be that in this period of prosperity we have reached such a state? How was it that we didn't know? The members of the secretariat must give a full account of our financial and economic position.'

— 'Yehuda Shertok, of Kibbuz Yagur, is coming to conduct a choir rehearsal. All the singers must appear; we must not waste Yehuda's time and energy.'

— Several members complain of the crowded and insanitary conditions in the babies' house, and demand that the building be enlarged.

— Under the heading 'On the Edge of the Desert' there is a news item about contract work for the kibbutz tractor in Ruhama, at the southernmost point of Jewish settlement.

— 'This evening: advanced study group on Bialik's poetry; meeting of the members of the orchestra with the cultural committee.'

— 'How can it be that Y. has been allowed to go abroad to visit

---

[36] For a full biographical account of Sereni see Bondy, *The Emissary*.

[37] Segre, *Memoirs of a Fortunate Jew*, 121–4, 129–37, 180–1.

[38] Tsur, *The Kibbutz Me'uhad in the Settlement of Eretz-Israel*, i. 63–5, 136–7.

his parents at their expense? Is this not a gross infringement of the principle of equality?'

Finally, all the items in the newsletter of one day in July:

— The council discussed the implications of the proposed reduction in the Jewish Agency's settlement budget; decided on temporary members of the secretariat to replace the secretary and treasurer who were going abroad for short periods; approved a list of ten candidates to be accepted for membership by the general meeting; decided to relieve the member in charge of the Rehovot branch of the milk marketing co-operative as soon as a replacement could be found.

— News items about the purchase of hay for the dairy herd; delay in the work of the carpentry shop in building huts. Those living in tents are asked to be patient.

— 'Please do not walk on the flower beds which have recently been planted outside the dining hall.'

— 'The general meeting of the Youth Aliya group has decided that on one day in each week only Hebrew will be spoken.'

— 'This evening: PT group; advanced poetry class, a lecture on Hebrew poetry in the Spanish era.'

— 'The unfortunate phenomenon known as "removals" from the clothing store is still occurring. Unfortunately, it is sometimes hard to distinguish between "removing" and plain criminal activity. Is it simply a "removal" when somebody sews something over another person's number? We must put a stop to these undesirable customs. The management of the clothing store announces that it will publicly denounce anybody found committing such an immoral act.'

## Hulda[39]

No more than ten miles from Giv'at Brenner lay Hulda, a very different settlement: in the terminology of the time, not a kibbutz, but a *kvutza* (later to be affiliated to Hever Hakvutzot) with some seventy members and about a dozen children. The name the members adopted for their settlement was a local place-name, identical with that of the neighbouring Arab village.

The evidence as to the quality of life in Hulda in the 1930s is of a

[39] Much of the information about Hulda is derived from Oz, 'The Farmyard in the Forest'. My thanks to No'a Amit, who drew my attention to this work, and to Arye Avnon and other workers of the archives of Ihud Hakvutzot Vehakibbutzim and Gordonia, who supplied much supplementary information.

different type from that which we found in Giv'at Brenner. Like other small *kvutzot*, Hulda had no need for a written news-sheet; the account that follows is based largely on a piece of local historical research, in which a young woman born and educated in present-day Hulda used written sources and oral history to build up a picture of the development and way of life of the *kvutza*.

Hulda had been part of the earliest area of Zionist settlement, close to the Ben Shemen training farm. In its early years it, too, had been a training farm, managed by an expert, and the architecture and planning of the complex of buildings at its centre reflected this approach: the upper—and biggest—part of the imposing central building was to have been the living quarters of the manager and his family, while the workers lived in the small, dank, crowded cellars. After a short period, the farm was run by a succession of independent *kvutzot*. It was one of several Jewish villages which were abandoned as a result of the riots of 1929, and it became a point of honour with the Zionist movement to re-establish it.

This task was undertaken by the first organized group of Gordonia. They believed that they had a special mission, both in reviving the traditions of the 'classic' *kvutza* and in providing an example for similar groups of Gordonia graduates who would follow them. During their first year in the country this conviction led them to initiate a process of selection, in which they purged themselves of members considered by the majority to be unsuited to life in an élite community.[40] When the leaders of Hapoel Hatzair suggested that they take on the resettlement of Hulda, they accepted the task as a challenge to themselves and a symbol to their movement.

The challenge was much greater than even they expected. In the event, the Zionist authorities refused to recognize the site as suitable for permanent settlement, since it had neither sufficient land nor a source of water. Officially, therefore, the group was not a permanent *kvutza*, but a *pluga*, and consequently lacked the funds for building accommodation and developing the farm which were more readily granted to other groups. None the less, the members became emotionally attached to the site, and this prevented them considering a move to another, more propitious location. For several years they were forced to work far from home; groups would be scattered all over the country during the week, returning only on Fridays to celebrate the Sabbath eve and be together the following day. Relative stability came

[40] Ben-Avram, *Hever Hakvutzot*, 51–3.

in 1934, as the economy of the Yishuv improved. Members were employed in the planting and maintenance of 100 hectares of citrus orchards in the vicinity, and 16 hectares, with facilities for irrigation, were allocated to Hulda as an extension of its own farmland. The Zionist authorities began to explore the possibility of designating it a place of permanent settlement and allocating the resources which such a decision would entail. Although no final decision was made until 1936, the atmosphere changed radically, and during 1934 a second group of Gordonia graduates was absorbed.

With all these developments, this small and struggling community now seemed to be on the road to prosperity, in common with much of the Yishuv. But 1935 was a year of disaster: 45 of the 70 members were taken ill with typhus, and within ten days 3 of them died. Over the next four months almost all the kibbutz contracted the disease, and virtually all normal activities ceased. Those who had recovered visited their comrades in hospital in Tel Aviv and Jerusalem and tended those who were convalescing.

The typhus outbreak served to draw attention to the fact that despite Hulda's proud claim to be an exemplary community, some aspects of life there were far from satisfactory. A letter from the High Commissioner, Sir Alfred Wauchope, dating from the beginning of 1936, says: 'Yesterday we were hunting in the region of Hulda. This was my second visit, and it made no better impression than the first. I do not think that any Arab village would appear so dirty and neglected and so badly cultivated. [My companion] took one look at the inhabitants, and said that he thought the place was used for housing horses [rather than people].' This is clearly not meant as criticism of Jewish settlement or the kibbutz in general; for Wauchope was well acquainted with Jewish settlement, and was drawing the attention of the Jewish authorities to an exceptional case. Kupat Holim, the Histadrut medical organization, sent a doctor to investigate; his report mentions some factors which were common to the whole of the kibbutz movement (particularly the shortage of accommodation, with four or five people sleeping in a small room, and others in a large hall). Others were specific to Hulda: one was the legacy of the original planning of the walled farmyard, with living quarters, kitchen and dining-hall, cowsheds, and stables in close proximity. Yet others, such as the lack of proper drainage, were the result of neglect. His report concludes: 'The state of Hulda is indeed beneath criticism. The fault lies both with the settlement authorities,

who leave the place to its own devices, and with the members themselves, who have become indifferent to the insanitary state of the
settlement.'[41]

The verbal evidence of former members, some of whom claim that
the slovenliness which was the keynote of Hulda's physical condition
at this time was the main reason for their leaving the *kvutza*, tends
to show that the doctor's criticism was justified. One of them states:

I arrived in Hulda as part of a group who had brought some equipment,
including a horse. The horse ran away, but none of the kibbutz members
bothered to go and look for it. I worked in the orchards and every day I
found tools which people had left behind. At the end of the day's work they
would say 'Why bother to carry the tools home and then back again tomorrow?' The following day these people would be allotted to another job, and
the tools forgotten. . . . The last straw was that my wife and I had to sleep in
a large hall, together with a lot of unmarried people.[42]

It is true that the lack of support by the Zionist authorities was a
major factor in the creation of this sorry state of affairs. But other
kibbutzim managed to build up a relatively efficient and healthy
community even at the earliest stage of their existence, when they had
little or no income apart from what they could earn by outside work.
It must be remembered, however, that during Hulda's early years it
belonged to no kibbutz movement, and that Hever Hakvutzot, which
it eventually joined, was the weakest of the movements, and in an
early stage of development. Thus, Hulda was not only isolated; it was
alone, in a sense that the *plugot* of the Kibbutz Me'uhad and the
Kibbutz Artzi were not. Perhaps the legacy of the youth movement,
with its emphasis on spontaneity and its belief that intimate contact
with nature was itself an assurance of health, was at work; for the
state of affairs began to improve with the birth of the first children
(by 1936 there were thirteen, and ninety adult members). Apparently,
responsibility for the younger generation was a maturing influence.

One of the differences between the kibbutzim described here is
quite clearly a function of size. We have seen that by 1935 Giv'at
Brenner had developed a complex network of democratic institutions.
In 1935—and, indeed, until 1937—Hulda was still governed by the
general members' meeting, and there were only three elected officials:
the secretary, whose main task was the representation of the kibbutz

[41] Text of the letter and the sanitary report in Oz, 'The Farmyard in the Forest',
53–6.
[42] Evidence of Yitzhak Schuman, in Schuman, 'Reasons for Leaving', 9–11.

in its relations with outside bodies, the treasurer, and the work organizer. Matters of principle were decided by the general meeting; but its deliberations were greatly influenced by the existence of an unofficial but none the less most powerful leadership whose status stemmed from the time of the youth movement. Outstanding among this informal hierarchy was Pinhas Lubianiker (Lavon), the creator of Gordonia; at this time he was already engaged in almost full-time political activity outside the kibbutz and often represented it in negotiations with outside bodies. This state of affairs was accepted by the first group of members, who had together undergone the experiences of the early years—including the process of self-selection. In 1934, however, they were joined by a younger group, many of whom thought the founding members a closed and unsympathetic society, unwilling to accept criticism and set in their ways. As a result, about half the new members left shortly after their arrival. Others, including one who has described his feelings in a detailed piece of oral testimony, struggled for a number of years to change the social structure and customs. One major problem, in their eyes, was the way in which the decisions of the general assembly were applied and day to day priorities allocated. This was, in practice, in the hands of the elected officials of the kibbutz.

There was no budget for anything. Not even a fixed number of days for annual leave. . . . The work organizer decided who should have time off . . . and the treasurer decided everything [in the economic sphere]. . . . There, too, there was no principle, no system, no method of organization. You went to the treasurer and said, for example, 'I need a new bridle.' If he had no money to buy one, he simply didn't. . . .

For seven years we had the same treasurer. If it weren't for him, who knows whether we could have survived. . . . he bore a burden which ordinary people couldn't have stood. On the other hand, his methods weren't suited to a normal kibbutz and to normal relationships between comrades. So in 1938 there was a 'palace revolution', and he was replaced.[43]

In view of all the negative aspects of life in Hulda, one is tempted to ask why so many of its members did, in fact, stay, eventually weathered the storm, and turned it into a settled and even prosperous kibbutz; for the proportion of members of the original group who stayed in the kibbutz—many of them still alive at the time of writing—was very high indeed. The first part of the answer lies, no doubt, in the calibre and conviction of the people concerned. They saw

[43] Oz, 'The Farmyard in the Forest', 49–50.

themselves as an élite group, whose success or failure would influence scores, if not hundreds, of similar groups, and untold numbers in the youth movement. There were also elements in the nature of Hulda itself which held a very special attraction. In the words of a woman who was a key figure in the first group: 'How magical was this green corner, set in the midst of empty fields! Who can say whether it was this superb scenery, and the majestic peace which came upon the forest with the setting sun, that supported our faltering hands and bound them inseparably to the barren rocks'.[44] The imposing building, albeit unsuitable and insanitary, set in the almost mystical ambience of the Herzl Forest—the first major enterprise of the Zionist movement—bore deep symbolic significance. There was a challenge implicit in the rebuilding of a sacked village, and in survival in an isolated and frequently hostile environment. There was idealism in the feeling of building a society based on the principles which had inspired the veteran *kvutzot*, but free from the blemishes with which they had been tainted over the years. All these factors combined to counteract the disadvantages. The 'oppositionist' witness quoted above summed up the prevalent attitude well when he said:

At the end of 1936 Hulda had reached such a deep social crisis that a group of us told Pinhas [Lavon] to inform the Zionist authorities that if they didn't recognize Hulda as a point of permanent settlement we would leave. . . . Only someone like myself, who had arrived here five years after the founders, could bring himself to make such a threat. For the original settlers it was an impossibility—their loyalty to the place was quite extraordinary. And even in our case, the threat was really meant for external consumption; we didn't actually intend to leave.[45]

The pressure was successful, land and water were found, and from 1937 onwards Hulda was recognized as a permanent kibbutz. From that time on it entered a period of consolidation and prosperity, fulfilling many of the dreams of its founders.

## *Mishmar Ha'emek*[46]

The name Mishmar Ha'emek ('Guard of the Valley') was derived from the kibbutz's geographical position at the western end of the Jezreal

[44] Gitlis, *Hulda* (Tel Aviv, 1941), 75.
[45] Oz, 'The Farmyard in the Forest', 60.
[46] Copies of the Mishmar Ha'emek news-sheet, on which this section is based, are to be found in the archives of the kibbutz, and in the archives of Hashomer Hatzair at Giv'at Haviva.

Valley. Although the kibbutz had been settled at its permanent home since 1926, its members reckoned its anniversaries from the time of the foundation of its first group of members, in 1922. By either reckoning, it was the oldest kibbutz of the Kibbutz Artzi. By 1935 it was an established and flourishing settlement. Its balance-sheet showed a profit, and its economy was constantly expanding. The first educational institute of the Kibbutz Artzi was located in close proximity, and the members of Mishmar Ha'emek were deeply involved in its development. Several of the veteran members, including Ya'akov Hazan, who shared with Meir Ya'ari of Merhavia the leadership of the youth movement and the Kibbutz Artzi, were active in the kibbutz movement and the central institutions of the Histadrut. In many respects, therefore, it was what Hulda had aspired to be, but had not then succeeded in becoming: a showplace for the kibbutz movement and an example and inspiration to the youth movement which was already beginning to supply it with additional members.

The source for the following description of life in Mishmar Ha'emek at this time is, as in the case of Giv'at Brenner, the local news-sheet. It was published weekly (though with occasional gaps; there were twenty-two issues in the nine-month period covered here), and was written in a more personal and journalistic style. Reports from the various economic branches often took the form of interviews with the branch manager. The editor raised issues of public policy as well as providing information; indeed, he had a regular column, entitled 'Everyday Faults', which gave a detailed, though polemic, view of the negative aspects of life in the kibbutz. At the same time, a good deal of factual information was conveyed, ranging from the average daily temperature and quantities sent to market to the number of members on the work roster. From this we learn that at the beginning of 1935 there were 126 workers in the kibbutz, and about 140 at its end. During this period Mishmar Ha'emek was in the process of absorbing a group of new members, all from Hashomer Hatzair. In terms of size, therefore, it lies between the ever-expanding Giv'at Brenner and the deliberately small Hulda. It is also a good example of the 'organic' method of building kibbutz society—the slow and cautious meshing of pre-existing groups.

Despite these differences, analysis of the contents of the news-sheet shows many basic similarities between Mishmar Ha'emek and Giv'at Brenner. Here, too, news about the economic development of the kibbutz predominates, with many detailed reports about the progress and problems of the various branches. Cultural events, education, and health are also prominent, though less frequently mentioned than economic affairs. Although the proportions of these relatively minor subjects differ as between the two kibbutzim, the differences are not so great as to rule out the possibility that they stem from the style and areas of interest of the editors, rather than the activities themselves. In general, therefore, it may be said that though the members of the two settlements differed in age, movement origin, and ideology, their day-to-day activities were in the main similar.

None the less, some differences can be discerned. The first concerns the general meetings of the kibbutz. Whereas the general meetings at Giv'at Brenner were not reported, all but five of the twenty-two issues of Mishmar Ha'emek's news-sheet carry short accounts of the subjects discussed at the general meetings and the decisions reached. During the seventeen weeks thus covered, fifty-one meetings are reported, an average of three per week. In one sense, this is misleading, for the reports also cover eleven lectures or accounts of members' activities in the kibbutz movement or the political sphere, as well as ten parties, ceremonies, and celebrations of the kibbutz as a whole. So only thirty relate to business meetings. The subject most often discussed was education, including several discussions of the relationship between the kibbutz and the neighbouring educational institute, now entering its fifth year. Work problems, ranging from a general discussion of the situation to decisions on who would work in particular jobs, were dealt with on nine occasions, and economic questions (the annual economic plan, the establishment of new branches, the treasurer's report, and the allocation of budgets) on seven. Problems connected with members' parents appear six times. There were four discussions of matters connected with the kibbutz movement and the youth movement, and four of personal requests of individuals, or questions arising from personal problems. Housing appears twice, absorption of new members and health once each.

Here again, there seems to be little difference between the principal concerns occupying the members of these two kibbutzim. But there are significant differences in the framework in which they were dealt with. First, a terminological difference may be noted. When all of Giv'at Brenner's members met together in their dining-hall, the event was known as a meeting (*asefa*). A similar event in Mishmar Ha'emek would be called a discussion (*siha*). Even though the content of the meeting and the way in which its business was conducted might be very similar, Mishmar Ha'emek, in common with all the kibbutzim of the Kibbutz Artzi, used a word which evoked the intimate discussions of the youth movement, while the terminology of the big kibbutzim was a continuation of that of Gedud Ha'avoda and of Hechalutz.

The differences were not merely linguistic. The fact that cultural and political events were classed as 'discussions' points to the fact that they were open for the participation of all members, and in fact all members were expected to meet together in the dining-room for three evenings each week on average. At one point, the editor of the news-sheet complained that the number was sometimes as high as five—and this was too much! The social and cultural activities of Giv'at Brenner were more varied, and placed greater emphasis on small group activities. Unfortunately, there is no detailed record of the network of committees in Mishmar Ha'emek, parallel to that described above in Giv'at Brenner. A number of committees are mentioned, and their decisions published in the news-sheet. It seems likely, however, that many decisions which reached the general meeting of Mishmar Ha'emek would have been resolved in Giv'at Brenner by a decision of one of the committees.

Reference has already been made to the lectures and reports about political and educational matters connected with the Kibbutz Artzi and Hashomer Hatzair. This was partly because several members actually worked for the movement in these fields, though they usually returned to the kibbutz after a number of years. They considered it their duty to report on their activities to the kibbutz; and, as we have seen, many of the issues with which they dealt were decided on the basis of discussion within the kibbutzim of the Kibbutz Artzi. In Giv'at Brenner, very much less overt political activity is recorded at this stage, although several members played some part in the politics of the Kibbutz Me'uhad and the Histadrut. Nor is there specific reference to political discussions organized by the cultural committee, as in Mishmar Ha'emek. In short, it seems as if Mishmar Ha'emek was a more politically conscious and active society in 1935 than Giv'at Brenner.

A further interesting feature of life in Mishmar Ha'emek is the constant stream of distinguished visitors: as remarked above, this community had become a showplace of the Kibbutz Artzi. Many were well-known personalities in the Zionist movement, including such leaders as Chaim Weizmann, Menahem Ussishkin, and Otto

Warburg as well as lesser-known figures from the British, French, German, and South African Zionist federations. Stefan Zweig, the Austrian author, wrote to thank the kibbutz for the gift of an album 'which brings memories of two of our happiest hours in Palestine'. And the High Commissioner wrote in the visitors' book: 'It was a great pleasure to see again the good work, the enthusiasm, and the success of this settlement.'

The contrast between this comment and the same man's impression of Hulda needs no elaboration. But the impression should, no doubt, be moderated by an item in the Mishmar Ha'emek news-sheet. A note from the Commissioner's secretary, thanking the kibbutz for a gift of plums and regretting that he would be unable to visit again in the near future, is followed by the following editorial comment: 'Apparently the High Commissioner is a clever man. He goes to Haifa, and [by hinting that he may visit us] keeps the work organizer in a state of tension. He knows that he will immediately put people to work cleaning up the central area of the kibbutz. And we, in our innocence, thought that there was no hope of getting the place cleared up [again].' The note concludes with a sardonic phrase in Yiddish implying that non-Jews can do what Jews cannot. The implication is clear: a chance visit to Mishmar Ha'emek, like that to Hulda, might have left a quite different impression on the distinguished visitor. It may be added that the report of the health inspector contains a number of criticisms of the level of sanitation, and several recommendations similar to those made to Hulda.[47]

A selection from the editor's column 'Everyday Faults' shows that there was plenty of room for improvement. The shepherd threatened to strike because the treasurer would not buy him a new watch, so he could not return from the pasture in time for the evening milking. Heavy rains increased the risk of malaria, and proper precautions had not been taken. The builders were congratulated on completing the new lavatory, but were asked why building materials were still lying around outside to trip members up on nocturnal visits. And why was there no netting over the window, to keep the flies out? A tap near the centre of the kibbutz had been dripping for nearly two weeks; why had nothing been done? Under the heading 'To whom does it belong?' the editor asks who was responsible for cleaning up certain overgrown areas, who was supposed to keep the graveyard in order,

[47] Mishmar Ha'emek news-sheet 4 May 1935, 26 May 1935, 15 June 1935.

and who had thrown a new pair of women's shoes on to the rubbish pile.

In all of this it is possible to see tendencies in kibbutz life similar to those which appeared in an extreme form in Hulda at its lowest ebb. Here, they are viewed with humour, sometimes even with tolerance, and it seems as though there was a constant effort to put things right. A similar parallel can be found in the discussion about the 'members' committee' in Mishmar Ha'emek towards the end of 1935. There was at this time no allowance of 'private money' for members to use as they saw fit; all needs, ranging from fares for a journey to town to furniture for their rooms, were allocated from the budget of the members' committee, which was supposed to assess members' relative needs and satisfy them within the limits of the money available. During 1935 it appeared that almost all of the members had appeared before the committee for some reason; and it was beginning to be said that its task was impossible, and should be lightened by giving every member a small monetary allocation. In Hulda, the difficulties inherent in estimating the needs of the individual seemed to be a function of the lack of formal channels of decision; but the experience of Mishmar Ha'emek shows that the institutionalization of the system did not in itself solve the problem.

This section will conclude, as did that on Giv'at Brenner, with a summary of the notices appearing in one typical issue of the Mishmar Ha'emek news-sheet, that of 15 March 1935:

— The manager of the orchards reports that since the tractor has been working in the branch it has saved 120 work-days of human beings, and 130 of animals.

— An editorial greets the group which has just reached the kibbutz as reinforcement, and warns members that they will have to invest much time and patience in their absorption.

— 'Yields of cauliflower are smaller than expected, but the price is high.'

— 'Children from the neighbouring Arab village have paid a successful visit to the educational institute.'

— 'Implementation of precautions against malaria is dangerously late.'

— 'Why does the taste of soap remain in the dishes after they are washed?'

— 'Beware of bees when you go for a walk in the nearby wood.

Our population is growing, and so is the noise in the dining-room; please try to moderate it.'

— 'Detailed analysis of the past three months' expenditure on consumption shows among other things that all of the money allocated to help for members' parents has been spent. The parents' committee has discussed the matter, and will bring it before the general meeting.'

— 'The kitchen is in urgent need of repairs, in view of the coming of spring.'

— 'Over the past two weeks some 25 people have devoted spare time to planting trees in the centre of the kibbutz.'

— General meetings discussed the release of members to act as emissaries to the youth movement in Europe. Ya'akov Hazan reported on his visit to the movement abroad. The treasurer reports that the financial situation is satisfactory, and that not one of the budgets has been overspent. There are reports from nine agricultural branches, warnings to be careful when crossing the main road, and details of the Friday evening gramophone concert.

With all these indications of prosperity, figures published a few months later show that in Mishmar Ha'emek 14 per cent of the members were living in permanent buildings, 74 per cent in huts, and 12 per cent had no accommodation. The general meeting decided to put unmarried members to live with married couples at the decision of the housing committee and 'in rotation'.

*Comparisons and Conclusions*

The economic structure of Mishmar Ha'emek was different from that of Giv'at Brenner. As an old-established kibbutz expanding much less quickly, it was less dependent on outside work. In the year ending August 1935, only 9 per cent of the members worked outside the kibbutz, compared with 30 per cent in Giv'at Brenner. Its economy was almost entirely agricultural: field crops, dairy cows, chickens, sheep, bees, fruit trees and a nursery, fodder crops and vegetables. It had no industrial branch, but hired out its truck. Fifty per cent of the work-days during the year were devoted to productive branches, 34 per cent to service branches, 12 per cent to illness and maternity, and 4 per cent to holidays and idleness enforced by rain.

Despite the many differences between them, the general direction of economic progress in both Giv'at Brenner and Mishmar Ha'emek is clear: by consolidating existing branches and constantly seeking new sources of income they had both been able to expand continuously and establish a firm basis for future development. Hulda was to reach a similar stage some three or four years later. As for other aspects of their ways of life, some remarks made by David Ben-Gurion in 1929 are relevant:

Everyone knows that from the economic point of view the kibbutz has made great progress. The farm has developed, the members have learnt, and know how to work.... But, even so, many leave, and many of those who stay are dejected, not because of disillusion with the great ideals of the kibbutz, but because of the lack of attention to small details ...

I have been in Ein Harod during mealtimes several times, and each time I was astonished at the way people eat there after working hours. No one worries about the small details that make up the way of life. The individual is too neglected, too unnoticed. His special needs and inclinations do not get enough satisfaction. He is too restricted.... The kibbutz has not yet begun to pay attention to the need for continuous improvement in the quality of life of its members.[48]

Although these criticisms were specifically levelled at the 'big kibbutz', the example of Hulda proves that indifference to physical appearance and well-being, and neglect of public (and private) property, were not simply functions of size. The same applies to many other aspects of kibbutz life illustrated here. The three kibbutzim differed not only in size, but in their members' movement allegiance, national background, and age, in their geographical location and the degree of economic progress attained. These differences show quite clearly in the detailed picture presented here. At the same time, there are a number of common characteristics which can be discerned, though in different degrees, in all of them. Negative features such as the lack of proper sanitary conditions, shortage of housing, and the tendency to neglect public property are to be found side by side with deep loyalty to comrades and the kibbutz as an institution, willingness to work hard and forgo material luxuries, and a creative urge which found myriad ways of expression in work, in cultural life, and in social relationships.

[48] *Davar*, 11 Jan. 1929.

# 8

# Diversity and Unity: The Smaller Movements, 1930–1939

IT was noted in Chapter 5 that by the mid-1930s the kibbutz movements were beginning to be more heterogeneous than in previous periods, in terms both of the geographical and cultural origins of their members and of the type of youth movement from which they were recruited. The discussion there was limited to the variations which were already of some importance by 1935. In this chapter I shall describe the evolution of a number of movements which had been of relatively minor importance at that time, but were to come to prominence (in the kibbutz context) in the coming years.

## PIONEERING YOUTH MOVEMENTS IN THE DIASPORA

### Maccabi Hatzair–Brit Hatzofim[1]

During most of the pre-Hitler years, one of the biggest of the German Zionist youth movements was Maccabi Hatzair, the Young Maccabean movement. It differed from the other movements described here in that it had international affiliations unconnected with any of the pioneering movements or the kibbutz. In its early stages it was primarily a sports organization, like its parent organization, Maccabi, with little more ideological commitment than a general pro-Zionist stance. By the early 1930s it had branches in Germany, Czechoslovakia, Hungary, Lithuania, Palestine, and other parts of the Jewish world and was, in many respects, independent of its parent organization. In 1934, it joined with the section of the Zofim (Jewish scout movement) which did not accept the pioneering ideology of Hashomer Hatzair. The main strength of the united movement was in Germany, where it had 5,000 members, Czechoslovakia (2,500), and Palestine (2,500). Its cultural ambience was firmly rooted in Central Europe and its lingua franca was German.

[1] This section is based on Ben-Avram, *Hever Hakvutzot*, 182–203.

The movement's ideology centred on the notion of *Gemeinschaft*. This term has been used in two senses—to denote a small group or community, or the national community linked by firm ties of common culture and emotion. In Maccabi Hatzair's early years the idea of the national *Gemeinschaft* was used to justify its own version of Zionist ideology, which involved opposition to such divisive notions as the class struggle within the national framework. While many of these views were similar to those of A. D. Gordon, they were sometimes couched in terms reminiscent of the surrounding nationalist atmosphere, which undoubtedly influenced the movement in its earliest stage. Its more extreme expression was soon abandoned, but for many years the movement remained opposed to socialist ideas and symbols. It educated its members to join the Histadrut, but refused to commit itself to any of the parties within the labour movement.

From 1933, Hever Hakvutzot began to send educational emissaries to the constituent movements of Maccabi Hatzair, and by the end of that year there were about one hundred German immigrants in its *kvutzot*, most of them from this movement. Opposition to the idea of a 'mass collective organization' ensured its affinity to Hever Hakvutzot; and, despite its early declarations of equal support for moshav and *kvutza*, its members began to reach the *kvutzot* in increasing numbers, both through its training farms and as trainees in the framework of Youth Aliya. In 1935 it decided that the *kvutza* was 'the way in which youth can become rooted in agricultural work, and through which is created a just and honest way of life.'[2] But, unlike the major youth movements, it did not speak of the kibbutz as the only way of life suitable for movement graduates, nor did it make movement membership conditional on commitment to join a kibbutz. Many of the movement's leaders believed that a high proportion of German youth were not suited to agriculture or to collective living. None the less, over the next two or three years the great majority of immigrants from this movement found their way to the *kvutza*, at least as their first stop in Palestine.

When the members of Gordonia had first encountered the veteran *kvutzot* some five years earlier, they had found a weak and divided cluster of settlements which contrasted with the self-assurance of the youth movement. By 1934, this was no longer so. The union of Gordonia and Hever Hakvutzot had created a consolidated and growing movement, with well-defined political and ideological

[2] Ibid. 186.

attitudes. Gordonia was now an active force within Mapai, and the majority in Hever Hakvutzot supported its stance, or were at least reconciled to it. The leaders of Maccabi Hatzair rejected the politicization of the youth movement and remained faithful to the view espoused by Hashomer Hatzair in its early days: political parties were necessarily opportunistic and manipulative organizations, whereas the youth movement was a spiritual association (*Bund*). On the other hand, they believed, as did Hashomer Hatzair, that their movement could and should respond collectively to all the problems of life and society, including those in the political sphere. In Zionist politics they supported the General Zionists, and in Palestine Mapai, but always emphasized that these were purely tactical choices, not fundamental ideological commitments. In 1938 they tried a new tactic. They entered the political lists as a separate entity, though with no ideological platform, and presented a list of candidates to the Agricultural Conference of the Histadrut. Only a very small proportion of movement members voted for the list; and this proved what should have been clear for some time: that the differences between Maccabi Hatzair and Hever Hakvutzot were no longer accorded great importance by most of the movement's graduates. In 1935, some of them had already begun to speak of their ideology as being essentially socialist; and from this to support for Mapai was a very small step indeed.

In 1937–8, however, few of the movement's leaders were prepared to entertain the thought of full membership in Hever Hakvutzot, which would presumably include support for Mapai, with its class ideology and use of such symbols as the red flag and the Internationale. They had reached an arrangement whereby they were an integral part of Hever Hakvutzot in matters concerning the kibbutz, but retained their organizational and educational independence. But this did not satisfy the leadership of Hever Hakvutzot. As the number of immigration certificates available to German Jews grew in relation to those from Poland, the contribution of Maccabi Hatzair to the straitened manpower of Hever Hakvutzot became ever more important. The central bodies of Hever Hakvutzot demanded that they, and not the youth movement, should decide on the allocation of manpower. In the discussion that followed, the two sides used similar arguments to those used between the minority and the majority in the Kibbutz Me'uhad. The issue was no longer ideological, but practical: who had control over the most precious resource of the kibbutz?

Unlike the situation within the Kibbutz Me'uhad, or between Hechalutz and the autonomous youth movements, this power struggle was not accompanied by an ideological rift. On the contrary, it was already becoming quite clear to the leaders of Maccabi Hatzair that they would eventually become full members of Hever Hakvutzot. Therefore, when the leaders of the latter threatened to break off relationships with the youth movement if their authority over its groups were not accepted, Maccabi Hatzair acceded. At the conference of July 1938, it accepted most of the ideological platform of Hever Hakvutzot, although its leaders still had hopes of retaining their ideological independence as a youth movement. Soon afterwards, however, the war cut them off from their reserves in Europe. Resigning themselves to the inevitable, in 1941 they united with Gordonia. Within seven years they had created or reinforced seven of the thirty-five kibbutzim of Hever Hakvutzot.

## Hanoar Hatzioni and Ha'oved Hatzioni[3]

The most important segment of the group of movements which eventually combined to form Hanoar Hatzioni originated in Galicia as a breakaway movement from Hashomer Hatzair, following the formation of the Kibbutz Artzi in 1927. Rejecting the politicization of the youth movement in any sense other than its support for the aims of Zionism, they saw themselves as the successors of the original, non-political youth movements such as the Blau-Weiss, and Hashomer Hatzair in its earlier stages. Several groups, in various parts of Poland, adopted names such as Hashomer Hale'umi or Hashomer Hatahor (respectively, the 'national' and 'pure' Hashomer movement). Between 1928 and 1930, similar organizations, all of which aimed to use the methods of the youth movement while preserving its pristine, non-political character, had sprung up in several other countries. At the same time, a number of student organizations adopted an ideological stance similar to that of the youth movements while not sharing their educational methods, and began to explore the possibility of setting up groups for settlement in Palestine.

All these movements reacted to the 1929 riots and the renewal of economic activity and immigration in that year in much the same way as Hechalutz and its component movements: preparations for their

---

[3] This section is based mainly on Cohen, *Hanoar Hatzioni*.

members' immigration to Palestine were speeded up and activities in the Diaspora were intensified. At the beginning of 1931 the federation of general Zionist youth movements, then known as Histadrut Hanoar Ha'Ivri ('Federation of Hebrew Youth'), comprising some 150 educational groups in Galicia alone, and claiming about twenty thousand members, sent its first group to Palestine.[4] There were similar movements throughout Poland, as well as in Hungary and Romania; bearing a variety of names,[5] they all shared the same general ideological approach and enjoyed the support of the local Zionist movement. In September 1932, these groups formed an international federation which came to be known by the name Hanoar Hatzioni ('Zionist Youth').

Many of these movements began their independent existence at the point which Hashomer Hatzair and the other large movements had already reached: they accepted the pioneering ideal, demanded that all their graduates devote their life to work in Palestine, and prepared them in training farms for their future life. Their first training farm was established in the early 1930s, and by 1934 some 4,500 young people were undergoing training in Poland, Romania, Hungary, Czechoslovakia, Lithuania, Austria, Holland, Belgium, and France. They were very jealous of their ideological and organizational independence and refused to be swallowed up in Hechalutz. Aware of the struggle between the Kibbutz Me'uhad and the autonomous youth movements, they were anxious to keep aloof from such imbroglios. Their training farms were therefore organized in an independent framework, under the overall name of Hechalutz Haklal-Zioni ('General Zionist Hechalutz').

The refusal to enter the general framework of Hechalutz cost them dear. Reports from the training farms and discussions in the local Zionist movement are replete with accusations of discrimination against the pioneers of Hanoar Hatzioni, particularly in the allocation of immigration certificates. It is impossible to know to what extent these complaints were justified, but a contemporary document speaks of people spending six to seven years on the training farm—a period greater than any found on the farms of the general Hechalutz movement.[6] In 1938, as a result of Hechalutz's refusal to include their

---

[4] Cohen, *Hanoar Hatzioni*, 71.

[5] Among them Akiva, Yardenia, Herzlia, Hashomer, and Hatsofeh.

[6] Cohen, *Hanoar Hatzioni*, 160; and cf. times spent in training (ibid. 157, 177) with those in other movements in Otiker, *Hechalutz in Poland*, 155–8.

members in its illegal immigration operation, Hanoar Hatzioni organized one of its own.[7]

In ideological terms, the movement rejected not only the party affiliations of the Kibbutz Me'uhad, but its concept of the 'great and growing' kibbutz. In terms which recall many of its members' origins in Hashomer Hatzair, they spoke of 'organic kibbutzim', and restricted the numbers on their training farms to a few dozen. From 1930 onwards, groups of graduates of the movement's training farms began to reach Palestine. Their kibbutzim grew both in numbers and in strength, and by 1939 four kibbutzim (Usha, Tel Yitzhak, Kfar Glickson, and Beit Yehoshua) had achieved permanent settlement. They joined together in a framework known as Ha'oved Hatzioni ('The Zionist Worker'), which seemed at first to be an embryonic independent kibbutz movement. But it soon became apparent that its senior kibbutz, Usha, was unable to receive advice and help in its early stages from this association of young and inexperienced groups. After stubborn negotiations, Usha joined Hever Hakvutzot, while insisting on the independence of its youth movement. This proved to be a precedent for the other kibbutzim of the movement, which achieved a similar arrangement within Hever Hakvutzot over the coming years.

For the first few years of its united existence, Hanoar Hatzioni prospered, and the number of its kibbutzim grew. In 1934, however, it underwent a major setback. From its inception, the central movement and its affiliates received financial and political support from the General Zionists, in much the same way that the other youth movements were supported by local left-wing Zionist parties. In the early 1930s, the General Zionists could not properly be called a party. Many of the local Zionist federations were controlled by people who were sometimes called '*stam Zioniim*' ('simple' Zionists, parallel to the 'simple pioneers' in Hechalutz): men and women with no party or ideological affiliations except to the idea of Zionism. Gradually, however, there grew up blocs within this group based partly on regional and personal affiliations and partly on ideological differences. During the Fifth Aliya, two distinct camps formed within the General Zionist bloc: those who came to be known as General Zionists 'A' emphasized the constructive tasks of Zionism, and frequently allied themselves with the labour movement; the other group (General Zionists 'B') opposed socialism in any form, including the Histradrut

[7] Cohen, *Hanoar Hatzioni*, 313–19.

and the kibbutz, and were allied with the farmers of the *moshavot*.

The ideology of Hanoar Hatzioni was from the beginning close to that of the left wing of the General Zionists. They rejected the promotion of class interest, whether of workers or bourgeoisie, and opposed the 'class orientation' of the Histadrut: they refused to fly the red flag or celebrate the first of May as a workers' holiday and advocated the establishment of non-party employment offices. On the other hand, from the arrival of their first immigrant group their members had joined the Histadrut, and their kibbutzim played an active part in the struggle for Jewish labour.

Between 1932 and 1934 fierce controversy arose within Hanoar Hatzioni. Its origins were partly tactical—the central question was whether the movement should fight for its views within the General Zionist movement or create a separate political framework of its own—and partly rooted in personal differences among the leaders. In 1934 the movement split into two, and this event proved to be a catalyst for a schism in the adult General Zionist movement. The General Zionists remained divided, and the General Zionists 'A' eventually became the nucleus of the Israeli Progressive Party. The struggle within the youth movement weakened it very seriously; one kibbutz broke up under the pressure, and others suffered severe losses. The two factions reunited, in very different historical circumstances, ten years later.

Before leaving Hanoar Hatzioni completely, mention should be made of a small but dynamic offshoot: Akiva, which attempted to create a synthesis of religious and non-religious Judaism and to practise it in its kibbutzim. With the politicization of Hanoar Hatzioni in 1939, Akiva continued to develop independently as an unaffiliated movement and made considerable progress, particularly in Galicia; at the outbreak of war it was the third biggest pioneering youth movement in Poland.[8] The Holocaust destroyed its sources of growth, and it was unable to reinforce its only kibbutz, Beit Yehoshua, which subsequently became a moshav.

## The Smaller Countries

This period saw the growth of youth movements in a number of countries where they had previously been very small, or unconnected

[8] Nezer, *The Zionist Theory of 'Akiva'*; Perlis, *Pioneering Zionist Youth Movements*, 457.

as yet with the kibbutz movement. Their quantitative contribution at this stage was small, but several of them played a proportionately more important role after the destruction of the Jewish communities of Europe.

The development of the Zionist youth movements of Hungary, for instance, was quite different from that of the bigger countries.[9] Here, a youth movement drawing from the community at large, with no exclusive ideological commitment, gradually broke up into smaller movements, each affiliated to a world-wide federation. The three biggest were Hanoar Hatzioni, Hashomer Hatzair, and the religious youth movement. All of them began to establish agricultural training groups; and all suffered from persecution by the Hungarian authorities, who suspected them of spreading Communist doctrines. Their very lack of numbers, and the fact that many members came from assimilated homes and knew little Hebrew, led to difficulties in the acclimatization of those who reached Palestine. In 1939, however, when Hungary annexed new territories where there were active Zionist youth movements—Southern Slovakia, Carpatho-Russia, and Northern Translyvania—these movements began to flourish. Many of their members played an important role in the organization of illegal immigration in the early days of the war, and in resistance to the Germans. Those who survived the war revived those groupings and went on to make an important contribution to the growth of the kibbutz movement.

The development of the pioneering movements in the English-speaking countries was no less affected by the special characteristics of their Jewish communities. In the United States, a short-lived Hechalutz movement, appealing mainly to Yiddish-speaking immigrants, had been established before the First World War, and expanded under the leadership of David Ben-Gurion and Yitzhak Ben-Zvi during their war-time exile. It broke up when they left for Palestine together with a group of volunteers for the British army in 1918.[10] Small groups of Hashomer Hatzair and Gordonia were established in the early 1920s and sent a trickle of pioneers to the Yishuv, but they had little influence on the growing generation of English-speaking youth. As the Poalei Zion party became accustomed to the new cultural climate, its youth movement (Young Poalei Zion Alliance) gradually adopted a pioneering ideology, and some of its members

[9] See Eichler, 'Zionism and Youth in Hungary'.
[10] Teveth, *Ben-Gurion*, ch. 18.

left for Palestine in 1930, to join in the foundation of Kibbutz Ramat Yohanan. With the resuscitation of Hechalutz in 1932, aided by a succession of gifted emissaries from the Kibbutz Me'uhad, the way was open for the development of a relatively broad movement, to be known as Habonim ('The Builders'), which absorbed Gordonia in 1938 and reached some five thousand members at its peak in 1946. Training farms for the members of Habonim and Hashomer Hatzair were established. A group from Gordonia joined Kibbutz Kiriat Anavim during the 1930s, and members of American Hashomer Hatzair were among the founders of Kibbutz Ein Hashofet in 1937. Habonim members began to reach Palestine at about the same time, and took part in the establishment of Kibbutz Kfar Blum in 1943.[11]

In several other English-speaking countries the major pioneering youth movement was also Habonim. It originated in England, where a group of young Zionist students saw in it a way of combating the assimilationist tendencies which they believed to be the chief problem of Anglo-Jewry at the time. They were apparently unaware in any detail of the methods and history of the European youth movements, but used many of the same educational tools—scoutcraft, camping, and a general orientation on Palestine—in order to develop the self-respect and Jewish identification of the members.[12]

Graduates of Habonim set up similar organizations in other parts of the British Commonwealth, and by 1939 there were Habonim movements in South Africa, Australia, and New Zealand. During the late 1930s contact was made with Hever Hakvutzot and the Kibbutz Me'uhad, and emissaries were sent to Britain, as well as the United States. In each of these national sections there was a wide-ranging ideological controversy about the movement's function: was its primary task to combat assimilation and provide leadership for the local Jewish community, or to educate its members to emigrate to Palestine and the kibbutz? At the outbreak of war, Habonim had some five thousand members in the English-speaking countries outside the United States.

PIONEERING YOUTH MOVEMENTS IN THE YISHUV

From the time of the Second Aliya, young people born in Palestine had played a part in the labour movement, even though it was led by,

---

[11] See Riemer, 'Habonim in North America'.
[12] See D. Mendelssohn, 'Pioneering Youth Movements in England'.

and largely composed of, Jews born in the Diaspora. Some of the best known figures in Hashomer were born in Palestine or arrived at an early age with their parents. But these were a small minority compared with the majority of locally born Jews, who tended to adopt the attitudes of their parents, whether in town or in the *moshavot*. In the course of the Third Aliya such figures as Moshe Shertok (Sharett), eventually to be Israel's second prime minister, and Eliyahu Golomb, for many years the head of the Hagana, were beginning to find their way in public life. This period also saw the beginnings of the local youth movements which came to be of first importance to the labour movement and, in particular, to the kibbutz.

## The Scout Movement[13]

In its origins, the Scout movement (Tsofim) of the Yishuv was a prototype of the many local movements which were to develop during the 1920s and 1930s. The Federation of Jewish Scouts was founded in 1919 by a few adults who had been active in Jewish scouting movements in the Diaspora, and had created groups in Tel Aviv and Haifa. Their basic conception was similar to that of the British Scout Association: to promote physical health and good citizenship among adolescents through games, hiking, and other group activities. They used many of the methods and symbols common to Scouts the world over, and much of their educational material was translated or adapted from the standard English version. But from a very early stage they adopted certain practices and principles which marked them out from most Scout movements of the world. In most instances, Tsofim groups were co-educational; their members promised allegiance not to king and country but to their 'people, land, and language'; and, in contrast to the Scouts' allegiance to the religious establishment, the Tsofim movement was deliberately neutral towards Jewish religion and practice, although it always contained a number of orthodox groups.[14] Its structure was also rather different from that of the Scouts, and emphasized the small educational group in ways which showed its leaders' origins in and affinities with the European youth movements.

Most of the movement's leaders were teachers, and it enjoyed the support of the local educational authorities. Groups met largely in

---

[13] This section is largely based on Alon, *Jewish Scouting in Israel.*

[14] They are still a recognized part of the movement, and their graduates join the Kibbutz Dati.

high schools, and most members were high-school students. But, in the intensive atmosphere of the Yishuv in the 1920s, the aim of 'good citizenship'—even in the Zionist interpretation of that term which it had adopted—was vague, and for many insufficient. From its early days the movement was a recruiting ground for the Hagana; but this in itself could not be openly proclaimed as its major aim. In a conference held in 1926 there was a heated discussion about the desirability of translating the concept of 'national service' into terms of agricultural work and settlement. It was agreed that the movement's aim was:

self- and mutual education ... to the fulfilment of [the young Jew's] obligations to his people and the construction of his land, as a pioneer of the renewed Hebrew society, which is based on Hebrew culture, (productive) self-labour, public responsibility, mutual aid, and dignified and honest relationships between man and man.[15]

The phraseology could almost have been adopted by any of the pioneering youth movements. But most of the Scouts' leaders were steadfastly opposed to anything which might lead to its politicization, or too stringent a definition of the movement's demands of its members in later life. So both the phrase about productive self-labour and its practical interpretation were deliberately not clarified.

A crisis arose in 1926 as the result of the activities of a gifted leader, Dr Moshe Schwabe, who had been one of the leaders of Hashomer Hatzair in Lithuania. He educated the Jerusalem branch of the movement to the concepts of the 'free youth movement', including the revolt of the local group against the authoritarian leadership of the movement, and an increased awareness of political questions. The result was the secession of the Jerusalem branch, which formed the nucleus of a small movement called Legion Hatzofim ('the Scouts' Legion') and later joined Hamahanot Ha'olim (to be discussed in a later section). After a long period of uncertainty and stagnation, the movement was officially brought under the aegis of the education department of the Va'ad Le'umi, the chief executive body of the Yishuv, in 1935/6. The newly appointed director of youth activities revived and expanded the movement, and in 1936 a new, more centralized, constitution was adopted.

The renewal of the movement's activities coincided with the Arab Revolt. The situation of the Yishuv and the challenge of the political

[15] Alon, *Jewish Scouting in Israel*, 88.

youth movements, whose graduates were forming settlement groups, led to increasingly more concrete definitions of the idea of 'service to the community'. This was at first confined to a 'year of service', which the movement's graduates would spend in agricultural work before taking up their studies or professions. In 1938/9 groups began to work in different kibbutzim each year. In 1941, the group which was about to finish its year of service at Kibbutz Beit Hashita declared that it would constitute a permanent group whose aim was settlement as a kibbutz. This action naturally aroused fierce controversy in a movement which had been at such pains to define its social aims as broadly as possible. But in the atmosphere of the time it was an almost irresistible challenge to patriotic and idealistic young people. The path from youth movement branch to kibbutz was now defined much as in the older pioneering youth movements, though with a less stringent feeling of obligation on the part of the movement member. The first groups of the Scout movement founded two of the eleven kibbutzim set up in the Northern Negev in October 1946 (Be'eri and Hatzerim), and the formation of groups for settlements became an established practice.

## Noar Oved[16]

The Noar Oved ('Working Youth') movement was founded in 1924 with the help of the Histadrut. There was little social legislation in Mandatory Palestine, and the movement's primary function was the protection of young workers, many of whom were very badly exploited. At an early stage it took on itself a number of educational tasks, such as raising the standards of knowledge of its members, a high proportion of whom were illiterate or semi-literate, and helping them to acquire professional skills. It also educated to the values of the Histadrut: Zionism and socialism.

All these aspects of the movement's activities were interwoven when, in the course of the Fourth Aliya, groups of working youth were organized as working parties in the veteran kibbutzim of the Jezreel Valley. It was a method of providing work at a period of unemployment in the towns; and after working hours the groups undertook educational projects. Here, for the first time, they met with a new type of society, whose declared aim was the advancement of Zionism and socialism. As a result, a number of the movement's leaders began to see the kibbutz and the moshav as possible solutions

[16] This section is largely based on Admati, *Youth on the Rise*.

to the problems of working youth in the Yishuv. These ideas were strengthened by their contacts with some of the leaders of the Histadrut and the kibbutz movement—notably Berl Katznelson and Yitzhak Tabenkin—who encouraged them and provided practical advice and help. Thus, although the movement's main functions continued to be in the spheres of protection and education for young workers, by the late 1920s it was regularly organizing groups, at first for work and later for settlement, in the kibbutzim. The movement's first kibbutz, Na'an, was established in 1929, and the first moshav, Beit She'arim, in 1936. From the first, the Noar Oved's contacts and its kibbutzim's affiliations were with the Kibbutz Me'uhad; and the leaders of that movement saw it as the Yishuv's equivalent of Hechalutz—a mass working-class movement, orientated educationally on the kibbutz.

## *Hamahanot Ha'olim*[17]

Hamahanot Ha'olim was the result of an amalgamation of two groups: the Jerusalem Scouts who had left their parent movement in 1927, and Hahugim, which originated in Tel Aviv.

The Jerusalem group widened their contacts and created a small but fervent alternative movement, the Scouts' Legion (Legion Hatzofim), which continued to use the symbols and educational methods of the Tsofim, but emphasized the independence and individual development of its members, as against the more authoritarian atmosphere in the parent movement. The Legion developed a social ideology similar to that of the pioneering youth movements, though it rejected the view that its ideals could be realized only in the kibbutz. From 1928 onwards, small groups of its graduates began to engage in agricultural work, and the formation of a group for kibbutz settlement began to be mooted. But it was becoming clear that this movement in itself was unlikely to be strong enough to form an independent group. The solution was the formation of a joint group with graduates of another independent movement: Hahugim.

Hahugim ('The Groups') originated in a discussion group focusing on the problems of Zionism, the Jewish people, and the Yishuv organized by one of the teachers at the Herzlia High School, the élite school of Tel Aviv. The first such group began meeting in 1926, and gradually spread to other high schools in Tel Aviv and, within two years, to Haifa. By then it was an independent youth movement with

[17] This section is largely based on Kafkafi, *Years of the Mahanot Olim*.

an ideology of its own, very similar to that of the Zionist youth movements of Europe. It did not use the methods and symbols of scouting, but fostered the structure based on small groups which we have seen in other movements. A central feature of its educational approach was the 'hike', whose duration might be anything from a few hours in the younger groups to some weeks among the seniors; this was viewed as a vital means of renewing the town-bred youths' contact with nature and with the geography and history of the Land of Israel.

Graduates of Hahugim began preparing themselves for agricultural settlement in 1928, and the first group united with a group of the Scouts' Legion in 1929. The unification of the two educational movements was a natural development, and from April 1931 the united movement adopted the name Hamahanot Ha'olim (literally, 'the ascending camps', a phrase which was meant to combine the symbolism of scouting with that of *aliya*—immigration and exaltation).

From the first, it was clear that the new movement's *pluga* intended to settle as a kibbutz. From July 1930, when it moved from Hadera to Kfar Yehezke'el in the Jezreel Valley, there were intensive discussions about its social structure and future movement affiliations. A minority, mainly from the Scouts' Legion, were politically close to the Kibbutz Artzi; but the majority tended to favour the ideology of the Kibbutz Me'uhad and identified with the political attitudes of Mapai. These tendencies were intensified by their contacts with the leaders of the labour movement, especially by their discussions with their neighbours in Kibbutz Ein Harod. In April 1931, the group formally joined the Kibbutz Me'uhad, and in 1934 settled at Kibbutz Beit Hashita in the Jezreel Valley; though in the course of these developments minority groups left to join the recently established Hashomer Hatzair movement. In December 1932, Hamahanot Ha'olim took the final step from a 'free', uncommitted youth movement to deliberate education to the kibbutz movement: it decided, as had most of the European youth movements, that it was the duty of all its members to join a kibbutz in their adult life.

## Summary

In all movements discussed here there was a similar development, from a generalized ideology of youth and/or a sensitivity to social issues to the specific solutions propounded by the kibbutz movements. In each case, the quantitative contribution to the kibbutz movement was small at this early stage, but the foundations were laid for expansion during the war and after it. Much the same applies to the more clearly defined kibbutz youth movements which were established in the Yishuv in roughly the same period: Hashomer Hatzair was founded in 1930, and Gordonia in 1932, by graduates of those movements in the Diaspora, and developed with the help of youth leaders and material resources from the movements' kibbutzim. Each of them gradually built its local branches, and their graduates established settlement groups. By 1939, there were six local youth movements whose graduates formed groups to create new kibbutzim or reinforce existing settlements: the Scouts, Hamahanot Ha'olim, Noar Oved, and the local branches of the world movements Hashomer Hatzair, Gordonia, Hanoar Hatzioni, and Akiva. There were also local branches of Maccabi Hatzair, whose plan to found an independent kibbutz was cut short by the outbreak of war.[18]

## THE RELIGIOUS KIBBUTZ MOVEMENTS

The kibbutz movement was further diversified during the 1930s by the establishment of a number of settlements whose members lived according to the tenets of orthodox Judaism, and who founded a small kibbutz movement: the Kibbutz Dati ('Religious Kibbutz'). Like the other movements, this was reinforced by groups of young people educated in youth movements, in this case primarily B'nei Akiva, which had branches both in the Yishuv and the Diaspora. By 1940 the religious kibbutzim had a population of 1,428, no more than 4 per cent of the whole of the kibbutz population of some 36,000.[19] But they added to the kibbutz movement as a whole a new and distinctive element, attracting young people from a milieu in which they could well have been entirely isolated from the social ideals of the kibbutz, and creating a way of life unique both within the orthodox community and within the labour movement.

### The Kibbutz Dati[20]

Among the pioneers who arrived from Russia and Poland during the Third Aliya was a small number of religiously orthodox Jews. They

[18] Hor, 'The Contribution of Maccabi Hatzair'.
[19] Gertz, *Jewish Agricultural Settlement*, 28–9.
[20] The major source for this movement is Fishman, 'The Religious Kibbutz'. A more detailed historical account of early developments is to be found in Aminoah, *The Religious Labour Movement*.

formed a movement known as Hapoel Hamizrachi ('The Mizrachi Worker'). The ideals which had been crystallized in the non-orthodox labour movement—equality, mutual aid, and self-labour—seemed to them to be the social expression of the Torah, and they aimed to combine these principles with an orthodox way of life.

The aspiration of Hapoel Hamizrachi is to return to primal Judaism . . . to create a pure [way of] life lit by the splendour of the patriarchs . . . to revive the original, healthy Judaism, and recreate the historical types [exemplified by] the Tannaim and Amoraim, who combined work with the Torah.[21]

Groups of orthodox workers contracted for road-making in the Third Aliya, and agricultural work in the Fourth. In general, Hapoel Hamizrachi in its early stages rejected the idea of the kibbutz as a permanent way of life: it was thought to contradict the tenet of the sanctity of family life which was central to traditional Judaism. Thus, when its members began to create permanent agricultural communities, they founded moshavim. The movement's first moshav was founded at the end of 1922. Although both this and a number of its subsequent foundations eventually failed, from that year onwards its working groups and settlements were a permanent part of the labour movement.

The first group which inclined to kibbutz settlement originated in Podolia, a district of Poland where Hasidic influence was particularly strong. Arriving in the early days of the Fourth Aliya, they made a temporary home on Mount Canaan, near Safed, historically the centre of mystical Judaism. Accounts·of their communal experience at this spot are reminiscent of the period of Beitania Eilit in the development of Hashomer Hatzair. As a result of this experience they evolved an ideology which held that

the individual is powerless to perfect himself. Only in a kibbutz of comrades, in a regimen of life based on renunciation and the negation of egoism is it possible to attain the fundamental aim of life. The moral improvement of each individual can be accomplished only by common spiritual effort.[22]

This group attracted a number of kindred spirits, but failed to reach the stage of settlement: no women joined it, and it was virtually ignored both by the secular settlement authorities and by the Mizrachi

[21] Zeira, *Hapoel Hamizrachi* (Jan.–Feb. 1925), 29. Quoted by Fishman, 'The Religious Kibbutz', ch. 4 n. 90.
[22] From a letter of one of the members. Quoted by Aminoah, *Religious Labour Movement*, 38.

establishment, whose political and financial help was essential. It was, however, an indication of one spiritual and sociological source of the religious kibbutz movement.

During the 1920s and early 1930s the ideas of Hapoel Hamizrachi began to spread slowly in the Jewish communities of the Diaspora. From 1925, the pioneering elements in the young Mizrachi movement were organized in a world movement known as Torah Va'avoda (Torah and Labour). Its members sent a small but steady stream of pioneers to Palestine, and some of them formed groups with the intention of kibbutz settlement. By 1931, there were some five hundred religious pioneers undergoing training in six European countries; and this number increased dramatically, as with non-religious pioneers, with the rise of Hitler.

This was, in essence, a young adults' movement, similar to Hechalutz in that it combined recruiting and educational work among this age-group with the organization of training and emigration.[23] It was far from being universally welcomed by the orthodox establishment, in the Yishuv or in the Diaspora. The vast majority of orthodox Jews were opposed to Zionism in any form, on the grounds that it was an infringement of the divine will. The religious Zionists, mainly organized in the Mizrachi movement, were suspicious of any separatist movement of young people, and feared that it would lead to disrespect for their elders and the weakening of traditional values. But the movement gradually gained strength. It was represented on the central bodies of the world Mizrachi movement, and from 1935 one of its leaders sat on the executive committee of the world Zionist movement. Within the Yishuv, it was greatly strengthened by the support of the Ashkenazi chief rabbi, Abraham Isaac Kook, who believed that the activities of the non-orthodox (and, *a fortiori*, of the orthodox) pioneers were a necessary step on the path to the redemption of the Holy Land. But, although the religious pioneers were granted immigration certificates more or less in proportion to their numbers, until the changed circumstances of the tower and stockade period (1936–9) they received far less material and moral support from the adult party closest to them than did the secular pioneers.

[23] As so often among the smaller movements, neither the nomenclature nor the organizational structure was completely standardized. In several countries there existed both Torah Va'avoda, which performed an educational function, and Hechalutz Hamizrachi for the organization of the training farms, allocation of certificates, etc. Elsewhere, Bachad (Brit Halutzim Dati'im, 'Federation of Religious Pioneers') combined both functions.

Numerically, the main source of religious pioneers was Germany:[24] the German pioneering movement, Bachad (Union of Religious Pioneers) was formed by graduates of two 'classic' German youth movements—Ezra, a youth movement originally promoted by the adult orthodox community to combat the erosive effect of the Zionist movements, although it too eventually adopted a pioneering Zionist ideology; and the orthodox off-shoot of the Jung-jüdischer Wander-bund, one of the components of what was to become the largest non-orthodox pioneering movement.[25] This movement's approach was closer to that of the Torah V'Derekh Eretz movement, which aimed at combining religious orthodoxy with social and economic modernization, than to the ecstatic Judaism of the Polish hasidim. The experience of the closely knit *Gemeinschaft* became a central element in its theory and practice. But it was conceived of as one component of an overall ideology which aimed at the total transformation of society in accordance with the spirit of the Torah.

The fulfillment of the Torah is a collective task.... the Torah cannot be fulfilled in any Jewish community, but only by means of a *Gemeinschaft* of free workers among whom there are neither exploiters nor exploited.[26]

The kibbutz as a [social] unit rests on the foundation of the Torah of Israel.... We must determine our way of life [in such a way that] it will elevate us in the way of eternal truth, and the direction of the Torah.[27]

In 1929, a group of Bachad members began training at a farm in the village of Rodges, in Hessen, and when they arrived in Palestine were known as the Rodges group. They served as the focus of a number of religious *plugot* waiting for the opportunity of settlement. In 1935 these groups formed the organization afterwards known as the Kibbutz Dati ('Religious Kibbutz').

The movement's first permanent settlement was at Kibbutz Tirat Zvi, in the Beit She'an Valley. Founded by part of the Rodges group together with others of Polish and Palestinian origin as a 'tower and stockade' kibbutz (on which see Chapter 7), it soon became a focus

[24] In 1941, some 55% of the members of the Kibbutz Dati were of German origin, 17% Polish, 11% Czech, 6% Austrian, 3% Romanian, and 7% from other countries; *Alonim* (1941).
[25] Aminoah, *Religious Labour Movement*, 77–9; Schatzker, 'The Jewish Youth Movement in Germany', 280–2.
[26] *Grundriss eines Erziehungprogramms* (Hamburg, 1933), 12. Quoted in Fishman, 'The Religious Kibbutz', 105.
[27] Hamelnik in *Voice of the Immigrants* 'Kibbutzim of Hashomer Hadati' (Heb.), (Warsaw, 1930), 14–15. Quoted in Fishman, 'The Religious Kibbutz', 109.

for the Religious Zionist movement. Its members displayed great courage in withstanding attacks in one of the most dangerous areas of a threatened Yishuv. At the same time, they exercised their judgement and faith to find innovative solutions to a number of problems which arose from the attempt to build an independent community living according to the precepts of the Halakha. Their isolation was somewhat mitigated in 1939, when another religious kibbutz, Sdeh Eliahu, was founded nearby. This, the beginning of a bloc of religious kibbutzim in the Beit She'an area, was followed by the creation of a similar group in the Etzion area, near Jerusalem.

The Kibbutz Dati placed particular emphasis on education, beyond the sphere of its connection with the religious youth movements. From 1934, even before any of its members had settled permanently, the Rodges *pluga* adopted a Youth Aliya group, which subsequently became the founding nucleus of Kibbutz Sdeh Eliahu. This was but the first of a long series of such adoptions, in numbers proportionately greater than in the other kibbutz movements; indeed, at times there were more Youth Aliya trainees in its kibbutzim than adult members. In 1941, when the bulk of the Rodges group settled at Yavneh, this was also the occasion for the foundation of a yeshiva in the vicinity of the kibbutz.

## B'nei Akiva[28]

The B'nei Akiva movement, which aimed to educate young people below the age of 18 in the spirit of the Torah by the use of the educational approaches evolved in the secular youth movements, came on the scene relatively late and suffered badly in its early years from lack of the support of the orthodox establishment. Founded in Jerusalem in 1929 by a young rabbi who was concerned about the quality of religious education in its traditional forms, it was rejected not only by most of the local rabbis but even by many of the leaders of Hapoel Hamizrachi in the Yishuv. They held that religious children should be educated to tradition and obedience, rather than the 'revolt of the young' which was one of the hallmarks of youth movement ideology. Another controversial issue was the membership of boys and girls in the same movement; for, although they were separated in the educational groups, they met from time to time in the broader framework of the local branch (known as the *hevruta*, a Hebrew

[28] This section is largely based on Lev, *The B'nei Akiva Book.*

term equivalent to *Gemeinschaft*—a clear indication of the similarity between this movement and many of the others described above). As a result, members in several places were prevented from attending religious schools, and the movement's early development was dogged by lack of funds and suitable meeting-places. None the less, with the help of a few young and relatively liberal-minded rabbis it made gradual headway, and by 1934 had more than five hundred members, in five towns. During this period it attempted to make contact with similar groups in the Diaspora, many of which had developed from, or in parallel to, the secular pioneering movements. In 1936 the international B'nei Akiva movement was founded.

In the Yishuv, B'nei Akiva gradually developed in the same direction as other youth movements, and in 1931 its first *pluga* was established. Lacking institutional support and reserves of manpower, however, it broke up after two years, and the first group of this movement which achieved permanent settlement—a *pluga* which eventually formed part of the founding group of Kibbutz Sa'ad—was founded only in 1936. Since then, a small but steady stream of B'nei Akiva graduates has created and reinforced the kibbutzim organized in the Kibbutz Dati movement. In accordance with the special emphasis which all sectors of the Kibbutz Dati placed on educational matters, B'nei Akiva founded a network of *yeshivot* at high-school level, which became an important element in the religious education system of the Yishuv and later the State of Israel.

## Poalei Agudat Israel

One further group of religious pioneers should be mentioned. Until the mid-1930s the ultra-Orthodox movement, Agudat Israel, was implacably opposed to Zionism, and attempted to defeat it by political and educational means in the Yishuv and the Diaspora alike. From 1935 onwards, this attitude was modified, largely under the influence of groups of immigrants from Poland and Germany, and the movement began to co-operate with the institutions of the Yishuv and take a stand on questions of internal Zionist politics. Poalei Agudat Israel (the Agudat Israel Workers party) was established in 1933, and gave political and economic backing to small groups of ultra-orthodox pioneers, mainly members of the Ezra youth movement, which were formed from the mid-1930s onwards. In 1944 one of these groups established Kibbutz Hafetz Haim. The movement's second kibbutz, Sha'albim, was founded in 1951.

## YOUTH MOVEMENTS AND KIBBUTZ MOVEMENTS

All these developments emphasize a factor in kibbutz history that now became of overwhelming importance: the close connection between the kibbutz movements and the youth movements. These relationships were very varied, and merit detailed analysis.

The ideas and activities of the classic youth movement stemmed from the social and psychological conditions of adolescence in an industrial society. The almost instinctive protest against swift and massive urbanization, the appeal to spontaneity and the emotions as against the restrictive morality of the nineteenth-century ethos, the attraction of nationalism in the face of the bland and abstract universalism of the classical ideal—all these can be seen as the natural outcome both of nineteenth-century romanticism and of the social and economic conditions which made it acceptable in very wide circles. The particular appeal of these ideas to middle-class youth is undoubtedly connected with the fact that here, for the first time in history, was a socially recognized segment of society whose members were physically but not yet socially mature, and had the time and physical conditions to concern themselves with such matters. Historically, the spread of the Zionist youth movements among central and Western European Jewry is also a function of the influence of the German youth movements such as the Wandervogel and the Blau-Weiss. The themes enumerated above appear again and again in similar if not identical forms in the dozen or so Zionist youth movements which grew up during the late 1920s and 1930s. But they would scarcely have been able to flourish in those countries had there not been suitable conditions for them to take root.

These conditions were lacking in the catchment areas of Hechalutz: sociologically, among predominantly working class youth; geographically, in Russia and Poland. Young people who were forced on to the labour market in their early teens did not have the leisure or the energy for the intellectual pursuits of the German high-school students. They were more likely to see Zionism as the solution to their personal problems in a much simpler and more direct way than the Westernized Jew, who viewed it as an alternative to cultural and social assimilation into the surrounding society. Nor were they likely to develop the intensive, face-to-face relationships which were so important in the youth movement groups. At a time in their life when they could—indeed, had to—decide their own future, they preferred to join an organization with clearly defined aims. These conditions were more favourable to Hechalutz (and, in the Yishuv, to the Noar Oved) than to the classic youth movements.

Even in this context, however, it must be remembered that these distinctions were less far-reaching than they seemed at the time.[29] Although the German youth movements were characterized by an ideology of independence and an image of control by the young people themselves, they were from the first led by older people. Even their names and symbolism show that their commitment to Zionism was deeper than the ideology of youth culture, which held that they were free to make their own decisions on any subject. It is true that for a short time, in the formative period of each of these movements, their members made fundamental choices as the result of their common development, often in defiance of the youth leaders or public bodies which had hitherto supported them. But most of them soon formed new ties with a kibbutz movement, and frequently with one of the Zionist parties; and there can be no doubt that the emissaries from the Yishuv, the educational literature which they provided, and the example of the movement's graduates, played a vital role from this point on. Equally, many of the themes which characterized the classic youth movements appeared in Hechalutz, though often in a rather different form and at a different stage of the young person's development. In the course of time such movements as the Noar Oved adopted many of the educational methods of the youth movement, such as the small group and even scouting activities.[30] The love of nature, independence of thought and action, the fostering of the *Gemeinschaft*—even the aspiration to ideological independence—all appeared in Hechalutz, though usually at a later stage than in the youth movements, being part of the ambience of the training farm rather than of the educational movement.

There was therefore a wide range of youth movements, from the large-scale, committed Hechalutz to the small, selective, ideologically independent German groups such as the Werkleute. Between them come several different combinations. Gordonia used the classic youth movement methods from its inception but was committed to a political

---

[29] e.g. in articles by Meir Bogdanovitch (Sheli), secretary of the world Hechalutz movement, and Moshe Shapira, emissary of Gedud Ha'avoda, in Aug. 1924. *Hechalutz* (Warsaw), 5, 8–10, 11–17. A more sophisticated version of the same viewpoint is expressed in Schatzker, 'The Jewish Youth Movement in Germany'.

[30] Admati, *Youth on the Rise*, 102–8.

outlook and party. Maccabi Hatzair, Hanoar Hatzioni, and the Tsofim of Palestine struggled to preserve their political neutrality and demanded from their members a lesser degree of commitment to the kibbutz idea. Habonim and the Tsofim attempted to combine youth movement methods and ideology with a policy of wide recruitment. B'nei Akiva rejected the notion of 'the revolt of youth'. And these are but examples.

Although these variations continued to exist, by the end of the 1930s their importance was secondary to the fact that each movement had become a major source of manpower for a particular kibbutz movement, with a defined political and social ideology. Most of them reached this stage after a similar process of development. Initially, the specific nature and ideology of the movement would be stressed as a major reason for its separate existence. As their ideas crystallized, they would be seen to lead directly to the kibbutz; and then there would be attempts to combine commitment to the kibbutz idea with ideological and organizational independence, frequently to the extent of attempting to establish an independent kibbutz movement (an attempt which generally failed, with a few exceptions—primarily the Kibbutz Dati). In the end, most youth movements affiliated to an existing kibbutz movement, though almost all attempted to retain a degree of educational and, often, of organizational independence: instances of this are Netzah, Maccabi Hatzair, and the contact offices for German immigrants and for Habonim members within the Kibbutz Me'uhad.

The historical reasons for this process seem clear. The numerical peak of the youth movements in all their varieties came in the mid-1930s, when Palestine became the chief refuge for persecuted Jews, and the pioneering youth movements constituted one of the best ways to get there. It was at this period, too, that the kibbutz was beginning to receive general approval as one of the major instruments of Zionist policy—an approval which became almost universal during the tower and stockade period (1936–9). No less important than all these external circumstances was the fact that the principles of the kibbutz—social justice, the return to nature, service to the nation, and the development of a close-knit community—were inherent in the fundamental ideological stance of most of the youth movements.

Within this broad framework, there were differences of emphasis and ideology which were often crucial in deciding the relative strength of the various movements. The 'scouting' movements appealed more, at all times, to high-school students than to working-class youth; and this class division, reflected in the character of the different Jewish communities, frequently determined the geographical strength of the movements. Thus, Hashomer Hatzair remained much stronger in Galicia and, relative to the size of the local communities, in Romania and Hungary, than in Congress Poland;[31] and similarly orientated movements had a virtual monopoly of the pioneering movements in Czechoslovakia, Austria, and the English-speaking world. The division in the Yishuv was almost entirely on class lines—working youth to the Noar Oved, high-school students to the other movements.

From the mid-1930s onwards, as the political complexion of the kibbutz movements became increasingly important, this too became a factor in deciding the relative influence of the movements. From now on, their strength was a function not only of the social and cultural factors already mentioned, but of the dominant political culture in the countries concerned: for instance, despite its dynamic educational methods, Hashomer Hatzair had increasingly less appeal in democratic countries as its commitment to Marxism and sympathy with the Soviet Union increased.

One further factor has also to be taken into account. It might be thought that the spiritual climate of German Jewry, the classic breeding ground of the movements which tended to emphasize *Gemeinschaft* above all, would foster the growth of movements favourable to the small, intimate, or organic kibbutz. Similarly, Hamahanot Ha'olim was similar in many respects to Hashomer Hatzair and Maccabi Hatzair, and might well have developed an affinity for the type of social organization to be found in the Kibbutz Artzi or Hever Hakvutzot. But at virtually all stages of their development, the German movements were dominated by the Kibbutz Me'uhad, and Hamahanot Ha'olim affiliated to that movement very early in its development. The reason seems to lie in the personal influence of a number of adult figures who developed special relationships with these movements and their young leadership: in the case of Germany, the emissaries of the Kibbutz Me'uhad (Yitzhak Ben-Aharon, Enzo

---

[31] During the 1930s, Hashomer Hatzair made great efforts to recruit working-class members. It is not clear whether the figures of membership during this period, which reflect a certain degree of success, are the result of this policy, or of the increasing poverty of Polish Jewry as a whole. What is certain is that this movement contained a relatively high proportion of intellectuals, though not all of them acquired formal secondary education.

Sereni, and others); in Hamahanot Ha'olim, Berl Katznelson, Yitzhak Tabenkin, and, at a later stage, Gershon Ostrovsky.[32]

These, then, are the factors which decided the relative strength of the youth movements, and their relationship to the kibbutz: the cultural and social state of the Jewish communities; the immanent development of the movements; the changing place of the Yishuv and Zionism within Jewry, and of the kibbutz within the Yishuv; and a host of personal and ideological nuances. Most important of all, however, were the broad historical developments in the Yishuv. After the limitations on immigration beginning in 1936 the numerical development of the youth movements in all countries, with the one exception of Nazi Germany, accorded with the curve of immigration to Palestine. As it became known that there were far fewer certificates, membership of the movements and the numbers on all their training farms dropped almost immediately. As success had bred success in previous years, so failure now bred failure. The same phenomenon, though in a rather different form, occurred in the youth movements of the Yishuv: the success and prestige of the kibbutz and the kibbutz movements made them an acceptable educational model. It was this, in the final resort, which determined their organizational affiliations.

---

[32] Bondy, *The Emissary*, chs. 11, 12, and 14; Kafkafi, *Years of the Mahanot Olim*, 277–95.

# 9

# The Heroic Period, 1936–1939

## THE ARAB REVOLT

THE Italian invasion of Abyssinia and the economic recession which followed it brought the era of prosperity in the Yishuv to an end. It was a paradigm of the events which were to crowd into the coming years and form the framework for the development of the Yishuv and the kibbutz movement: links in the chain which eventually led to the Second World War, many of which had no immediate connection with the Yishuv or even the Jewish people, but which vitally affected the fate of both. In this chapter we shall be primarily concerned with the development of the kibbutz movement as a function of the changing fortunes of Zionism and the Yishuv. But it should never be forgotten, as the actors in the drama could never forget, that these events took place against the sombre background of the preliminaries to the coming world conflict. In July 1936 the Spanish Civil War, widely believed to be a practice-ground for the coming struggle, broke out. From the early 1930s the Nazi regime had been strengthening its hold on Germany, and its influence in the other countries of Europe: dictatorial and antisemitic regimes were established in Hungary in 1932, in Latvia in 1934, in Poland in 1935, and in Romania in 1937. In March 1938, Germany annexed Austria to the German Reich. The reluctance of the European powers to oppose the expansion of Nazi Germany led to their acquiescence in the German territorial demands on Czechoslovakia in September of that year; and when this was followed in March 1939 by the occupation of Prague, Britain and the other democratic powers confined themselves to verbal protests, and a guarantee (widely believed to be of little effect) of the territorial integrity of Poland. In April 1939, the Republican forces in Spain were finally defeated, and a campaign of vicious repression of all political opposition put into effect. This record of victories for the enemies of democracy was halted only with Britain's and France's declaration of war in September 1939; at this stage (the 'phoney war') in a tentative and not entirely convincing fashion.

For the Jews, this period was a series of unallayed disasters, during which the number of Jewish refugees increased dramatically. Two events stand out even against this almost completely black record: the Evian Conference of July 1938, which increased the number of refugees admitted into the democratic countries, but in numbers which bore no proportion to the millions who were in mortal danger; and the Kristallnacht of November 1938, which showed quite clearly that the Nazis were in earnest about their threat to persecute the Jews physically and with demonstrative brutality.

All these events emphasized the growing strength of the dictatorships, the hesitations of the democratic powers, and the perilous situation of the Jewish people. On the other hand, while they buttressed the Zionist claim to be the only certain response to Jewish powerlessness, developments in the Yishuv and the Zionist movement seemed to show that this contention was itself far from being unquestionable. The status of the Zionist enterprise in the Palestinian triangle had already been called into question after the riots of 1929, and the twice-yearly struggle with the Mandatory government for the allocation of immigration certificates was a constant reminder that the British support for Zionism could be reversed in a moment if the circumstances changed. That is what happened in 1936.[1]

The outbreak of what came to be known as the Arab revolt in April 1936 came as no less of a surprise to most of the Zionist leaders than the riots of 1929. It was, however, preceded by a number of local attacks on Jewish life and property by the irregular forces led by Iss al-Din al-Qassem; in perspective, these seem to have been the first organized attempt at an ideologically motivated guerilla struggle against Zionism. Al-Qassem was killed in November 1935. In April 1936, there took place what seemed at first to be a repetition of the 1929 riots. Concentrations of Jewish population in Jaffa, Beit She'an, Hebron, and smaller communities were attacked, and some ten thousand people were forced to flee in search of homes and jobs elsewhere

[1] For a general account of the Arab Revolt and the reaction of the Yishuv, see Dinur, *History of the Hagana*, vol. ii, pts. 2 and 3. The growth of the Arab nationalist movement and the politics of the revolt are described by Y. Porat, *The Palestine Arab National Movement*. On the tower and stockade settlements, see Orren, *Settlement amid Struggles*. On political and military developments in 1938–9, see Bauer, *From Diplomacy to Resistance*, ch. 1.

in the Yishuv. On this occasion, however, the Arab protest lasted longer and was better organized than that seven years earlier. The Arab Higher Committee proclaimed a general strike, which lasted until October 1936. At the same time, attacks on Jewish settlements, individuals, and means of communication took place all over the country, developing into a widespread partisan battle. After a cease-fire from October 1936 to September 1937, the revolt was resumed. At first it had a considerable degree of success, particularly in the summer of 1938. But during 1939 the increasing efficiency of Jewish and British defence methods, and dissension among the Arab community that led to pervasive internecine conflict and terror, had their effect. By May 1939, when the British government's White Paper on Palestine was published, Arab attacks on Jews had almost ceased. Since this document envisaged an independent Arab-controlled Palestine within ten years, it seemed superfluous to fight for aims which had, in effect, been achieved. The Arab revolt was over.

Militarily, the British were at first ill equipped materially and mentally to deal with a partisan revolt of the type they were now faced with. Gradually, however, they improved their tactics; they learnt to use their superior force in hilly areas, and began to employ methods of attack instead of static defence. This, combined with the threat of martial law and the economic damage caused by the boycott, brought the first stage of the revolt to an end after some six months, during which more than three hundred people had been killed. In the second stage of the revolt, the British themselves, whose proposal to partition the country was seen as a betrayal of Arab interests, were under attack no less than the Jews, and they acted with increasing rigour and initiative.

The Jews' defence effort was hampered by a number of factors. The Jewish defence force, the Hagana, was an illegal body, and suffered very badly from lack of funds and arms. The arms permitted by the British to the Jewish settlements were few in quantity, and were supposed to be used only under very stringent conditions. There were some Jews in the Settlement Police, virtually all of whom were members of the Hagana or co-operated with it; but their numbers were very small, and began to be significant only when the British began recruiting them in larger numbers in 1936. Moreover, the Jewish defence forces themselves were divided. A group of the Hagana's most experienced officers had seceded from it several years earlier, and created a small paramilitary organization of their own,

known as Irgun Beit ('Organization B'), which advocated more
aggressive tactics towards the Arab population and did not accept the
discipline of the Hagana.

The Jews were at first no less confounded by the turn of events
than the British. They concentrated on protecting the major areas of
Jewish population, and in this, together with the parallel efforts of
the British police and army, they were reasonably successful. But the
Arabs attacked two of their weakest points: fields, farm buildings, and
other forms of unprotected property, particularly in rural settlements;
and interurban transport, which almost invariably had to pass through
hostile areas. The Jews' first reaction was to concentrate on the
protection of human life, defend closely populated areas, and fortify
Jewish settlements against attack. Gradually, however, they evolved
more aggressive tactics, whereby specially selected groups attacked
the Arab forces at their places of muster or retreat. The leading figure
in this development was Yitzhak Sadeh, one of the founders of Gedud
Ha'avoda, who had been a Hagana officer since the early 1920s. He
worked in the first instance with a 'mobile platoon' in the Jerusalem
area, and later used similar tactics in the defence of the settlements
of the Jezreel Valley.

One of the major questions arising from the need for Jews to defend
the Jewish community was whether to take retaliatory measures
against the Arab population, on the pattern of the Arab attacks against
the Jews. From the first, the commanders of the Hagana opposed
such tactics on moral, strategic, and political grounds: morally, they
opposed any attempt to punish innocent people for acts of the Arab
guerrilla forces; strategically, they doubted the value of such actions,
and feared that they would lead to an escalation of intercommunal
strife; politically, they believed that the moral stance of the Jewish
community was an invaluable asset in international public opinion,
and in the eyes of the British legislators who controlled the fate of
the Yishuv. The policy which stemmed from these arguments was
known as 'self-restraint'. It was reaffirmed by the high command of
the Hagana in August 1936, but rejected by the breakaway organization Irgun Beit, which carried out a number of actions against the
civilian Arab population. In April 1937, after the recommencement
of the Arab revolt, most of the members of this minority force rejoined
the Hagana. A small group formed the IZL (Irgun Zva'i Le'umi,
'National Military Organization'), under the command of David
Raziel. This body, which was close to the Revisionist Party, retained

its independence of policy and action until the establishment of the State of Israel.

Politically, the British reaction to the Arab revolt was almost a repetition of 1929: the government appointed the Peel Commission to look into its underlying causes, and suggest a permanent solution to the problem of Palestine. By the beginning of January, what was to be its main recommendation—the partition of Palestine, and the creation of separate Jewish and Arab states—was already known. By the time the report was published in July 1937, the Zionist movement was in the throes of a fierce and divisive controversy on the partition issue. The Arabs had no such doubts, and reacted to the Peel Commission's report by renewing their military activities. From 1937 to 1939 the British government and the Zionist movement moved simultaneously in opposite directions. Some of the Zionist leaders, notably Ben-Gurion and Weizmann, believed that the partition proposal gave the Jews two essential things which they would be unlikely to achieve otherwise in the foreseeable future: Jewish sovereignty, albeit over a sadly diminished area of Palestine; and control over immigration—the issue which was most vital in view of the plight of European Jewry. Other Zionist leaders, among them Berl Katznelson and Yitzhak Tabenkin, opposed partition: some insisted on the principle of the indivisibility of the Land of Israel; others maintained that the proposed Jewish state would be so small as to be unviable, and could certainly not accommodate a sufficient number of Jewish refugees. The Zionist Congress of 1937, while rejecting the partition proposals, agreed that the executive should continue negotiations in the hope of achieving a more favourable proposal. The British Government, seeking a way of retreat from the partition proposals, appointed the Woodhead Commission to investigate their practicability. Its recommendations were negative. At the end of the St James conference of 1939, which had been convened supposedly to bring about agreement between the hostile parties, the British government announced its new policy: in ten years an independent Palestinian state would be established, one-third of whose citizens would be Jews, and the immigration schedules would be adjusted to this plan. The White Paper of 1939 which announced this policy also proposed far-going restrictions on the purchase and settlement of land by Jews.

The White Paper went even beyond the Zionist leaders' worst expectations. It was considered in all sections of the Zionist movement and the Yishuv to be a betrayal of the undertaking which the British themselves had assumed in the Balfour Declaration of 1917. Preparations were made for a civil revolt, including non-payment of taxes, the establishment of independent Jewish municipal institutions, and the open flouting of the provisions of the White Paper. The outbreak of the war prevented the implementation of these decisions. Ben-Gurion declared that the Yishuv would support the British war effort as if there were no White Paper, and fight the White Paper as if there were no war.

## THE KIBBUTZ MOVEMENT AND THE DEFENCE OF THE YISHUV

### *Kibbutzim, Kibbutz Movements, and the Arabs*

Kibbutz members and kibbutz movements came into contact with the problem of the relationships between Jews and Arabs on three different, though often overlapping, levels. Virtually every kibbutz was located in the vicinity of one Arab community or more, and there were a great many local and personal contacts. Each of the kibbutz movements dealt with the Arab question in its political programmes and actions. And all were forced to defend themselves and thus to contribute to the defence of the Yishuv.

There is no standard pattern of relationships between the kibbutzim and their Arab neighbours. They were affected by the attitudes of the communities concerned, the personal attitudes of particular individuals, geographical distance, and so forth. In many cases there were commercial relationships which bred personal acquaintance and even friendship. Moshe Hass of Hulda recalled many years after:

We learnt a few words of Arabic [in our first year in the country]. Nobody was particularly aware of the need. But when we got to Hulda, our encounter with the Arabs was quite successful. Not that we turned them into Zionists, but we managed to create excellent personal relationships on a face-to-face level, particularly with the people of Arab Hulda.

One of these was the manager of the local railway station. He was an outspoken anti-Zionist, always ready for a political argument or hostile remark. But in his personal relationships with the kibbutz members he was warm and friendly; he would escort home women who arrived at the station after dark, and help with the technical problems connected with railway consignments. He was a familiar figure to all the members of Hulda, and was often invited to their Passover celebrations. Moshe Hass's reminiscences continue:

We did a lot of trading with one of the local villagers, a man named Isma'il, who [also] became part of our surroundings. When we were imprisoned[2] for our activities in the Hagana, many of the Arabs from the village used to come and visit us—we didn't known what to do with all the foodstuff they brought us. Isma'il in particular brought everything he could think of. And when we were released, the whole village—not just one or two we happened to be in contact with—held a celebration, replete with speeches and recitations by the school children, and so forth.[3]

This last incident was probably unique. But neighbourly relationships between Jews and Arabs, in various degrees of breadth and intensity, were very frequent among the kibbutzim, even in those which had been, or even were being, subject to physical harassment and theft.[4] Usually some of the members—often the *mukhtar*, or security officer—specialized in knowledge of the local language and customs. This tradition was begun by the members of Hashomer, who emphasized the importance of local knowledge both in terms of 'know your enemy' and because they believed that the Jews must return to their cultural roots in the East. It was profoundly ambiguous: the very people who were knowledgeable about the kibbutz's neighbours, often to the extent of real friendship, were usually those who became responsible for problems of local defence; it was hard for them to adopt any other attitude than that encapsulated in the popular Hebrew saying, 'respect him but suspect him'. The occasions on which personal acquaintance and friendship had proved ephemeral in times of tension were legion; and the best known of them—the slaughter of the Jewish community of Hebron by those among whom they had lived in overt friendship for generations—was fresh in the consciousness of the whole Yishuv. In a profound sense, therefore, even the best of local contacts and friendships were dependent on the underlying political relationships between the two communities.

The kibbutz movements were deeply divided on the political aspects of Jewish-Arab relationships. The Kibbutz Artzi considered

---

[2] This took place in 1943; but the incident is described here as illustrating an aspect of local relationships which was common throughout the 1930s and indeed until 1948.

[3] El'ad, *Moshe Hass*, 48–9.

[4] See e.g. Dorsinai, *From the Banks of the Dnieper to Ma'ayan Harod*, 74–7, 112–13.

Palestine to be, in the words of Buber, 'a land of two peoples', and
proposed political solutions based on this assumption: in the 1920s
and early 1930s, joint trade union activity, with the distant perspective
of a 'binational society' in the Middle East; later, a binational state,
to be backed by the strengthening of cultural ties and deepening
understanding between the two peoples. The Kibbutz Me'uhad
believed that conflict between the two peoples was inevitable, and
that the interests of the Yishuv required it to be strong numerically,
economically, and militarily. The members of Hever Hakvutzot were,
to echo Moshe Hass's words, not particularly conscious of the
problem. When it presented itself as part of their day-to-day life, they
dealt with it on the local and personal level. Their political attitudes
were, on the whole, those of the leadership of Mapai, and not fundamentally different on this issue from those of the Kibbutz Me'uhad.

These differences date from a very early stage in the development
of the movements. From the time when the leaders of Hashomer
Hatzair had begun to formulate their political attitudes they had seen
themselves as part of the Zionist left, and were attracted to the concept
of the joint Arab–Jewish trade union; the leaders of Ahdut Ha'avoda
(particularly Tabenkin) constantly emphasized the need for the
Yishuv to rely on its own strength, rather than its moral superiority
or the support of a great power; and Hapoel Hatzair tended to rely
on the wisdom and influence of Weizmann in Zionist politics. But,
in addition to these overtly political considerations, there were some
influences engrained in the political culture of those who formed and
led the movements in their early years.

For Tabenkin, as for Berl Katznelson (who had grown up in the
same town),[5] the Arabs were *goyim*: non-Jews, with a different, and
presumably hostile, background. For the great majority of the Kibbutz
Me'uhad, the lesson of history was that the Arabs might be negotiated
with from strength, but could not be changed by fine words or friendly
actions. For the founders of Hashomer Hatzair, the *goy* was not an
inscrutable and hostile being. They had studied with non-Jews,
perhaps even numbered many among their friends. Therefore, they
believed that human relationships and rational discussion with their
Arab neighbours were possible, and could be politically fruitful.[6]
Moreover, although Hashomer Hatzair had long since adopted

[5] Shapira, *Berl*, 68-9, 99-100.
[6] At a later stage (from the beginning of the 1940s) Hashomer Hatzair established
a Department for Arab Affairs whose work was based on this outlook.

Marxist ideology, it still retained something of the youth movement approach, as expressed in the belief that social relationships could be altered by educational work with individuals and small groups. And indeed, in many localities this approach led to the creation of direct contacts between Jews and Arabs, not only on the ideological or political level. On this issue, the members of Gordonia were closer to the Kibbutz Me'uhad than to Hashomer Hatzair, while the graduates of the German youth movements (and some individuals, such as Enzo Sereni) tended to follow a more pacific line, even though they were politically affiliated to the Kibbutz Me'uhad.

The influence of national origins and political environment on political culture can be discerned in the Israeli youth movements no less than the European. It is exemplified in the discussion in Hashomer Hatzair at the time of the creation of Tel Amal, the first tower and stockade kibbutz (discussed in detail later in this chapter). Ya'akov Hazan, true to his movement's traditional approach, warned the settlement group against the danger of provoking the local Arabs. The settlers themselves, the first group of locally born Hashomer Hatzair graduates, replied that they were willing and able to demonstrate their strength, even if opposed.[7] They had grown up and acquired their basic attitudes in an atmosphere of underlying danger; the riots of 1929 had taken place when they were in their early teens. It is, therefore, not surprising that they tended to view the Arabs—and especially those they did not know—as potential enemies. Though they accepted the movement line on the eventual settlement of the Arab–Jewish conflict, their instincts were to deter any show of violence by a demonstration of strength rather than of pacific intentions.

Despite this wide range of political attitudes and personal and communal relationships, nobody in the kibbutz movement doubted that self-defence under attack must have overriding priority. I shall preface my account of the reactions to the 1936 disturbances with some remarks about previous periods.

## The Tradition of Defence

The kibbutzim were well acquainted with problems of security. As we have seen, their very origins were connected with the paramilitary organization Hashomer, and this tradition was kept alive in many ways. The men of Hashomer joined Gedud Ha'avoda, and continued

[7] Orren, E., *Settlement amid Struggles*, 17–18.

to see the security of its settlements as their special responsibility: when the founders of Ein Harod put up their tents in 1921, former members of Hashomer provided a cavalry escort; and in the settlements of Upper Galilee the organization continued to lead an underground existence until 1929, even though it had formally disbanded ten years earlier.[8] The story of Hashomer was spread throughout the Diaspora at an early stage, and became part of Zionist mythology. From 1919 the names of Trumpeldor and Tel Hai provided a similar legend, giving inspiration and example to the Hechalutz movement and the kibbutz movement as a whole. The experiences of self-defence, heroism, and death under fire were not confined to one particular part of the kibbutz movement. Degania and Kinneret also had their local heroes: the grave of Joseph Saltzmann, killed by raiding Bedouin from Transjordan in 1913, is still to be found at the entrance of Kibbutz Kinneret; and when, in the same week, Moshe Barsky of Degania was killed under similar circumstances, his parents wrote the kibbutz a letter which also became part of kibbutz mythology, suggesting that their other son come to take his place.[9]

Those who perpetrated these attacks were usually referred to as 'robbers' or 'gangs': sometimes they were individuals, sometimes Bedouin tribes who considered such activities to be a legitimate method of livelihood. Their object was robbery, whether of farm equipment or livestock, money, or crops at harvest time. But, from a very early stage, Jews came under attack by groups with religious and/or nationalist motivation. This had happened at the beginning of Zionist settlement in the Jezreel Valley (Merhavia, 1911), and again in the riots of 1920 and 1921 in Jerusalem, Jaffa, Petah Tikva, and elsewhere.

The 1929 riots were of this type. Although the Zionists referred to the attackers (quite correctly) as 'mobs', this did not detract from their menace, or from their ominous character as presages of more effective Arab resistance to the growth of the Yishuv. Their chief victims were the urban communities in Jerusalem, Hebron, and Safed; but a number of rural settlements were also attacked, among them three kibbutzim. Ramat Rahel, the Jerusalem *pluga* of Gedud Ha'avoda, was destroyed, as were Hulda and Mishmar Ha'emek—the latter after its members had successfully defended themselves, but were evacuated at the order of the local police force. Several other kibbutzim

---

[8] Dinur, *History of the Hagana*, vol. ii. pt. 1, ch. 15.
[9] Gadon, *The Kvutza and the Kibbutz*, i. 100; ibid. 81–2.

were attacked, but succeeded in defending themselves, despite losses of life and property.

Like the rest of the Yishuv, the kibbutz movement quickly returned to normal life after the damage of the 1929 disturbances had been repaired. One historian remarks that between 1923 and 1934 'neither the ordinary kibbutz members nor the leaders of the movement were particularly concerned with problems of defence'.[10] This comment refers specifically to the Kibbutz Me'uhad; but, since this was at all times the most defence-conscious of the kibbutz movements, it certainly applies, *a fortiori*, to the other movements.

This lack of preparedness was intensified, within the kibbutz movement and outside it, by a degree of political myopia. The 1929 riots were thought of as the work of primitive mobs, egged on by unscrupulous religious demagogues, which could easily have been put down had the Mandatory government been prepared to use firm punitory measures. Similarly, Qassam's forces, which attacked a number of settlements in the Jezreel Valley—particularly kibbutzim and moshavim—were described as 'gangs' with no regard for their political aims or the possibility that they might prove to be the inspiration of a much wider movement. Militarily, therefore, the 1936 disturbances found the kibbutzim quite unprepared. In particular, defence had hitherto been conceived of as a purely local function: each settlement had to find the manpower to defend itself, while the Hagana helped by providing training and, as far as it could, weapons, and help in time of need. It was only under the pressure of the events of 1936–9 that the Hagana, and the kibbutz movement under its aegis, evolved a strategy for defence against a prolonged and concerted attack in many areas and on the lines of communication between them.

Inevitably, the disturbances of 1936 led to profound changes in the relationships between the kibbutzim and their Arab neighbours. From now on military prudence dictated that the whole of the Arab community should be considered potentially hostile, and that only proved friends be trusted. Contacts with neighbouring villages were still maintained wherever possible, but this was increasingly seen to be no less an attempt to maintain sources of intelligence in the area than a genuine attempt at friendship. The kibbutzim, in common with the rest of the labour movement, were faithful to the principle of 'self-restraint', and refrained from attacking non-combatants. But a

[10] Brenner, *The Kibbutz Me'uhad in the Hagana*, 33.

detailed knowledge of happenings in neighbouring villages made it possible for the Hagana to distinguish between friendly, neutral, and hostile elements, and take preventive or punitive measures against those who supported the rebels. Here again, the boundary between fostering friendship and knowing one's enemy could be very unclear.

In the process of adaptation to the new conditions, the kibbutzim were aided by a number of important factors. The first was the existence of the tradition of self-defence, and the awareness of its importance, as already mentioned. This was not only a matter of education and ideology; many of those who had been active in defence matters in Hashomer or in their kibbutzim in earlier years retained their interest and maintained their skills even during more peaceful periods. One of the best known was Haim Sturman, who had begun his activities in Jewish self-defence at the time of the Second Aliya in Jerusalem. He had been a member of Hashomer, and was responsible for the planning of its settlements in Upper Galilee. He joined Gedud Ha'avoda at an early stage and was one of the founders of Kibbutz Ein Harod. There he worked in agriculture, but throughout the years was responsible, with a small group of members, for the defence of the kibbutz. With the outbreak of violence in 1936 he joined the district defence committee of the Hagana, and was intimately concerned both with the planning of the defence of existing settlements and with the military aspects of new settlement in the Jezreel and Beit She'an valleys. It was while returning from a tour of this area in 1938 that his car was blown up by a landmine, and he was killed together with two other Hagana officers.

Although Sturman was famous throughout the Yishuv for his heroism and efficiency in defence matters, he was only one of a large group of kibbutz members who now began to devote themselves completely to defence, in the framework of the Hagana. In this, they had the backing of their communities and of the kibbutz movement as a whole. This is not surprising; for the kibbutzim, by their very number and dispersal, to a large extent comprised the front of the intermittent but bloody war which had, in effect, begun with the demonstrative protests of the Arab tenants in the Hefer Valley against Jewish settlement in 1930–1. The chronicle of the incidents which comprised the struggle covers almost every area of kibbutz settlement. Moreover, in much of the kibbutz movement the concern with defence matters was not only a matter of self-interest, but of basic ideology.

The most extreme and outspoken advocate of this viewpoint was Yitzhak Tabenkin.

The conference of the Kibbutz Me'uhad at Yagur took place in October 1936, almost a year later than originally planned, for travel was dangerous and every available person was needed for defence. In the discussion on the problems of security, Tabenkin quoted a passage from the book of Nehemiah as symbolic of the period:

'They which builded on the wall, and they that bare burdens ... every one with one of his hands wrought in the work, and with the other hand held a weapon.' ... That is the reality. It is particularly terrible ... for the kibbutzim, for those whose whole life, and the life of their community and their children, is devoted to the liberation of our people, to construction and labour.... This is a tragic contradiction, but an unavoidable one.... The image of man which informs our way of life, our self-education, the education of our children ... is bound up with the conquest of the soil, of land and sea—the image of a Jew who knows how to use his strength against violence, to harness his strength in self-defence. We must develop our inner forces and initiative not only for colonization ... but in order to turn ourselves into defenders....

We educate ourselves to self-restraint, to avoid any form of retribution against the innocent; but, at the same time, to active, independent self-defence, limited only by our own abilities.... The idea of self-defence will be realized when it ceases to be [dependent on] the will of a small group of people, and becomes the responsibility of all our settlements; then the kibbutz will become a pioneering nucleus of work, defence and settlement.[11]

Tabenkin emphasized the tradition of Jewish self-defence, whose development he traced from Poland and Russia in the early years of the century through Gedud Ha'avoda to the Kibbutz Me'uhad. In the less aggressively minded Hever Hakvutzot, where the semi-pacifist teachings of A. D. Gordon were still influential, the need for self-defence was also accepted, though less readily:

Since Shlomo and Hanoch were murdered, something has changed in the *kvutza*. People's facial expression is different, more emotional. The light-heartedness, the resounding laughter which was the expression of our care-free attitude, is silent.... Every now and again the 'clown' of the *kvutza* tries to make people laugh, to 'renew our days as of old'. But his laugh echoes in isolation, and calls forth no response. A circle is formed for a dance, and breaks up at once, as if all around were saying 'Stop!' And even so we carry on. Life flows in its normal channels, the dining-room is full and active as

[11] Kibbutz Me'uhad, *Eleventh Council*, 133–4, 139. The biblical quotation is from Nehemiah 4: 17.

ever; work goes on, building continues, the task is not halted ... but look around and you will see: none the less, something has changed. Something has happened among the hills of Nazareth, and the date is engraved deep in our memory....

The rifle has become a working tool. We don't move without it. Our concepts have changed: we men of the *kvutza* were not particularly enthusiastic about arms; indeed, we always tended to disparage them. Now, the rifle is as essential as our working tools—perhaps more so. It is good to have a rifle in one's hand, it gives one security. Our brethren in Germany and Poland are much less fortunate.[12]

## *Hulda: Security Problems*[13]

It is instructive to examine the way in which the people of Hulda, whose way of life in time of peace was described in a previous chapter, coped with problems of defence. Their special situation made them particularly sensitive to matters of security. Their very existence in Hulda was the result of Arab hostility. The original settlement had been attacked in 1929 and evacuated at the orders of the British, though its defenders were prepared to stay and fight. The declared intention of the Gordonia group, most of whom reached the spot in September 1931, was to restore the settlement in defiance of its neighbours' hostile intentions. Thus, the question of defence was part of its *raison d'être*. The fact that its nearest neighbours were four Arab villages, and the closest Jewish settlement some five miles away, was a daily reminder of this.

None the less, for several years the men and women of Hulda lived in a state of comparative security. They drew water daily from a well in the neighbouring Arab village of Hulda. Much of their income was derived from work in nearby orange groves, which involved long journeys each morning and evening. And, as we have seen, though their contact with most of their neighbours was slight, they maintained good personal relationships with a number of local Arabs, mainly those with whom they had business of various sorts.[14]

Thus, although the political and military situation was potentially explosive, little attention was paid at this time to matters of defence. The Jewish National Fund, which owned the surrounding forest, paid the wages of one guard, and the kibbutz supplied another each night. Officially, their only weapons were two old-fashioned rifles

[12] Weismann, 'In These Days'.
[13] This section is largely based on Oz, *History of Hulda*, ch. 8.
[14] Ibid. 58–9.

supplied by the British authorities to be used only in the case of actual attack. The same proviso applied to a sealed case of several more modern weapons which was supplied in 1934.

It seems, however, that problems of defence were not the most pressing of Hulda's priorities at this time. Guard duty was no doubt viewed as a precaution against theft rather than politically inspired attack. There is no reason why the graduates of Gordonia, with its pacifist inclinations, should have been more sensitive to such dangers than their neighbours in Giv'at Brenner, where an article written in July 1935 describes the lax state of security in the kibbutz: the night guard was laden with trivial duties, was often inexperienced and insufficiently briefed, and the area he had to cover was far too wide.[15]

With the outbreak of the Arab revolt in April 1936, four policemen (two British and two Arabs) were sent as the official guards of the kibbutz. The members viewed this development with mixed feelings: although the number of their defenders had increased, they placed little trust in them; and the *mukhtar*, as the kibbutz member in charge of defence matters was known, now had no discretion to act even in time of attack, but was under the command of these outsiders.

Arab Hulda was now openly hostile. Water was drawn from the well under guard for some weeks, until the problem was solved by the acquisition of a truck with a water tank which made a daily journey of some eight miles, under heavy guard, to a source of water on Jewish-owned land. During the summer of 1936, the kibbutz was frequently under attack from snipers, and one attempt by an organized band to storm the buildings was repulsed. The only means of contact with the outside world was by light signals to nearby Jewish settlements. In the summer of 1936 the children and most of the women were evacuated for three months, but living in a state of tension eventually became a matter of routine. Eighteen kibbutz members were enrolled as supernumerary police and engaged in full-time defence duties. Since only six of them were paid by any outside body, this was a heavy burden on a community which numbered sixty-six at the beginning of these events (although another twenty-five were absorbed in the course of the year).

Many of the members worked outside the kibbutz, and the way to and from work in the orange groves (more than seven miles) had to be checked meticulously, morning and evening, for mines. The worst blow came when the orange grove, in which the young men and

[15] Daily news-sheet, Giv'at Brenner, 2–3 July 1935.

women of Hulda had invested so much work and money, was uprooted overnight by hostile forces. Hulda was fortunate in that none of its members was killed during the disturbances, but it paid a heavy toll in social and economic terms. The constant need to devote a quarter or more of the productive workers to defence matters, repeated thefts of produce and interruptions to work, and the unremitting tension of living in a state of siege—added to the precarious state of the kibbutz even before 1935—all had their effect.

At the end of 1936 a group of members announced that, unless they received more concrete support from the settlement authorities, they would leave the kibbutz.[16] As a result, they were recognized by the Jewish Agency as a permanent settlement and granted the basic budget to which a group of this size was entitled. Water had been discovered in the vicinity, and they were given a share in its use. Their recognition as a settled kibbutz also afforded them rights to extra land, including a young citrus grove. One of the conditions for the change in their status was that they leave the forest where they had seen so much suffering, but which for many, especially the veteran members, was the focus of their devotion to the place. They moved to a nearby site, more easily defensible and closer to their new lands. A new group of youth movement graduates was successful absorbed. Slowly they began to work their way out of their state of poverty and moral depression. The siege had led, indirectly, to their salvation.

### Defending the Yishuv

I mentioned earlier the concept of the 'mission' of the kibbutz: the belief that the kibbutz was a serving élite, prepared to take on the most urgent tasks of the Yishuv and the Jewish people as a whole. During this period, this principle found new applications in the field of self-defence. Two examples may be given. In May 1936, after the shock of the first wave of attacks on Jewish settlements, the leaders of the Hagana and of the kibbutz movement began to advocate 'breaking out of the barricades': up to now, they had used methods of static defence which ensured the safety of the inhabitants but left their fields and property at the mercy of the attackers; now they were to adopt more active measures. The 'field units' which were the practical expression of this idea developed from the 'mobile platoon' which had been based on Kibbutz Kiriat Anavim and functioned in

---

[16] See account of Hulda in ch. 7, above.

the area around Jerusalem. These units, which were based on kibbutzim in the areas which they served, were manned by Jewish Special Police who were employed and paid by the British but were also under the discipline of the Hagana. A high proportion of them, including their officers, were recruited from the kibbutzim. They began operations, under the overall command of Yitzhak Sadeh, in December 1937 and continued to function until mid-1939. From mid-1938 they co-operated with the British forces, and their standards of training and self-confidence were vastly increased by the work of Captain Orde Wingate, an eccentric pro-Zionist British officer who helped to develop the tactics evolved by Sadeh. In all of these units and operations, not only were the operational bases generally located in kibbutzim; a very high proportion of the fighting men were also kibbutz members.[17]

There can, however, be no doubt that the most important development in the field of Jewish self-defence, and the kibbutzim's most striking innovation in this sphere, was the system of agricultural settlement known as 'tower and stockade'.

## TOWER AND STOCKADE

The aims of the Arab revolt were clearly political: to prevent the normal functioning of the Yishuv and to halt the growth and expansion of the past four years. One of these aims was easy enough to achieve. If the British government could be persuaded that the continuation of Jewish immigration threatened the peace of the country, immigration schedules would be reduced, and the Mandatory government would become the ally of the Arab nationalist movement in its attempt to prevent the growth of the Jewish population. There were several precedents for this, notably after the riots of 1921 and 1929.[18] The other target of the Arab struggle was the expansion of Jewish settlement, and the attacks on Jewish rural areas were a clear indication of the importance attached to this sector. From the Jewish point of view, therefore, it was of vital importance to show that even under conditions of armed struggle the Yishuv was willing and able to continue the policy of settlement.

[17] On these Special Night Squads, the Field Squads, Sadeh, and Wingate, see Dinur, *History of the Hagana*, vol. ii, pt. 2, chs. 47 and 48.

[18] For a detailed account of changes in the immigration policy of the British administration, see Gurevich *et al.*, *Jewish Population of Palestine*, 20–42.

By now, the ideological opposition to the kibbutz which had caused so much controversy and distress in the early 1920s was no longer a factor in planning new settlement. At the Zionist Congress of 1935, the Labour faction was the most powerful element, and Ben-Gurion was elected chairman of the Jewish Agency Executive, thus ensuring full political backing for the foundation of kibbutzim and moshavim alike. Moreover, the Jewish National Fund had reserves of land. The problem was how and where to build new settlements at a time when the fields of established kibbutzim were being burnt nightly by marauders, their orchards uprooted, and their members attacked on their way to and from work. The first reaction was to confine settlement to relatively safe areas; and the first two villages set up after the Arab strike (Kfar Maccabi, in the hinterland of Haifa Bay, and Kfar Hittim, in Lower Galilee) were far from the trouble centres such as the Jezreel Valley and the more isolated parts of the coastal plain. The breakthrough in methods of settlement came in December 1936, as the result of the initiative of a group from the Hashomer Hatzair movement in the Yishuv who had begun to cultivate a stretch of land in the Beit She'an area in the hope that they would shortly be able to build a new kibbutz there.

The Beit She'an Valley was politically and strategically a most sensitive area.[19] By the terms of the Mandate, the Zionist movement was to have been offered state-owned land for settlement, and most of the area came under this category. But it had for many years been occupied by Arab tenant farmers, and in 1921 the Mandatory government reached an agreement with them which protected their rights for fifteen years, with an option to purchase the land. Nevertheless, over the next ten years the Jewish National Fund managed to buy much of the land from its occupants, though until 1936 none of it was settled by Jews. Not only would such settlement reaffirm the right which the Zionists believed that the British had unjustly denied them; it would also strengthen the settlements of the eastern Jezreel Valley, now under constant threat of attack, and help to seal off the retreat route across the Jordan. Such an event would be a resounding moral and political defeat for the Arab nationalist forces, who had claimed all along that the Jews had no rights in the area and had made their land purchases by guile.

During the fighting in early 1936, the temporary building which the potential settlers had put up had been destroyed, and the fields

[19] Stein, *The Land Question*, 207.

laid waste. They retired to the nearest kibbutz, Beit Alpha, and in the autumn, when the fighting had died down, decided to return as soon as possible to resettle their land. The settlement authorities were doubtful, and the Hagana agreed only when one of the group suggested a novel strategy: they would arrive at dawn, under the protection of armed police, and erect a stockade and a watch-tower to protect themselves. The settlement of Tel Amal in this way went off without a hitch and became the model for establishing more than fifty settlements up to the outbreak of the Second World War.

Here is a contemporary description of the first day of settlement:

The day of settlement is fixed in advance, after the removal of all the many obstacles, and completion of the practical preparations: consolidation and evacuation of the appointed lands, confirmation that the necessary funds are available, the agreement of the (British) authorities, which it is not easy to obtain, and preparation of the defensive equipment.[20] For some time before settlement day, feverish preparations are under way so that all the material for the camp, the buildings and everything else needed on the spot will be ready on time. In a near-by kibbutz or moshav members of the settlement group, together with volunteers and mobilized members (Jewish members of the Settlement Police) from the neighbouring kibbutzim, prepare all the components of the new settlement: the sides of the defence stockade, the watch-tower, huts for accommodation, a searchlight, equipment for the barbed-wire fence, and all the basic tools required for work and defence. At the point of departure there is a powerful feeling of expectation. The members of the settlement group are to meet there. During the night, they and their hosts will finish off all the preparations, plan the final operative details, and allocate the different tasks to the forces available. During the night they load all the equipment on trucks which have been mobilized from all the settlements in the area. Long before dawn, the whole convoy—in trucks and carts, some by vehicle and some on foot—moves off to the appointed spot. They are accompanied by many friends and comrades, dozens of police brought along from the kibbutzim in the neighbourhood, representatives of the settlement

[20] *Consolidation*: Many of the lands acquired for settlement were bought in small lots, not always contiguous, which had to be consolidated into a continuous area by a process, often long and tortuous, of further purchase and exchange. *Evacuation*: The policy of the Zionist authorities was to ensure that those who occupied the land, whether legally or illegally, should be compensated, financially or by the exchange of land, and should leave the area before it was settled by the Jews. This, too, was a long and complex process, and not always successful. *Agreement of the authorities*: This was necessary in order to ensure the protection of settlement police while the fortifications were being erected. British policy tended increasingly to frown on the expansion of Jewish settlement.

authorities and the Histadrut, and the commanders of the Hagana's forces in the district. They take with them barrels of water, food, and first-aid equipment. In many cases the local branch of Hapoel [the Histadrut sports organization, often a cover for Hagana activities] and others from the nearest town take an active part in the work.

At first light, work begins. First are the mowers, who cut down the thistles and weeds and clear the way for the builders. The camp's perimeters are marked out, stakes driven in the ground, and a double wall erected round the camp. The gravel is carried from the trucks in baskets, and poured between the walls. Here, in the long line, passing the baskets from hand to hand, are old and young, veterans and newcomers, men and women, all pouring with sweat and all radiating good spirits. In a short while the tower is erected, proclaiming afar that a new Jewish settlement has sprung up.

At the same time, another group is putting up the huts, which grow taller every hour until they are finally completed. Yet another group is laying down two barbed-wire fences round the camp, while others dig trenches and prepare defence posts, ready to receive any enemy. The technicians assemble the searchlight on the tower, and prepare it for its task. The women give out food and water as the work goes on, for time is short and the day is coming to an end. By evening the camp is standing in its appointed place; the tiny, new-born settlement shines forth far into the wilderness around. Speeches are made, words from heart to heart, by all those who took part in the operation—the new settlers and their neighbours, representatives of the settlement bodies and the Histadrut—and the song of these workers and builders bursts forth into the silent evening. The searchlight sends its first message to the neighbouring settlements.

Even if rain or storms hinder the work, it still goes on. For nothing can stop this act of creation for which they have been longing and waiting for so many days.[21]

The elements enumerated above—official protection on the first day, completion of tower and stockade by nightfall, direct visual communication with a neighbouring settlement, and reasonably swift access in time of emergency—were a formula for maximum security. At first they were considered indispensable, but they were later somewhat modified with the growth of confidence in the settlers' power to withstand attack, and with changes in the political circumstances. Thus, many settlements were erected despite the distance from their nearest Jewish neighbours and consequent difficulties of communication; and in 1939 several kibbutzim were founded without the prior knowledge of the British authorities.[22]

[21] Koller, in *UAW Report* (1939), 182.
[22] Orren, *Settlement amid Struggles*, 62–3, 86–9.

## Strategic Settlement

Several tower and stockade settlements were none the less attacked, some on the first day of their establishment; in a few cases the attackers even managed to penetrate the outer defences of the kibbutz. But all of them managed to survive, though in some cases with severe losses. The improvised defences of Tel Amal proved to be a brilliant tactical innovation.

Just a month after the foundation of Tel Amal there began a political development which made the creation of new settlements in dangerous areas of even greater importance to the Zionist cause. In January 1937, one of the Peel Commission's members spoke to Chaim Weizmann about the possibility of partitioning the country. Although this suggestion led to a deep rift among the Zionist leadership, it united the whole of the movement on one central issue of settlement policy. Moshe Shertok (Sharett), then the head of the Jewish Agency's political department, put it succinctly:

Under present circumstances, there was only one thing to do—to alter the map of the Land of Israel by creating new settlements: (a) in order to make a solution of the Palestine problem by partition or cantonization as difficult as possible; (b) to ensure that even if there is a decision in favour of partition or cantonization, the damage it does will be minimized. . . . From the political point of view, I know of no more pressing task, no more effective weapon, than founding settlements in [border] areas, and thereby creating facts.[23]

This was a radical departure in settlement policy. Up to now, the major factor in deciding the order of settlement of available land had been its economic possibilities, together with a general aim of creating geographic blocs of Jewish villages. From now on, such decisions would be taken in the framework of a generally agreed 'settlement strategy', aimed at extending the boundaries of any possible Jewish state as much as possible and increasing the security of the existing population.

Thus began an unprecedented burst of settlement activity, carried out with frenetic speed. From 1932 to 1936, sixty-six new Jewish settlements were established, an average of just over one per month. From 1937 to 1939, the average increased to 1.7, and that at a time when the planning and physical preparations for settlement were vastly more difficult, and operations frequently had to be postponed for security reasons. The ownership and financial backing of settlement

[23] Sharett, *Political Diary*, ii. 172–3.

in the period of prosperity had been very varied: land and citrus orchards were at a premium, and many private purchasers, developers, and speculators engaged in land purchase. From May 1936, the Jewish National Fund was virtually the only agency able and willing to buy land. As a result, land values dropped, and the concentration of ownership made it possible to decide on national priorities: but the need to ensure that every new site was militarily defensible added greatly to the cost of settlement in terms of money, time and planning activities.[24]

In concrete terms, the pattern of Jewish settlement in 1935 was roughly in the shape of an N, running along a fairly broad coastal strip from Be'er Tuvia in the south to Haifa, thence along the Jezreel Valley to Lake Kinneret, and from there northwards along the Jordan to Upper Galilee. The area allocated to the Jews by the Peel Commission was based on this configuration, with the addition of Western Galilee for future development. The establishment of a bridgehead in the Beit She'an valley pointed to the possibility of extending the easterly line of the N southwards; and similar moves were initiated in other areas.

Careful inspection of the map (see endpapers) and of the course of the disturbances reveals that the N itself was very far from being solidly settled. Settlement strategy had therefore to take into account the strengthening of existing areas no less than the opening of new regions. The danger of attack was always present, and the tower and stockade system was used as a matter of course in establishing new settlements from December 1936 until September 1939. In this way, six new areas of Jewish settlement were opened up:

1. Ten new villages were established in the Beit She'an area, and five in the region of Lake Kinneret, joining the Beit She'an group with the established kibbutzim of the Jordan Valley. The new kibbutzim in this latter area were east of the line demarcating Jewish territory in the Peel Report (along the Jordan River, continued northwards into Lake Kinneret), though still within the borders of Mandatory Palestine. They formed both a bridgehead into Transjordan and a protective cover for the Palestine Electricity Company's works at the southern end of Lake Kinneret.

2. Four kibbutzim were set up in the Huleh area (eastern section

---

[24] Stein, *The Land Question*, 174–80, 202–11; Rayman, *The Kibbutz Community*, 32–7.

of Upper Galilee), protecting both the headwaters of the Jordan and the approaches to Lake Huleh, a concession for whose drainage had been granted to a Jewish company in 1934.

3. Two kibbutzim were set up in the Ju'ara area, south-east of Haifa, as the beginning of an attempt to create a line of settlements which would join the Jewish food-growing area of the Jezreel Valley to the coast without passing through the Arab-controlled hinterland of Haifa. At the same time, an attempt was made to increase the number of Jews living in this latter area, as well as the town itself; for it was clear that in any future political settlement, Haifa would be of enormous importance both because of its port and as the end of the oil pipeline from Iraq. Therefore, although this area was relatively quiet from the military point of view at this time, ten settlements were established there, reaching from Haifa Bay in the north to the Zevulun Valley in the east and the Mediterranean coast in the south.

4. Three kibbutzim were set up in the south. The names of two of them, Sha'ar Hanegev ('Gateway to the Negev') and Negba ('To the Negev') expressed their purpose. Although this vast arid area had been excluded from the Jewish state by the Peel Commission, the Jewish counter-proposals suggested that it should remain mandated territory, with the intention of preserving it for future Jewish development.

5. On the other hand, Western Galilee had been included in the tentative Jewish state; but it was only in 1937–8 that land was bought and settlement begun outside the recently founded *moshava* of Naharia. Three tower and stockade settlements were established in this region.

6. Finally, one new kibbutz was set up on the approaches to Jerusalem, to give some support to the isolated Kiriat Anavim and Motza. In addition to these new regions, seventeen settlements were established in areas which were already overwhelmingly Jewish: eleven on the coastal plain from Gedera to Hadera and its hinterland, five in Lower Galilee, and one in the Jezreel Valley.

Naturally, these overall statistics do not reveal the special reasons for giving priority to a particular spot, or the dangers involved in its settlement. For instance, the establishment of Moshav Sdeh Warburg, not far from Kfar Saba, in 1938, did not open up a whole new area to Jewish settlement, as did the foundation of Hanita on the Lebanese border; but it went some way to reducing the isolation of Kibbutz Ramat Hakovesh, which had been under attack almost continuously since 1936, and was virtually under siege; it suffered some twenty attacks during the disturbances, and fourteen of its members were killed.[25] None the less, the regional analysis does point up the changes which this massive effort at settlement made in the map of Palestine, and in the lines which any future partition of the country would have to follow. In the words of one historian:

The inclusion of geostrategic factors in Jewish land-purchase ... reflected the advanced stage of the Jewish state's evolution perhaps more than any other change in settlement policy. By 1939, and before events in Europe focused the world's attention on the Jewish condition, a geographic nucleus for a Jewish state was present in Palestine.[26]

It should, however, be added that without the actual process of settlement, Jewish land ownership would have been of little political import. It was the fifty-three tower and stockade settlements which determined the shape of the geographic nucleus of the Jewish state. This operation did not emerge fully-fledged as a result of long-term planning. Rather, it evolved in the course of events, as the Zionist leaders—particularly Ben-Gurion, Berl Katznelson, and Shertok— realized that partition was a real possibility, and grasped the strategic implications of the tower and stockade. Others were slower to adopt such an adventurous policy. Those responsible for the detailed planning and economic support of new settlement demurred on the grounds of financial difficulties and doubts about the economic viability of kibbutzim and moshavim founded under such conditions; they would have preferred to go more slowly, and intensify settlement in areas already settled rather than break into new and untried districts. Some of the opposition was also clearly motivated by political doubts as to whether such actions might not ruin whatever chance there might be of political rapprochement between Jews and Arabs.[27] In the end, the fact that the policy was approved not only by the principal leaders of the Zionist movement, including Chaim Weizmann, but also by the high command of the Hagana, overcame all objections of principle while leaving a good deal of room for disagreements about the details of execution and the priorities at any given stage. It was a time of grave emergency, both military and political, and the Yishuv rallied almost unanimously behind its leaders.

---

[25] Detailed reports in the Kibbutz Me'uhad archives, Ef'al, Ramat Hakovesh files.
[26] Stein, *The Land Question*, 211.     [27] Orren, *Settlement amid Struggles*, 22–8.

The Revisionists were the exception. As we have seen, the IZL remained independent of the Hagana, and during 1938 carried out a number of attacks on concentrations of Arab civilians which were in stark contrast to the policy of 'self-restraint'; the leaders of the labour movement claimed that it was these actions which provoked retaliations in kind and led to the escalation of the summer of 1938. The Revisionists did not view the policy of increased settlement as an appropriate reaction to the Arab attacks; they believed that all its successes were worthless if not supported by appropriate political and military actions.

In August 1939, Berl Katznelson summed up the achievements of the past three years in words which would have been accepted by the great majority of the Yishuv, of almost every political persuasion:

Because we chose a policy of self-restraint, we took the honourable path of creating in this country a sort of Jewish militia, which is destined to serve as the kernel of something even more important. Because we chose a policy of self-restraint, we were able to defend what already existed and create new settlements. . . . Through the policy of self-restraint even a hostile administration and the British Army gained respect for the Jew, as a just and courageous human being. In this protracted war we have succeeded in achieving something even more important: we did not evacuate a single position. There is a rule in war: shorten the front as much as possible . . . that is the doctrine of evacuation, which the government and the military and honourable Jewish gentlemen urged on us. We did not take their advice . . . deliberately, clear-sightedly, we lengthened the line. . . . Not in the safe, easily defended areas, but at the most difficult points, on the borders.[28]

## Kibbutz Settlement

The kibbutz movement played an essential part in the tower and stockade operation. From the beginning, there were at hand groups of idealistic and self-sacrificing young people who enthusiastically accepted the policies of self-restraint and constructivism and were prepared to take on themselves the practical work of settlement and defence: these were the *plugot* of the kibbutz movements, and the parallel groups, known as *irgunim*, waiting for settlement in moshavim. Although the closely knit kibbutz group could well be thought to be more suited to such an operation than the individualist moshav members, this was not the reason that kibbutz groups predominated;

[28] From Katznelson's speech at the Zionist Congress, Aug. 1939. *Writings*, ix. 66.

for almost all the moshav groups adopted the social structure of a kibbutz in their early period of settlement. Numerically, however, the graduates of the kibbutz-orientated youth movements far outweighed the potential moshav members. As a result, thirty-six kibbutzim were established in this period, as against eighteen moshavim (including two *meshakim shitufi'im*, or co-operative farms). On the whole, too, the legends which were created in and about this period referred to the kibbutz rather than the moshav.

The best known example of such a legend is undoubtedly that of Hanita. Founded in March 1938, in conditions of exceptional danger, Hanita marked the northern border of Palestine and was established to prevent infiltration of hostile forces from Lebanon. This evoked a wide range of popular responses: current reportage, short stories, songs, poems, and even an opera. Children wrote letters to Hanita's brave defenders. Zionist personalities visited them. In short, it became a sort of contemporary national shrine, embodying the individual, social, and political values which were thought to be the epitome of the Yishuv at its best: courage and devotion, co-operation and equality, patriotism and self-sacrifice.[29]

This myth-making, while typical of a nation at war, was far from being pure propaganda: some seventy kibbutz members were killed by enemy action.[30] Even in the places where there was no actual fighting, the first period of settlement was very much harder than during the relatively relaxed conditions of earlier years. We have a contemporary description from Kibbutz Maoz ('Fortress') in the Beit She'an Valley, a week after the establishment of the kibbutz:

Half of the people have beds, and the other half lie down at night in different corners, on piles of wood, corrugated iron, and so forth. But all of us have been covered in dust and intolerable dirt for these many days. The 'dining-room' is an awning with no sides, which spoils our appetite, and the girls find it hard to cook properly in the temporary kitchen. And on top of all this, our two hours' break at midday is not so much rest as a constant shift of body and soul from one patch of shade to another....

Being shut up in this tiny stockade confines our horizons. During the day we move around outside the wall, though under guard, but in the evening— all inside! And the forecast is that we shall have to live like this for at least a year....

[29] For an account of the establishment of Hanita and the accompanying myth-making see Rayman, *The Kibbutz Community*, ch. 1 and app. 2.
[30] *UAW Report* (1939), 373–7.

In the evenings, during or after supper, as we sit round the trestle tables, sometimes someone starts up a song. Once we tried to dance a hora together— but the clouds of dust clung to our clothes, our bodies, and our very skin, and put a stop to our enthusiasm. But it doesn't really matter: our spirits are high ... little by little, step by step, we shall build and be built.[31]

The spirit and enthusiasm of the young settlers sprang not only from their confidence in their own future, but from their belief that they were making an important political statement. Kibbutz Maoz, for example, was founded, as a political gesture, earlier than originally planned, on the day before the publication of the Peel Report. One of the settlers wrote:

During the [first] day I spoke to Raffi, and we both said: 'What *hutzpa!* What we're doing is plain *hutzpa!*' Here, close to Beit She'an, the day before the publication of the report of the Commission, when it's quite clear that this area, south of Beit She'an, is going to be outside the Jewish state, in the heart of an Arab area, we've staked our claim.[32]

As so often happens in periods of heightened national consciousness and struggle, there were many points of correspondence between the myth and the reality.

## Kibbutz Settlement: Policy and Practice

The general atmosphere of national unity and discipline did not prevent controversy and conflict on details and priorities. Some of them particularly affected the kibbutz movements. Throughout the period, the tensions between them continued, though in a somewhat different form from the power struggles of the early 1930s. From about 1937, the relations between the movements in Hechalutz became less tense. Apparently all the movements, and particularly the Kibbutz Me'uhad, had come to the realization that their major problem was to ensure the quality of their membership, through education and a process of selection, rather than to attempt to increase their strength at the expense of the other movements. Each movement therefore

[31] From a letter from Yitzhak Zvi, one of the first settlers, to the members of the group of the Mahanot Olim movement in Ra'anana. Printed in the newsletter of the *pluga*, no. 146, 15 July 1937 and preserved in the archives of Kibbutz Maoz Haim (as Kibbutz Maoz was later renamed in memory of Haim Sturman, who was killed while investigating the best location for further settlement in this area), box 560. The last words quoted are part of a song popular in all the youth movements.

[32] Yitzhak Avrahami to Shlomit Nahmani, 8 July 1937. Copy in archives of Kibbutz Maoz Haim.

began to increase the number of emissaries to the training kibbutzim and to initiate a series of seminars designed to deepen their members' ideological consciousness. The result was a marked improvement in the number of members remaining in the kibbutzim on their arrival in the country.[33]

It would be wrong to attribute this improvement to one factor alone. A further cause was no doubt the reduction in the membership of the pioneering movements with the decrease in immigration certificates from 1936 onwards: there were now relatively few whose prime motivation for joining the movement was the certificate, rather than the movement or the kibbutz. Above all, however, it was the change in atmosphere in the country from 1936 onwards that made a fundamental impact on many of the new immigrants. Whereas in the period of prosperity life in the kibbutz had been a conscious rejection of the dominant atmosphere in the Yishuv for the sake of an ideal, it was now that ideal which dominated the Yishuv. A young pioneer who left the kibbutz in 1934 was betraying his friends and his movement. In 1937–9, he would feel that he was also betraying his country.

Nevertheless, tensions between the movements remained. Many of them, as we shall see in the next chapter, were in the political sphere, others intimately connected with the problems of settlement and defence; for each of the movements was anxious to settle as many of its groups as possible, and the demand for the right to occupy new points of settlement often led to acrimonious controversies in the executive bodies of the Histadrut and the Jewish Agency. By now, each of the movements had a similar policy on absorption: to create kibbutz communities by joining groups of different national origin. In certain other respects, however, the differences between them proved to be significant.

The ideology and public image of the Kibbutz Me'uhad was one of greater flexibility than the other movements, and it was able to adapt itself more readily to the changing needs of the Yishuv. In consequence of its centralized structure, it had been able to create special groups, often composed of people from existing communities, for new or particularly difficult tasks. Thus, from April 1934 there had been a group at the Dead Sea potash works at Sodom—work which was particularly hard because of the intense heat and isolation, but ensured the presence of Jewish workers, and possible future

[33] Sarid, *Hechalutz in Poland*, 546–7, 567–70.

settlement, in this strategically important spot. Similarly, *plugot* working in the ports of Haifa and Tel Aviv played an important part in replacing the striking Arab workers in 1936. Even before the disturbances of 1936, the leaders of the Kibbutz Me'uhad had called on its members to volunteer for the police, which was largely staffed by Arabs, and by March 1937 thirty members had answered this call. It is true that careful examination of the facts reveals a certain dissonance between the Kibbutz Me'uhad's aspirations to devote itself to the needs of the Yishuv, which were often accompanied by a rhetoric of success, and its actual achievements. For instance, the main practical consequence of the call to 'conquer the sea' was the establishment of *plugot* which worked, with varying degrees of success, in the ports; and eight months after the decision of the central committee of the Kibbutz Me'uhad to mobilize fifty policemen, only thirty had answered the call.[34] But these relative failures are understandable in view of the tremendous effort required simply to maintain and expand the existing settlements and groups. The Kibbutz Me'uhad lived in a state of perpetual tension between its aspiration to put itself completely at the service of the Yishuv and the practical limitations which sprang from its relative weakness; the other two movements were almost exclusively concerned with building agricultural communities, and saw their other occupations as ancillary to this main objective.

In one matter, however, the Kibbutz Me'uhad displayed an uncharacteristic conservatism. The conditions of the tower and stockade campaign called for extensive settlement, even if the kibbutzim thereby created would be relatively weak. The policy of creating 'great and growing' kibbutzim conflicted with this aim, for it concentrated in one place forces which could well have been employed to create more new settlements. On at least one occasion this conflict led to a direct clash with the planning authorities of the Histadrut. In 1939, Avraham Harzfeld, one of those responsible for agricultural planning on behalf of the Histadrut's Agricultural Centre, said:

Sometimes this approach [of the Kibbutz Me'uhad] clashes with vital issues connected with the political interests of the Yishuv, and then the whole of the [labour] movement loses by it.... The Kibbutz Me'uhad did not go to [settle at] Hanita, it didn't want to go there; and your attitude to Hanita is symbolic, as I see it....

[34] Tsur, *The Kibbutz Me'uhad*, i. 168–71, 191–3, 197–202, 267–70.

Do you really believe that the additional fifty people that you bring to Na'an every year are more important than the settlement of a new site? The final development of Na'an or Giv'at Brenner ... is assured. But we are in danger of losing [a settlement] which we don't yet have....

I would take whole groups of people out of Yagur and other places and send them to create new kibbutzim.[35]

Like all the other kibbutz movements, the Kibbutz Me'uhad sent a group of its members to take part in the dangerous operation of establishing Hanita and defending it in its first weeks of existence. But the small area available, the poor quality of its land, and its isolation rendered it unsuitable for the development of a large kibbutz; and the Kibbutz Me'uhad central committee decided not to send a group for permanent settlement there. It was settled by an independent group which eventually affiliated to Hever Hakvutzot. A similar clash within the Kibbutz Me'uhad itself arose on the question of the resettlement of Mahanaim in Upper Galilee. Both the settlement authorities and a group close to the spot were interested in carrying out this plan, but the central committee of the Kibbutz Me'uhad objected strongly, on the grounds that the place was not suitable for a large and varied community.[36]

The results of this policy show clearly in the statistics of settlement. Although between 1935 and 1939 membership of the Kibbutz Me'uhad increased at a far greater rate than that of the other two movements, it established only twelve new tower and stockade settlements, as against the ten each of Hever Hakvutzot and the Kibbutz Artzi. If the national priority in these years was to establish new settlements as quickly as possible in as many places as possible, it seems that the other movements fulfilled this task more efficiently than the Kibbutz Me'uhad (see Tables 12 and 13).

## HECHALUTZ AND ILLEGAL IMMIGRATION[37]

Throughout the Mandatory period, the six-monthly 'schedule' of immigration certificates was a bone of contention between the British

[35] In the conference of the Kibbutz Me'uhad at Na'an, 1939. Quoted by Kanari, 'The Kibbutz Me'uhad's Way', 118. Harzfeld's account is confirmed by the discussions in the Agricultural Centre of the Histadrut, 21 Aug., 28 Aug., and 23 Oct. 1938; Labour Movement Archives, box iv. 253, minute book, 51.

[36] Kanari, 'The Kibbutz Me'uhad's Way', 120–1.

[37] The account of pre-war illegal immigration is primarily based on Avneri, *From Velos to Taurus.*

TABLE 12. New Jewish Settlements, October 1936–September 1939

| | Oct.–Dec. 1936 | 1937 | 1938 | 1939 | Total |
|---|---|---|---|---|---|
| Kibbutzim | | | | | |
| Kibbutz Me'uhad | 1 | 5 | 2 | 4 | 12 |
| Kibbutz Artzi | 1 | 2 | 4 | 3 | 10 |
| Hever Hakvutzot | 1 | 2 | 5 | 2 | 10 |
| Ha'oved Hatzioni | – | – | 1 | 1 | 2 |
| Kibbutz Dati | – | 1 | – | 1 | 2 |
| Total | 3 | 10 | 12 | 11 | 36 |
| Other | | | | | |
| *Moshav shitufi* | – | 1 | 1 | – | 2 |
| *Moshav ovdim* | 1 | 3 | 3 | 5 | 12 |
| Middle-class moshavim | – | 1 | 2 | – | 3 |
| Other | – | 1 | – | – | 1 |
| Total | 1 | 6 | 6 | 5 | 18 |

*Sources:* Gurevich *et al., Jewish Population of Palestine*, 381–2; Orren, *Settlement amid Struggles*, 241–2.

TABLE 13. Increase of Kibbutz Membership,[a] March 1936–September 1939

| Year | Kibbutz Me'uhad | Kibbutz Artzi | Hever Hakvutzot | Other | Total |
|---|---|---|---|---|---|
| 1936 | 5,386 | 2,835 | 1,407 | 1,007 | 10,635 |
| 1939 | 8,687 | 4,685 | 2,862 | 1,605 | 17,839 |
| Growth | 3,301 | 1,850 | 1,455 | 598 | 7,204 |
| % of total growth | 45.8 | 25.7 | 20.2 | 8.3 | 100 |

*Sources:* Zak, *Report on the Kibbutzim, 1936*, 4; id., *The Kibbutz Movement in Numbers*, 1938/9, 13.

[a] Adult workers only

government and the Zionist movement. The labour movement, which was dependent on the allocation of certificates for working-class immigration and was in direct touch with the potential immigrants in the training kibbutzim in Europe, was particularly sensitive to the implications of this. There had always been attempts by individuals and small groups to by-pass the immigration regulations; but, in general, the Zionist movement rejected any such attempts on principle.

The first serious suggestion to adopt illegal immigration as a matter of policy was made by Yitzhak Tabenkin in 1928, at a moment of exasperation with the modesty of the demands made by the leaders of the Zionist movement.[38] But no practical steps were taken until the spring of 1934. This was a particularly frustrating time in the history of Polish Hechalutz. The sudden increase in immigration from the spring of 1932 had combined with the threatening situation of the Jews of Europe to bring a huge influx of new members. The training kibbutzim were full, but the number of immigration certificates available was far from sufficient to ensure a reasonable turnover. Two special factors no doubt intensified the feeling of frustration in the Polish movement: the justified demand for certificates on the part of the German movement, which had hitherto been numerically negligible; and the disappointingly small increase in the number of certificates in 1933/4, after the spectacular rise in the previous year.[39] This was the period of overcrowding, illness, and malnutrition which Berl Katznelson saw on his visits to Poland. The movement's demands to find ways to reduce the pressure on the training kibbutzim became increasingly strident.

In April 1934, three young kibbutz members about to leave for Poland as emissaries to the youth movements were asked by Eliahu Golomb, one of the senior officers of the Hagana, to begin to organize illegal immigration. Despite their inexperience and lack of funds, they managed to hire a Greek ship (the *Velos*) together with its captain. With the help of the Hagana they brought 350 prospective pioneers to Palestine and landed them safely without the knowledge of the authorities. A second attempt, two months later, failed; Hechalutz, which had taken upon itself the organizational burden of the operation, was left in very severe financial straits. As a result, and in view of the gradual increase in legal immigration over the coming two years, this was the last such attempt made by Hechalutz for some time.

[38] Histadrut, Minutes of the Twentieth Council (1928), 53. Cf. Near, *Kibbutz and Society*, 203.

[39] From Apr. 1932 to Mar. 1933 some 6,500 workers' immigration certificates were granted: 61% of the Jewish Agency's demands. The corresponding figure for Apr. 1933–Mar. 1934 was 11,000: only 33% of the number requested, which took the situation in Germany into account; Gurevich *et al.*, *Jewish Population of Palestine*, 30.

The economic crisis of autumn 1935 and the Arab revolt which followed led to drastic reductions in the immigration schedule. Yet again, the average period in the training kibbutzim began to go up; and this at a time when every able-bodied man and woman was urgently needed to take part in the settlement and defence of the Yishuv. The decision of the British government in the summer of 1937 to limit the monthly schedule to one thousand, including all types of immigrants—a crippling blow to any expectation of increased numbers of certificates for Hechalutz in the near future—was the final straw. The leading figure in the *Velos* operations had been a young member of Kibbutz Giv'at Hashlosha, Yehuda Barginsky. Towards the end of 1937, the central committee of the Kibbutz Me'uhad asked him to renew his activities. He hired a boat and a captain in Greece. But the matter had to be brought to the notice of the leaders of the labour movement in order to ensure financial and political backing.

Politically, this was a very sensitive question indeed. The official leaders of the Yishuv were engaged in several simultaneous sets of negotiations with the British authorities: they were demanding a revision of the Peel proposals in order to make the suggested Jewish state viable; an increase in the immigration schedule; and more whole-hearted co-operation with the Jewish community and the Hagana in putting down the Arab rebellion. Each of these issues affected their stance on the question of illegal immigration. Those who favoured partition were afraid that open defiance of the British would harden their attitude. Those responsible for the complex and difficult discussions about the immigration schedule feared that it would be even further reduced if the unofficial immigrants were discovered. And the British authorities were hardly likely to put more trust in the Yishuv if they found that its leaders were deceiving them on this vital matter. On the other hand, each of these questions was in itself a matter of controversy within the Histadrut and the Zionist movement. By and large, those who opposed the partition proposals—Katznelson, Tabenkin, and some of the officers of the Hagana—supported the initiative of the Kibbutz Me'uhad; while Ben-Gurion, Shertok, Sprinzak, and others who supported the idea of partition opposed it. The result, repeated in the discussions which took place at intervals over the coming two years, was a tied vote. In effect, this meant that the Kibbutz Me'uhad and Hechalutz were allowed to continue the operation, but with no official support from the Histadrut or the

Jewish Agency. The aid which they received had to be mobilized through their supporters in these institutions, often using their contacts with wealthy Jews in Palestine and the Diaspora. From an early stage, however, they had friends in the command of the Hagana. Without their goodwill the whole operation would have been impossible, for it was through the Hagana that support teams for the voyage were mobilized, communications established and gradually improved, and—above all—arrangements made for receiving the immigrants on the coast and dispersing them throughout the Yishuv without the knowledge of the British. No less important was the wholehearted approval of Berl Katznelson, who was not only an authoritative figure within the Hagana but was able to find resources from outside the labour movement, and even outside the Zionist establishment.

Accepting, though never reconciled to, this semi-official status, the emissaries of the Kibbutz Me'uhad created an organization which succeeded in bringing to Palestine groups of pioneers from all the European countries. They became experts in appraising the seaworthiness of ships and the trustworthiness of their crew, in negotiating with (and bribing) officials and ministers in Greece, Italy, Yugoslavia, and even in Nazi Germany and Austria. They gradually created standard patterns of organization and behaviour for the groups of 'tourists' who were sometimes forced to spend a month or more in crowded conditions, with a minimum of food and water, until they were able to reach shore unimpeded by the coastal police. On the whole, too, they were successful in evading the agents of the CID who attempted to check their movements before the boats set out; although the protests of the British government made their operations increasingly difficult in Greece, Italy, and other countries where ships and port facilities could be hired. Between January 1938 and September 1939 they organized sixteen voyages and brought to the country 5,300 immigrants, of whom some 3,500 completely evaded the immigration authorities. The official number of immigration certificates in this period was 3,500.

Meanwhile, the political situation in the Yishuv was changing. The British abandonment of the partition proposal and the White Paper of 1939 brought Ben-Gurion to a radical reappraisal of his views. In November 1938 he suggested that the Zionist movement should organize massive illegal immigration, which would bring about a breakdown of the British administration. This move was opposed both by the moderates in the Zionist camp and those who had been involved in illegal immigration over the past year—the commanders of the Hagana and the emissaries of the Kibbutz Me'uhad. They were afraid that open defiance of the British would make it impossible for them to continue their clandestine operation: ships would be confiscated, their crews imprisoned, and embarkation made even more difficult—and all this for doubtful political gains.[40]

Ben-Gurion's extreme suggestion was rejected by the Histadrut and the Zionist movement. But it was now no longer possible to keep the operation out of the accepted (though unofficial) range of activities of the Zionist movement. In March 1939 Shaul Meirov (Avigur), a former commander of the Hagana and a member of Kibbutz Kinneret, arrived in Europe to help in the operation. In July of the same year, the Institution for Independent Immigration (Mossad le'Aliya Beit) was created, with Avigur at its head. Thus, a campaign which had originated at the joint initiative of the leaders of Hechalutz and a group of activists within the labour movement received the blessing of, and (no less important) a measure of financial support from, the Zionist movement.

In order to see these undoubted achievements in perspective, it must be added that the Mossad le'Aliya Beit was not the only framework for illegal immigration in these years. Shortly after the first voyage of the *Velos*, the Revisionist party organized a similar operation. This, too, had no follow-up during the years of prosperity; for, although the Revisionists had by now left the Zionist Organization, they found ways of obtaining certificates for their members. In March and September 1937 they sent two more boatloads, with much publicity; and there can be no doubt that the knowledge of their activity increased the discontent in the training kibbutzim, and helped to stimulate Barginsky and others to promote the Hechalutz operation. From 1937 until September 1939, the Revisionist movement (now known as the New Zionist Organization) brought to Palestine some six thousand immigrants, in fourteen voyages. Their organization was not as efficient as that of Hechalutz. Apart from their first two boatloads, many of their passengers were not affiliated to any Zionist organization and were chosen because of their ability to pay rather than because of the qualities of endurance and discipline possessed by the graduates of the Hechalutz training farms. Many

[40] Teveth, *Ben-Gurion*, 674–9, 725–30; Bauer, *From Diplomacy to Resistance*, 61–7; Avneri, *From Velos to Taurus*, 180–9.

suffered greatly through the insanitary and crowded conditions and the inhumane attitude of the crew. Almost all the organizers of their operations were at some stage accused of corruption and removed from their posts. And their support organization in Palestine, depending as it did on a small group of political supporters, was less competent than the Hagana at evading interception by the British. In several cases, however, the Hagana gave logistic support to Revisionist and non-party ships which arrived with no local back-up. None the less, they succeeded almost as well numerically as Hechalutz in bringing refugees from persecution to a safe haven. A further nine thousand people who had no chance of obtaining official certificates were brought by private operators, or by groups of Zionist and other organizations.

Viewed against this background, the Hechalutz operation must be seen as the beginning, and the central part, of a general movement which, in the face of physical and mental hardship, and despite the determined opposition of the British authorities, saved some twenty thousand Jews from destruction by the Nazis and their allies. The illegal operations of Hechalutz were from the first organized by kibbutz members, with the backing of the activist group in the Histadrut and the Hagana. The selection of the candidates was in the hands of the Hechalutz authorities, and the numbers allotted to each movement were broadly in accordance with the proportions in the training farms. The whole operation was, however, almost entirely controlled by the members and emissaries of the Kibbutz Me'uhad. The group which organized the voyages of the *Velos* was chosen by Eliahu Golomb and included two members of Hever Hakvutzot. But as the organizational framework grew, virtually all its members were recruited from the Kibbutz Me'uhad; and on more than one occasion Barginsky and others resisted attempts to increase the participation of other movements in the controlling groups.[41] After the creation of the Mossad, the other kibbutz movements began to take a more active part in its work; but the bulk of those prominent in its activities continued to come from the Kibbutz Me'uhad.

Compared with the millions who stayed in Europe, the tens of thousands of refugees saved by the illegal immigration movement up to 1939 may seem relatively insignificant. At this stage, however, this was the Yishuv's and the Zionist movement's last desperate chance

[41] Avneri, *From Velos to Taurus*, 72, 98–9, 124–5.

to save some part of European Jewry. The boast of the kibbutz movement, and particularly of the Kibbutz Me'uhad, to have played a leading part in this effort, was well justified.[42]

[42] In view of the figures quoted above, it appears that Shabtai Teveth's contention that illegal immigration was not effective, since the British deducted the number of arrivals from the quota of certificates, does not apply to this period; Teveth, *Ben-Gurion*, 727–8.

# 10

# Economics, Politics, and Society, 1936–1939

## THE KIBBUTZ ECONOMY

THE economic recession of late 1935 was the beginning of seven lean years for the economy of the Yishuv. Almost overnight, prosperity was followed by a slump in the building trade reminiscent of that in the Fourth Aliya, and a similar increase in unemployment. From 1934 onwards the changing conditions of world trade had led to a decline in the profitability of citrus, and a corresponding decrease in new plantings. The Arab revolt of 1936, together with the restrictions on the number of new immigrants, sharply reduced the volume of economic activity and increased the number of unemployed. Thus, between 1936 and 1941 there was an overall decline in both the gross national product and the level of production per person. An economic historian of the period sums it up as follows:

All of the increase in personal income which had been achieved in the prosperous years of the Fifth Aliya had disappeared as though it had never been. On the other hand, the final result of the cycle of boom and slump in the thirties was that, while the population increased by 150% compared with 1931, the level of income which had been achieved at the beginning of the period remained steady at its end.[1]

The recession of the late 1930s was not like that of the mid-1920s, which had mainly affected the towns and the building trades. The citrus branch, then in a stage of expansion, was now undergoing a crisis, and offered no prospects of employment to those who found none in the towns. Thus, the kibbutz movement could not offer a way out, as it had to some extent a decade earlier. Nor was there a massive wave of emigration, as there had been in the earlier recession. However bad the situation was, the prospects for Jews attempting to enter other countries were even worse; and the Jewish population

---

[1] Halevi, *Economic Development*, 36.

increased steadily, though at nothing like the rate of 1932–6. Table 14, which gives total Jewish population, the rate of unemployment, percentage increase in production per head, and the share of agriculture in total Jewish production, tells the story succinctly. The decrease in the percentage of agriculture in total production was caused mainly by the difficulties in the citrus sector. This was the result of the effects of the world depression on the British market, to which local exports were sent according to the economic policies of the Mandatory government. Prices declined continuously from 1930 onwards, and from 1934 no more than 7–8 per cent of total Jewish investment was invested in citrus, as compared with more than 30 per cent in previous years.[2]

The consequences of the Arab revolt were not completely negative for Jewish agriculture, however. The strike of 1936 made it clear that the Jewish economy, which had been interwoven with that of the Palestinian Arabs and of the neighbouring countries, had to become as independent as possible, and there was rapid growth in the agricultural branches which provided basic foodstuffs for the Jewish population. The effect of these changes on the national level was considerable, though not as great as the authorities of the Yishuv had hoped. By 1939, local growers produced some 96 per cent of the vegetables consumed by the Yishuv (apart from potatoes, of which they grew 39 per cent). They also increased the production of dairy and poultry products considerably; but in neither of these branches were they able to satisfy even half of the local demand, in competition with the much cheaper produce of the Arab sector and the neighbouring countries.[3]

The belief of the kibbutzim in the mixed economy, and their consequent reluctance to become too dependent on citrus, now paid off. The structural changes which the new situation demanded were, in effect, a development of existing tendencies rather than a remodelling of the kibbutz's economic pattern. Thus, the overall effect of these changes on the kibbutz economy was very similar to that of the changes in the security situation on its status in the Yishuv, for it played a leading part in developing the agricultural branches which had now become a national priority.

Although the development of the citrus branch came to quite a rapid halt, there was still fruit to be tended and harvested in the

---

[2] Horowitz, *Development of the Palestinian Economy*, 62, 70–2.    [3] Ibid. 42–50.

TABLE 14. Economic Indices, 1933–1941

| Year | Population | Unemployed[a] | Change in production (%) | Contribution of agriculture to production (%) |
|------|-----------|--------------|--------------------------|-----------------------------------------------|
| 1933 | 210,700 | 400 | + 20.5 | 13.0 |
| 1934 | 255,500 | 400 | + 2.8 | 10.6 |
| 1935 | 322,000 | 2,475 | + 1.8 | 9.5 |
| 1936 | 371,000 | 8,058 | − 9.8 | 9.5 |
| 1937 | 389,000 | 8,427 | − 8.9 | 10.5 |
| 1938 | 403,000 | 11,289 | − 9.1 | 8.9 |
| 1939 | 432,000 | 15,045 | − 5.4 | 9.0 |
| 1940 | 460,100 | 24,873 | − 1.9 | 7.3 |
| 1941 | 474,200 | 15,377 | + 12.5 | 6.5 |

*Source:* N. Halevi, *The Economic Development of the Jewish Community of Palestine,*
*1917–1947* (Heb.), (Jerusalem, 1979), Tables 2, 4, and 5.
[a] The unemployment figures are for those 'seeking work', not the totally unemployed;
this figure is more relevant to the situation of the kibbutzim, whose members were
not registered as unemployed.

existing groves. The labour force in this branch had always been predominantly Arab. During the strike of 1936–7, there was an acute shortage of labour. New immigrants were sent to the citrus areas, and the young kibbutzim which had for years suffered from under-employment found work for all their members. In the spring of 1937, building workers, students, and high-school children were all recruited for work in the citrus groves. Although many of the employers who had previously relied on Arab labour returned to their former practice shortly after the end of the strike, the majority of the places of work taken over by groups of kibbutz workers remained in their hands; and the crop of 1938/9 was harvested entirely by Jewish workers.[4] In consequence, the proportion of kibbutz members employed in work outside the kibbutz—particularly in the citrus branch—remained almost steady throughout the period, despite the rapid absolute growth in the number of kibbutzim and their population. Similarly, the tendency to develop small industrial enterprises, particularly in the young kibbutzim and *plugot*, was continued and intensified. The results can be seen in Table 15.

[4] *Mibifnim* (May 1939), 26–8; *UAW Report* (1939), 245–6; ibid. (1945), *a*.

TABLE 15. The Kibbutz Economy: 1935/6 and 1939
(permanent kibbutzim)

| | 1935/6 | | 1939 | |
|---|---|---|---|---|
| | % work | % income | % work | % income |
| Agriculture | | | | |
| Arable crops | .. | 10.0 | 4.3 | 7.7 |
| Fodder | .. | 4.0 | 3.3 | 3.2 |
| Vegetables | .. | 5.8 | 6.7 | 5.5 |
| Fruit orchards | .. | } 10.2 | 8.8 | 11.1 |
| Nurseries | .. | | 1.9 | 1.0 |
| Poultry | .. | 8.6 | 3.0 | 6.8 |
| Dairy cattle | .. | 22.1 | 5.8 | 12.0 |
| Sheep, honey | .. | 2.0 | 2.2 | 2.1 |
| Total | 46.9 | 54.9 | 36.0 | 49.4 |
| Industry | 8.0 | 15.8 | 9.0 | 17.7 |
| Outside work | 32.4 | 21.8 | 30.0 | 27.4 |
| Investment | 4.5 | – | 9.0 | – |
| Other[a] | 8.3 | 7.8 | 16.0 | 5.5 |

*Sources: Yalkut,* 3 (1935/6), 9; 11 (1938/9), 71; Zak, *The Kibbutz Movement in Numbers, 1938/9,* 16–17; and see table 8 above.
.. No figures available.          [a] Mainly payment for defence-linked occupations.

Many of the changes in the structure of the kibbutz economy were due to the members' sensitivity to the fluctuations of the market, and their desire to adapt to the needs of the Yishuv in conditions of intercommunal strife. They also received various forms of support from outside their own ranks; for instance, the investments in vegetables and poultry were backed by the Anglo-Palestine Bank, through the good offices of Tnuva, the Histadrut co-operative marketing agency.[5] The overall result was that, despite the dangers and physical effort which these years involved, they brought about a marked improvement in the economic situation of the kibbutz movement as a whole, and in particular of the established settlements. One indication is the rapid mechanization of kibbutz farming: between 1935 and 1939, the number of tractors in the kibbutzim increased from 105 to 188; of combine harvesters from 24 to 60; and of motor vehicles from 101 to 188.[6] Another emerges from an examination of the annual

[5] Halevi, *Economic Development,* 41.
[6] *Yalkut,* 11 (Oct. 1940), 22.

balance sheets of the kibbutzim. A comparative analysis of the decade ending in 1939, as presented in Table 16, shows a steady progression from overall loss by all kibbutzim to a state in which more than two-thirds of them showed a profit. Other economic indicators, such as the degree to which the kibbutzim were able to finance their economic development from their capital savings and the proportion of long-term as against short-term loans, point in the same direction.[7] Even though the young kibbutzim which were not yet fully established are included in these figures, they indicate clearly that the years of crisis for the Yishuv were years of consolidation and development for the kibbutz economy.

TABLE 16. Profits and Losses of Kibbutzim, 1929–1939

| Year | No. of Kibbutzim | | Total profit or loss (P£) |
|------|------|------|------|
| | With loss | With profit | |
| 1929 | 23 | 0 | − 114,161 |
| 1937 | 22 | 18 | − 9,719 |
| 1939 | 16 | 47 | + 30,681 |

Source: *UAW Report* (1939), 222. Zak, *The Kibbutz Movement in Numbers, 1938/9*, 12, 24.

Nevertheless, life in the kibbutzim was not easy. The housing situation had not eased to any substantial degree. Work in agricultural and service branches alike was hard, and the accepted standards unsparing. The constant threat of attack by Arab forces combined with uncertainty about the future of the Yishuv—and, indeed, of the world—served to increase tensions and anxieties. The only respect in which the kibbutzim had attained a reasonable standard of living was in the level of nutrition, which was satisfactory by accepted international standards and higher than that of agricultural workers outside the kibbutz. This standard was maintained from 1935, when it was first investigated, until wartime conditions led to its reduction.[8]

[7] Zak, *The Kibbutz Movement in Numbers, 1938/9*, 7–10, 21–2. Comparative figures for previous years in *UAW Report* (1939), 215.
[8] *Yalkut*, 17 (Sept. 1941), 8–12. On the deterioration in nutrition during the war see *UAW Report* (1945), 71–2.

## Water[9]

The economic progress of these years enabled many kibbutzim to accumulate sufficient capital to strike out in new directions. But no part of the agricultural economy could develop without a sufficient supply of the element which is essential to the intensification of farming in a semi-arid climate such as that of Palestine: water. Even in the wettest parts of Palestine, the dry season lasts for more than half the year. The possibility of irrigation is therefore the key to the development of modern, intensive farming. One of the reasons for the large proportion of land devoted to relatively unprofitable arable crops in the early days of kibbutz settlement was the lack of water. From the time of the Second Aliya, experiments were made with various forms of irrigation. For example, there was a pump on the land of the Kinneret farm, and during the First World War the land adjacent to it was hired out to individuals and small groups who grew vegetables and other irrigated crops. But, despite the proximity of the veteran kibbutzim to the Jordan River, and to Lake Kinneret with its abundance of water, these resources were scarcely tapped until the completion of a regional irrigation project in the early 1930s. From 1931, an aqueduct brought water to all the kibbutzim in the area, and the pace of economic development was heightened considerably.

This project was financed and managed by the Zionist movement. Its success was an impetus to other schemes, which took a variety of organizational forms: co-operative enterprises run by the settlements in a given area; public companies supported by the Histadrut and the Jewish Agency; and, from 1934 onwards, companies financed by private capital but managed by the Histadrut and the settlements in a particular region.[10] The Palestine Economic Corporation (a profit-making concern backed by public and private capital)[11] financed the Palestine Water Company, which pumped water and sold it to the settlements. During this period, this body undertook to operate a number of pumping stations which the settlements themselves were unable to complete. Two companies—Gilboa, which operated in the area round Kibbutz Ein Harod, and Emek, which aided settlements in much of the Jezreel Valley—were established in 1934, partly with loans from public bodies, including the Zionist movement's Keren

---

[9] This section is based on *UAW Report* (1939), 28–40.

[10] Ibid. 28–9, 33.

[11] Ulitzur, *National Capital and Construction in Palestine, 1918–1937*, 12.

Hayesod, and the Jewish Agency's department for resettling German Jews; but the bulk of the money came from a loan made by the British company ICI with the active intervention of its chairman, Lord Melchett—an indication of growing confidence in the Yishuv's economic potential.

All these projects were fairly small, sometimes serving only one or two settlements. With the expansion of Jewish settlement to new areas, where the possibilities of economic development were now often secondary to political and strategic considerations, it became apparent that in many cases irrigation projects had to be developed on a regional, perhaps even a national, level. Mekorot ('Sources'), a company founded jointly by the Histadrut, the Jewish Agency, and the Jewish National Fund, with financial support through an issue of shares, undertook to develop the water resources for a wide area ranging from Afuleh in the east to Kiriat Haim in Haifa Bay. Headed by a dynamic team which included Levi Shkolnik (Eshkol) of Kibbutz Degania Beit, for many years one of the central figures in the Histadrut's Agricultural Centre, this company eventually became the national water authority of the Yishuv. At this stage, however, it was no more than an ambitious regional project.[12]

The result of this activity, which was rightly considered by all those concerned with the development of the Yishuv to be the key to the future of its agriculture, was a vast expansion of irrigated land. The kibbutzim and moshavim together had 1,200 hectares under irrigation in 1929, and 1,600 hectares in 1935; by 1939 there were more than 3,400 hectares of irrigated land in the kibbutzim alone.[13]

### DEMOGRAPHIC DEVELOPMENTS

In Table 12, above, the results of the developments discussed in chapter eight are beginning to appear. Only five years earlier, virtually every kibbutz had belonged to one of the three major movements. Now there began to appear smaller movements, whose proportion in the total was even greater if their *plugot* are taken into account. Another variation of the kibbutz idea which now appeared for the first time was the *meshek shitufi* (co-operative farm), whose members worked their land in common, as in the kibbutz, but lived in family

[12] Ulitzur, *National Capital and Construction in Palestine, 1918–1937*, 30–1.
[13] *Yalkut*, 1 (1936), h; Horowitz, *Palestinian Economy*, 40; *UAW Report* (1945), 40.

units and distributed their earnings in accordance with the size of the family.

There were other variations which were not reflected in the official statistical tables. Smaller youth movements such as Habonim and the Werkleute, whose graduates began to reach the country in this period, joined the major kibbutz movements and left no trace in the official statistics. Moreover, both within the major movements and outside, there was a great diversification of geographical origins. In chapter four I pointed out the importance of differences in cultural traditions which stemmed from diverse national origins, and their effect on the development of kibbutz ideology. Almost all these variations had been between three geographical areas: Russia, Galicia, and the rest of Poland. Now, with the growing strength and reputation of the kibbutz, and the overwhelming distress of European Jewry, there began to appear significant concentrations of Jews from Germany and from the other countries of Central and Western Europe—in particular, Czechoslovakia and the Baltic states—and even the United States; and from the early 1930s, groups of Palestine-born Jews began to create youth movements of their own, and to build kibbutzim.

Until 1930, the pattern was standard: the members of virtually all the kibbutzim established until that date had been born in Eastern Europe—Russia, Poland (including Galicia), Romania, Lithuania—and educated in one of the major youth movements (Hechalutz, Hashomer Hatzair, Gordonia), and joined one of the three major kibbutz movements. Other movements and national groups existed, but they were minorities within the major movements or national groupings, and those of their members who joined the kibbutz were assimilated into a largely homogeneous population. Thus, there was a small group of German Jews in Ein Harod, the founders of Heftziba originated in Czechoslovakia, and those of Beit Zera in Germany; but each of these groups was, or became, a minority in a predominantly East European community and movement.

The first break with this pattern came in 1930, with the establishment of Kibbutz Na'an by a group from the Noar Oved movement. But large-scale deviations from the standard pattern only began with the speeding up of the rate of settlement from 1936 onwards. During the period of tower and stockade operation, only eleven new kibbutzim conformed to the standard pattern. Nine were established by groups of Yishuv-born youth in the framework of the major kibbutz movements, while another thirteen deviated in other ways from what had until then been the norm: some came from Western countries, directly or through Youth Aliya; others were members of the new, smaller movements.[14]

This development is yet another indication of the degree to which the kibbutz had become central in Zionist aspirations and actions during these years. All these youth movements reached the conclusion that their educational ideal must be, in words whose contents appear in literally dozens of different forms throughout the pioneering youth movements, 'Jews who are prepared to devote themselves to their people. The highest form of this devotion is the realization of the Zionist idea through *halutziut* (pioneering).'[15] In the situation and atmosphere created by the tower and stockade operation, the function of the kibbutz as the most effective and elevated expression of this pioneering spirit seemed unquestionable. So a whole series of groups and movements, of widely different national origins and with a broad range of ideological beliefs, began to find their way to the kibbutz—often being careful to preserve their special character and aspirations. Within three or four years, the tripartite division of the kibbutz movement was modified by the beginnings of a thorough-going diversification.

### The Kibbutz Population in 1939

Table 17 shows the population of the kibbutzim in the autumn of 1939. The sum total of all categories was 24,105. At this point, the total Jewish population of Palestine was 445,457.[16] The proportion of the kibbutz population in that of the Yishuv was therefore 5.41 per cent as compared with 4.43 per cent in 1936.

### THE KIBBUTZ IN POLITICS[17]

In these perilous and stormy years, the kibbutz movements, each in its own way, mobilized their physical, educational, and spiritual forces

[14] Shoshani, *The Kvutza and the Kibbutz*, ad rem.
[15] Maccabi Hatzair, 1939; quoted by Ben-Avram, *Hever Hakvutzot*, 186.
[16] *Encyclopedia Judaica*, ix, 701.
[17] The developments in the labour movement during this period, and particularly the split in Mapai and its background, have been the subject of more research than almost any other aspect of the political history of the Yishuv. The works most relevant to our subject are Asaf, 'The Political Conflict in Hakibbutz Hame'uhad'; Kanari, 'The Kibbutz Me'uhad's Way'; Kedar, 'Policy of Kibbutz Me'uhad'; Shapira, *Berl*; and Yishai, *Factionalism in the Israeli Labour Movement*.

TABLE 17. Kibbutz Population, September 1939

| Kibbutz and population type | Kibbutz Me'uhad | Kibbutz Artzi | Hever Hakvutzot | Other[a] | Total |
|---|---|---|---|---|---|
| Permanent settlements | 25 | 23 | 21 | 10 | 79 |
| Members[b] | 7,331 | 3,331 | 2,360 | 1,195 | 14,217 |
| Children | 2,058 | 838 | 694 | 292 | 3,882 |
| Youth Aliya[c] | 537 | 344 | 409 | 68 | 1,358 |
| Total | 9,926 | 4,513 | 3,463 | 1,555 | 19,457 |
| Temporary *plugot* | 10 | 13 | 8 | 7 | 38 |
| Members[b] | 1,356 | 1,354 | 502 | 410 | 3,622 |
| Children | 143 | 35 | 20 | 15 | 213 |
| Youth Aliya[c] | 26 | 2 | 0 | 36 | 64 |
| Total | 1,525 | 1,391 | 522 | 461 | 3,899 |
| All kibbutzim | 35 | 36 | 29 | 17 | 117 |
| Members[b] | 8,687 | 4,685 | 2,862 | 1,605 | 17,839 |
| Children | 2,201 | 873 | 714 | 307 | 4,095 |
| Youth Aliya[c] | 563 | 346 | 409 | 104 | 1,422 |
| Total | 11,451 | 5,904 | 3,985 | 2,016 | 24,105[d] |

*Sources:* Zak, *The Kibbutz Movement in Numbers, 1938/9.* (Shatil, *The Economy of the Communal Settlement*, 370, gives rather different figures. I have preferred Zak's, which are based on the balance-sheets of the kibbutzim for 1938/9 and are given in some detail.)

[a] Including the Kibbutz Dati (Religious Kibbutz Movement) and Ha'oved Hatzioni (attached to Hano'ar Hatzioni and the General Zionist Movement).
[b] Including candidates for membership. Normal minimum age, 17–18.
[c] Including similar training groups.
[d] Including 749 parents of members not included in other figures.

to the national cause in an all-out effort to ensure the survival of the Yishuv and play their part in the defence of European civilization. Such intensive efforts sprang from a profound belief in the aims and values of the kibbutz. But some of these aims and values were themselves the source of deep disagreement within the Yishuv, and within the kibbutz movements themselves—disagreement which frequently expressed itself in political terms. Thus, concurrently with their effort to promote the national cause, these years were also a period of dynamic and complex political activity and controversy for the kibbutzim. In this process, the most dramatic and far-reaching developments were connected with the politics of the Kibbutz Me'uhad. They were the result of a series of events which that movement's leaders neither initiated nor welcomed.

## The Call for Kibbutz Unity[18]

I noted earlier that despite the growing similarities between the movements in many aspects of kibbutz life, there was no significant demand for them to unite. When such a demand did arise, it came unexpectedly, from a personality who had never himself been a member of a kibbutz: Berl Katznelson. It will be recalled that in 1934/5 the agreement between Ben-Gurion and Jabotinsky, the Revisionist Leader, had been rejected after a heated controversy within Mapai and the Histadrut. For Katznelson, this event had been traumatic. The Kibbutz Me'uhad had emerged as a leading force on the national level, capable of uniting, if only on one issue, a group of what had hitherto been deemed disparate elements (including groups outside Mapai, such as Hashomer Hatzair and Left Poalei Zion) and defeating what had until then been an invincible combination within the labour movement: Katznelson and Ben-Gurion. To Katznelson's mind, this incident was a continuation of the process which he had sensed in the ongoing, and still unresolved, controversy about Hechalutz: the Kibbutz Me'uhad, and Hechalutz as its agent, had become an independent educational movement to which no others—neither himself, nor the central organs of the Histadrut— were allowed access. Now it appeared that this movement was not only an educational force, but a political one. Katznelson was convinced that the only way to prevent this situation from recurring was by breaking down the organizational and ideological barriers between the kibbutz and the rest of the labour movement. As a first, and vital, step to 'the rehabilitation of the labour movement', he proposed a merger of all the kibbutz movements, beginning with Hever Hakvutzot and the Kibbutz Me'uhad. A number of elements combined to prompt the campaign for labour unity which Katznelson waged with vigour and conviction, but with no success, for some five years from 1935. One of his prime arguments was that unless the labour movement had the leadership which only the kibbutz movements, supported by Hechalutz, could provide, it was doomed to lose its inspiration and fall into the hands of self-seeking bureaucrats. He hoped to renew the harmony between the small group of veterans of the Second Aliya—particularly himself, Ben-Gurion, and Tabenkin—whose pristine vision of a 'workers' commonwealth' he believed to be the basis of the practical policies of the labour movement.

[18] Shapira, *Berl*, ch. 13.

And he was undoubtedly motivated by a considerable degree of apprehension for his personal influence. For some fifteen years, Katznelson had been the acknowledged spiritual leader of the labour movement, and more. No important move was made in the Yishuv without consulting him, no appointment made without his approval. More important, he had had an inestimable degree of influence on the younger generation in the labour Zionist movement, in Palestine and the Diaspora, and had established a vast network of friends, colleagues, and disciples. Now, he found that one of these friends, Yitzhak Tabenkin, and the movement which he led, had become an organized opposition within Mapai. The last straw for him had been the Kibbutz Me'uhad's obstruction of his attempt to regain his influence in Hechalutz through an independent department of the Histadrut. He still approved of many of the aims of the Kibbutz Me'uhad—its expansionism, its readiness to serve the needs of the Yishuv, its rejection of the 'provincialism' of the other two kibbutz movements. But he now believed that these characteristics could be promoted only by breaking down the organizational barriers which confined them to one movement only and made them part of an exclusive creed.[19]

Tabenkin and the other leaders of the Kibbutz Me'uhad were not prepared to abandon their position of pre-eminence in order to please Katznelson. But there were others within their movement who did find his views more attractive. Over the years Tabenkin had buttressed his leadership by devoting a great deal of time to educational work, both with groups of young people and through personal contact with many of the central figures in the kibbutzim and *plugot*. His constant demands for 'pioneering tension' within the Kibbutz Me'uhad, his overwhelming public persona, his gift for combining universal elements culled from history, philosophy, political theory, Jewish folklore and culture, literature, and other spheres with concrete demands, and thereby giving the individual in the smallest kibbutz the feeling that he was playing a significant part in making history—all this ensured his dominance in the movement at large.

This dominance was increased by the personal loyalty and devoted work of the talented group of men and women who constituted the organizational framework of the Kibbutz Me'uhad. The democratic

[19] Ibid. 206–25.

structure of the movement was simple:[20] a council, composed of representatives of the kibbutzim and *plugot*, was held every six months, and a conference roughly every two years. In practical terms, the movement was administered by a secretariat, theoretically appointed from time to time by the council but in fact chosen by Tabenkin in consultation with the other members of the secretariat—virtually all of them his comrades from the days of Kibbutz Ein Harod, or former followers of his in the youth movements. Though they were formally elected, the process was, in fact, co-option.

In one sense, therefore, the Kibbutz Me'uhad was always ready to give Tabenkin the absolute loyalty which he had demanded at the Yagur conference of 1933. But a number of circumstances combined to erode its monolithic character. The first of these is what may be described as natural resistance. The members of the Kibbutz Me'uhad had been educated to continuous effort, and usually answered readily to Tabenkin's demands. But there were occasions when he encountered opposition. In many kibbutzim, situations arose in which the kibbutz, or groups within it, wanted to stop absorbing new members in order to consolidate their community or economy. Others objected to having some of their best members mobilized for work in another *pluga*, or in the central institutions of the movement. Others again wanted, or refused, to absorb particular groups. There were even cases of 'rebellion'—refusal to accept the decisions of the movement's central bodies—on these and other grounds. Indeed, Tabenkin's own style laid him open to criticism, for his demands were often recognized to be exaggerated and impractical, even by those close to him.[21]

These creakings in the movement machinery were made even worse by the existence of groups with special reasons for dissatisfaction with the dominance of Tabenkin and his followers: the group of veterans who had opposed the establishment of the 'country-wide kibbutz' in the early 1920s; Netzah, still guarding its independence and steadily increasing its membership; and the German Jews who were now a significant minority in the movement. These were not only separated from the central leadership by their different cultural background, which led Tabenkin to describe them as 'half assimilated'; prominent among them was a group of former youth movement leaders, whose

[20] Hadari, *The Kibbutz Me'uhad*, 26–7; Kanari, 'The Kibbutz Me'uhad's Way', 66–9.
[21] Kanari, 'The Kibbutz Me'uhad's Way', ch. 3.

approach to matters of education and absorption policy was similar to that of Netzah. Their demand for control of their own movements and their own immigrant groups led to constant friction with the secretariat.[22]

The situation came to a head at the 1936 conference of the movement at Kibbutz Yagur. Here, the central group demanded a firm assertion of the principle that the administrative organs of the kibbutz had authority over its constituent parts. They had their way, but only after a bitter debate in which all the oppositionist elements, who had up to now resisted the central committee sporadically and on specific issues, supported each other and argued their case on ideological grounds.[23]

This was bad enough for the leading element in the Kibbutz Me'uhad. Even worse was the discussion on the unity of the kibbutz movement. The secretariat had wanted to keep this subject off the agenda. It was only discussed cursorily, and the advocates of unity spoke rather badly. None the less, a resolution suggesting that the question be examined sympathetically received the support of almost one-third of the delegates.[24]

The leadership was astonished. There had been currents of opposition in the movement since its foundation, but this was the first time that so large a group had united against the leadership, and on an issue which seemed to Tabenkin and his allies to threaten the very existence of the movement as they understood it. And this it certainly did. The question of unifying the kibbutz movements had been discussed several times over the past decade within Ein Harod and the Kibbutz Me'uhad, and up to now its leaders' conclusions had always been the same: they were prepared for unity, but on condition that the other partners accept their principles. In 1936, the Kibbutz Artzi was not a potential partner: its political independence, and the principle of ideological collectivism, made this quite clear. Hever Hakvutzot might be prepared to join with the Kibbutz Me'uhad, but only on condition that the special character of the *kvutzot* were preserved. Such a condition would, of course, completely change the character of the Kibbutz Me'uhad: it would mean, for instance, that the leadership would have to give up that degree of authority which they had just demanded at this very conference, and would call in

[22] Kedar, 'The German Aliyah as an Apolitical Opposition'.
[23] Kibbutz Me'uhad, *Eleventh Council*, 51–129.
[24] Ibid. 149–79.

question the whole of the educational and organizational structure of the Kibbutz Me'uhad's youth movement.[25]

The conference rejected the call for unity by a large majority. In political terms, however, the discussion was an unexpected, though incomplete, victory for Katznelson, and a warning of grave danger to the leadership. An opposition, hitherto fragmented and rather incoherent, had appeared, had stood up to be counted, and had proved to be much stronger than anybody had suspected. Moreover, the theme of unity was psychologically compelling: it had been one of the leitmotifs in the ideology of the labour movement, and of Tabenkin himself, from the days of the 'non-party group' in the Second Aliya onwards. And it was advocated by none other than Berl Katznelson, whom Tabenkin still saw as a personal friend as well as a relative,[26] a political ally, and even an honorary member of the kibbutz movement.[27]

After the conference Katznelson continued to advocate the idea of kibbutz unity, with the help of a group of supporters in the Kibbutz Me'uhad. But, concurrently with this discussion, other events were taking place which at first eclipsed it completely. The controversy was revived at a later stage in a quite different context.

## The Partition Controversy

After the Yagur conference came the Peel Commission and the partition controversy. Ben-Gurion and Weizmann, convinced that the establishment of a Jewish state, however small, would afford a real chance of saving a substantial number of European Jews from disaster, led the pro-partition campaign within the Zionist movement. Tabenkin, and with him virtually the whole of the Kibbutz Me'uhad, took an extreme and unambiguous stand: they were completely opposed to partition in any form.

The special emphases of the Kibbutz Me'uhad were in large measure a function of its underlying social philosophy and aspirations. In dozens of speeches and articles, its leaders maintained that without extensive areas for agricultural settlement the character of Jewish society in Palestine would be fatally flawed:

In the wake of partition, the centre of gravity of the [Zionist] movement will move away from the aim of [agricultural] settlement. The trend will be

[25] Near, *Kibbutz and Society*, 325–31.
[26] They were cousins.
[27] Kibbutz Me'uhad, *Eleventh Council*, 150–1; Shapira, *Berl*, 217.

towards the town: to commerce, tourism, all the functions of the middleman.
Those will be the major means of livelihood—to be missionaries of [bourgeois]
culture, commissars of commerce. . . . The citizens of this country, who are
to be doomed to strangulating confinement, will move towards a totalitarian
nationalism, a chauvinism which will lead to thoughts of uprooting the
present inhabitants, perpetual education to militarism. . . . We can already see
the beginnings of the militarism, whose slogan is 'More officials! More
officers! The man of the future is the intellectual, the military man, the civil
servant.'
    That is the image of the state—without its major hallmark, without the
support of millions of workers and farmers, but with the need to fulfil all the
'governmental' functions of a state, particularly those that are thought to be
'superior'—defence of the borders, preparedness for war, construction of the
'governmental' apparatus.[28]

    Tabenkin and his disciples were not opposed to the idea of a Jewish
state. But they believed profoundly that this particular Jewish state—
truncated, threatened with military and economic destruction, unable
to realize any schemes for extensive agricultural development—would
of necessity be militaristic and capitalistic, 'a copy of the pale of
settlement, with its ways of life and livelihood'.[29]

    To this sociological forecast was added an emotional dimension,
not specific only to the Kibbutz Me'uhad and its youth movements,
but very much emphasized in their educational thought and practice.
The knowledge and love of the Land of Israel, in all its aspects and
all its areas, had always been one of its principal educational aims; for
instance, the first book published by the publishing house of the
Kibbutz Me'uhad, established in 1939, was a popular book on the
geography of Palestine.[30] The members of its youth movements had
tramped and camped in the wildest and most remote parts of the
country, and had made them part of their national consciousness. The
feeling of historical continuity, that they were returning to (or growing
up in) the biblical Land of Israel, applied no less to districts currently
not inhabited by Jews than to those which were natural candidates
for inclusion in a Jewish state after partition. This view of the Land
of Israel, one and indivisible, was strengthened by economic and
geographical arguments about the need for extensive areas in order
to carry out widespread settlement schemes; and this, again, inter-
locked with a maximalistic view of Zionism: Jewish Palestine must

[28] Tabenkin, 'To Clarify the Way', *Mibifnim*, 8–9 (Aug.–Sept. 1937), 2–10.
[29] Ibid. 9.
[30] Braslavsky (Braslavy), *Do You Know the Land?*

afford a refuge for great numbers of Jews, not only for the minority urgently in need of rescue. In Tabenkin's slogan: 'Zionism is the movement of national liberation of the Jewish people, [whose aim is] the upbuilding of its country: the great majority [of Jews]—of whom the great majority will be composed of working people—[must settle] in its land, and the great majority of that land will be under their control.'[31]

In one sense, therefore, this issue was similar to that of the agreement with the Revisionists, through which the Kibbutz Me'uhad first appeared as a leading force in the politics of the labour movement: it combined the interests of the Kibbutz Me'uhad itself with a clear and partisan view of the national interest. At the time of the earlier controversy many of the arguments adduced were identical with those of others in the labour movement. Now, the anti-partition forces were to be found in most of the Zionist camp, ranging from Hashomer Hatzair to the Revisionists, and they shared a wide range of common attitudes. Thus, although the leaders of the Kibbutz Me'uhad were very cautious about extending their organizational contacts beyond the labour movement, it had became a major force in the prime national issue of the day.

In August 1937, the Zionist Congress decided that, despite its opposition to the Peel proposals, the executive should continue negotiations with the British government in the hope of attaining a better settlement. Tabenkin acceded to this formulation for tactical reasons, although his opposition to partition in any form remained unchanged. The British government itself rejected the principle of partition in November 1938. It was only in March 1939, in the shadow of the failure of the St James' Conference, that Ben-Gurion adopted the policy of 'fighting Zionism' which brought him close to the Kibbutz Me'uhad's attitude to Zionist policy.[32]

Meanwhile, however, fundamental damage had been done to the relationship between the leaders of Mapai and those of the Kibbutz Me'uhad. In addition to rejecting Katznelson's suggestion for labour unity, the latter had for two years waged a public campaign against the proposal which Ben-Gurion saw as the only way of saving the Zionist cause, and decried it as an unmitigated catastrophe. For the second time, it had waged a bitter struggle against the policy of the party's acknowledged leaders.

[31] *Mibifnim* (Dec. 1937), 9.     [32] Bauer, *From Diplomacy to Resistance*, 47.

## The Beginnings of 'Faction B'

The fourth conference of Mapai took place in Rehovot in May 1938, at the height of the partition controversy.[33] Questions of Zionist policy played a relatively minor part in the overt agenda. Katznelson again advocated the unity of the kibbutz movement, but it was already too late. Not only was the party deeply split on such issues as partition and the organization of Hechalutz; the very way in which the conference was managed—with time allocated to each kibbutz movement, the moshavim, and the towns according to the strength of each sector—showed that the divisions within the party were well on the way to being institutionalized. Although there was a formal decision in favour of the unity of the kibbutz movements, beginning with the pioneering youth movements of the Yishuv, no real attempt was made to impose this against the will of the movements concerned. In the negotiations which followed, it became clear that there had been no real change of attitude. Any change would have to come from inside the movements, and not be imposed from without.[34]

The leaders of the Kibbutz Me'uhad used the party conference to launch a frontal attack on the leadership of the party. The kibbutz movements had for many years complained that both Mapai and the Histadrut were less unified bodies than coalitions of professional politicians and local and interest groups. At the Rehovot conference the Kibbutz Me'uhad's demands for democratization of the Histadrut and the party were pointed and concrete. On questions of Zionist policy, and particularly the partition debate, party policy was effectively controlled by the political committee—a nominated body, on which the Kibbutz Me'uhad, for instance, was not represented. The policy discussions which preceded the Zionist Congress had taken place in the party's central committee, appointed by the (elected) conference some five years earlier: demands for a party conference before the Zionist Congress had been refused, and even now the conference agenda dealt with such apparently secondary issues as the unity of the party and the kibbutz.

In fact, these issues were not secondary. Behind the demand for kibbutz unity lay the political reality. Hever Hakvutzot was virtually unanimous in its support of the Zionist leadership, and its amalgamation with the Kibbutz Me'uhad would have seriously weakened that movement's anti-partition stance; and the unification of the youth movements would certainly have broken the Kibbutz Me'uhad's control of Hechalutz. For Katznelson, the call for unity was a step towards renewing the spirit of harmony within the labour movement; for Ben-Gurion, a means of ensuring discipline and majority rule.

The discussion at Rehovot revealed another facet of this problem. In chapter six we saw that as early as 1933 the Kibbutz Me'uhad was groping towards ways of increasing its involvement in the politics of the labour movement. At the same time, the leaders of that movement saw the kibbutz as a reservoir of activists who could and should play a greater part in party affairs. One major result of this confluence of interests was that in 1936, on Ben-Gurion's initiative, Yitzhak Ben-Aharon of Kibbutz Giv'at Haim was appointed secretary of the Tel Aviv Labour Council—the local executive body of the Histadrut.[35]

In 1936, Ben-Aharon was a talented and dynamic young man: at the age of 30 he already had several years of public activity behind him. He had been one of the central figures in the Hashomer Hatzair movement in Romania, and was a founding member of Kibbutz Giv'at Haim in the Hefer Valley.[36] For several years he had been advocating greater involvement of the kibbutz in politics;[37] and he himself had been secretary of Mapai in Tel Aviv, as well as an emissary to Hechalutz in Germany.

In Tel Aviv it was possible to see, in concentrated form, some of the most intractable problems of the Yishuv and its labour movement in the late 1930s. Since the end of 1935, the Yishuv had been in a state of economic crisis. During 1938, at least 6 per cent of the Jewish work-force was unemployed. Although the Histadrut took a number of initiatives, such as the establishment of an unemployment fund and an attempt to establish rotation of employment, by 1938 there were many who had been unemployed or partially employed for years, and there was no solution in sight.[38]

[35] Kedar, 'Policy of Kibbutz Me'uhad', 453.

[36] Ben-Aharon's youth, in the framework of the early days of the youth movement, is described in his autobiographical work, *Listen Gentile!* Giv'at Haim was one of the kibbutzim of Netzah; but, unlike the other Netzah groups, most of its members, including Ben-Aharon himself, remained close to the policies of the leaders of the Kibbutz Me'uhad.

[37] See his remarks in the consultation between the leaders of the Kibbutz Me'uhad in the spring of 1935. Repr. in Near, 'The Kibbutz and the Outside World', 393–5.

[38] Halevi, *Economic Development*, table 2; cf. Kedar, 'Policy of Kibbutz Me'uhad', 9. The official figures ignore seasonal fluctuations which meant that the state of affairs was often worse than reported.

Tel Aviv was not only an area of particular distress, it was also politically of great importance to the labour movement: it had the biggest branch of Mapai in the country, and a tradition of rebelliousness and anti-establishment politics dating from the Third Aliya.[39]

Ben-Aharon found not only unavoidable suffering in Tel Aviv: he discovered corruption and self-seeking among the local Histadrut establishment, particularly in the building workers' co-operative, the biggest single employer of labour in the building trade. Its managers held power in the local labour council and enjoyed the support of Ben-Gurion and the central Histadrut authorities. The opposition elements were divided, and ideologically remote from the constructive socialism of the kibbutz and the official Mapai approach; their style of thought and speech was uncouth. At first they saw Ben-Aharon as part of a Histadrut establishment which was basically indifferent to the interests of the urban workers.

By the time of the Rehovot conference, Ben-Aharon had been working in Tel Aviv for almost two years and was firmly convinced that the Histadrut machine was supporting the most corrupt elements in the local labour movement. The opposition group had won the elections to the labour council by a lightning recruiting campaign, but were being kept from power by a series of manipulations. Thus, the rhetoric of the Kibbutz Me'uhad about the lack of democracy in the party and Histadrut now had a much wider application than in previous years: its leaders saw themselves as the allies of an urban working class unfairly treated in matters of social policy, just as the Kibbutz Me'uhad was unfairly treated in matters of Zionist policy and settlement.[40]

At Rehovot, the party leaders turned this parallel on its head: both the Kibbutz Me'uhad and the Tel Aviv rebels were accused of particularism, of promoting their own interests as against those of the party as whole. In the light of its representatives' experiences in Tel Aviv, the Kibbutz Me'uhad began to see itself as the ally and spokesman of the unemployed and underprivileged in the Histadrut and the party.[41]

In informal discussions at the Rehovot conference an alliance was formed between the Kibbutz Me'uhad and the oppositionist elements

[39] Tzahor, *On the Road to Yishuv Leadership*, 150–3, 227–8, 244.
[40] Kedar, 'Policy of Kibbutz Me'uhad', 260–2.
[41] Shapira, *Berl*, 236–7; Kedar, 'Policy of Kibbutz Me'uhad', 284–6, 293–5.

from Tel Aviv. It became permanent and institutionalized in September 1938 when, in the course of a seemingly interminable series of elections in Tel Aviv, Ben-Aharon stood for election at the head of a combined list, known from now on as *Si'a Beit*—'Faction B'. Over the next four years, this faction continued to struggle for power in Tel Aviv, against the obstinate resistance of the national leadership of Mapai and its local allies. Meanwhile, the alliance between the urban sections and the Kibbutz Me'uhad was strengthened. In the elections to the party conference in 1942, Faction B emerged as a national grouping, with a clear ideology and platform of its own. The Kibbutz Me'uhad was now deeply involved in the life of the party. But this involvement had greatly intensified the trend already discernible at Rehovot in 1938, and turned the party into a federative body: each of the factions promoted its own policy, and their relative strength was decided by elections based on proportional representation. Ben-Gurion, foreseeing the political struggles ahead of the Yishuv, demanded the abolition of the factions in order to enable the party to make clear and unequivocal decisions.

At his urging, the Mapai conference at Kfar Vitkin in 1942 voted for the abolition of the factions. Faction B remained in existence, but its days in the party were clearly numbered. It was an independent entity in all but name, and even formed tactical alliances on Histadrut affairs with some of Mapai's left-wing rivals. In 1944 the formal break was made, and the Kibbutz Me'uhad stood at the centre of an independent party—l'Ahdut Ha'avoda (The Movement for Labour Unity).

## Faction B in Mapai: Some Issues

These developments, from the rejection of Katznelson's appeal for unity through the establishment of Faction B to the split in Mapai, were under the exclusive control of the majority in the Kibbutz Me'uhad. They suffered a set-back in July 1939, when a motion in favour of unification of the kibbutz movements won a tiny majority at the movement's conference; but this was nullified by the re-election of the central committee, whose members were overwhelmingly in the Tabenkin camp. By the next conference, in 1941, the forces were more or less stabilized: about one-third of the movement belonged to the pro-unity opposition. From now on the Kibbutz Me'uhad, while organizationally still united, was divided politically: the majority supported Tabenkin and his henchmen, and the minority were loyal to the leadership of Mapai.

Retrospectively, it seems that in the latter months of 1939 there were few differences of policy between these two groupings. The partition controversy was no longer relevant, though it was to be revived in a different form in a few years' time. Both Ben-Gurion and Katznelson were pursuing an 'activist' policy in reaction to the 1939 White Paper. Until the outbreak of war, Ben-Gurion had been advocating a civil rebellion; both now supported illegal immigration, and intensive settlement in defiance of the Mandatory restrictions on land purchase. All of these policies were very much in line with the basic attitudes of the Kibbutz Me'uhad leadership. But the dynamics of the unification campaign, which had led directly to the creation of Faction B, prevented any overall reconciliation between them.

It sometimes seems as if these two sets of relationships and tensions worked in separate dimensions. In 1940, at the height of the bitter controversy about the Tel Aviv branch of Mapai, one of the members of Mapai's central committee remarked that he could scarcely credit that that was what concerned the party at that particular time.[42] This remark could be generalized to cover much of the jockeying for position and ideological self-justification which occupied both majority and minority during this period. But there were some issues which linked the world of factional strife directly with that of the struggle for the survival of the Jewish people.

One of these was the question of Zionist orientation. Two strands can be discerned in the thought of Tabenkin and his disciples from a very early stage. One, which I have dwelt on, is the aspiration to Jewish independence in matters of defence, and, as far as possible, in Zionist policy: the policy described from 1933 onwards as 'orientation on ourselves'—that is, on the social and economic strength of the Yishuv—in contrast with Weizmann's pro-British policy, or the pro-Soviet orientation advocated by such parties as Left Poalei Zion. The other was an admiration for the Soviet Union, as the home of socialism. Until 1933, this admiration had been very strongly tempered by criticism of Communist policy towards the Jews, and of the internal characteristics of the Soviet regime. From 1933 onwards, the leading

[42] Shapira, *Berl*, 243.

group in the Kibbutz Me'uhad began increasingly to see the Soviet Union as the only power able and willing to lead the world in the struggle against Fascism. This change in Tabenkin's attitude was marked by a well-known article, 'Marx the Symbol', published in 1933, in which he said that the international situation called for the closing of the ranks. Marx (and, by implication, Communism as a social system) must now be the symbol of the struggle against the forces of reaction.[43]

Within the majority in the Kibbutz Me'uhad there were those who approved almost completely of the Soviet Union and its regime, with the exception of its anti-Zionist stance. The most extreme of these was Lev Leviteh, of Ein Harod, a member of the movement's inner circle from its inception, who spoke of an article in the Histadrut newspaper critical of the Moscow trials as 'depressing evidence of the decline of Socialist and working-class values in our movement'.[44] Others, while less extreme in their defence of the Soviet Union, saw it as the only force seriously determined to save the world from the threat of Fascism and Nazism. Tabenkin himself remained constant to the line he had followed from 1934 onwards: in addition to its military potential as the defender of the workers of the world, the Soviet Union was an example of a socialist society in its internal structure, and had a right to protect itself: the Molotov–Ribbentrop alliance was, therefore, not only a 'pardonable necessity', but also an example of the 'national egoism' which was the only possible pattern of relations between states.[45]

The reluctance of the leaders of the Kibbutz Me'uhad to approve of recruitment of kibbutz members to the British army at the beginning of the war can be seen as a convergence of these lines of thought. The need to strengthen the Hagana as an independent Jewish fighting force was a clear expression of 'orientation on ourselves'. It was without doubt strengthened by the suspicion that Britain was primarily defending not the freedom of the world but its own imperial interests. In Tabenkin's words, 'There is no fundamental moral difference between Nazism and England and France ... the mobilization of forces in Palestine [strengthens] distant forces for an anti-Russian front.'[46]

[43] Tabenkin, 'Marx the Symbol'.
[44] Kibbutz Me'uhad *Eleventh Council*, 121–2.
[45] E. Kafkafi, 'The Notebooks of Yitzhak Tabenkin'.
[46] Ibid. 256–7.

*The Kibbutz Artzi*[47]

By 1946 the Kibbutz Artzi, like the Kibbutz Me'uhad, stood at the centre of a political party, with its own platform and a well-defined constituency outside its kibbutzim. But there were significant differences both between the political aims of the two movements and in the way in which they became involved in party politics.

In the late 1920s and early 1930s, one of the chief questions at issue between the leading group in Hashomer Hatzair and those who sought to 'tighten the movement line' was the demand to turn the movement into an independent political party. This demand had been rejected; but the tension between the constructivist tendency in the movement and the demands of the left for increased political involvement continued. The question of the broadening of the political framework arose in an acute form in 1935. From the time of the establishment of Mapai in 1930, there had been a series of discussions between that party and the leaders of Hashomer Hatzair on the possibilities of unity between the two. All had foundered on the question of ideological collectivism: the leaders of Mapai were not prepared to accept into their ranks an organized group which would vote *en bloc* and turn the party into a federative movement; and Hashomer Hatzair was not prepared to be swallowed up in a mass party. One such discussion, which took place in January 1935, left the leadership of Hashomer Hatzair with a feeling of isolation within the labour movement. Their natural allies, the Kibbutz Me'uhad, were waging a joint struggle with them against the leadership of Mapai on the question of the agreement with the Revisionists. But it was clear that the Kibbutz Me'uhad saw its place within Mapai; and without this or some other public support, the Kibbutz Artzi would have no real political power beyond its own, necessarily limited, numerical strength. At this point, an approach was made by a group of urban workers, many of them ex-members of Hashomer Hatzair and its kibbutzim, who accepted the movement's political line and suggested an alliance. The reaction was very guarded. Some of the leaders of Hashomer Hatzair still hoped that it would find a way to join Mapai and believed that an alliance with outside forces would close that option. Others were opposed to an alliance with—and, thereby, legitimation of—people who had left the kibbutz. None the less, the majority agreed, though hesitantly, to the establishment of the Socialist League as the urban

[47] This section is based on Zait, 'From Kibbutz Movement to Party Organization'.

ally of the Kibbutz Artzi. Despite some initial tensions, this group was completely loyal to the policies of Hashomer Hatzair and the Kibbutz Artzi from its formation in 1936 until the foundation of the Hashomer Hatzair party in 1946—even though its influence in forming those policies was restricted to a modicum of representation on the Kibbutz Artzi's political committee. However, it established itself as a small but significant political force, attacking the Histadrut establishment and demanding a more aggressive policy in trade union affairs, democratization of the Histadrut, and an end to corruption and inequality in Histadrut-controlled enterprises. During the war years it gained strength, and in 1946 was merged into the Hashomer Hatzair party.[48]

In parallel, the movement continued to develop and define its characteristic policies. One of these continued to be opposition to the Histadrut bureaucracy and support for militant trade union tactics in the urban sector. Another was its special sensitivity to the Arab problem.[49] Though its support for the joint Jewish-Arab trade union was never abandoned, after the Arab revolt it no longer seemed to be the main path to agreement; none the less in 1940 it established an Arab department and formed a cadre of activists who studied Arab languages and customs, and attempted to make contact on the personal and political level.

In matters of Zionist policy, Hashomer Hatzair allied itself with the Kibbutz Me'uhad in opposing the partition proposals, emphasizing that statehood at this stage would put an end to any hope of Arab–Jewish rapprochement. Its own alternative was, however, not as yet clearly defined. It was only during the early 1940s, under the pressure of Ben-Gurion's demand for a 'Jewish commonwealth' after the war, that it began to advocate a binational state, as distinct from the much vaguer concept of a binational society.

This movement, like the Kibbutz Me'uhad, conducted a constant internal dialogue on the question of its attitude to the Soviet Union. Although its ideology was unreservedly Marxist, it was highly critical of what its leaders described as the distortions of socialism in Soviet Russia. Ideologically, most of them saw themselves as part of the Austro-Marxist school. With the worsening of the international situation, they also emphasized the need for international solidarity with

[48] Zait, 'From Kibbutz Movement to Party Organization', 177.
[49] Id., *Zionism and Peace*, ch. 6.

the Soviet Union, in order to prevent the destruction of the only socialist society in the world. But this did not prevent them from criticizing the Moscow trials, the Communists' destruction of the Catalan anarchist movement, the Molotov–Ribbentrop pact, and the Russian invasion of Finland.

This was the attitude of the principal leaders of the Kibbutz Artzi, foremost among whom were Meir Ya'ari and Ya'akov Hazan. Throughout its history, however, there were groups within the movement whose attitude towards Soviet Russia was more indulgent. Their leaders were largely men and women of the younger generation, most of whom had arrived in Palestine in the early 1930s and had been active in the agitation to 'tighten the line'. Prominent among them were Mordechai Oren and Ya'akov Riftin, both often members of the Kibbutz Artzi's central executive bodies. Their influence combined with the generally left-leaning views of the younger members of the movement to restrain it from taking a strong anti-Soviet line, and kept its doubts about the genuineness of British opposition to Hitler alive in the early years of the war. On this matter, and the related question of the mobilization of movement members to the British armed forces, members of the Kibbutz Artzi commonly expressed views similar to those of Tabenkin, as quoted above.

In short, by 1939 the leadership of the Kibbutz Artzi, like that of the Kibbutz Me'uhad, was definitely on the left wing of the labour movement, in two significant respects: their Marxist ideology, which was common coin in their educational movements; and their tendency to sympathize with the policies and social system of the Soviet Union. They were far from the standpoints of movements such as Left Poalei Zion, which opposed the concept of constructive Zionism, or of the anti-Zionist Communist movement. But, equally, this aspect of their ideology cut them off from the mainstream of labour Zionist thought as expressed mainly in Mapai, which was both non-Marxist and deeply anti-communist.

## *Hever Hakvutzot*[50]

The politics of Hever Hakvutzot were less stormy than those of the other two movements, though no less deeply felt. On the whole, the members of the veteran *kvutzot* were prepared to leave politics to the small minority who were interested in such matters; and, apart from

---

[50] This section is based on Ben-Avram, *Hever Hakvutzot*, pts. 2 and 3.

a few party activists such as Joseph Baratz, these were largely the graduates of Gordonia. In the first few years of its partnership with Hever Hakvutzot, this movement developed a theory of socialism of its own, largely derived from Eduard Bernstein and Henri de Man.[51] Thus, it was ideologically at odds both with the other two kibbutz movements and with the great majority of the leadership of Mapai, most of whom thought in class terms, if not necessarily in the classical Marxist categories. Hever Hakvutzot's allies, the ex-members of Hapoel Hatzair, were definitely in the minority in Mapai. Both Ben-Gurion and Katznelson preferred the dynamism and public consciousness of the Kibbutz Me'uhad to the introverted *kvutzot*. So it looked at first as if Gordonia, with the backing of Hever Hakvutzot, would settle down to being a tolerated but not very influential minority group within the party.

In the mid-1930s, it suddenly found itself in the midst of a radical political change. This was heralded by the controversy about the use of violence against the Revisionists, in which the former unanimity of the veteran Ahdut Avoda leaders was broken, and Katznelson was allied with his erstwhile opponents of Hapoel Hatzair—including Gordonia—against Tabenkin and Ben-Gurion. The kibbutz movement was also divided on this issue: the Kibbutz Me'uhad against Hever Hakvutzot. In the campaign against the agreement with the Revisionists, this constellation was repeated, this time with the Kibbutz Artzi ranged on the side of the Kibbutz Me'uhad, and Hever Hakvutzot supporting Katznelson and Ben-Gurion. So it is not surprising that, when Katznelson began to count heads in his struggle against the hegemony of the Kibbutz Me'uhad, he saw Hever Hakvutzot as a possible ally; and, equally, that his opponents within the Kibbutz Me'uhad saw his call for unity as a means of restoring his leadership, through an alliance between Hever Hakvutzot and the minority within their own movement. In June 1936, when the leaders of Hever Hatvutzot met with Katznelson and Ben-Gurion to discuss the question of kibbutz unity, they were amazed to hear Ben-Gurion reaffirm his preference for the Kibbutz Me'uhad 'which continues the tradition of Ahdut Ha'avoda'. One of the leading graduates of Gordonia remarked: 'I don't want to say that we are the most loyal, but we certainly support the general policy of the party leadership. Your line is ours.'[52]

---

[51] Margalit, The *Gordonia Youth Movement*, chs. 3, 6, and 8.
[52] Ben-Avram, *Hever Hakvutzot*, 159–62.

And so, in most respects, it was. Most of the members of the movement supported Ben-Gurion in the partition controversy; and in 1938 Pinhas Lubianiker (Lavon), the founder and leader of Gordonia, was appointed joint secretary of Mapai, together with Joseph Bankover of the Kibbutz Me'uhad, in an attempt to balance the political forces in the party machinery. Katznelson's call for kibbutz unity received a mixed reception in Hever Hakvutzot. As we have seen, many of the veteran members, including some of those whose original party loyalties had been to Hapoel Hatzair, disapproved of the separatism of Gordonia, and were opposed to its union with their movement. Two of the leading figures in this group were Levi Shkolnik (Eshkol) and Kadish Luzinsky (Luz; later minister of agriculture and chairman of the Knesset in the state of Israel) of Degania Beit—a *kvutza* which had always demurred from the cult of 'intimacy', and had had a more dynamic policy of social and economic expansion than its senior neighbour, Degania Aleph. In 1933, when the negotiations with Gordonia were at their height, Luzinsky made a far-reaching suggestion for co-operation between the kibbutzim in the Jordan Valley: to own and work their lands in common, while each community remained in control of its own social structure. At that time, the *kvutzot* refused to give up their right to control their own economic destinies, and preferred the union with Gordonia—including its political implications—to Luzinsky's plan.[53] In 1938, after the Rehovot conference of Mapai had called on Hever Hakvutzot and the Kibbutz Me'uhad to explore the possibility of unification, Luzinsky, together with some of the leaders of the minority in the Kibbutz Me'uhad, suggested a scheme which went some way towards accepting the Kibbutz Me'uhad's approach. It envisaged a united, disciplined movement, but allowed the *kvutzot* to retain their own social structure and limited size. This suggestion was rejected by the majority of Hever Hakvutzot: they were prepared to create a new movement in which both forms of settlement had equal rights, but were not prepared to be treated as a 'tolerated minority' within a movement dominated by the big kibbutzim.[54]

None the less, the discussions before and during the unification controversy showed that there was a powerful minority within the movement which was aware of, and even welcomed, the social and economic trends which were reducing the distance between the

[53] Ibid. 75–84.     [54] Katznelson, *Efforts towards Unity*, 113–18.

structure of *kvutza* and kibbutz—in practice if not always in ideology. This group included some of the younger members of Gordonia, who emphasized the need for the kibbutz movement—including their own organization—to take on national duties which it had hitherto declared less important than the development of agricultural settlement. 'The facts of life are more important than formulae and [ideological] definitions';[55] and these facts pointed to the breaking down of the traditional distinctions.

Hever Hakvutzot's declaration of conditional support for a unified kibbutz movement was primarily a political act, prompted by support for Berl Katznelson and the general principle of labour unity. But it seems probable that, had the Kibbutz Me'uhad been prepared to enter into serious negotiations, an organizational basis for unification could have been found even at this early stage. Hever Hakvutzot's separate existence was a function of its politics no less than—indeed, perhaps more than—its special concept of the structure and functions of the kibbutz community. In questions of Zionist policy, the leaders of Gordonia and the other activists of Hever Hakvutzot carried on the Hapoel Hatzair tradition by supporting the Weizmann line, and reacting with suspicion to the activism of Ben-Gurion and the Kibbutz Me'uhad alike. As we have seen, this in no way affected their participation in the tower and stockade operation, which exactly fitted their belief that agricultural settlement was the heart of the Zionist enterprise. But most of them supported Weizmann and Ben-Gurion on the partition issue; and, from the outbreak of war, their members volunteered for the British forces in proportions significantly greater than those of the other two movements. With the secession of Faction B in 1944, Hever Hakvutzot and its associated youth movements became a central force in the dominant grouping in Mapai.

## Summary

These years saw the continuation of the trends which were noted in previous chapters. The primary aims of all the kibbutz movements were still the creation and development of kibbutzim, education in the framework of the youth movement, and absorption of immigrants. But each of them had also adopted clear policies on public issues in the Yishuv, the Zionist movement, and, indeed, the world. Moreover,

---

[55] Ben-Avram, *Hever Hakvutzot*, 141–2, 144.

each of them had either created institutional means of promoting these policies or was groping its way towards such means: Hever Hakvutzot as part of the Mapai establishment, the Kibbutz Artzi as an independent political force with a growing body of organized supporters in the towns, the Kibbutz Me'uhad as the leading partner in an oppositional faction of Mapai. With the expulsion of Faction B from Mapai and its regrouping as l'Ahdut Ha'avoda in 1944, and the establishment of the Hashomer Hatzair party in 1946, both the Kibbutz Me'uhad and the Kibbutz Artzi would have created, though with some reluctance, a similar political structure: an independent party controlled by a kibbutz movement.

A comparison of Table 18 with Table 11 above shows something of the changes which had taken place since 1935. Table 18 reveals a growing similarity between the standpoints of the Kibbutz Me'uhad and the Kibbutz Artzi: they were divided only by the questions of separate political organization and of partition. It would, however, be a full decade until these issues were resolved or perceived to be irrelevant.

## SOCIAL DEVELOPMENTS

Previous chapters have described the kibbutz community at specific points of time, until 1935. This section traces a number of trends in the social development of the kibbutz during the second half of the 1930s, occasionally outlining their continuation until the end of the Second World War.

### Women in the Kibbutz

In chapters 3 and 6 we noted the ways in which the kibbutz attempted, not always successfully, to combine the principle of equality between the sexes with the preservation of the family unit. There remained certain tensions between the family and the broader kibbutz community which were not always resolved in favour of the family. In some educational circles, particularly those of Hashomer Hatzair, the tendency to see the parents as a 'pathogenic factor' in the life of the child lingered on for many years.[56] The institution of the 'primus'[57] is perhaps the most extreme example of the penalization of the family unit for the benefit of the wider community. The same tendency

---

[56] e.g. Golan, *Collective Education*, 20–2.
[57] See 'The Third One', above, ch. 5.

TABLE 18. Political Attitudes, 1935–1939: Kibbutz Movements and Labour Leaders

| | Kibbutz movements | | | | Labour leaders | | |
| --- | --- | --- | --- | --- | --- | --- | --- |
| | Kibbutz Me'uhad (leadership) | Kibbutz Me'uhad (opposition) | Gordonia/ Hever Hakvutzot | Kibbutz Artzi | Ben-Gurion | Katznelson | Sprinzak |
| Support for Ben-Gurion–Jabotinsky agreement | − | − | + | − | + | + | + |
| 'Comprehensiveness' in Hechalutz | + | − | − | − | ± | − | − |
| Support for unification of kibbutz movement | − | + | ± | − | + | + | + |
| Trade-union militancy | + | ± | − | + | − | − | − |
| Agricultural settlement | + | + | + | + | + | + | + |
| 'Self-restraint' in defence | + | + | + | + | + | + | + |
| Partition of Palestine | − | − | + | − | + | − | + |
| Binationalism | − | − | − | + | − | − | − |
| Sympathy to USSR | + | − | − | + | − | − | − |
| Belief in mass party | + | + | + | − | + | + | + |

*Notes:* +: supported; −: opposed; ±: neutral, wavered, or changed policy.

expressed itself, though less dramatically, in the custom whereby, well into the 1940s, married couples seldom sat together in the dining room or other public places; and in the words used to denote 'husband'—*haver* (comrade) or *ish* (man) rather than *ba'al*, which in Hebrew also has the connotation of 'lord' or 'owner'.[58]

All this made for the social equalization of the sexes. But it was not as far-reaching as appears in the accepted image. It is true that the kibbutz community gave every woman the opportunity to engage in agriculture: a month's maternity leave was given as a matter of course, and the child care system enabled mothers to return to their previous work immediately thereafter. But, as noted in chapter 2, the pattern set in the Second Aliya, whereby men worked in the 'productive branches' and women in the 'services', still applied in the veteran kibbutzim in the mid-1920s, though often not in the plugot where there were few children.[59] Moreover, from the earliest days of the kibbutz its democratic institutions were almost entirely dominated by males: women spoke far less in the general meetings, were rarely elected to the central decision-making bodies of the kibbutz (secretariat, economic committee), and virtually never held such administrative posts as farm manager or secretary. In Ein Harod, in the mid-1930s a group of women demanded that one-third of the places on all the kibbutz committees be reserved for women. The suggestion was adopted, and eventually became a guide-line for the whole of the kibbutz movement.[60] But administrative positions, particularly in the economic sphere, remained the virtual monopoly of the men.

While the Third Aliya established the image of sexual equality in the kibbutz, it also saw the beginnings of its decline. In 1923, the proportion of children to adult members of the established kibbutzim was 13.6 per cent. Ten years later, it had increased to 43 per cent, and by 1941 had reached about 47 per cent.[61] As the number of children grew, the proportion of workers needed in the children's houses rose steeply and the proportion of women working in agriculture fell. The principle of communal child care was one of the cornerstones of kibbutz society. But it was put into practice not by

---

[58] e.g. Lieblich, *Kibbutz Makom*, 113.
[59] Rosen, 'Changes in the Status of Women', 77.
[60] Bat-Rahel, *The Path in which I Went*, 94–6.
[61] *Pinkas Hahistadrut* (Jan.–Feb. 1923), table A; *UAW Report*, 1939, 197; *Yalkut*, 1942, 10.

the community as a whole, but by the women alone—a fact still expressed semantically in the word *metapelet* (child care worker), which is used almost exclusively in the feminine gender.

By the end of the 1930s the pattern was clearly established. To a very great extent, men engaged in traditional male occupations— agriculture, and ancillary trades such as carpentry and metal work —while women worked in the kitchen, the laundry, and the children's houses. These differences were also reflected in the administrative institutions of the kibbutz. Just as there were 'women's branches', there were also 'women's committees'—notably those dealing with education, clothing, and the distribution of consumer goods. They were usually elected to such bodies as the economic committee, if at all, by virtue of the 'rule of the third'.[62]

One other area in which kibbutz women are often believed to have achieved emancipation in the kibbutz is that of defence. In the Second Aliya period, this was true only to a limited extent. In Hashomer, most of the wives were not involved in defence matters; and there is no evidence that the situation in the *kvutzot* was different. At the time of the riots of 1929, women took little or no part in the defence of the kibbutzim, and this led to a reaction after the outbreak of the Arab Revolt in the mid-1930s. From then on, it was one of the shibboleths of kibbutz thought (particularly in the Kibbutz Me'uhad) that women had a right and a duty to take their place in the fighting line alongside the men. And, indeed, much was achieved: kibbutz women learnt to handle weapons, did guard duty, and were full members of the Hagana.[63] None the less, their numbers were always small compared with those of the men, and in most cases they were given special, non-combatant (though often very dangerous) tasks, such as radio operation. In the description of a tower and stockade settlement in chapter 9 women were seen mainly in ancillary occupations. It seems, then, that apart from short periods when there were few or no children, the kibbutzim never achieved occupational and political equality in the terms to which they themselves aspired. And this state of affairs tended to perpetuate itself, by influencing the expectations of coming generations—both those joining the kibbutz from the youth movement, and those born and educated in the kibbutz.

The developing attitudes of the kibbutz members themselves to

[62] Bassevitz, *Eleventh Council*, 69.
[63] Brenner, *The Kibbutz Me'uhad in the Hagana* (Heb.), (Tel. Aviv, 1980), 157–65.

questions of sexual equality are also part of the historical record. Towards the end of the Second Aliya, Joseph Bussel declared that emancipation had been achieved. This view was generally accepted until some time in the mid-1930s when such phenomena as the 'rule of the third' point to a growing degree of dissatisfaction. This feeling erupted at the beginning of the tower and stockade period, with the demand that women share the burden of defence equally with the men. It is not clear whether this was the result of a general attitude, or of an élite group under the influence of the (male) leaders of the kibbutz movement; for the call to involve women in guard duty was first sounded by Yitzhak Tabenkin, his wife, and the wife of Avraham Tarshish, one of his close supporters.[64] But it quickly became the declared policy of all the kibbutz movements.

On the whole, however, the accepted wisdom in the late 1930s and 1940s was that, despite a good many difficulties during the formative period of the kibbutz, its women had fought for their emancipation and achieved it in the main, although there were still some areas in which it was as yet incomplete. This is undoubtedly the general message of two anthologies on the subject which were widely circulated and used in the pioneering youth movements at the time.[65]

The reasons for these developments are still a matter of theoretical controversy, which will not be discussed here. It should, however, be pointed out that at each stage kibbutz thought developed against the background of ideological attitudes in the world at large. In most countries, the earliest demands of the feminist movements were both for the rights of the woman as against her husband and for 'securing to women an equal participation with men in the various trades, professions, and commerce'.[66] Women's emancipation was one of the demands of the Russian revolutionary movement which deeply influenced the pioneers of the Second and Third Aliya; and both here and in the German feminist movement the influence of such thinkers as August Bebel, who 'encouraged a positive attitude towards women's participation in the labour market' was dominant.[67] In this context,

[64] Y. Tabenkin, 'On the Question of Our Defence' (Heb.); E. Tabenkin, 'On Women's Part in Defence'; Bat-Rahel, 'Is it Fated'. And cf. Brenner, loc. cit.

[65] Katznelson-Shazar, R., *Words of Working Women*; Poznansky and Shehori, *Women in the Kibbutz*.

[66] From the Declaration of Sentiments at the Seneca Falls Convention, New York State, 1848. Reprinted in O'Neill, *The Woman Movement*, 111.

[67] Evans, *The Feminists*, 158, 182.

the demand of women in the Labour Zionist movement to take part in the conquest of labour does not seem exceptional, although the particular trades which they sought to enter were certainly so. The other major issue of feminism the world over—votes for women—had been conceded in the kibbutzim from their very beginnings. So they could well claim to be an extreme example of the success of feminism, with only minor obstacles in the path to complete sexual equality. The decline of the feminist movement in the world after the achievement of political emancipation in many countries[68] meant that there was little external ideological stimulus to challenge the view that the problem of the women was very largely solved in kibbutz society. It was only with the new wave of feminism sparked off by the publication of Simone de Beauvoir's *Le Deuxième sexe* in 1949 and the American women's movement of the 1960s that the question was raised again, in different dimensions, outside the kibbutz movement and within it.

## Culture

In the earlier chapters of this book it was emphasized that self-created cultural activities were a vital element in creating and maintaining the social cohesion of the kibbutzim. This was a function both of their isolation and of their determination to build a self-sufficient community, with cultural values and customs of its own. In time, many of these local creations spread throughout the kibbutz movement; and there were added to them ideas and activities which could only be put into practice within a wider framework of co-operation between neighbouring kibbutzim, or in the country-wide movement.

Folk song and dance have been part of the cultural ambience of the kibbutz from its earliest days. The ecstatic sing-song and *hora* were not only to be found in Degania and Geva; they recur in descriptions of the life of every kibbutz in its first years. Folk song was not an indigenous creation of the kibbutz. The members brought with them a whole repertoire—sometimes rooted in Jewish culture, at others in that of the peoples among whom they lived; at times sung in the original version, frequently translated and adapted. This process was broadened by the constant accession of waves of immigrants from different countries, and particularly from the youth movements, in all of which folk song was a recognized educational medium. All of

---

[68] Evans, *The Feminists*, 211–28.

these elements were refined, selected, and fused in the local repertoire of each kibbutz: one song 'naturally' followed another as a result of long usage; local variations in words or melody became part of the accepted canon. Each of the youth movements created its own song-books, many of them with eclectic selections from half a dozen national repertoires. Thus, in one of the best known, there are songs in Hebrew, German, and Yiddish. Many of them are of Russian origin, others are taken from the Hasidic repertoire, while others again originated with the German youth and student movements—although the words would often be adapted to bear a Zionist message.[69] These songs soon became known outside the ranks of the pioneering movements themselves. In 1924, for instance, there appeared a thin volume entitled *Hahalutzim* (The Pioneers),[70] containing twenty folk songs, illustrated by silhouettes created by one of the founders of the Bezalel art school in Jerusalem. Most of the songs were satirical, though a few bore an explicit Zionist message. Their fate illustrates the process described here. All of them grew out of the ambience of the 'period of the roads'. Most of them have fallen into disuse, but two or three can still be heard today in the youth movements and kibbutzim, and on Israeli radio and television.

Folk dance developed hand in hand with song, and for very similar reasons. As practised in the kibbutzim, neither could be very sophisticated: social solidarity demanded that all should be able to dance, often at a very rough and ready level. Equally, the communal sing-song was frequently louder than it was tuneful. But at the same time the more talented members of the kibbutzim were seeking more aesthetic ways of expressing the same motifs: choirs, dance groups, and, with the gradual rise in standards of living during the 1930s, musical instruments such as the piano, and the beginnings of instrumental groups. In the mid-thirties Yehuda Shertok (Sharett) of Kibbutz Yagur, a talented violinist, composer, and conductor, was spending much of his time working with local choirs in different kibbutzim of the Kibbutz Me'uhad.[71] There were also a number of composers of folk music whose compositions, rooted in the everyday experience of their own communities, became part of the general repertoire. Such activities developed over the years, until in the bigger kibbutzim they reached professional standards. Concerts—often

[69] Schonberg, *Songs of the Land of Israel.*
[70] Narkiss, *The Pioneers.*
[71] His visits to Giv'at Brenner are mentioned in ch. 7, above.

including music, dance, dramatic performances, and the like—would be given for the benefit of all the kibbutzim in the area. During the 1930s, the members of the *pluga* which eventually settled at Afikim in the Jordan Valley set up a travelling amateur dramatic group known as 'Blue Shirt', on the model of the artistic and propaganda troupes of Soviet Russia, which specialized in satirical revues on topical subjects.[72] For most kibbutz members visits to theatres or concerts in town were rare luxuries; but the central dramatic companies of the Yishuv gave special performances in areas where there were a number of kibbutzim and moshavim.

The kibbutz engendered a good deal of writing. Much of it was ideological or political, but there was also some purely literary creation. Most appeared in local news-sheets, but there are short stories, poems, and literary reportage in almost every issue of the kibbutz movements' (usually quarterly) journals during the late 1930s, and in 1937 there were enough young writers in the Kibbutz Me'uhad alone to hold a special conference.[73] Several books by kibbutz members or about kibbutz life had appeared; and some of these authors, such as Nathan Bistritzky-Agmon, Yehuda Ya'ari, and David Maletz were in the process of achieving a country-wide reputation.[74]

As in other areas of cultural activity, much of this literary creation sprang from to the day-to-day life of the kibbutzim; for instance, many short stories, poems, and other literary works by authors who subsequently became known to a wider audience were first written in the house journal of an individual kibbutz or kibbutz movement. From about 1937 the number of local kibbutz news-sheets grew constantly. Naturally, their standards varied, from ungarnished accounts of administrative decisions to extensive literary or political expression; but by the end of the 1950s such a journal was a more or less standard feature of every kibbutz.

Kibbutz writing, as indeed other forms of cultural expression, was increasingly in Hebrew, and by the end of the Third Aliya Hebrew was firmly established as the common language. This necessitated much effort, and many hours of formal and informal teaching, particularly at times of mass immigration; and in many kibbutzim a whole host of other languages could be heard on the pathways and in

---

[72] Tsur *et al.*, *Beginning of the Kibbutz*, 227–8; Ucko, 'Songs of the Youth Movements', 257–65.

[73] Reported in *Mibifnim*, 4/6 (June 1937), 142–3.

[74] Shur and Goldemberg, 'Kibbutz and Literature'.

the dining-hall. But the increasing number of children whose mother tongue was Hebrew ensured that every parent learnt the language, and this allowed constant enrichment of forms of cultural expression. All of this took place in a framework of continuous cultural activity, centred largely on the Sabbath and the Jewish festivals, through which the different kibbutz communities expressed both their own internal solidarity and their spiritual links with the Jewish people.

From their earliest days, the men and women of Degania had celebrated the Sabbath as a day of rest, though their way of doing this was far from that of their orthodox parents. As the *kvutza* developed, it became clear that a number of agricultural and service branches would have to function even on the day of rest: livestock had to be fed, cows milked, children looked after, food provided for all. With the expansion and diversification of the farm, there was constant pressure to use the Sabbath for urgent work not connected with such vital needs. In 1933, Joseph Baratz protested against

the disruption of the Sabbath by special working days.... In the name of the prospect of wind and rain, in the name of dry heat which may spoil the flour, in the name of dew and rot which endanger the fodder, and so on and so forth—in all of these natural disasters I see only an excuse for sullying our working lives with secularism, boorishness and uncultured behaviour....

In the kindergarten and the school there are special ceremonies to mark the beginning of the Sabbath ... the children are full of joy and happiness ... and what a contrast there is between ... the children's reception of the Sabbath on the Friday evening and the parents' deeds on the Saturday: they are off to the harvest in their working clothes, even to work on tractors or with the hoe. The pressure is certainly very great. 'We don't manage', people say. But when have we ever managed? ... The devaluation of the Sabbath rest is a sign of moral, cultural, and social decline. This is the finest, most humane value which we have derived from our Judaism. It is time to put a stop to this phenomenon.[75]

Despite the protests of Baratz and others, the shortage of labour in the kibbutz movement as a whole from the early 1940s onwards brought about a constant erosion of the 'sanctity of the Sabbath' as a day of complete rest for the whole community. Not only were there frequent corvées for special purposes; the Sabbath work schedule was often not very different from that of the week, with the children's houses open as usual, and many branches functioning in accordance with seasonal demands. The social rights of the individual were

[75] J. Baratz, 'On the Sabbath and the "Shabbaton".'

preserved; a record was kept of his work, and he could 'take a Sabbath' when it was convenient. But the community as a whole could scarcely be said to be resting.

In his condemnation of the 'secularization' of the Sabbath, Baratz referred to the *kabbalat shabbat* ('Reception of the Sabbath'). In traditional Judaism this is a religious ceremony, practised in the synagogue or the home at the beginning of the Sabbath, shortly before dark on Friday evening. The Friday evening meal was a special occasion, both in culinary and social terms, from an early period in the development of the kibbutz, but it was devoid of any specific cultural content. In the course of the 1930s, the *kabbalat shabbat* began to acquire a standard form in many of the veteran kibbutzim: there were readings from the Bible, songs connected with the Sabbath, often some reference to a current event or an anniversary. In some places the traditional ceremony of the lighting of the Sabbath candles became part of the tradition.

These cultural forms spread through the kibbutz movement. As appears from Baratz's article, they were first introduced as part of the preparation for the Sabbath in school and kindergarten, and only later adopted by the adult community.[76] This process took place at roughly the same time in a number of kibbutzim, as did the controversy which accompanied it. In an article written in 1938, David Smetterling (Gil'ad), one of the intellectuals of Degania, wrote:

One of the main sources of criticism . . . is the reading of part of the 'weekly portion'[77] from the Bible which opens the *kabbalat shabbat*. . . . But there are certain groups who are unable to digest this custom. They are afraid that it will develop into a religious rite, of the sort which we have worked so hard to avoid. I must reply that the Bible is not a forbidden work because it has religious elements in it. . . . The fact that we preserve our connection with Jewish culture through our Bible readings need not prevent us from using other elements in our own cultural heritage; or, indeed, that of any other people or language.[78]

In many respects, the *kabbalat shabbat* is a paradigm of the changing attitudes towards Jewish tradition in the kibbutz movement. Similar developments can be seen in the case of the festivals. From the first, they formed an acknowledged part of the life of the community; but

[76] Shua and Ben-Gurion, *Sabbath Anthology*, 254–6.
[77] This custom derived from the reading of set chapters from the Bible each week in the synagogue.
[78] Gil'ad, 'On Sabbath Celebrations in Degania'.

they were celebrated primarily as the agricultural festivals which most of them were. Other elements were emphasized in accordance with the cultural needs and predilections of the time: Passover, the time of the Exodus from Egypt, was the Festival of Freedom; Purim, as in the Diaspora, a time for light-hearted merry-making. Here, too, certain trends can be discerned in the whole of the kibbutz movement, though there are many local variations. Each kibbutz created its own tradition; but there was a growing tendency to use traditional Jewish themes, and, often, to learn from other kibbutzim. Thus, until the mid-1930s the Passover Haggada was a local production, entirely humorous in most cases, and with very little reference to the special cultural content of the festival. In 1935, the first 'serious' kibbutz Haggada was written and read (in Giv'at Brenner). This form of production, which still contained many contemporary and local references, but was based on the traditional framework, gradually became standard throughout the kibbutz movement, although it was not until 1943 that the Kibbutz Artzi issued the first all-movement Haggada, to be followed in the next few years by the other movements.[79]

None of this took place in a vacuum. The effort to learn and teach Hebrew as one of the aims of practical Zionism was common to the whole of the labour movement in the Yishuv from the Second Aliya onwards. The *kabbalat shabbat* developed parallel to the *oneg shabbat* ('Sabbath delight') conducted weekly in Tel Aviv by the poet Haim Nahman Bialik, and Bialik himself encouraged his many friends and pupils in the kibbutzim to do likewise. The kibbutz movement was part of the Yishuv, and was deeply influenced by the general cultural atmosphere. None the less, the cultural creations of the kibbutzim were distinctive both in their intimate connection with the community which created them and in the conscious process through which they evolved.

### *The Religious Kibbutzim*[80]

Much of what has been said about cultural activities applies also to the religious kibbutzim. But in their case there was an added dimension. Whereas the Judaism of the non-religious kibbutzim was confined to the cultural sphere, these young men and women constantly strove to express in their way of life their faith in God, and their acceptance of the *halakha*—the precepts of orthodox Judaism. It was taken for

[79] Steiner, 'Kibbutz Haggadot'; Herzog, 'The Kibbutz Hagadah'.
[80] Fishman, 'The Religious Kibbutzim'.

granted that there should be a synagogue in the kibbutz, that food should be kosher, that the Sabbath should be observed according to the strict dictates of the halakha, and so forth.

This basic precept implied a challenge far greater than may appear at first glance. For to be an orthodox kibbutz did not simply mean being a kibbutz, with certain additional ceremonies and rituals. In the Diaspora, Jews had found myriad ways of dealing with the exigencies of everyday life while obeying the halakha. They were not permitted to light fires or switch on electricity during the Sabbath; but those who could afford to employ a *shabbos-goy*[81] could enjoy warmth and light. If they were farmers, they did not have to obey the laws which commanded them to leave the land fallow every seven years, for these laws applied only to the Land of Israel. These options, and many others, were closed to the religious pioneers. Not only could they not afford to employ others to do work which their religion forbade them to do, but they believed themselves to be laying the foundations of an independent Jewish state: if that state were, as they wished, to be based on the *halakha*, they must find ways of life and work which did not depend on others. So many of the traditional solutions of the Diaspora, which depended on the symbiosis of Jew and non-Jew, would not work. There were committees for religious affairs both in each settlement and at the level of the central movement. Some of their members had studied for the rabbinate, and were able to suggest their own solutions; but, in each case, they turned to rabbinical authorities outside the kibbutz for confirmation of their ideas.

Here are some examples of practical problems and their solutions.[82] Some of the most vital questions were connected with security: could kibbutz members bear weapons, ride horses, fill sandbags, and use radio sets for communication, on Sabbaths and festivals? In a way, these were the easiest problems to solve in the framework of the halakha. By the use of the halakhic principle that 'the saving of life takes precedence over the Sabbath', it was established that in circumstances of immediate or potential danger to life, it was permitted to take part in defensive operations, including all those mentioned above. The people of Tirat Zvi, a tower and stockade kibbutz, said their Sabbath prayers at their posts, but did not hesitate to

---

[81] A 'sabbath gentile'; one employed to do work forbidden to Jews on the Sabbath.
[82] Not all these problems had been solved during the period under discussion here, but they illustrate a process which began with the first religious *plugot*.

continue their preparations for the coming attack or to resist it when it came. A similar approach was applied to the maintenance of the infrastructure of the kibbutz: water, electricity, and the like. Although the use of electricity by the individual on the Sabbath was severely restricted, as in any orthodox household, it was agreed that health and security dictated that the settlement should be assured of these basic requirements.

Agricultural problems were more difficult to solve. The problem of milking on the Sabbath was at first one of the most intractable. The solution adopted by the orthodox farmers of the Yishuv, employing non-Jews, was clearly unacceptable. So was that suggested by certain rabbis, to milk the cows in order to prevent their suffering, and throw the milk away. Instead, they adopted a solution suggested by a German rabbi, and agreed to by the chief rabbi of Tel Aviv: they milked into a pail containing food, and ate the resulting porridge themselves. This was clearly only a temporary solution, however, for it could not hold for a large, modern dairy herd. Investigation of halakhic sources led to another practice, adopted in 1942: the milk was poured into pails containing chlorophyll. This made it unsuitable for drinking, but it could be used for cheese and other dairy products. It was only in 1950, with the technological progress of the branch, that a solution was adopted which still holds today: machinery (and, of late, automation) enables the cows to be milked without direct contact with the cowman.

Similar problems arose in the matter of the injunction to leave the land fallow every seventh year. In its early stages the religious kibbutz movement saw no alternative but to go along with the procedure of the orthodox establishment, which has been followed ever since: to permit the Jews to cultivate the land through its fictitious sale to a non-Jew. The ultra-orthodox kibbutzim of the Agudat Israel movement were not satisfied with this solution. They developed a system of hydroponic agriculture, which enabled them to grow certain crops while leaving the land uncultivated.

In these and many other instances, rabbinical authority was sought and given, although in some cases there were rabbis who found the solution unacceptable. But at all stages the workers, ideologists, and halakhic experts of the religious kibbutz movement were active in seeking and promoting ways of procedure which would enable them to lead a secure, economically sound, and socially stable way of life in accordance with halakhic principles.

Thus, by a combination of ingenious interpretation and re-interpretation of the *halakha*, technological innovation, and, not infrequently, compromise, the religious kibbutz evolved a way of life which enabled them to live as orthodox Jews, to develop a thriving agricultural and, later, industrial economy, and to create a model for a modern, efficient, and self-sufficient orthodox Jewish society. And, in fact, many of the solutions which they evolved were subsequently adapted to the wider framework of the State of Israel; for instance, in the standing orders of the Israeli army on observance of the Sabbath.

## Education[83]

The organizational pattern of child care established in the Second and Third Aliya continued to be the basis of kibbutz education throughout this period. The babies' house and 'toddlers' group' in early childhood were succeeded by the kindergarten, until the beginning of formal schooling at the age of six. There was, however, one important difference between the early *kvutzot* and the kibbutzim of the middle and late 1930s: during the 1930s the number of children in proportion to adults grew apace. In the formative period of kibbutz education, child care would normally be the responsibility of a known and trusted member of the community, herself usually a mother, who would work with the children on a regular basis and thereby gain their trust and confidence. From the 1930s onwards, however, child care was subject to all the strains of the manpower situation in the kibbutzim: the task was often given to young and inexperienced women who had to gain the requisite skills in the course of their work, and sometimes at the cost of the children.

In later years, many of the children recalled some of the results of this situation. In some kibbutzim they were compelled to eat according to the dictates of the *metapelet*, and punished for non-compliance. In others, there were open conflicts between parents and *metapelot*. Young, inexperienced child workers found it difficult to deal with the fears engendered by the night in the children's house. It was even harder to cope with the psychological strain to which both they and the children were subject when the kibbutz or its neighbours was under attack, or when parents were absent. One woman remembered the nursery in Giv'at Brenner:

[83] R. Porat, *Together but on our Own.*

There was no light at night, it was quite dark ... I shall never forget the call of the jackals, and the rhythmic sound of the Arabs' water-pump ... We were all scared, all the children ... the woman on night duty used to go around with a torch, and that also scared us, for it cast great long shadows. When one of the children cried, she would come in with her torch, and it made all sorts of frightening patterns ... it was being together with other children that gave us a sense of security ... when I was scared, I used to do all sorts of things to wake up my neighbour. Her being there made me feel more secure than the nightwatch woman did.

The same woman tells of her fears after a fire in the kibbutz. She was given some sort of tranquillizer, but made to feel ashamed of her emotions, which she thereafter managed to conquer and conceal. But when one of the kibbutz members was killed by a mine, all of her fears returned, together with those of the other children.

Do you think anyone talked to me about it? It's as if it was a forbidden subject. I had a wonderful mother, and I told her of my fears. But she also didn't discuss it with me, just listened to what I had to say. And after the incident of the fire, I wouldn't talk to the *metapelet* about it ... [After an attack on a funeral during the riots] we stood on the wall, and watched, and suddenly heard the shots. The nursery teacher suddenly shouted 'Get under the beds' ... We saw the guards coming home, bent double: imagine it, people were killed, there was a funeral, shots, people crawling home, lights out—and nobody said a word to us! Talk about death was taboo. We were scared, but we didn't dare to talk about it.[84]

Clearly, such incidents were due in large part to the adults' own difficulties in coping with situations of physical hardship and danger. But they also stemmed from the lack of experience of child care of both workers and parents. In many cases they had no other way of dealing with harassing situations, and an unfamiliar educational structure, than by reverting to the social ethos which they themselves had learnt as children. It was only in the late 1930s that the kibbutz movements began to develop a network of experienced and, increasingly, professional advisers to help in such situations. And on the whole the child care system worked well, and was not subject to serious revision until the early 1960s, when the question of where the children were to sleep at night became an important issue.

In the course of the 1930s the tripartite division of the school system according to kibbutz movements became firmly established. The 'Educational Institute' of the Kibbutz Artzi at Mishmar Ha'emek

[84] Ramot, *The Adventures of a Bell*, 164, 171, 173–4.

was at first the only school in the movement. When it was established in 1931, its twenty-seven pupils, ranging in age from 5 to 8, were the total school population of the movement. Gradually, each kibbutz began to establish its own school for the younger age-groups, and by 1939 there were six such schools. The Institute now began at fifth grade level (age 10); and, as the number of older children in the local schools grew, this was eventually raised to the seventh grade (age 12).

According to the original conception of the founders of the Educational Institute, one such school was to have served the whole of the Kibbutz Artzi. Until 1940, the relative proximity of the movement's kibbutzim enabled this arrangement to proceed smoothly. But, as the number of children in more distant kibbutzim grew, it proved necessary to create similar institutions in different areas, thus ensuring closer contact between the children, their educators, and their home kibbutzim. As the movement expanded geographically, so did the number of educational institutes, each serving from two to five kibbutzim in a given area. By 1948 there were six such institutes.[85]

Apart from the Kibbutz Artzi, none of the kibbutz movements established boarding schools for their children. In the Kibbutz Me'uhad, the general tendency was to establish a school in each kibbutz, and by 1945 there were nine such schools. The size of the kibbutzim, the number of their children, and their constant effort to increase their populations—by the absorption both of adult members and of Youth Aliya groups—ensured a sufficient critical mass to make such schools viable, and in many cases to absorb children from smaller kibbutzim in the neighbourhood. This tendency was reinforced by Segal's theory of the importance of integrating the school in the kibbutz community, which spread throughout the movement during the 1930s; and, although Segal himself dealt mainly with problems of the primary school, this doctrine was generally interpreted to include the high-school level also. The exception was the joint school of Ein Harod and Tel Yosef, which for a short period also served children from the neighbouring Geva (of Hever Hakvutzot).

In Hever Hakvutzot, in whose kibbutzim there were rarely enough children to form an autonomous school, there was little alternative to continuing the tradition which had been set in the Jordan Valley in the 1920s and relying on co-operation between neighbouring kibbutzim. During the 1930s there were a number of examples of district schools in which kibbutzim of both Hever Hakvutzot and the Kibbutz

[85] *Hedim*, 58 (July 1958), 3.

Me'uhad, and even of the ideologically more separatist Kibbutz Artzi, participated; but none of them survived the political tensions of the late 1930s and early 1940s. Degania and Kinneret's joint school came to function as a common primary school for the whole of the Jordan Valley. In 1940 a separate high school was established, also supplying the needs of all the kibbutzim in the area.

The district school was a realistic solution for the settlements of Hever Hakvutzot in the Jordan Valley, where they were relatively numerous. Several of its kibbutzim were both small in numbers and isolated. Most were able to keep a local primary school in existence, though often with great difficulty; but at both primary and secondary level they were forced to make a series of attempts at co-operation with neighbouring kibbutzim, many of which were bedevilled by political tensions. It was only in the 1950s that a general solution was found, with the establishment of a number of district high schools in a wider movement framework.

One important addition to the structure of kibbutz education came about in 1940, with the foundation of the Kibbutz Teachers' Seminary in Tel Aviv. Created and run by leading educationalists from all three movements, it aimed to provide a cadre of teachers and *metaplot* at all levels who would combine academic training with understanding of the special nature of kibbutz society and education.

In all three movements there was a continued preoccupation with what may be called social education, which can be traced back to the very earliest discussions of educational questions within the kibbutz movement. In all varieties of kibbutz education, the concept of the 'children's community' was of crucial importance, though the form it took depended on local circumstances and movement background. In some schools, virtually all the extracurricular activities, from the children's farm to the celebration of Sabbaths and festivals, were run by the children, organized in general meeting and committees modelled exactly on the adult kibbutz. In others, the model was the youth movement, with the leader as a central figure in the children's social activities. In the early 1930s one of the questions discussed by the management of the Mishmar Ha'emek Institute was how to ensure that the pupils should take part in youth movement activities without their clashing with the very intensive life of work, learning, and social interaction directed by the teachers and *metaplot*. The solution was to create a branch of the Hashomer Hatzair movement within the school, whose youth leaders would be the older children. In the 1930s, the elder children of both the other movements created local branches of the Noar Oved youth movement, as the natural framework for their extracurricular activities. It gradually became apparent that educational programmes and activities suited to the town children who were the majority of the movement's members were not necessarily suited to kibbutz youth. In the early 1950s both these movements created special divisions for the children of kibbutzim, formally affiliated to the Noar Oved but in practice largely independent.

## Patterns of Consumption[86]

From the first, the distribution of material goods and services within the kibbutz was based on the principle 'to each according to his needs', within the limits permitted by the community's economic situation. For many years this limitation ensured that the definition of 'needs' was minimal. Clean clothing was taken from the communal laundry as needed, with no regard to individual preference or even size. The minor necessities of life—soap, toothpaste, and the like—were also distributed 'at need'. Furniture was minimal, often primitive and home-made. The individual's consciousness of the economic situation was held to ensure that his demands would not be exaggerated. In the first years of Degania, a box was placed in the dining-hall in which the treasurer would put small sums from time to time in case any of the members felt a special need which was not fulfilled in the ordinary way. For periods of months the money remained untouched.

The asceticism of the early days was not a matter of principle, though in many cases it fitted the character and predilections of the members. It sprang from the economic realities of the time. As the standard of living of the Yishuv gradually rose, and the economic basis of the kibbutzim became firmer, the minimal definition of needs became increasingly problematic. For instance, as the standard of clothing rose, the principle that all clothes belonged to all members was seen to be both unaesthetic and wasteful. It was modified first by classifying the clothes roughly according to size, and then by ensuring that each member had a set of clothes of his own.

These changes did not come about easily, for by the 1920s the principle of 'communal consumption' had become one of the central tenets of kibbutz ideology. Any change, such as a decision to build

---

[86] Ronen, 'Changes in the Gratification of Individual Needs'.

individual shelves and mark each person's clothes, was seen by some as the beginning of the end of the kibbutz.[87] Eventually, however, all kibbutzim adopted this system. They learnt by experience that, after the very earliest period of complete identification of the individual with the community, many members who neglected and wasted the resources of the community were more considerate of their own property. Clothes and other material goods were distributed 'according to need'; and the degree of need was assessed by the person in charge of the relevant store, the treasurer or the secretary. As the kibbutzim grew in size and in the variety of their members' requirements, this system too was seen to be problematic. The description of arbitrary allocation of goods in Hulda in the 1930s in Chapter 7, above, is no doubt coloured by the personal experiences of the author. But it points to a problem inherent in the principle 'to each according to his needs': the difficulty of making an objective assessment of the needs of the individual at any but the most rudimentary level, and the danger of arbitrary decisions by the elected officials of the community. In the bigger kibbutzim, attempts were made to tackle this problem at a very early stage by putting decision-making into the hands of committees, rather than individuals. But here, too, there was much room for disagreement and arbitrary judgement. During the 1930s, with the general rise in the standard of living of the Yishuv and the comparative prosperity of the kibbutzim, there was increased pressure to raise standards of consumption, and further erosion of the tacit agreement to keep them to a minimum. In response to these pressures, an attempt was made to introduce an objective standard of individual needs: the norm. In its first manifestation, this was a standard of clothing to which each member was entitled. When a particular article wore out, or was spoilt or lost, it was replaced. The global budget of the clothing store was based on an assessment of the needs for new clothes and replacement, in order that all the members should have a standard level of clothing.

This did not apply to all consumer goods. Such things as toilet necessities were originally distributed according to need: each member received soap, razor blades, etc., according to perceived need. When experience showed that this system tended to be wasteful, a different sort of norm—a weekly or monthly allocation, of standard quality and quantity—was introduced. Housing was allocated according to a rough criterion of need, with higher standards for married couples

[87] For example, in Kvutzat Hasharon in the early 1930s; Tsur *et al.*, 306–7.

and older people than for the young and unmarried.

All the problems so far mentioned are, in a sense, intrinsic to the kibbutz system. Others have an external source. During the 1930s members began to receive gifts in kind and money from friends and relatives, or to use for their own purposes resources which they had obtained outside the kibbutz. In some of its manifestations, this phenomenon was manageable. Gifts of clothing could be taken into account when estimating the degree to which the individual's possessions conformed to the norm. But, even so, they were a disturbing factor; in a period when kibbutzim were buying clothes wholesale, usually in a standard cut (sometimes even standard colour) for the sake of economy, they were a constant reminder of the gap in material standards between the kibbutz and the outside world, and a stimulus to attempt to close it, perhaps even at a cost to the economic welfare of the community as a whole.

'Private money' was much more difficult to deal with. As early as 1929 it was being discussed, and condemned, in several kibbutzim. Two years later one of the leaders of the Kibbutz Me'uhad said: 'Private money in the kibbutz is illegal. It has stolen into the kibbutz. In its early stage it was of no importance; the men of the Second Aliya used to send back any money which their parents sent them.... Gradually we have reached a state in which private money is a serious phenomenon.'[88] There is no evidence that this phenomenon subsequently disappeared at any period, though estimates of its seriousness may vary. One reason for this is the inherent difficulty in tracing its existence; unlike clothes and other material objects, small amounts of money, and even private bank accounts, are not immediately obvious in the course of daily life. There are, perhaps, deeper reasons for the failure to tackle the problem effectively over the years: the feeling that the degree of inequality it occasions is trivial compared with the overall egalitarianism of kibbutz society; and, above all, the suspicion that the needs which are thus fulfilled are not necessarily illegitimate, even though the kibbutz cannot fulfil them at the time. Typical of this attitude is a remark made at the Kibbutz Me'uhad conference in 1936: 'We must take care of the members' minor needs, and we have still not stopped treating them as unimportant. We cannot fight against private money as long as we have not freed the individual from the need to worry about these needs by himself.'[89]

---

[88] *Mibifnim* (Nov. 1931). Quoted by Ronen, 'Changes in Gratification', 30.
[89] *Eleventh Council*, 78.

Although questions of consumption receded into the background from 1936 to 1945, when absolute priority was given to military affairs, there is plenty of evidence to show that many of the trends already noted gained momentum during this period.[90] In particular, the lack of time and inclination on the part of the kibbutz authorities to deal with matters which were considered to be relatively unimportant at a time of national emergency led to a widespread increase in 'private arrangements' for providing items neglected by the official system. The cumulative effect of this process was, according to one estimate (no doubt tendentious) that 70 to 80 per cent of the veteran members of the kibbutz movement had to rely on outside sources in order to reach the accepted standard.[91] It was only after the Second World War that these issues became the subject of a widespread public debate in all the kibbutz movements.

[90] Ronen, 'Changes in Gratification', 34–43.
[91] *Hedim*, 3/4 (Sept. 1947); and cf. Kibbutz Me'uhad, *Eleventh Council*, 79.

# 11

# *Comments and Conclusions*

THIS chapter will sum up the processes and events described in the previous pages, and analyse them at a rather more general level.

## ECONOMICS

One of the chief motives of the founders of the early kibbutzim, and a prime condition for their survival, was the ability to make a living without reliance on charity. This motif was a constant factor in their ideology and practice throughout these years.

On the evidence available from this period, it is difficult to assess to what extent they were successful. The conditions which shaped the kibbutz were not those of competitive capitalism. Settlements were founded on unproductive and insufficient land, and had to be worked under conditions of physical insecurity. Working capital was hard to come by, and often obtained at rates of interest far higher than are normally considered appropriate for agriculture. New settlers had to learn their trade while earning their keep. Consequently, the simplistic view of the early period—that economic success could be achieved by hard work alone—was replaced by more realistic views. It came to be acknowledged that without considerable investment— in land purchase and improvement, irrigation, housing, equipment, and the means of survival in the early years of settlement—no form of colonization could succeed. Settlers without capital, whether in kibbutz or moshav, had to turn to outside sources for loans that would be repaid when their economies had become firmly established. The degree to which such aid was granted depended largely on factors such as the fortunes of the Zionist movement and the political complexion of its leadership.

Some estimate can nevertheless be attempted. In terms of technological development, whether measured in mechanization, crop yields, or efficient use of manpower, the kibbutz was a progressive force in the economy of the Yishuv. In purely financial terms, the kibbutz economy showed considerable skill in adapting to changing conditions, surviving periods of economic contraction as in the mid-1920s and late 1930s and exploiting the intervening boom period of the mid-1930s. By the mid-1930s the debts of the veteran settlements were consolidated with the help of the national funds, and they began repaying their debts. This must certainly be counted an economic success. But only three or four years later, many of them began to amass further debts in order to cover the extra expenses which arose from absorption and defence. It seems that there was a contradiction between the aspiration of the kibbutz to serve the nation and its function as a purely economic enterprise.

One reason why the kibbutzim were prepared to incur such financial risks was that, perhaps subconsciously, they relied on the backing of the Zionist authorities. From a very early stage, the Zionist movement (later the Jewish Agency) accepted the ultimate financial responsibility for settlement and other national aims such as defence. The contribution of the settlers themselves in hard work, self-sacrifice, creativity, and the constant acquisition of know-how was certainly of prime importance, however. The combination of these pioneering values with national capital was the key to the survival and economic progress of the kibbutzim.

## SOCIAL DEVELOPMENTS

In some respects, kibbutz society changed fundamentally during these years. The individual kibbutz was no longer the uncomplicated social organism of the Second Aliya, with its simple, face-to-face relationships. All, including those described as 'small' or 'intimate', had grown and become institutionalized, with at least the rudiments of a network of committees and elected officials similar to that of the biggest kibbutzim. To no small extent, Lavi's concept of the 'big *kvutza*' had been adopted by the whole of the kibbutz movement.

That a single kibbutz was unable to exist without the support of outside bodies such as the Zionist movement and the Histadrut had been clear from a very early stage. The 1930s added another element—the kibbutz movement, which was now seen to be part of the essential backing needed for the individual community. There was also the modest beginning of practical co-operation between the kibbutz movements, with the establishment of *Brit Hat'nua Hakibbutzit* (the Kibbutz Movement Association); but the emphasis remained on the three main kibbutz movements, each with its own youth movement and political connections. Here again was a degree of institutionalization scarcely dreamt of by the founders of the early *kvutzot*.

Culturally, the kibbutzim had developed far beyond the wild *hora*-dancing of the early days. Creative artists living in the kibbutz whose subject-matter was the lives of their own community had produced and published their first works in the fields of literature, graphic art, and folk song and dance. The typical expression of kibbutz culture, however, was in the everyday conversation of its members, the local news-sheets, wall- and oral newspapers—all of them in the Hebrew language, adopted by generations of immigrants, often after the investment of very strenuous efforts; in the weekly celebrations of the Sabbath, now becoming a regular feature in many kibbutzim; and in the annual cycle of Jewish and nature holidays, in new forms and ceremonies which were often adopted by the Yishuv as a whole. Not all of the kibbutz movement answered to the ideal of an 'intellectual proletariat'; but this ideal was widely adopted, and realized in many instances.

Cultural activity is connected intimately with education, and the association with the youth movement is one of the most unique and characteristic features of kibbutz society. It not only ensured demographic continuity and growth, but also guaranteed that the great majority of kibbutz members underwent a process of selection and training which would ensure their acceptance of the kibbutz ethos. A natural continuation of this process was the evolution of a unique system of child care and education designed to ensure that those born on the kibbutz would continue the same tradition.

In summing up these changes, one must ask whether the very different society of the late 1930s was faithful to the principles of the tiny communal groups of the Second Aliya. On the whole, the answer is affirmative. This was a largely egalitarian and democratic society whose members were hard-working, creative, and ready for a high degree of self-sacrifice in order to advance the interests of the Yishuv and the Jewish people as they saw them; and among its aims were such specific imperatives of the Second Aliya as the 'conquest of labour' and the rejection of any form of exploitation. It had many blemishes: the 'ideal relationships' of the early *kvutzot* had been replaced by a much broader, often more superficial, social nexus; there was a degree of inequality, both economically, in such matters as 'private money', and socially, in the differing degrees of influence as between individuals and social groupings. Moreover, the very growth of the kibbutz unit, and its interdependence with the movement and its institutions, meant that representational, rather than direct, democracy was practised at several levels. The general picture, however, is of a society faithful to the elevated ideals evolved a quarter of a century earlier, and striving to apply them in arduous and rapidly changing conditions.

### THE KIBBUTZ AND THE OUTSIDE WORLD: IDEOLOGICAL VARIANTS

Much of this book has been concerned with the relationship between the kibbutz and the world around it. This question was virtually always considered in the context of Zionism. It was a basic assumption of all the kibbutz movements that the anomalous situation of the Jewish people could be solved only by a return to the Land of Israel, and that the major task of the kibbutz was to take part in this enterprise. The implications of this standpoint for relationships with the British and the Arabs were matters of political controversy; but the justice and desirability of Zionism were not questioned. There were occasions when it appeared as if there was a conflict between the interests of Zionism and those of socialism as then conceived of— particularly in relation to the Soviet Union. Under these circumstances, the leaders of the kibbutz movement almost invariably chose Zionism;[1] and the major exception, the left wing of Gedud Ha'avoda, was remembered long after as a dire warning of the dangers of deviation. As for the socialist way of life of the kibbutz community, all the kibbutz movements maintained that it was both an end in itself and a means for waging the struggle for the fulfilment of Zionism more efficiently.

The situation of the kibbutz movement in 1939 exemplifies these themes most dramatically. When Zionism, and its practical application in the form of agricultural colonization, was under physical attack, the kibbutzim changed their way of life, their criteria for settlement, and the demands which they made of their members, in accordance with the new national priorities. They began to speak and think of their communal way of life, with its social solidarity, inner discipline, and adaptability, as a major advantage in the organization of

[1] Ben-Avram, 'The Kibbutz as a Zionist Phenomenon'.

settlements under siege—as, indeed, it was. And they applied to matters of defence the same devotion and ingenuity which they had previously shown in tackling economic and social problems.

Although the general formula according to which kibbutz life was both end and means commanded general agreement, the kibbutz movements were far from unanimous on questions concerning the relationship between the kibbutz and the outside world. The main approaches to this question can be grouped roughly in five clusters: those in which the kibbutz is viewed as a model; kibbutz holism; kibbutz Marxism; variants of the idea of pioneering; and the approaches which emphasize the educational functions of the kibbutz.[2]

## Models

The early *kvutzot* maintained that they were attempting to create an exemplary society. The individual kibbutz aims at perfection in the relationships between its members, in economic matters, and in its social and cultural activities. If it is successful, others will do likewise. Joseph Baratz said in 1923: 'Our way of life is suitable for the masses— and, indeed, for all mankind. But ... it is obvious that the masses ... are not yet suited to communal life.' When historical conditions produced a generation which could live up to its standards, it would become a model for others to copy.[3]

## Holism

The first reasoned alternative to the concept of the model is one which I have labelled kibbutz holism: the belief that the kibbutz can and must expand until it comprises the whole of the Yishuv. The classical statement of this view was in Gedud Ha'avoda's aspiration to create a 'general commune of all the Jewish workers of the Land of Israel'; but it underlies many of the declarations and actions of the Kibbutz Me'uhad throughout this period. Though today such an aim may seem ludicrously overambitious, in periods of rapid expansion such as the Third Aliya or the late 1930s it certainly did not look like an impossible dream.

Holism was couched in the prophetic mode: it was both a forecast of the future and an expression of approval of that future. But it also

---

[2] For a fuller treatment of this subject see Near, 'Paths to Utopia', on which this section is largely based.

[3] Shatz, *On the Edge of Silence*, 92, 98. Baratz, as reported in Katznelson, *The Kvutza*, 19.

existed purely as a value judgement: not that the kibbutz would necessarily encompass the whole of society, but that it should. This view was encapsulated in Tabenkin's punning phrase: the moshav (and, *a fortiori*, other, less desirable, forms of settlement) must enjoy equality of rights (*shivyon z'khuyot*); but it should not be viewed with equanimity (*shivyon nefesh*).[4] In this version of holism, the reinforcement and expansion of the kibbutz are the only permissible aim. All of its relationships with the outside world—in politics, in the educational sphere, in the struggle for government support—are directed to this end. This attitude underlay many of the claims of the kibbutz, and particularly of the Kibbutz Me'uhad, to priority in such matters as allocating land for settlement, capital loans, etc.

Throughout the interwar period the very existence of these concepts was a source of strength to the kibbutz movement. Under conditions of poverty, political weakness, and military danger, the vision and forecast of an all-kibbutz society created a confidence which was certainly not self-evidently grounded in the real situation of the kibbutz.

## Kibbutz Marxism

Three classical doctrines can be described as 'kibbutz Marxism'. In the Kibbutz Me'uhad's interpretation of constructive socialism, the class struggle was expressed in competition between various social forms—the kibbutz, the moshav, the town, and the *moshava*. The revolution would consist in the victory of the kibbutz—in other words, the elimination of all other social forms. The Kibbutz Artzi's 'theory of stages' accepted the need for a proletarian revolution as prophesied by Marx, but postponed it until after the completion of the 'constructive stage' of Zionism. Towards the end of its Zionist phase, the left wing of Gedud Ha'avoda defined the chief task of the kibbutz as political education and organization, while its social and economic activities were to provide a material basis for this revolutionary activity. The kibbutz was an avantgarde in the classical political sense of the term—a Leninist revolutionary party.

The Leninist view disappeared with the Gedud, to return at a much later date. The other two versions of kibbutz Marxism were still current in 1939.

[4] Yitzhak Tabenkin, in an interview with Baruch Ben-Avram and the author, May 1971. Tabenkin claimed that these words appear in his published works, but I have been unable to verify the reference.

## Pioneering

There are several variants of the idea of pioneering (*halutziut*). This concept was derived from an incident described in the Book of Joshua, when the vanguard (*halutzim*) 'went before the host' at the siege of Jericho (Joshua vi: 8–13). In 1932, one of the leaders of the Kibbutz Me'uhad said: 'We are not teachers or leaders. We are merely pioneers, going along the road before the host.'[5] Here, the kibbutz is conceived of as a forerunner of the new society, doing on a small scale today what the whole of the people, moved by the ineluctable forces of history, will do in the future. Close to this view, though not identical with it, is the idea that the kibbutz is a growth point. 'The pioneering cells of the new society' will 'create the core of the future socialist economy'.[6] They seek 'new spiritual sources, and arouse hidden cultural forces which will be the basis of the new society'.[7] In a third interpretation, the pioneer does not go before the host, but at its head: showing the masses not necessarily where they will go, but where they should go. In other words, the kibbutz was thought to have a function of leadership, even outside the Marxist avantgardist context.[8] This view was to be found in Hashomer Hatzair and in certain parts of the Kibbutz Me'uhad.

Radically different from these approaches is one put forward by Ben-Gurion in 1924: 'To be a pioneer means not demanding rights, but amassing duties.' An extreme version of this view is the saying, widely in use in the 1930s and considered an expression of pride, that the current generation of pioneers is 'dung for future generations!'[9] Pioneering in this interpretation is not leadership but service.

In light of the experience of the tower and stockade period this last version of the pioneer concept became dominant in the whole of the labour movement. But the others remained, sometimes side by side with it, but often in contexts where the meaning was ambiguous.

## Education

The special relationship with youth and the youth movement was a central part of the ideology of the Kibbutz Artzi from its earliest days.

---

[5] Bar-Yehuda, *Mibifnim* (7 Dec. 1932), 12.

[6] *Ideological Premises of the Kibbutz Artzi*, 1927, sec. 3.

[7] Horowitz, 'Kibbutz and Party', 279.

[8] Benari, *Mibifnim*, 16 (1927), 338.

[9] Katznelson-Shazar, *Words of Working Women*, 189; and cf. Tsur *et al.*, *The Beginning of the Kibbutz*, 199.

The other movements reached similar practical conclusions, but on different ideological grounds. Those kibbutzim or kibbutz movements, such as Gedud Ha'avoda, which broke off their connection with the youth movement soon entered into a decline; and from the time of the birth of the first child in Degania, questions of child care and education were perceived as central to the survival of the kibbutz.

The spirit of this education can perhaps best be gauged by contrast with a statement by one of the leaders of the Kibbutz Me'uhad: 'Our pioneering education will not be wasted, even in the case of those who cannot join the kibbutz for various reasons. It will make them faithful to the realization of Zionism and Socialism, and give them respect for and understanding of co-operative living wherever it may be.'[10] This was said by a man who was considered to be something of a maverick in his own movement, and his point of view certainly did not command general assent in any of the kibbutz movements or the pioneering youth movements in this period. On the contrary: they demanded that all their graduates join the kibbutz, and condemned those who left as 'deserters', or 'educational failures'. The social theory which underlay their educational practice was kibbutz holism, or the overriding importance of strengthening the kibbutz as a social or political avantgarde.

## POLITICS

All the kibbutz movements saw their political activities as one way of ensuring their own interests: in particular, advancing their claims to land for settlement, and supporting their youth movements. Such an attitude was inherent in each of the ideological stances enumerated above; for there was general agreement, both within the kibbutz movement and outside it, on the congruence between the interests of the kibbutz and those of the nation as a whole.

Other elements in the politics of the kibbutz movements were parallel to different concepts of the nature of pioneering. Two variants correspond to the idea of pioneering as service: non-commitment, as advocated by most in the veteran *kvutzot* and by many of the senior members of the Kibbutz Me'uhad; and the view that kibbutz members—and, in particular, the representatives and emissaries of

[10] Liebenstein (Livneh), *Mibifnim*, 42 (Aug. 1929), 13.

the kibbutz movements—should work to strengthen the party they supported. This was undoubtedly the dominant view among those party leaders who were not themselves kibbutz members.

Most of the other variants of kibbutz politics derived from the concept of pioneering as leadership. They were the kibbutz party, as exemplified by Gedud Ha'avoda and the Kibbutz Artzi (with certain semantic and organizational reservations); the kibbutz-dominated party, of which the only example at this stage was the Socialist League; and the kibbutz faction, through which the movement attempted to influence the party within which it operated—Gordonia in the early 1930s, until it adopted a politics of service, and the Kibbutz Me'uhad from roughly 1932 onwards. In 1939 the Kibbutz Me'uhad was in the process of evolving another variant, the kibbutz-dominated faction—exemplified in Faction B until its expulsion from Mapai in 1944.

By 1939 the kibbutz movements themselves had assessed the effectiveness of most of these approaches. In practice if not in principle, the politics of interest was widespread. But this did not mean that the other viewpoints were automatically abandoned. The model of the kibbutz party had been universally rejected—by general agreement in the case of Gedud Ha'avoda, implicitly by the Kibbutz Artzi with the foundation of the Socialist League—and the Kibbutz Artzi was developing a kibbutz-dominated party as its major form of political activity. The concept of the faction, too, had been tried and rejected, though for more than one reason: by Gordonia because it no longer had a distinctive policy of its own within Mapai; and by the Kibbutz Me'uhad for both ideological and pragmatic reasons—ideologically, because its leaders needed to combat the accusations of separatism and self-interest involved in their position; pragmatically, because they needed allies within the party if they were to promote their policies.

Viewed objectively, it is difficult to sum up the comparative effectiveness of these approaches, except to say that the concept of politics as interest was both effective and justified as long as there was a general consensus—even if not in the Yishuv as a whole, certainly in its majority parties—on the national importance of the kibbutz. In one sense, the kibbutz movements did Mapai little service; its members served the party only in relatively minor positions, and do not seem to have been particularly effective. It is already possible to see the effects of the 'service' doctrine in the mobilization of talented young kibbutz members to positions in the Histadrut and Mapai: among others, Joseph Baratz, Pinhas Lubianiker (Lavon), and Yitzhak Ben-Aharon in Mapai, and Levi Shkolnik (Eshkol) in the Histadrut. But at this stage, it was still too early to assess the effect of these appointments. In another sense, however, the very fact that the kibbutzim, with the national prestige they had acquired in the days of tower and stockade settlement, acted within the political framework of the labour movement undoubtedly enhanced that movement's influence in the Yishuv and Zionist circles in general.

One point may be made in conclusion. The attempt to ensure that the kibbutz movement should play an independent and active part in national politics, by whatever method, undoubtedly deepened and perpetuated differences between movements whose origins were in quite different spheres. No doubt the state of the world and the Zionist movement made some such development unavoidable. But from the point of view of the development of the kibbutz, it was divisive and, as we shall see in the coming volume, in the long run almost destructive.

## REFLECTIONS

Thirty years is a long enough time to enable us to discern historical trends and attempt to assess underlying influences in the development of the kibbutz movement. I shall therefore conclude this summary with a number of reflections on some more general questions which arise from the events described and analysed above.

One of the questions most frequently asked about the kibbutz is whether its practice is derived from ideology or from pragmatic considerations. In my analysis of the events of the Second Aliya I maintained that there is no simple answer: the founders of the early kibbutzim were motivated by a clear set of principles and values, but had no detailed ideology of communal life or blueprint for their future society. In later years this changed. The youth movement graduates who formed the bulk of the kibbutz movement from the early 1920s onwards had very clear ideas about what the kibbutz should be, and these were derived from well-defined ideological systems.

None the less, these systems too were more open-ended than might appear from an examination of the views of these young people, who often came from the Diaspora with a fully formed world-view. One of the reasons for this was the gap between ideal and reality, whether between the ideals of youth and the practice of maturity, or between an idealized version of the Land of Israel and the land itself. One major historical example is the meeting between the first graduates of Gordonia, with their exalted concept of the *kvutza*, and the real *kvutzot*; but each generation of youth movement graduates—including those who have had personal contact with kibbutzim—is familiar with this phenomenon.[11]

In every generation a number of those who found the real kibbutz different from their ideal became disillusioned and left. Those who remained did not automatically abandon their ideas when their original applications were seen to be unrealistic or dysfunctional. They engaged in a complex process of adaptation to reality while preserving much of their ideology.

One result of this process was a phenomenon which recurred often in the history of the kibbutz, and which I shall call, for lack of a less ungainly phrase, the ideologization of the improvised. It is often said that in the Yishuv and Israel there is nothing as permanent as the temporary. The factor I am describing is a variant of this rule. An action or institution which was originally a pragmatic solution to a particular problem was not only perpetuated by repetition; it was sanctified (in secular terms) by use. The creation of the system of child care and the institutionalization of the *metapelet*, and the 'communal sleeping' of children are but two instances among many. Indeed, according to one version, the kibbutz itself originated as the result of the operation of this factor, which perpetuated and gave ideological backing to a pragmatic solution to the problems of the conquest of labour. I do not believe that it is possible to generalize to the whole of the kibbutz movement in this way; but it is certain that this process was at work in the thoughts and actions of such people as Miriam and Joseph Baratz, who came to the *kvutza* with no preconceived theory of communal life, but were converted in the course of their experience. Since these young people's cast of thought tended to emphasize the universal implications of their everyday actions, neither innovation nor continuity was held to be warranted without ideological justification; hence the ideologization of their improvisations.

Ideologies were not formed in a vacuum, however. The congruence between variations in the political and cultural background of the kibbutz movements (and particularly the youth movements) and their

[11] Near, 'Utopian and Post-Utopian Thought'.

overt ideologies has often been pointed out in this volume. In many cases, the conflicts can be interpreted as a secular variant of *cuius regio eius religio*; and, even without the sanction of ideology, differences in culture (including political culture) between kibbutzim of different national origins recurred throughout the history of the kibbutz movement. The differences between youth movements in Eastern and Western Europe, dissensions on the nature of movement democracy, clashes on absorption policy, the growing political division in the Kibbutz Me'uhad—all these were justified and rationalized on an ideological level; but they were all ultimately connected with the national origins of the different sectors of the kibbutz movement.

None the less, the very fact that all of these sectors adopted a similar way of life points to a basic unity of ideology and attitudes. Many specific solutions to the problems of nation- and society-building were prompted by circumstances of time and place; but they were adopted in the light of an underlying social philosophy which informed the thought and actions of all the kibbutz movements. The evolution of this philosophy can be explained in part by the historical background against which the kibbutz developed: socialist and anarchist thought in late nineteenth-century Russia, and the polarization of the Western world in the 1930s. But these factors had produced no lasting social form comparable to the kibbutz in any other society. Even in the *soi-disant* socialist part of the world, and in the movements which advocated myriad varieties of socialist and revolutionary doctrine, the kibbutz was virtually a unique phenomenon. There had been similar social experiments in the early years of the Soviet regime, and some still existed in the late 1930s in North America and Republican Spain. But none of them achieved either the extent or the success of the kibbutz movement.[12] It is therefore legitimate to ask why the kibbutz was created and successfully developed at this particular place, and by these particular people. Part of the answer will be found in the detailed narrative of the events of these thirty years; but there may also be a deeper reason for the dominance of communal and co-operative ideas in the Zionist movement, and the leading role of the labour movement in the Yishuv. The leaders of these movements formed their fundamental social attitudes in a society shot through with values of mutual aid and social responsibility. The ghettoes and small towns of Eastern Europe were far from being egalitarian

---

[12] Oved, *Two Hundred Years of American Communes*; id., 'Communal Experiments'.

societies, but they displayed a degree of care for the needy and sick,
social interdependence and mutual aid, which made them precursors
of the welfare state. In this sense, the contention that the kibbutz is
the successor of the *shtetl*,[13] in spirit if not in social structure, is well
founded. In so far as they were in control of their own communities
the Jews regulated their lives according to principles of social justice
and mutual aid which derive ultimately from the world outlook of
Biblical Judaism. In the acquisition of wealth, the laws of capitalism
applied; in its distribution, they were modified by principles of social
justice. It is not surprising, therefore, that Jews so readily adopted
social doctrines such as socialism and anarchism, which aspired to
apply these very values to society at large. In this light, the kibbutz
is an extreme expression of the values of labour Zionism, which is the
continuation of Jewish social tradition.[14]

### ACHIEVEMENTS AND APPREHENSIONS

Within some thirty years, the kibbutz movement had grown from one
struggling group of pioneers, uncertain of their personal future or of
that of the social form they were in the process of evolving, to a well-
established sector of the Yishuv, with a population of close on twenty-
five thousand people, in 117 groups ranging geographically from the
northern border of Palestine to the northern approaches to the Negev,
and from the Mediterranean to the new settlements along the Jordan
Valley. Its members had successfully withstood periods of unemployment and hunger, physical isolation and armed attack, as well as
the perils of prosperity with its consequent loss of numbers. They
knew well that all of these threats were likely to recur, perhaps with
even greater intensity. But they had already created a history, and a
series of legends, which gave them strength in the present and confidence in the future. Moreover, they knew that they were not alone:
the past three years had confirmed their place, in their own eyes as
in those of the Yishuv and the whole Zionist movement, as an essential
factor in the defence and development of Jewish Palestine. And, above
all, their reserve forces in the Diaspora and the Yishuv seemed
assured. There were more than a hundred thousand people in the
pioneering youth movements, some two thousand in the kibbutzim
in the framework of Youth Aliya, and twice that number of their own

---

[13] Diamond, 'Kibbutz and Shtetl'.
[14] For an extreme statement of this view, see Barzel, *To Be a Jew*, ch. 4.

children. They were under no illusions about the dangers ahead of them. There was no guarantee that the Allies would win the war, or that its outcome would be immediately favourable to the Zionist cause. But, whatever the course of the struggle to come, they were convinced of the rightness of their cause, and that they would play a major part in bringing about what they saw as the only solution to the problems of the Jewish people.

The coming years would see some of these expectations fulfilled, others—especially their hope for the continuation of massive support from the Diaspora—tragically disappointed, to a degree which none of them even began to envisage.

The second volume will deal with these processes: the experience of the kibbutz movement in the face of war and the Holocaust, the struggle for the State of Israel, and the changes which followed the establishment of the state.

# *Appendix 1:* The Kibbutz Movement in 1939

| | Year founded[a] | Movement allegiance in 1939[b] | Location[c] |
|---|---|---|---|
| Afikim | 1932 | KM | G4 |
| Amir | 1939 | KA | G1 |
| Ashdot Ya'akov[d] | 1924 | KM | G4 |
| Ayelet Hashahar | 1916 | KM | G2 |
| Beit Alpha | 1922 | —[e] | G5 |
| Beit Ha'arava | 1939 | KM | G8 |
| Beit Hashita | 1936 | KM | G4 |
| Beit Oren | 1939 | KM | E3 |
| Dafna | 1939 | KM | G1 |
| Dalia | 1939 | KA | E4 |
| Dan | 1939 | KA | G1 |
| Degania Aleph | 1910 | HK | G4 |
| Degania Beit | 1920 | HK | G4 |
| Eilon | 1938 | KA | F2 |
| Ein Gev | 1937 | KM | G3 |
| Ein Hahoresh | 1931 | KA | D5 |
| Ein Hamifratz | 1938 | KA | E3 |
| Ein Harod | 1921 | KM | F4 |
| Ein Hashofet | 1937 | KA | E4 |
| Ein Shemer | 1927 | KA | E5 |
| Evron | 1936 | KA | E2 |
| Gan Shmuel | 1913 | KA | E5 |
| Gesher | 1939 | KM | G4 |
| Geva | 1921 | HK | F4 |
| Ginegar | 1922 | HK | F4 |
| Ginossar | 1937 | KM | G3 |
| Giv'at Brenner | 1928 | KM | D8 |
| Giv'at Haim | 1932 | KM | D5 |
| Giv'at Hashlosha | 1925 | KM | D7 |
| Gvat | 1926 | KM | F4 |
| Hanita | 1938 | HK | E2 |

| | Year founded[a] | Movement allegiance in 1939[b] | Location[c] |
|---|---|---|---|
| Hazorea | 1936 | KA | E4 |
| Heftziba | 1922 | KM | G5 |
| Hulata | 1938 | KM | G2 |
| Hulda | 1930 | HK | D8 |
| Kfar Gil'adi | 1916 | KM | G1 |
| Kfar Glickson | 1939 | OZ | E5 |
| Kfar Hahoresh | 1933 | HK | F4 |
| Kfar Hamaccabi | 1936 | HK | E3 |
| Kfar Masaryk | 1938 | KA | E3 |
| Kfar Menahem | 1939 | KA | D8 |
| Kfar Ruppin | 1938 | HK | G5 |
| Kinneret | 1918 | KM | G4 |
| Kiriat Anavim | 1920 | HK | E8 |
| Kvutzat Hasharon[f] | 1926 | HK | F4 |
| Kvutzat Schiller[g] | 1928 | HK | D8 |
| Ma'abarot | 1933 | KA | D5 |
| Ma'aleh Hahamisha | 1938 | HK | E8 |
| Ma'apilim[h] | 1939 | HK | D4 |
| Ma'ayan Tzvi | 1938 | HK | E4 |
| Mahanaim | 1939 | KM | G2 |
| Maoz Haim | 1937 | KM | G5 |
| Massada | 1937 | HK | G4 |
| Merhavia | 1911 | KA[i] | F4 |
| Mesilot | 1938 | KA | G5 |
| Mishmar Ha'emek | 1926 | KA | E4 |
| Mishmar Hasharon | 1933 | HK | D5 |
| Mishmar Hayam[j] | 1939 | KM | D4 |
| Mishmarot | 1933 | HK | E5 |
| Mizra | 1923 | KA | F4 |
| Na'an | 1930 | KM | D8 |
| Negba | 1939 | KA | C9 |
| Neveh Eitan | 1938 | HK | G5 |
| Ramat David[k] | 1926 | HK | F4 |
| Ramat Hakovesh | 1932 | KM | D6 |
| Ramat Rahel | 1926 | KM | F8 |
| Ramat Yohanan[l] | 1932 | HK | E3 |
| Sarid | 1926 | KA | F4 |
| Sdeh Eliahu | 1939 | KD | G5 |
| Sha'ar Ha'amakim | 1935 | KA | E3 |
| Sha'ar Hagolan | 1937 | KA | G4 |
| Shefaim | 1935 | KM | D6 |
| Tel Amal (Nir David) | 1936 | KA | G5 |

| | Year founded[a] | Movement allegiance in 1939[b] | Location[c] |
|---|---|---|---|
| Tel Yitzhak | 1938 | OZ | D6 |
| Tel Yosef | 1921 | KM | F4 |
| Tirat Tzvi | 1937 | KD | G5 |
| Usha | 1937 | OZ | E3 |

[a] Year of permanent settlement by a kibbutz group.

[b] HK: Hever Hakvutzot; KA: Kibbutz Artzi; KD: Kibbutz Dati; KM: Kibbutz Me'uhad; OZ: Ha'oved Hatzioni; Pagi: Poalei Agudat Israel.

[c] See end-papers.

[d] Formerly Gesher.

[e] Beit Alpha, which had been politically divided since its establishment, split permanently in 1940: the group that supported Mapai moved to Ramat Yohanan, and Beit Alpha affiliated to the Kibbutz Artzi.

[f] Later merged in Yif'at.

[g] Gan Shlomo.

[h] Later Neveh Yam.

[i] From 1911 to 1929 Merhavia was inhabited by a series of independent *kvutzot*; it was then taken over by the third settlement group of Hashomer Hatzair and affiliated to the Kibbutz Artzi.

[j] Later merged into Ma'ayan Zvi and Sdot Yam.

[k] Formerly Ayanot.

[l] Formerly Ramat Hatzafon.

# Appendix 2: Guide to Other Settlements Mentioned in this Volume

|  | Settlement type | Location[a] | Year founded[b] | Movement allegiance[c] |
|---|---|---|---|---|
| Afuleh | Town | F4 |  |  |
| Atarot | Moshav | F8 |  |  |
| Be'er Sheva | Town | D11 |  |  |
| Beitania | *Moshava* | G4 |  |  |
| Beit Ha'emek | Kibbutz | E2 | 1951 | KM/IKK |
| Ben Shemen | Training farm | D7 |  |  |
| Gedera | *Moshava* | D8 |  |  |
| Hadera | *Moshava* | D5 |  |  |
| Hafetz Haim | Kibbutz | D8 | 1944 | Pagi |
| Haifa | Town | E3 |  |  |
| Hebron | Town | E10 |  |  |
| Jaffa | Town | D7 |  |  |
| Jerusalem | Town | F8 |  |  |
| Kfar Blum | Kibbutz | G1 | 1943 | KM/IKK |
| Kfar Malal[d] | Moshav | D6 |  |  |
| Kfar Saba | *Moshava* | D6 |  |  |
| Kfar Vitkin | Moshav | D5 |  |  |
| Kfar Yehezke'el | Moshav | F4 |  |  |
| Kinneret | *Moshava* | G4 |  |  |
| Kinneret | Training farm | G4 |  |  |
| Migdal | *Moshava* | G3 |  |  |
| Moledet | Moshav shitufi | G4 |  |  |
| Motza | *Moshava* | E8 |  |  |
| Nahalal | Moshav | E4 |  |  |
| Nazareth | Town | F4 |  |  |
| Netanya | *Moshava* | D5/6 |  |  |
| Petah Tikva | *Moshava* | D7 |  |  |
| Ramot Hashavim | Moshav | D6 |  |  |
| Rehovot | *Moshava* | D8 |  |  |
| Sa'ad | Kibbutz | C10 | 1947 | KD |
| Safed | Town | G2 |  |  |
| Sdeh Warburg | *Moshava* | D6 |  |  |

|  | Settlement type | Location[a] | Year founded[b] | Movement allegiance[c] |
|---|---|---|---|---|
| Sejera | Training farm | G3 |  |  |
| Sejera | *Moshava* | G3 |  |  |
| Sha'albim | Kibbutz | E8 | 1951 | Pagi |
| Tel Adashim | Moshav | F4 |  |  |
| Tel Aviv | Town | D7 |  |  |
| Tel Hai | Kibbutz | G1 | 1916 | Gedud |
| Tiberias | Town | G3 |  |  |
| Yif'at | Kibbutz | F4 | 1952 | IKK |
| Zichron Ya'akov | *Moshava* | E4 |  |  |

[a] See end-papers.

[b] Kibbutzim only.

[c] Kibbutzim only. Gedud: Gedud Ha'avoda; IKK: Ihud Hakvutzot Vehakibbutzim; KD: Kibbutz Dati; KM: Kibbutz Me'uhad; Pagi: Po'alei Agudat Yisrael.

[d] Ein Hai.

# *Map*
## The Kibbutz Movement in Context, 1939

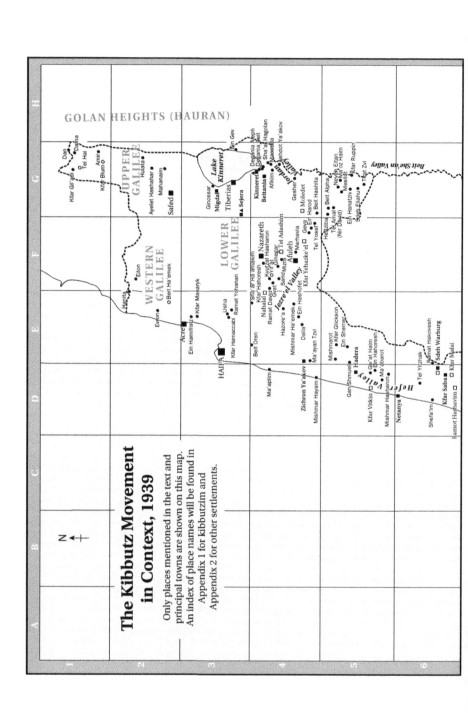

## The Kibbutz Movement in Context, 1939

Only places mentioned in the text and principal towns are shown on this map. An index of place names will be found in Appendix 1 for kibbutzim and Appendix 2 for other settlements.

N

GOLAN HEIGHTS (HAURAN)

UPPER GALILEE

WESTERN GALILEE

LOWER GALILEE

Lake Kinneret

Yarmuk Valley

Beit She'an Valley

Jezre'el Valley

Hefer Valley

HAIFA

Dan
Dafna
Kfar Gil'adi
Tel Hai
Amir
Kfar Blum
Hulata
Mahanaim
Ayelet Hashahar
Safed
Hagita
Eilon
Evron
Beit Ha'emek
Acre
Ein Hamifraz
Kfar Masaryk
Usha
Kfar Hamaccabi
Ramat Yohanan
Beit Oren
Ma'apilim
Zichron Ya'akov
Mishmar Hayam
Ma'ayan Tzvi
Dalia
Mishmar Ha'emek
Hazore'a
Ramat David
Nahalal
Gvat
Kfar Hahoresh
Sha'ar Ha'amakim
Ginegar
Kvutzat Hashomron
Nazareth
Tel Adashim
Sarid Mizra
Ein Hashofet
Kfar Yehazke'el
Gevat
Memavia
Afuleh
Tel Yosef
Ginossar
Migdal
Tiberias
Sejera
Kinneret
Beitania
Deganiah Aleph
Deganiah Beit
Sha'ar Hagolan
Masada
Ashdot Ya'akov
En Gev
Gesher
Moledet
Harod
Beit Hashita
Beit Alpha
Heftziba
Tel Amal (Nir David)
Neveh Eitan
Ma'oz Haim
Neslit
Eih Hanatziv
Sdeh Eliahu
Tel Tzvi
Kfar Ruppin
Kfar Glickson
Mishmarot
Ein Shemen
Gan/Shmuel
Giv'at Haim
Hadera
Kfar Vitkin
Ein Hahoresh
Mishmar Hasharon
Ma'abarot
Netanya
Tel Yitznak
Shefa'im
Ramat Hakovesh
Sdeh Warburg
Kfar Malal
Kfar Saba
Ramot Hashavim

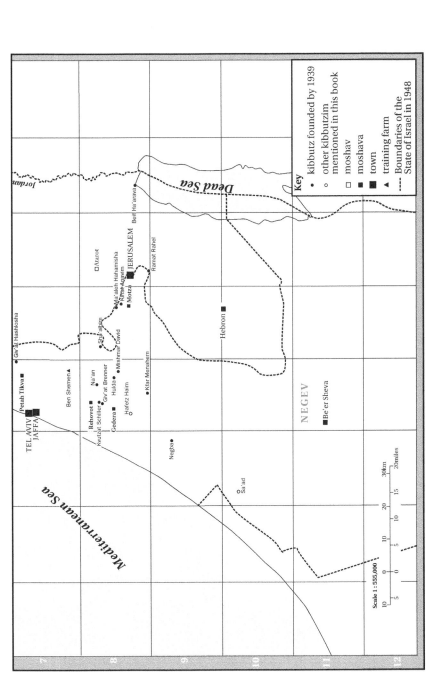

# Glossary

PRONUNCIATION is phonetic. The accent is usually on the last syllable. The consonant clusters kh or ch, and sometimes h, are pronounced as in Scottish loch or German *ich*. In these cases they appear in **bold** lettering in the headword.

Ahdut Ha'avoda ('Labour Unity'): Party in the Yishuv, founded in 1919. Its original components were the Poaÿei Zion party, a group of workers previously unaffiliated to any party, and a minority from Hapoel Hatzair. It had a majority in the Histadrut from 1921 to 1930. Socialist, but not dogmatically Marxist. Supported Gedud Ha'avoda and the Kibbutz Me'uhad, but with reservations. Leaders: David Ben-Gurion, Berl Katznelson, David Remez, Yitzhak Tabenkin. Merged with Hapoel Hatzair in 1930 to form Mapai.

*ahuza* (holding; pl. *ahuzot*): Farm in Palestine bought by an individual in the Diaspora (usually through an association which promoted saving schemes for this purpose), and worked by others in its first years, until it could yield a satisfactory crop.

Akiva: European Jewish youth movement that attempted to combine an element of (non-orthodox) religion with pioneering. Attached politically to the General Zionist movement.

*aliya* (lit., 'ascent' [to the Land of Israel]; pl., *aliyot*): Immigration, or wave of immigration, to Palestine or Israel. The accepted chronology is: First Aliya: 1882–1903; Second: 1904–1914; Third: 1918–1923; Fourth: 1924–1928; Fifth: 1929–1936; Sixth: 1936–1939.

Ashkenazi (pl. Ashkenazim): Jew originating in Eastern or Central Europe, as distinct from the Sephardi Jews of Middle Eastern or Asian origin.

Bachad (Brit Halutzim Dati'im, 'Association of Religious Pioneers'): Umbrella orthodox movement corresponding to the non-religious Hechalutz.

Bar Giora (name of the leader of the Jewish revolt against the Romans, 66–70 CE): Small clandestine movement devoted to Jewish self-defence, 1907–9. Its members became the leaders of Hashomer.

Bilu (Hebrew acronym of the Biblical phrase, 'House of Jacob, let us arise and go up'): Small movement, mainly of students, in First Aliya period, whose members undertook to settle in Palestine. Though its practical achievements were few, in later years it came to symbolize the First Aliya.

B'nei Akiva ('Children of Akiva'): Youth movement of orthodox Jews, affiliated to the Hapoel Hamizrachi party. Its graduates join the Kibbutz Hadati.

Brit Habirionim (League of Ruffians): Extreme nationalist Zionist movement, centred in Palestine, and loosely connected with the Revisionist party. Its leaders preached violence against the British and the Histadrut. Its spiritual leader was Abba Ahimeir.

Dror ('Freedom'): (*a*) A small group of Zionist activists who left Russia for Poland in the early 1920s. Played a major part in the leadership of Hechalutz and, after arriving in Palestine, of the Kibbutz Me'uhad. (*b*) A movement formed in 1939 by the unification of Hechalutz Hatzair and Freiheit; affiliated to the Kibbutz Me'uhad.

General Zionists: Originally, members of the Zionist movement in the Diaspora with no party affiliations. From 1931, organized as an autonomous Zionist party. It was subject to many schisms, and from 1934 there were two parties, which came to be known as General Zionists A (pro-Histadrut) and B (anti-Histadrut).

Gordonia: Zionist youth movement, founded 1924 in Galicia. Drawing its inspiration from Aharon David Gordon, it advocated non-Marxist socialism. From 1932, associated with Hever Hakvutzot. Leader: Pinhas Lubianiker (Lavon).

Hagana ('defence'): Clandestine Jewish defence organization in the Yishuv, from 1920. Controlled at first by Ahdut Ha'avoda, and from 1921 by the Histadrut. In 1931 its controlling body was broadened to include representatives of all parts of the Yishuv.

Haggada: The text read at the ceremony on the eve of Passover.

Ha'ikar Hatzair ('The Young Farmer'): Small Zionist movement of immigrants from the United States, active during the Second and Third Aliya. Among its leaders was Eliezer Yaffe of Nahalal. Advocated immigration to Palestine and moshav settlement.

*halakha*: Code of religious and ritual precepts governing the way of life of orthodox Jews.

Hamahanot Ha'olim (lit., 'the ascending hosts', or 'camps': an untranslatable name symbolizing a synthesis of scouting and Zionism): Zionist youth movement in the Yishuv, associated from 1932 with the Kibbutz Me'uhad.

Hanoar Hatzioni ('Zionist Youth'): Non-socialist pioneering youth movement, active in eastern and central Europe from the early 1930s.

Ha'oved Hatzioni ('The Zionist Worker'): Organization of settlements of Hanoar Hatzioni youth movement. Non-socialist, but supported the Histadrut. Leader: Moshe Kolodny (Kol).

Hapoel Hatzair ('The Young Worker'): Anti-Marxist socialist Zionist party, founded in Palestine in 1905. Advocated revival of Hebrew culture, immigration to Palestine, and agricultural work. Supported *kvutzot* (as against big kibbutzim) and moshavim. Leaders: A. D. Gordon, Joseph Sprinzak, Haim Arlosorov. Combined with Ahdut Ha'avoda in 1930 to form Mapai.

Hashomer ('The Guard'): Organization for Jewish self-defence active from 1909 to 1920, when it dispersed in favour of the Hagana. Leaders: Israel Gil'adi, Yitzhak Ben-Zvi, Manya and Israel Shohat.

Hashomer Hatzair ('The Young Guard'): Pioneering Zionist youth movement founded in 1913. Adopted Marxism in the 1920s; later educated to Mapam. Today as then, its graduates join the kibbutzim of the Kibbutz Artzi. Leaders: Meir Ya'ari, Ya'akov Hazan.

*havura*: (*a*) In the Third Aliya, an umbrella organization uniting a number of *plugot*. (*b*) In the period of unemployment during the Fourth Aliya, an individual *pluga* or group of *plugot*.

Hechalutz ('The Pioneer'): Founded in 1917 as an organization for educating young people (minimum age: 17–18) for immigration to Palestine. Organized training farms, allocated immigration certificates to trainees, etc. Other Jewish youth movements were affiliated to Hechalutz from the late 1920s onwards, so that it came to function as an umbrella organization.

Hechalutz Hatzair ('The Young Pioneer'): Pioneering youth movement, educating to membership of Hechalutz, immigration to Palestine, and kibbutz membership. Attached to the Kibbutz Me'uhad.

Histadrut (officially Hahistadrut Haklalit shel Ha'ovdim Ha'ivri'im Be'eretz-Yisrael—General Organization of Jewish Workers in the Land of Israel): Central organization of the labour movement, founded in January 1921. Combines trade union functions and constructive activities—ownership of industries and co-operative enterprises, support for kibbutzim and moshavim, etc.—with cultural activities and social services. General secretaries in the period considered here: 1921–35, David Ben-Gurion; 1935–44, David Remez.

Hovevei Zion ('Lovers of Zion') : Organization founded in Eastern Europe in the 1870s for promoting Jewish culture and Zionist ideas. Supported 'practical Zionism' and colonization activities in Palestine from 1881 to 1914.

Irgun Zva'i Le'umi (IZL) ('National Military Organization'): Independent underground military organization active from 1931 to 1948 and loosely associated with the Revisionist party. Pursued an activist anti-British policy in opposition to the Histadrut and the Hagana.

Jewish Colonization Association (JCA): Organization founded in 1891 by Baron Maurice de Hirsch, to encourage the migration and pro-ductivization of distressed Jews. From 1899 to 1924, it supported *moshavot* founded by Baron Edmond de Rothschild, and went on to give much support to non-kibbutz settlement.

Jewish National Fund: Founded by the Zionist Organization in 1901 in order to raise funds from the Jewish people and buy land which would remain under public ownership while leased to those who cultivated it. All kibbutzim and moshavim were founded on lands owned by the JNF or by the JCA/PICA (*q.v.*).

Keren Hayesod ('Foundation Fund'): Founded by the Zionist Organization in 1920 in order to raise capital for Zionist settlements, including kibbutzim and moshavim, in their early years.

kibbutz (community): (*a*) federation of communal groups (*plugot, havurot,* etc.) and/or settlements (e.g. the Kibbutz Me'uhad). (*b*) Large communal settlement, combining agriculture with industry, as opposed to the small entirely agricultural *kvutza*. (*c*) Comprehensive name for communal settlement.

Kibbutz Artzi (shel Hashomer Hatzair) ('National Kibbutz [Movement] of Hashomer Hatzair'): Kibbutz movement founded in 1927 by graduates of Hashomer Hatzair. Leaders, political attitudes, etc.—as for Hashomer Hatzair.

Kibbutz Me'uhad ('United Kibbutz [Movement]'): Kibbutz movement founded in 1927 by the unification of Kibbutz Ein Harod with a number of smaller groups. Principles: large kibbutzim based on agriculture and industry, and continuous expansion. Among its leaders: Yitzhak Tabenkin, Aharon Tzisling, Yitzhak Ben-Aharon, Israel Galili.

*kvutza* (group): (*a*) Communal working group, whose members contracted to work for a defined time or objective. (*b*) Small, permanently settled, purely agricultural communal group.

*meshek shitufi* (co-operative farm; pl. *meshakim shitufi'im*): Alternative name for moshav shitufi.

Mizrachi: Orthodox Zionist organization, founded in 1902 and affiliated to the Zionist movement. Gave political backing to the Kibbutz Dati.

moshav: *see moshav ovdim.*

*moshav ovdim* (workers' village; often called simply 'moshav'—pl. 'moshav-im'): Smallholders' settlement, based on family holdings and a wide measure of co-operation in marketing and purchasing.

# Glossary 413

*moshav shitufi* (co-operative moshav): Settlement farmed communally (like a kibbutz). Members live in family units, and income is distributed according to family size.

*moshava*: Village based on family units, with no institutionalized co-operation.

Netzah (No'ar Tsofi Halutzi, 'Pioneering Scouting Youth'): Independent youth movement created by the Russian Hashomer Hatzair after its break with the main movement in 1930. Affiliated to the Kibbutz Me'uhad from 1927.

Noar Oved ('Working Youth'): Major youth movement of the Histadrut, combining educational and trade union functions. Groups of its graduates joined the Kibbutz Me'uhad from 1929 onwards. Most prominent leader: Israel Galili.

PICA: Colonizing organization founded by Edmond de Rothschild in 1924. Took over responsibility for many *moshavot*, and supported about a dozen kibbutzim and moshavim.

*pluga* (pl. *plugot*): Communal group whose members worked as hired labourers, usually with the intention of settling permanently as a kibbutz when land became available.

Poalei Zion (pronounced 'tseeon', 'Workers of Zion'): Socialist (mainly Marxist) Zionist party. Originated in the Diaspora at the turn of the century. The Yishuv branch became the leading group in the labour movement from 1906 until 1919, when it disbanded to join Ahdut Ha'avoda. Leaders: David Ben-Gurion, Yitzhak Ben-Zvi. In 1920 the world movement split, and the leftist faction became a very small independent party (Left Poalei Zion).

Sephardi (pl. Sephardim): Jew of Middle Eastern or Asian origin, as opposed to the Ashkenazim of Eastern Europe.

Socialist League (*Liga Sotzialistit*): Political party active from 1936 to 1944, allied to Hashomer Hatzair.

Torah: The laws, teachings, and religious tenets of Judaism.

Yishuv: Jewish community of Palestine before the establishment of the State of Israel.

Youth Aliya: A scheme established in 1934 to bring young refugees from the Nazis to Palestine and educate them. Many were absorbed in the kibbutzim.

# References

AARONSOHN, R., 'Stages in the Development of the Settlements of the First Aliyah' (Heb.), in M. Eliav and Y. Rosenthal (eds.), *The First Aliyah* (Jerusalem, 1981), i. 25–83.

ADMATI, M., *Youth on the Rise: Hanoar Haoved, 1924–1931* (Heb.), (Tel Aviv, 1974).

AHAD HA'AM (Asher Ginzberg), 'This is not the Way' (1869); 'Truth from the Land of Israel' (1891–3), *At the Parting of the Ways* (Heb.), (Berlin, 1921), 1–13, 26–53.

AHARONOVITZ, Y., 'To Clarify the Situation' (Heb.), *Hapoel Hatzair*, 2/3 (4 Nov. 1909), 3–9.

ALMOG, S., 'Redemption in Zionist Rhetoric', in R. Kark (ed.), *Redemption of the Land of Eretz-Israel: Ideology and Practice* (Heb.), (Jerusalem, 1990), 13–32.

ALON, H., *Jewish Scouting in Israel, 1919–1929* (Heb.), (Tel Aviv, 1976).

AMINOAH, N., *The Religious Labour Movement* (Heb.), (Jerusalem, 1931).

AMIT, Y., BEN-NAHUM, D., and DROR, L., *From Beginning to End: The History of the Hashomer Hatzair Movement in Lithuania* (Heb.), (Tel Aviv, n.d.).

ASAF, Y., 'The Political Conflict in Hakibbutz Hameuchad [sic], 1939–1951' (Heb.), Ph. D. thesis (Tel Aviv, 1987).

AVNER [Yitzhak Ben-Tzvi], 'The Question of Collective Settlement' (Heb.), *Ha'ahdut*, 2/35 (26 July 1911), 3; 2/36 (3 Aug. 1911), 5.

AVNERI, A. L., *From 'Velos' to 'Taurus': The First Decade of Jewish 'Illegal' Immigration to Mandatory Palestine (Eretz-Israel), 1934–1944* (Heb.), (Tel Aviv, 1985).

AZATI, A., 'Hashomer and its Attitude to Settlement' (Heb.), *Hakibbutz*, 9–10 (1983–4), 321–34.

BARATZ, J., 'On the Sabbath and the "Shabbaton"' (Heb.), *Niv Hakvutza*, 6 (1933), 21–3.

BARATZ, M., 'From Petah Tikva to Um Juni' (Heb.), *Niv Hakvutza*, 7/2 (May 1958), 356–8.

—— 'Early Days in Degania' (Heb.), *Meshek Bakar Vehalav*, 162 (Oct. 1979), 74.

BARTAL, I. (ed.), *Book of the Second Aliya* (Heb.), vol. ii (Jerusalem, forthcoming).

BARZEL, A., *To Be a Jew* (Heb.), (Tel Aviv, 1978).

BASSOK, M. (ed.), *The Book of Hechalutz* (Heb.), (Jerusalem, 1940).

—— (ed.), *Hechalutz Hatzair* (Heb.), (Ein Harod, 1944).

BAT-RAHEL, Y., 'Is It Fated?' (Heb.), *Mibifnim* (June 1936), 70–1.

—— *The Path in which I Went* (Heb.), (Tel Aviv, 1981).

BAUER, Y., *From Diplomacy to Resistance: A History of Jewish Palestine, 1939–1945* (New York, 1973).

BEIN, A., *History of Zionist Settlement* (Heb.), 5th edn. (Ramat Gan, 1976).

—— (ed.), *Arthur Ruppin: Memoirs, Diaries, Letters* (London, 1971).

BEN-AHARON, Y., *Listen Gentile!* (London, 1947).

BEN-ARYEH, Y., 'Geographic Aspects of the Development of the First Jewish Settlements in Palestine' (Heb.), in M. Eliav and Y. Rosenthal (eds.), *The First Aliyah* (Jerusalem, 1981), i. 85–96.

BEN-AVRAM, B., *Hever Hakvutzot: Its Social and Ideological Development* (Heb.), (Tel Aviv, 1976).

—— 'The Formation of the Kvutza Ideology' (Heb.), pt. 1, *Shorashim*, 3 (1982), 37–80; pt.2, *Shorashim*, 4 (1984), 39–71.

—— 'The Kibbutz as a Zionist Phenomenon', in Y. Gorni, Y. Oved, and I. Paz (eds.), *Communal Life: An International Perspective* (Ef'al–New Brunswick, 1987), 243–8.

BEN-AVRAM, B., and NEAR, H., *The Third Aliya: Historical Aspects* (Heb.), (Jerusalem, forthcoming).

BEN-GURION, D., 'Hechalutz in Russia' (Heb.), *Kuntres* (20 Feb. 1924), 11–14; (7 Mar. 1924). 6–12.

BEN HAVA [Moshe Smilansky], 'The Galilean Worker' (Heb.), *Hapoel Hatzair*, 1/7–8 (1908), 5–6.

BEN-TZVI, Y., SHOHAT, Y. (eds.), MEGGED, M., and TWERSKY, Y. (eds.), *The Book of Hashomer* (Heb.), (Tel Aviv, 1957).

BEN-YEHUDA, B. 'Life in Degania During the First World War' (Heb.), *Davar*, 14 Oct. 1960, pp. 6, 11.

BENARI, N., 'Ein Harod as a Cultural Movement' (Heb.), *Mibifnim*, 17 (Sept. 1925), 337–9.

BERNSTEIN, D., *The Struggle for Equality: Urban Women Workers in Prestate Israeli Society* (New York, 1987).

BLOOM, S., 'The Woman in the Labour Movement in the Period of the Second Aliya' (Heb.), MA thesis (Tel Aviv, 1980).

BONDY, R., *The Emissary: A Life of Enzo Sereni* (London, 1978).

*Book of Ginegar* (Heb.), [no author cited] (Ginegar, 1947).

*Book of the Shomrim* (Heb.), [no author cited], (Warsaw, 1934).

BRASLAVSKY [Braslavi], J., *Do You Know the Land?* (Heb.), (Ein Harod, 1939).

BRASLAVSKY, M., 'On the Roads' (Heb.), *He'atid* (June 1932), 133–4.

—— *The Labour Movement of the Land of Israel* (Heb.), 3 vols. (Tel Aviv, 1955–9).

—— *Workers and their Organizations in the First Aliya* (Heb.), (Tel Aviv, 1961).

BRENNER, U., *The Kibbutz Me'uhad in the Hagana* (Heb.), (Tel Aviv, 1980).

CARMEL, A., 'The Character and Uniqueness of Hashomer Hatzair in Germany' (Heb.), MA thesis (Haifa, 1987).

COHEN, A., *The Halutz Resistance in Hungary, 1942–1944* (Boulder–New York, 1986).

COHEN, Y., *Hanoar Hatzioni: The Growth of a Movement* (Heb.), (Tel Aviv, 1976).

DAN, H. (ed.), *The Book of Klosova* (Heb.), (Lohamei Hageta'ot, 1987).

DAYAN, S., *Twenty-Five Years of Degania* (Heb.), (Tel Aviv, 1935).

*Degania Beit: History and Writings* (Heb.), [no author cited] (Degania, 1946).

DIAMOND, S., 'Kibbutz and Shtetl: the History of an Idea', *Social Problems*, 5/2 (1957), 71–99.

DINUR, B.-Z. (ed.), *History of the Hagana* (Heb.), 3 vols. (Tel Aviv, 1956–72).

DORSINAI, Z., *From the Banks of the Dnieper to Ma'ayan Harod* (Heb.), (Tel Aviv, 1974).

EHAD MIHAKOMMUNA [Joseph Baratz], 'The First Two Years' (Heb.), *Hapoel Hatzair*, 12/38–9 (18 July 1920), 21.

EICHLER, H., 'Zionism and Youth in Hungary between the World Wars' (Heb.), Ph. D. thesis, Bar Ilan University (Ramat Gan, 1982).

EL'AD, G. (ed.), *Moshe Hass: Man of Encounter–Pioneer and Fighter* (Heb.), (Tel Aviv, 1985).

ELIAV, M., and ROSENTHAL, Y. (eds.), *The First Aliyah* (Heb.), 2 vols. (Jerusalem, 1981).

EREZ, Y. (ed.), *The Book of the Third Aliya* (Heb.), (Tel Aviv, 1964).

ETTINGER, Y., 'The Communal Groups at the Beginning of 5679' (Heb.), *Kuntres* (12 Aug. 1919), 5–6.

EVANS, R. J., *The Feminists* (London, 1977).

EVEN-SHOSHAN, Z., *History of the Labour Movement in the Land of Israel* (Heb.), (Tel Aviv, 1962).

FIALKOV, A., and RABINOVITCH, Y., *Yitzhak Tabenkin* (Heb.), (Tel Aviv, 1982).

FISHMAN, A., 'The Religious Kibbutz: A Study in the Interrelationship of Religion and Ideology in the Context of Modernization' (Heb.), Ph. D. thesis (Jerusalem, 1975).

FISHMAN-MAIMON, A., *The Working Women's Movement in the Land of Israel* (Heb.), (Tel Aviv, 1929).

FOGIEL-BIJAOUI, S., 'Motherhood and Revolution: The Case of the Kibbutz Women, 1910–1948' (Heb.), *Shorashim* (forthcoming).

FRANKEL, J., *Prophecy and Politics: Socialism, Nationalism and the Russian Jews, 1862–1917* (Cambridge, 1981).

FRANKEL, R., 'The Evolution of the Kvutza and the Kibbutz' (Heb.), seminar paper, Department of Jewish History, Tel Aviv University (Tel Aviv, 1972).

—— 'Joseph Bussel, The Hadera Commune and the Birth of the Kvutza', *Zionism*, 1 (1980), 83–103.

FRANKEL, R., BEN-AVRAM, B., and NEAR, H., 'Ideological Motives in the Formation of the Kvutza during the Period of the Second Aliya' (Heb.), *Cathedra*, 18 (Jan. 1981), 111–29; 23 (Apr. 1982), 187–91.

FRIEDMAN, A., 'From the Distant Past', in B. Katznelson (ed.), *At Work* (Heb.), (Jaffa, 1918), 22–32.

GADON, S. (ed.), *Paths of the Kvutza and the Kibbutz* (Heb.), vol. i (Tel Aviv, 1958).

GEDUD HA'AVODA, ex-members of in the Kibbutz Me'uhad (eds.), *Gedud Ha'avoda* (Heb.), (Tel Aviv, 1931).

GERTZ, A. (ed.), *Jewish Agricultural Settlement in Numbers* (Heb.), (Jerusalem, 1946).

GIL'AD, D., 'On Sabbath Celebrations in Degania' (Heb.), *Niv Hakvutza* (Mar. 1937), 90–1.

GIL'ADI, D., *The Yishuv in the Period of the Fourth Aliya* (Heb.), (Tel Aviv, 1973).

GIL'ADI, Y., 'History of the Movement' (Heb.), *Hashomer Anthology*, 5–20.

GITLIS, M., *Hulda* (Heb.), (Tel Aviv, 1941).

GOLAN, H. 'The First Year of Gedud Ha'avoda', paper read at the Third Conference on Kibbutz Research, Jordan Valley College, Oct. 1990.

GOLAN, S., *Collective Education* (Heb.), (Tel Aviv, 1961).

GORDON, A. D., 'An Irrational Solution' (1909), (Heb.), *Nation and Labour* (Jerusalem, 1962), 88–102.

——*Letters and Notes* (Heb.), (Jerusalem, 1954).

——*Nation and Labour* (Heb.), (Jerusalem, 1962).

GORNI, Y., OVED, Y., and PAZ, I., *Communal Life: An International Perspective* (Ef'al–New Brunswick, 1987).

*Grundriss eines Erziehungprogramms* [no author cited] (Hamburg, 1933).

GUREVICH, D., and GERTZ, A., *Jewish Agricultural Settlement in Palestine (General Survey and Statistical Abstracts)* (Heb.), (Jerusalem, 1938).

GUREVICH, D., GERTZ, A., and BACHI, R., *The Jewish Population of Palestine: Immigration, Demographic Structure, and Natural Growth* (Heb.), (Jerusalem, 1944).

GVATI, H., *A Century of Settlement* (Heb.), (Tel Aviv, 1981).

HABASS, B. (ed.), *Book of the Second Aliya* (Heb.), (Tel Aviv, 1947).

HADARI, H., *Kibbutz Ein Harod, 1923–1927: Decisions and Documents* (Heb.), (Tel Aviv, 1977).

——*The Kibbutz Me'uhad: Decisions and Documents, 1927–1933* (Heb.), (Tel Aviv, 1982).

HADOMI, L., 'Literary Representations of Patterns of Involvement: Content Analysis of Form and Content of the Kibbutz Short Story, 1920–1969' (Heb.), Ph. D. thesis (Jerusalem, 1974).

HALEVI, N., *The Economic Development of the Jewish Community of the Land of Israel, 1917–1947* (Heb.), (Jerusalem, 1979).

HALPRIN, H., 'On the Question of Planning in New Settlement' (Heb.), *Hameshek Hashitufi*, 29 (Mar. 1934), 81–2.

*Hashomer Anthology* (Heb.), [no author cited], (Tel Aviv, 1937).

*Hechalutz Anthology* (Heb.), [no author cited], (Warsaw, 1930).

*Herut: An Anthology of Letters by Members of Kibbutz Herut who Met an Untimely Death* (Heb.), [no author cited], (Giv'at Brenner, 1941).

HERZOG, H., 'The Kibbutz Haggadah' (Heb.), *Hakibbutz*, 3–4 (1976), 237–46.

HISTADRUT, *Minutes of the Twentieth Council* (Heb.) (1928), mimeo.

—— *UAW Report* (Reports of the Union of Agricultural Workers to Histadrut Conferences), (Heb.), (Tel Aviv, 1923–45).

HOR, E., 'The Contribution of Maccabi Hatzair to the Palmach and Jewish Settlement' (Heb.), (Land of Israel Department, Haifa University, 1988).

HOROWITZ, D., 'Kibbutz and Party' (Heb.), *Mihayeinu*, 67 (1926), 278–80.

—— *The Development of the Palestinian Economy* (Heb.), 2nd edn. (Jerusalem, 1948).

*Hovrot Statistiot.* Statistical publications of the Agricultural Centre of the Histadrut.

IDELSON (Bar-Yehuda), I., 'With the Stream or Against It?' (Heb.), *Mibifnim* (7 Dec. 1932), 8–12.

*Israel Bloch*, memorial booklet (Heb.), [no author cited], (Tel Aviv, 1966).

ITAI, A., *The Saga of Hashomer Hatzair in the USSR: Noar Tzofi Halutzi— Netzah* (Heb.), (Jerusalem, 1981).

ITAI, A., and NEISTAT, M., *The History of a Movement: Netzah in Latvia* (Heb.), (Tel Aviv, 1972).

KAFKAFI, E., 'Ideological Development in the Kibbutz Me'uhad during the Period of the Cold War' (Heb.), Ph. D. thesis (Tel Aviv, 1986).

KAFKAFI, Y. (ed.), *Years of the Mahanot Olim* (Heb.), 2 vols. (Tel Aviv, 1975–85).

KANARI, B., 'The Kibbutz Me'uhad's Way as an Alternative to the Histadrut and the State of Israel Orientation: The Struggle and the Collapse' (Heb.), Ph. D. thesis (Tel Aviv, 1986).

—— 'Planned Economy: Zionist and Socialist-Zionist', paper read at the Third Conference on Kibbutz Research, Jordan Valley College, Oct. 1990.

KANIEL, Y., *Continuity and Change: The Old and New Yishuv in the Period of the First and Second Aliya* (Heb.), (Jerusalem, 1982).

KAPLANSKY, S., 'Co-operative Settlement' (1910), *Vision and Realization* (Heb.), (Merhavia, 1950), 406–13.

—— *Vision and Realization* (Heb.), (Merhavia, 1950).

KARK, R. (ed.), *Redemption of the Land of Eretz-Israel: Ideology and Practice* (Heb.), (Jerusalem, 1990).

KATZNELSON, B., *Writings* (Heb.), 11 vols. (Tel Aviv, 1946–9).
—— (ed.), *At Work* (Heb.), (Jaffa, 1918).
—— (ed.), *The Kvutza* (Heb.), (Tel Aviv, 1924).
—— (ed.), *Efforts towards Unity* (Heb.), (Tel Aviv, 1945).
KATZNELSON-SHAZAR, R. (ed.), *Words of Working Women* (Heb.), (Tel Aviv, 1930).
KEDAR, A., 'The German Aliyah as an Apolitical Opposition in the Kibbutz Me'uhad During the Fifth Aliyah', *Cathedra*, 16 (July 1980), 133–52.
—— 'The Policy and Ideological Development of Hakibbutz Hame'uchad [sic] (1933–1942)', (Heb.), Ph. D. thesis (Jerusalem, 1983).
KIBBUTZ ARTZI, *Ideological Premisses*, repr. in Margalit, *Hashomer Hatzair from Youth Bund to Revolutionary Marxism* (Heb.), (Tel Aviv, 1968), 301–2.
*Kibbutz Me'uhad Anthology* (Heb.), [no author cited], (Tel Aviv, 1932).
KIBBUTZ ME'UHAD, *On Questions of our Movements in the Diaspora* (Heb.), mimeo (Ein Harod, 1933).
—— *Report of Kibbutz Me'uhad Council, Yagur, 1933* (mimeo).
—— *Eleventh Council of the Kibbutz Me'uhad, Yagur, 1936* (Heb.), (Ein Harod, 1937).
—— 'Minutes of the Founding Conference', ed. H. Hadari, *Shorashim*, 2 (1980), 224–66.
KOLATT, I., 'Ideology and Reality in the Labour Movement in the Land of Israel, 1905–1919' (Heb.), Ph. D. thesis (Jerusalem, 1964).
LAQUEUR, W., *A History of Zionism* (London, 1972).
—— *Young Germany: A History of the German Youth Movement* (New York, 1962).
LASKOV, S., *Yosef Trumpeldor: A Biography*, 2nd edn. (Heb.), (Jerusalem, 1982).
LAVI, S., 'Choosing Members' (Heb.), *Mihayeinu*, 12 (Nov. 1921), 1, 79–80.
—— *My Story in Ein Harod* (Heb.), (Tel Aviv, 1947).
LEV, Y. (ed.), *The B'nei Akiva Book* (Heb.), (Tel Aviv, 1938).
LIEBENSTEIN (Livneh), E., 'Labour Festivals and Religious Tradition' (Heb.), *Mibifnim*, 35 (July 1928), 1–5.
—— 'For Unity', *Mibifnim*, 42 (Aug. 1929), 13.
LIEBERMAN, T., *Chapters in a Life* (Heb.), (Tel Aviv, 1970).
LIEBLICH, A., *Kibbutz Makom* (New York, 1981).
LUBIANIKER (Lavon), P., 'Our Position in Hechalutz' (Heb.), *Gordonia* (June 1929).
MAIMON-FISHMAN, A., *Fifty Years of the Working Women's Movement* (Heb.), (Tel Aviv, 1958).
MALETZ, D., 'On the Way to a Cultural Ambience' (Heb.), *Kibbutz Me'uhad Anthology* (Tel Aviv, 1932), 197–211.
MALKIN, S., *With the Second Aliya* (Heb.), (Tel Aviv, 1929).
MANIV, B. (ed.), *Dror Anthology* (Heb.), (Efal, 1981).
MANNING, P. K. (ed.), *Youth: Divergent Perspectives* (New York, 1973).

MARGALIT, E., *Hashomer Hatzair from Youth Bund to Revolutionary Marxism* (Heb.), (Tel Aviv, 1971).

—— *Commune, Society and Politics* (Heb.), (Tel Aviv, 1980).

—— *The Gordonia Youth Movement: Conception and Way of Life* (Heb.), (Tel Aviv, 1986).

MARON, S., *Kibbutz as a Communal Household* (Ef'al, 1987).

MENDELSOHN, E., *The Jews of Eastern Central Europe Between the World Wars* (Bloomington, 1983).

MENDELSSON, D., 'The Development of the Pioneering Youth Movements in England, 1929–48' (Heb.), MA thesis (Jerusalem, 1987).

MINTZ, M., *The Lame and the Nimble: The Story of the 'Dror' Group in Russia* (Heb.), (Tel Aviv, 1983).

*My Notebook* (Heb.), [no author cited], (Warsaw, 1918, and later editions throughout the 1920s).

N.Y., 'With the Festival' (Heb.), *Mibifnim* (June 1932), 42–5.

NARKISS, M. (ed.), *The Pioneers* (Heb.), (Jerusalem, 1924), selection of silhouettes by Meir Gur-Aryeh.

NEAR, H., 'Hever Hakvutzot Vehakibbutzim' (Heb.), *Baderech*, 6 (Dec. 1970), 141–53.

—— 'The Kibbutz and the Outside World' (Heb.), Ph.D. thesis (Jerusalem, 1977).

—— *Kibbutz and Society* (Heb.), (Jerusalem, 1984).

—— 'Utopian and Post-Utopian Thought: The Kibbutz as Model', *Communal Societies*, 5 (Fall 1985), 51–67.

—— 'Paths to Utopia: The Kibbutz as a Movement for Social Change', *Jewish Social Studies*, 48/3–4 (Summer–Fall 1986), 189–206.

—— 'The Languages of Community: Terminology and Reality in the History of the Kibbutz' (Heb.), *Hatzionut*, 13 (1988), 123–46.

—— 'Redemption of the Soil and of Man: Pioneering in Labour Zionist Ideology, 1904–1935' (Heb.), in R. Kark (ed.), *Redemption of the Land of Eretz-Israel: Ideology and Practice* (Jerusalem, 1990), 33–47.

—— 'Authority and Democracy: Varieties of Political Culture in the Kibbutz Movements in the 1930s' (Heb.), *Yearbook of the Institute for the Study of Contemporary Jewry* (Jerusalem, forthcoming).

—— 'Joseph Baratz', in Z. Tzahor (ed.), *Second Aliya Book* (Heb.), biographical volume (Jerusalem, forthcoming).

—— 'Towards Workers' Settlement', (Heb.), in I. Bartal (ed.), *Book of the Second Aliya*, vol. ii (Jerusalem, forthcoming).

NEZER, R. (ed.), *The Zionist Theory of the Hebrew Youth Movement 'Akiva'* (Heb.), (Tel Aviv, 1986).

O'NEILL, W. L., *The Woman Movement: Feminism in the US and England* (London, 1969).

OPHIR, A. (ed.), *Afikim* (Heb.), (Afikim, 1951).

—— *Elik: Streams of Life* (Heb.), (Tel Aviv, 1957).

OPPENHEIM, Y., *The Hechalutz Movement in Poland, 1917–1929* (Heb.), (Jerusalem, 1982).

ORREN, E., *Settlement Amid Struggles* (Heb.), (Jerusalem, 1978).

OTIKER, I., *The 'Hechalutz' Movement in Poland, 1932–1935* (Heb.), (Lohamei Hageta'ot, 1972).

*Our Community* (Heb.), [no author cited], (Haifa–Jedda road, 1922).

OVED, Y., *Two Hundred Years of American Communes* (New Brunswick–Oxford, 1988).

—— 'Communal Experiments During the Spanish Civil War' (Heb.), (Ef'al, 1989), mimeo.

OZ, F., 'The Farmyard in the Forest: The History of Kvutzat Hulda, 1931–1938.' (Heb.), (Brenner School, 1979), mimeo.

PAUCKER, A., GILCHRIST, S., and SUCHY, S. (ed.), *The Jews in Nazi Germany, 1933–1943* (Tubingen, 1986).

PAUL, L., *Angry Young Man* (London, 1951).

PERLIS, R., *The Pioneering Zionist Youth Movements in Nazi-Occupied Poland* (Heb.), (Lohamei Hageta'ot, 1987).

PINES, D., *Hechalutz in the Crucible of the Revolution* (Heb.), (Tel Aviv, 1938).

PORAT, R., *The History of the Kibbutz: Communal Education 1904–1939* (Norwood, Pa., 1985).

—— *Together but on our Own: The Creation of Schools in the Kibbutz Movement* (Heb.), (Tel Aviv, 1987).

PORAT, Y., *The Palestine Arab National Movement: From Riots to Rebellion, 1929–1939* (London, 1977).

POZNANSKY, M., and SHEHORI, M. (eds.), *Women in the Kibbutz* (Heb.), (Ein Harod, 1944).

PREUSS, W., 'Problems Related to Wages in Palestine' (Heb.), *Hameshek Hashitufi*, 2/17 (6 Sept. 1934), 210–13.

RABINOVITCH, J., 'Social and Economic Life in the Merhavia Co-operative' (Heb.), *Hapoel Hatzair*, 14 (Nov.–Dec. 1920), 6–11.

RABINOVITCH, Y., *Principles of the Kibbutz Me'uhad* (Heb.), (Tel Aviv, 1953), mimeo.

'RACHEL' [Lilia Bassevitz], 'The Third One' (Heb.), *Mibifnim*, (Oct. 1934), 69–73.

RAMOT, L., *The Adventures of a Bell: The Beginnings of Collective Education in Giv'at Brenner, 1928–1938* (Heb.), (Tel Aviv, 1982).

RAPHAELI, A., *In the Struggle for Salvation* (Heb.), (Tel Aviv, 1956).

RAYMAN, P., *The Kibbutz Community and Nation Building* (Princeton, 1981).

REINHARZ, J., 'Hashomer Hatzair in Germany (I), 1928–1933', *Yearbook of the Leo Baeck Institute*, 31 (1986), 173–208.

—— 'Hashomer Hatzair in Nazi Germany', in A. Paucker, S. Gilchrist, and S. Suchy (eds.), *The Jews in Nazi Germany 1933–1943* (Tubingen, 1986), 317–50.

REINHARZ, S., 'Toward a Model of Female Political Action: The Case of Manya Shohat, Founder of the First Kibbutz,' *Women's Studies International Journal*, 7/4 (1984), 275–84.

RIEMER, Y., 'From Youth Party to Youth Movement' (Heb.), occasional paper of Yad Tabenkin (Ef'al, 1985), mimeo.

—— 'Habonim in North America: Synchronic Table', occasional paper of Yad Tabenkin (Ef'al, 1985), mimeo.

RO'I, Y., 'Relations between Jews and Arabs in the Moshavot during the First Aliya', in M. Eliav and Y. Rosenthal (eds.), *The First Aliyah* (Heb.), (Jerusalem, 1981), i. 245–68.

ROKHEL, H., 'From Daily Life' (Heb.), in ex-members of Gedud Ha'avoda in the Kibbutz Me'uhad (eds.), *Gedud Ha'avoda* (Tel Aviv, 1931), 219–51.

RONEN, J., 'Changes in the Gratification of Individual Needs among the Kibbutz Membership: A Historical Perspective' (Heb.), MA thesis (Tel Aviv, 1980).

RON-POLANI, Y., *Until Now* (Heb.), (Tel Aviv, 1971).

ROSEN, A., 'Changes in the Status of Women in Workers' Settlements' (Heb.), MA thesis (Tel Aviv, 1984).

ROSOLIO, D., 'The Controversy in the Labour Movement over the Agreement between Ben-Gurion and Jabotinsky, October 1934–March 1935' (Heb.), MA thesis (Tel Aviv, 1971).

ROTH, C., WIGODER, G., POSNER, R., RABINOWITZ, L. I., ELIAV, B., and KATZ, M., *Encyclopedia Judaica* (Jerusalem, 1972).

RUPPIN, A., *The Zionist Organization's Agricultural Settlement in Palestine (1908–1924)* (Heb.), (Tel Aviv, 1925).

SARID, L. A., *Hechalutz and the Youth Movements in Poland, 1917–1939* (Heb.), (Tel Aviv, 1979).

SCHAMA, S., *Two Rothschilds and the Land of Israel* (London, 1978).

SCHATZKER, H., 'The Jewish Youth Movement in Germany, 1900–1933' (Heb.), Ph.D. thesis (Jerusalem, 1969).

SCHONBERG, J. (ed.), *Songs of the Land of Israel* (Heb.), (Berlin, 1935).

SCHUMAN, I., 'Reasons for Leaving the Kibbutz in favour of the Moshav during the Thirties' (Heb.), seminar paper, Haifa University, 1987.

SCHWARANTZ, Y., *An Underground Pioneering Movement in Nazi Germany* (Heb.), (Lohamei Hageta'ot, 1969).

SCHWEID, E., *The World of A. D. Gordon* (Heb.), (Tel Aviv, 1970).

SEGAL, S., and FIALKOV, A., *The Fields of Grochov: The Story of Kibbutz Grochov* (Heb.), (Lohamei Hageta'ot, 1976).

SEGRE, D. V., *Memoirs of a Fortunate Jew* (London, 1987).

SHAFIR, G., *Land, Labor and the Origins of the Israeli-Palestinian Conflict, 1882–1914* (Cambridge, 1989).

SHAFRIR, D., *Life's Furrows* (Heb.), (Tel Aviv, 1975).

SHAPIRA, A., 'The Dream and its Shattering: The Political Development of Gedud Ha'avoda, 1920–1927' (Heb.), *Baderech*, 3 (Dec. 1968), 34–63; 4 (Aug. 1969), 33–62.

—— 'The Debate in Mapai about the Use of Violence' (Heb.), *Hatzionut*, 5 (1975), 141–81.

—— *Futile Struggle: The Jewish Labour Controversy, 1929–1939* (Heb.), (Tel Aviv, 1977).

—— *Berl: The Biography of a Socialist Zionist* (Cambridge, 1984).

SHAPIRO, Y., *The Formative Years of the Israeli Labour Party* (London, 1976).

SHARETT, M., *Political Diary*, vol. ii: *1937* (Heb.), (Tel Aviv, 1971).

SHATIL, Y., *The Economy of the Communal Settlement in Israel: Principles and History* (Heb.), (Tel Aviv, 1955).

SHATNER, D. (ed.), *To Our Hill: The History of Kvutzat Geva, 1921–1981* (Heb.), (Geva, 1981).

SHATZ, Z., *On the Edge of Silence* (Heb.), (Tel Aviv, n. d.)

SHEFER, U., 'Nahalat Yehuda and the Beginnings of the Moshav' (Heb.), unpublished paper (Tivon, 1984).

SHILO, M., 'Degania: First Model of Collective Settlement on Nationally Owned Land' (Heb.), *Cathedra*, 39 (1986), 87–96.

—— *Experiments in Settlement* (Heb.), (Jerusalem, 1988).

SHOHAT, M., 'In the Beginning' (Heb.), *Mihayeinu*, 93 (June 1929), 617.

SHOSHANI, E., *The Kvutza and the Kibbutz in Israel* (Heb.), (Tel Aviv, 1973).

SHUA, Z., and BEN-GURION, A. (eds.), *Sabbath Anthology* (Heb.), (Tel Aviv–Beit Hashita, 1984) (mimeo).

SHUR, S., and GOLDEMBERG, H., 'Kibbutz and Literature: A Bibliographical Note', (Heb.), *Hakibbutz*, 13 (1990), 243–5.

SLUTSKY, Y., *Introduction to the History of the Israeli Labour Movement* (Heb.), (Tel Aviv, 1973).

STEIN, K. W., *The Land Question in Palestine, 1917–1939* (Chapel Hill–London, 1984).

STEINER, N., 'Kibbutz Haggadot' (Heb.), *Studies in Bibliography and Booklore* (1965), 10–33.

TABENKIN, E., 'On Women's Part in Defence' (Heb.), *Mibifnim* (June 1936), 80–7.

TABENKIN, Y., 'On the Question of Our Defence' (Heb.), *Mibifnim*, 44 (Dec. 1929), 3–4.

—— 'To Clarify the Way' (Heb.), *Mibifnim*, 8–9 (Aug.–Sept. 1937), 2–10.

—— *Devarim: Collected Speeches* (Heb.), vol. i (Tel Aviv, 1967).

TAMIR, N. (ed.), *People of the Second Aliya* (Heb.), 2 vols (Tel Aviv, 1970).

*Tanhum* (Heb.), [no author cited], (Degania Aleph, 1969).

TEVETH, S., *Ben Gurion: The Burning Ground, 1886–1948* (Boston, 1987).

TRUMPELDOR, J., *Hechalutz: Its Nature and Immediate Aims* (Russian), (Petrograd, 1918). Heb. trans. in M. Bassok (ed.), *The Book of Hechalutz* (Jerusalem, 1940).

TSUR, M., ZEVULUN, T., and PORAT, H. (eds.), *The Beginning of the Kibbutz* (Heb.), (Tel Aviv, 1981).

TSUR, Z., *The Kibbutz Me'uhad in the Settlement of Eretz-Israel* (Heb.), 3 vols. (Tel Aviv, 1979–84).

TZAHOR, Z., *On the Road to Yishuv Leadership* (Heb.), (Jerusalem, 1981).

—— (ed.), *Second Aliya Book* (Heb.), biographical volume (Jerusalem, forthcoming).

ULITZUR, A., *National Capital and Construction in Palestine, 1918–1937* (Heb.), (Jerusalem, 1939).

WEINER, H., 'The Co-operative Blau-Weiss Works, 1924–1926' (Heb.), *Hatzionut*, 7 (1981), 214–39.

WEISMANN, S., 'In These Days' (Heb.), *Niv Hakvutza*, 18 (Mar. 1938), 57.

WEST, B., *Hechalutz in Russia* (Heb.), (Tel Aviv, 1932).

WILKANSKY, Y., *On the Way* (Heb.), (Jaffa, 1918).

WURM, S. (ed.), *Bussel Memorial Book* (Heb.), (Tel Aviv, 1960).

YA'ARI, M., 'Rootless Symbols' (Heb.), *Hedim* (1923), 93–6. Repr. in *Mekorot Hashomer Hatzair*, 1 (1984), 60–9.

Yagur Council. *See* Kibbutz Me'uhad, *Report of Kibbutz Me'uhad Council.*

*Yalkut.* Journal published by Brit Pikuah Leko'operatzia Hakla'it.

YISHAI, Y., *Factionalism in the Israeli Labour Movement* (Heb.), (Tel Aviv, 1978).

ZAIT, D., 'From Kibbutz Movement to Party Organization' (Heb.), Ph. D. thesis (Tel Aviv, 1985).

—— *Zionism and Peace* (Heb.), (Tel Aviv, 1985).

ZAK, S., *Report on the Kibbutzim to Bank Hapoalim, 1935* (Heb.), (Tel Aviv, 1936), mimeo.

—— *The Kibbutz Movement in Numbers: 1938/9* (Heb.), (no place of publication, n.d.). Copies in Kibbutz Me'uhad archives, Ef'al.

ZEMAH, S., *In the Beginning* (Heb.), (Tel Aviv, 1946).

ZERTAL, M., *Spring of Youth: Hashomer Hatzair in Warsaw, 1913–1943* (Heb.), (Tel Aviv, 1980).

# Index

426      *Index*

Ben-Gurion, David—*contd*
in Moscow 98
in partition controversy 303
on pioneering 392
at Poalei Zion conference 21
on sectoral parties 195
on Second Aliya 12
and strategic settlement 322
Ben-Gurion–Jabotinsky agreement 211–
12, 218, 346, 352, 362, 366
Ben-Zvi, Yitzhak 26, 36 n., 281
Berman, Moshe 23–4, 26
Biluim 11
binationalism 203, 218, 360, 366
*see also* Arabs; Kibbutz Artzi
Blau-Weiss 113, 127, 128
B'nei Akiva 292–3
Borochov, Ber 13
Brandeis, Louis Dembitz 95, 132
Brit Hat'nua Hakibbutzit (Kibbutz
Movement Association) 387
Brith Olim 127–8, 227–9
British Army, recruitment to 358, 361, 364
Buber, Martin
influence on: Blau-Weiss 113; Brith Olim
127–8; Hashomer Hatzair 114;
Werkleute 228–9
Bussel, Joseph 28–9, 38–9, 44–5
on communal child care 50
on general meeting 38
on new immigrants 52
on permanent settlement 35
on sexual equality 86, 369
on small *kvutza* 44

child care
in Hashomer 47–9
in kibbutzim 50–1, 185, 237–8, 367–8,
378–9, 396
children, number of 80, 138, 236–7, 345
citrus fruit 133–4, 176, 178, 179–81,
187–8, 336–8
clothing 39, 184, 382–4
communal experience, intensive
at Beitania Eilit 115–16
at Degania 40–1
at Ginegar 80–1
Lavi on 70
on Mount Canaan 289
in second Hashomer Hatzair kibbutz
246
in training kibbutzim 109–10
communal settlement, ideology of 28–31

communes
Hadera 28–9, 31
Rehovot 18–19
in Second Aliya 18–20, 32–4, 35
*see also* Gedud Ha'avoda (general
commune)
Communism and Communists 13, 98–9,
118, 128, 152, 201, 213, 218, 357–8,
361
in Gedud Ha'avoda 142–3
community, varieties of kibbutz 1, 5, 37–
41, 80–5, 246–73, 387–9
*see also* communal experience; culture;
Giv'at Brenner; Hulda; Mishmar
Ha'emek; ways of life
comprehensiveness (*klaliut*) 129–30, 210, 366
'conquest groups' 26–7, 31, 32–4, 37
Um Juni 27–8, 31, 34 n.
'conquest of labour' 16–18, 73, 94, 135, 145,
201–3, 370
*see also* hired labour; trade unions
consolidation loans 171–2, 183
consumption, organization of 19, 23, 39,
271, 382–5
*see also* living standards
contract work *see* Hashomer; *havura*;
*kvutzot*; outside work; roads
co-operative scheme (Jordan Valley) 363
*see also* Merhavia
culture 1, 39–41, 83–4, 249–55, 370–5, 388
dance and song 40–1, 260, 370–1, 388
diaries, communal 84, 249–50
drama 372
Hebrew language and literature 39, 55,
120, 252, 258, 260, 372–3, 375, 388
literary creation 372
music 260, 371–2
news-sheets, local newspapers 250–1,
267, 372, 388
politics as 208–9
reading, libraries, reading-rooms 249–51
sport 83
*see also* festivals; Sabbath

defence
of *kvutzot* and kibbutzim 307–12, 368:
Hulda 308, 312–14; under Ottoman
rule 8, 25, 31, 38, 308
of Yishuv 301–3, 307–11, 314–15, 323
*see also* Bar Giora; Hagana; Hashomer;
Irgun Beit; Irgun Zva'i Le'umi;
Raziel; Sadeh; self-restraint; Sturman;
tower and stockade

*Index compiled by Henry Near*

Printed and bound by CPI Group (UK) Ltd, Croydon, CR0 4YY

09/06/2025

14685814-0002